PRAISE FOR APPLIED SECURITY VISUALIZATION

"If we subscribe to the sage advice of Confucius, 'What I hear, I forget. What I see, I remember. What I do, I understand,' then Raffael Marty's Applied Security Visualization *will surely bring us much wisdom. Marty embraces the security visualization discipline with panache, fluid grace, and exquisite detail...a must read for sec vis experts and novices alike."*

—Russ McRee, HolisticInfoSec.org

"Collecting log data is one thing, having relevant information is something else. The art to transform all kind of log data into meaningful security information is the core of this book. Raffy illustrates in a straight forward way, and with hands-on examples, how such a challenge can be mastered. Let's get inspired."

—Andreas Wuchner, Novartis

"This book starts with the basics of graphing and visualization and builds upon that with many examples of log analysis, compliance reporting, and communicating security information. I recommend this book for anyone with the task of analyzing volumes of security and compliance data who must then report their findings in a clear and concise manner."

—Ron Gula, CTO, Tenable Network Security

"Raffael Marty truly shows you the ropes to security visualization from the very basics to complete case studies. The broad range of use-cases and the wealth of hands-on examples throughout the book continuously inspire you to new visualization applications in your domain of competence."

—Jan P. Monsch, Senior Security Analyst

"Amazingly useful (and fun to read!) book that does justice to this somewhat esoteric subject—and this is coming from a long-time visualization skeptic! What is most impressive, is that this book is actually 'hands-on-useful,' not conceptual, with examples usable by readers in their daily jobs. Chapter 8 on insiders is my favorite!"

—Dr. Anton Chuvakin, Chief Logging Evangelist, LogLogic

Applied
Security
Visualization

Applied Security Visualization

Raffael Marty

⩗Addison-Wesley

Upper Saddle River, NJ · Boston · Indianapolis · San Francisco
New York · Toronto · Montreal · London · Munich · Paris · Madrid
Capetown · Sydney · Tokyo · Singapore · Mexico City

The publisher offers excellent discounts on this book when ordered in quantity for bulk purchases or special sales, which may include electronic versions and/or custom covers and content particular to your business, training goals, marketing focus, and branding interests. For more information, please contact:

U.S. Corporate and Government Sales
(800) 382-3419
corpsales@pearsontechgroup.com

For sales outside the United States please contact:

International Sales
international@pearsoned.com

This Book Is Safari Enabled

The Safari® Enabled icon on the cover of your favorite technology book means the book is available through Safari Bookshelf. When you buy this book, you get free access to the online edition for 45 days.

Safari Bookshelf is an electronic reference library that lets you easily search thousands of technical books, find code samples, download chapters, and access technical information whenever and wherever you need it.

To gain 45-day Safari Enabled access to this book:

- Go to http://www.awprofessional.com/safarienabled
- Complete the brief registration form
- Enter the coupon code EIKH-5PEJ-VV59-7QII-9SDH

If you have difficulty registering on Safari Bookshelf or accessing the online edition, please e-mail customer-service@safaribooksonline.com.

Visit us on the Web: www.awprofessional.com

Library of Congress Cataloging-in-Publication Data:

Marty, Rafael, 1976-
  Applied security visualization / Rafael Marty.
    p. cm.
  Includes index.
  ISBN 0-321-51010-0 (pbk. : alk. paper) 1. Computer networks—Security measures 2. Information visualization. 3. Computer security. I. Title.

  TK5105.59.M369 2008
  005.8—dc22
                           2008023598

ISBN-13: 978-0-321-51010-5
ISBN-10:   0-321-51010-0
Text printed in the United States on recycled paper at RR Donnelley, Crawfordsville, Indiana.
First printing August 2008

Editor-in-Chief
Karen Gettman

Acquisitions Editor
Jessica Goldstein

Senior Development Editor
Chris Zahn

Managing Editor
Kristy Hart

Project Editor
Andy Beaster

Copy Editor
Keith Cline

Indexer
Erika Millen

Proofreader
Jennifer Gallant

Publishing Coordinator
Romny French

Multimedia Developer
Dan Scherf

Book Designer
Chuti Prasertsith

Composition
Nonie Ratcliff

Graphics
Tammy Graham
Laura Robbins

Contents

Preface

This book is about visualizing computer security data. The book shows you, step by step, how to visually analyze electronically generated security data. IT data must be gathered and analyzed for myriad reasons, including GRC (governance, risk, and compliance) and preventing/mitigating insider threats and perimeter threats. Log files, configuration files, and other IT security data must be analyzed and monitored to address a variety of use-cases. In contrast to handling textual data, visualization offers a new, more effective, and simpler approach to analyzing millions of log entries generated on a daily basis. Graphical representations help you immediately identify outliers, detect malicious activity, uncover misconfigurations and anomalies, and spot general trends and relationships among individual data points. Visualization of data—the process of converting security data into a picture—is the single most effective tool to address these tasks. After all...

A picture is worth a thousand log entries.

To handle today's security and threat landscape, we need new analysis methods. Criminal activity is moving up the network stack. Network-based attacks are becoming more sophisticated, and increasingly attacks are executed on the application layer.

Criminal techniques have adapted. Are you prepared to deal with these new developments? Are you aware of what is happening inside of your networks and applications? In addition to monitoring your networks, you must make sure you are taking an in-depth look at your applications. Because of the vast amount of data that requires analysis, novel methods are needed to conduct the analysis. Visualization can help address these complex data analysis problems.

WHAT THIS BOOK COVERS

Follow me on an exciting journey through security data visualization. We will start with the basics of data sources needed for security visualization. What are they? What information do they contain, and what are the problems associated with them? I then discuss different ways to display data in charts or more complex visualizations, such as parallel coordinates. You will learn which graphical methods to use and when. The book then takes you through the process of generating graphical representations of your data. A step-by-step approach guarantees that no detail is left out. By introducing an **information visualization process,** visualization of security data becomes a simple recipe, which I apply in the core of this book to analyze three big areas of security visualization: perimeter threat, compliance, and insider threat. These chapters are hands-on and use-case driven. Open source visualization tools and libraries are discussed in the last chapter of the book. You can find all the tools introduced on the accompanying CD. Without dealing with installations, you can immediately start analyzing your own security data.

The book is a **hands-on** guide to visualization. Where it covers theoretical concepts and processes, it backs them up with examples of how to apply the theory on your own data. In addition to discussing—step by step—how to generate graphical representations of security data, this book also shows you how to analyze and interpret them.

The goal is to get you excited and inspired. You are given the necessary tools and information to go ahead and embed visualization in your own daily job. The book shows example use-cases that should inspire you to go ahead and apply visualization to your own problems. If one of the chapters covers a topic that is not your responsibility or focus area (for example, compliance), try to see beyond the topic specifics and instead explore the visualizations. The concepts may be valid for other use-cases that you want to address.

WHAT THIS BOOK DOESN'T COVER

This book covers visualization of computer security data. I do not discuss topics such as binary code or malware analysis. I don't get into the topics of steganography (the art or science of hiding information in images) or system call visualizations. This book is about time-based data and system status records. The data visualized is data you use to operationally secure an organization.

This book is not a compendium of security data sources and possible visual representations. It uses existing visualization methods—charts, parallel coordinates, treemaps, and so on—that are supported by many tools and applications. The book is composed of a sample set of data sources and use-cases to illustrate how visualization can be used.

AUDIENCE

I wrote this book for security practitioners. I am introducing new ways to analyze security data to the people who can implement them. Whether you are analyzing perimeter threat issues, investigating insider crimes, or are in charge of compliance monitoring and reporting, this book is meant for you.

The reader should have a basic understanding of programming to follow the Perl and UNIX scripts in this book. I assume that you are familiar with basic networking concepts and have seen a log file before. You don't have to be an expert in IT security or compliance. It helps to have an understanding of the basic concepts, but it is definitely not a prerequisite for this book. Most of all, I want you to read this book with an open mind. Try to see how visualization can help you in your daily job.

STRUCTURE AND CONTENT

This book follows a simple organization. It introduces basic visualization and data graphing concepts first. It then integrates those concepts with security data and shows how you can apply them to security problems. In the following list, I briefly describe each chapter:

- Chapter 1: Visualization

  Visualization is the core topic of this book. The first chapter introduces some basic visualization concepts and graph design principles that help generate visually effective graphs.

- Chapter 2: Data Sources

  Visualization cannot exist without data. This chapter discusses a variety of data sources relevant to computer security. I show what type of data the various devices generate, show how to parse the data, and then discuss some of the problems associated with each of the data sources.

- Chapter 3: Visually Representing Data

  Data can be visualized in many different ways. This chapter takes a closer look at various forms of visualizations. It first discusses generic graph properties and how they can help encode information. It then delves into a discussion of specific visualizations, such as charts, box plots, parallel coordinates, links graphs, and treemaps. The chapter ends with a discussion of how to choose the right graph for the data visualization problem at hand.

Acknowledgments

Many people have shaped my journey into the world of security data visualization. It all started with my cryptography professor, Ueli Maurer. He awakened my curiosity about computer security. His war stories inspired me to learn more about the topic. He was also responsible for introducing me to my first internship in the Silicon Valley. What was intended as a stay of seven months turned, two years later, into my new home.

After my internship, I was fortunate enough to receive an introduction to security research. The internship at IBM Research's Global Security Analysis Lab (GSAL) taught me my first log analysis skills. I am still in touch with many of my old colleagues, and one of them even served on my review committee. Thanks Andreas, Dominique, James (thanks for all the tips and tricks around UNIX; I shall never forget sash), Marc, Morton, and all the other people at the IBM Rüschlikon lab for fueling my interest in intrusion detection and log analysis.

I cannot thank Toby Kohlenberg enough for everything he did for me. Toby is responsible for putting me in touch with my first U.S. employer. He also connected me with many people in the security arena that, today, are invaluable contacts. And that is not enough. Toby also introduced me to my first writing gig—a chapter for Syngress's Snort book.[1] I first met Toby on a mailing list. Over time, we became close friends. Toby, thanks!

My fascination with visualization started during my employment at ArcSight. The event graph feature in the product first fascinated me because of its artistic value. After a

---

[1]   www.syngress.com/catalog/?pid=4020

while, I realized that there had to be more, and I started visualizing all kinds of data. After a while, the developers stopped implementing my feature requests. At that time, Christian Beedgen, the lead developer at ArcSight, and I started working on AfterGlow.[2] This gave me a way to implement the visualization features that I needed to analyze my log files. Christian wrote all of the original AfterGlow code. I merely added some more features to configure the graphs in different ways. Thanks, Christian. Many other ArcSight colleagues are responsible for my knowledge of log analysis. Ken Tidwell, my first boss at ArcSight, was a great mentor in many ways, and I attribute a lot of what I know to him.

Greg Conti let me write two chapters of his book *Security Data Visualization*.[3] He beat me to market by more than an arm's length with a book about the topic. Greg and I had numerous discussions about visualization, which were always inspiring. Thanks, Greg.

This book comes with a CD for visualization (DAVIX)[4] that contains all the tools discussed in this book. Jan Monsch approached me and asked whether I was interested in helping out with the development of DAVIX. I cannot tell you how excited I was. Jan did a great job with the CD. What an amazing project. Jan, thanks for having me onboard.

I had discussions about visualization with so many people. To just name a few: Jake Babbin (thanks for some great discussions of perimeter threat visualization), Vincent Bieri (thanks for the numerous discussions about visualizing risk), Neil Desai (thanks for the piece of AfterGlow code), Ross Graber (thanks for the feedback on compliance and fraud; that fraud examiner handbook is scary), Dave Anderson (thanks for having an early look at my compliance chapter and patiently explaining the auditor jargon to me), Peter Haag (thanks for helping me with nfdump, NetFlow-related questions, and the DoS example graphs), Greg Stephensen (thanks for introducing me to treemaps and inspiring my insider threat work), Mike Murray (thanks for entertaining my crazy ideas about the human psyche and looking over my introduction to the visualization chapter), Advizor Solutions—especially Doug Cogswell (thanks for allowing me to use your product for some of the graphs in the book), Ralph Logan (thanks for endorsing my book proposal and providing me with some visualization examples), Alain Mayer (thanks for the discussions about treemaps and vulnerability data visualization), Kathy Dykeman (thanks for inspiring me with examples of visualization outside of the computer security world and the many hours you had to listen to my visualization talk), Beth Goldman (thanks for helping me clean up the graph decision process). And thanks to all the people who contributed to http://secviz.org.

---

[2] http://afterglow.sf.net

[3] http://nostarch.com/securityvisualization.htm

[4] http://davix.secviz.org

Thanks to all of my friends, especially Quinton Jones, who always encouraged me to finish the book and who were my company when I was writing at Farley's, the local coffee shop.

A huge thanks goes out to the best review committee that I could have hoped for. Adam O'Donnel, Andrew Jacquith, Diego Zamboni, Jan Monsch, and John Goodall. Your feedback was absolutely amazing.

I want to also thank the folks at Pearson who have been fantastic to work with. Starting with Jessica Goldstein, who didn't think twice when I proposed the book project to her. She has been a great coordinator and motivator along the way, as were Karen Gettman, Andrew Beaster, Romny French, and Chris Zahn. Chris, your feedback was invaluable.

And finally, I want to thank my parents, who during my entire life always let me make my own decisions. Thanks for all the encouragement and support!

There are many more people who were instrumental in my journey. My sincerest gratitude to you all.

About the Author

Raffael Marty is Chief Security Strategist and Senior Product Manager for Splunk, the leading provider of large-scale, high-speed indexing and search technology for IT infrastructures. As customer advocate and guardian, he focuses on using his skills in data visualization, log management, intrusion detection, and compliance. An active participant on industry standards committees such as CEE (Common Event Expression) and OVAL (Open Vulnerability and Assessment Language), Marty created the Thor and AfterGlow automation tools and founded the security visualization portal secviz.org. Raffy's passion for security visualization is evident in the many presentations he gives at conferences around the world. Prior to writing *Applied Security Visualization*, he contributed to a number of books on security and visualization. Before joining Splunk, Raffy managed the solutions team at ArcSight, served as IT security consultant for PriceWaterhouseCoopers, and was a member of the IBM Research Global Security Analysis Lab.

Visualization

"I saw it with my own eyes!"

This sentence usually expresses certainty and conviction. It is a strong sentence. It is stronger than saying, "I heard it with my own ears." Often, this sentence is interpreted as expressing the speaker's conviction that she is privy to some truth. And we treat that conviction as authentic. It must have happened if she saw it. We want people to say this about the security data we analyze. We want them to look at a picture of our work product and have that experience. A picture says more than a thousand words. A visual representation of data can communicate a lot of detail in a way that is instantly accessible and meaningful.

More of the human brain is devoted to visual processing than to any other sense. It is the "broadband" access to understanding. This ability of the human mind to rapidly process visual input makes information visualization a useful and often necessary tool, enabling us to turn data into information and knowledge.

Images are very interesting. They are different from the written or the spoken word in many ways. It is not just the bandwidth of information that can be transferred. There is a much more interesting phenomenon called the **critical faculty** or the **skepticism filter.**[1] When you listen to someone speak, or while you are reading these words, you are constantly asking yourself, "Is he saying the truth? Does this match up with my experience?" If you look at a picture, this skepticism filter does not seem to be there in the first

---

[1] Barnett, E. A. *Analytical Hypnotherapy: Principles and Practice* (Glendale, CA: Westwood Publishing Company, 1989).

moment. We trust a photograph. Do we? At first glance, we seem to. However, the closer we look, the more detail we start seeing, the more we analyze the picture, and the more skeptical we get. What is happening?

For the brain to process an image and understand its contents, it has to formulate sentences and words around the image. The image, and more specifically color, is put into sentences.[2] The longer we look at an image, the more sentences the brain constructs. And the more sentences, the more reason we give our brain to apply the skepticism filter.

What does this all have to do with visualization, you might wonder? When we visualize data, we have to make sure that the output is going to be as simple and clear as possible. We have to make sure that the viewer needs as few sentences as possible to interpret the graph. This not only decreases the time that someone needs to process and understand a visualization, it also minimizes the surface area for viewers to apply the skepticism filter. We want them to trust that the image correctly represents the data.

This chapter explores visualization, encourages you to visualize security data, and explains some of the fundamental principles that anybody who is trying to communicate information in a visual form should understand.

WHAT IS VISUALIZATION?

The proverb says, "A picture is worth a thousand words." Images are used to efficiently communicate information. An image can capture a sunset in all of its beauty. It would be impossible to capture the same impression in words. I like to say that

A picture is worth a thousand log records.

Instead of handing someone a log file that describes how an attack happened, you can use a picture, a visual representation of the log records. At one glance, the picture communicates the content of this log. Viewers can process the information in a fraction of time that it would take them to read the original log.

Visualization, in the security sense, is therefore the process of generating a picture based on log records. It defines how the log records are mapped into a visual representation.

---

[2]   A. Franklin et al., "From the Cover: Categorical perception of color is lateralized to the right hemisphere in infants, but to the left hemisphere in adults," *PNAS* 105, 2008, 322–3225.

WHY VISUALIZATION?

Why should we be interested in visualization? Because the human visual system is a pattern seeker of enormous power and subtlety. The eye and the visual cortex of the brain form a massively parallel processor that provides the highest-bandwidth channel into human cognitive centers.

—Colin Ware, author of *Information Visualization: Perception for Design*

Visual representations of data enable us to communicate a large amount of information to our viewers. Too often, information is encoded in text. It is more difficult to immediately grasp the essence of something if it is just described in words. In fact, it is hard for the brain to process text. Pictures or images, on the other hand, can be processed extremely well. They can encode a wealth of information and are therefore, well suited to communicate much larger amounts of data to a human. Pictures can use shape, color, size, relative positioning, and so on to encode information, contributing to increased bandwidth between the information and the consumer or viewer.

Many disciplines are facing an ever-growing amount of data that needs to be analyzed, processed, and communicated. We are in the middle of an information explosion era. A big percentage of this information is stored or represented in textual form: databases, documents, websites, emails, and so forth. We need new ways to work with all this data. People who have to look at, browse, or understand the data need ways to display relevant information graphically to assist in understanding the data, analyzing it, and remembering parts of it. Browsing huge amounts of data is crucial for finding information and then exploring details of a resultset. Interaction with the visualizations is one of the key elements in this process. It is not just the expedited browsing capabilities that visualization has to offer, but often a visual representation—in contrast to a textual representation—helps us discover relationships well hidden in the wealth of data. Finding these relationships can be crucial.

A simple example of a mainstream visualization application is the Friend Wheel, a Facebook[3] application that generates a visualization of all Facebook friends (see Figure 1-1). Each person who is a friend of mine on Facebook is arranged in a circle. Friends of mine who know each other are connected with a line. Instead of me having to explain in written form who my friends are and what the different groups are that they belong to, this visualization summarizes all the relations in a simple and easy-to-understand picture.

---

[3] Facebook (http://facebook.com) is a social networking platform.

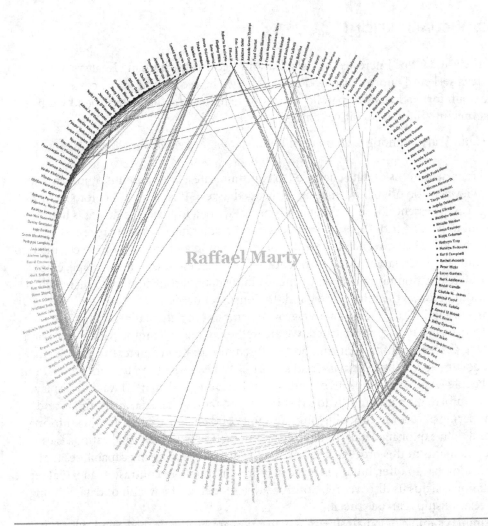

Figure 1-1 The Friend Wheel visualizes friend relationships on Facebook.

There is a need for data visualization in many disciplines. The Friend Wheel is a simple example of how visualization has gone mainstream. The data explosion and resultant need for visualization affects computer security more than many other areas. Security analysts face an ever-increasing amount of data that needs to be analyzed and mastered. One of the areas responsible for the growth in data is the expanded scope of information that needs to be looked at by security people. It is not just network-based device logs anymore, such as the ones from firewalls and intrusion detection systems. Today, the entire stack needs to be analyzed: starting on the network layer, going all the way up to the applications, which are amazingly good at generating unmanageable amounts of data.

VISUALIZATION BENEFITS

If you have ever analyzed a large log file with tens of thousands of entries, you know how hard it is. A visual approach significantly facilitates the task (as compared to using text-based tools). Visualization offers a number of benefits over textual analysis of data. These benefits are based on people's ability to process images efficiently. People can scan, recognize, and recall images rapidly. In addition, the human brain is an amazing pattern-recognition tool, and it can detect changes in size, color, shape, movement, and texture very efficiently. The following is a summary of visualization benefits:

- *Answers a question:* Visualization enables you to create an image for each question you may have about a dataset. Instead of wading through textual data and trying to remember all the relationships between individual entries, you can use an image that conveys the data in a concise form.

- *Poses new questions:* One interesting aspect of visual representations is that they cause the viewer to pose new questions. A human has the capability to look at a visual representation of data and see patterns. Often, these patterns are not anticipated at the time the visual is generated. What is this outlier over here? Why do these machines communicate with each other?

- *Explore and discover:* By visualizing data, you have a new way of viewing and investigating data. A visual representation provides new insights into a given dataset. Different graphs and configurations highlight various different properties in the dataset and help identify previously unknown information. If the properties and relationships were known upfront, it would be possible to detect these incidents without visualization. However, they had to be discovered first, and visual tools are best suited to do so. Interactive visualizations enable even richer investigations and help discover hidden properties of a dataset.

- *Support decisions:* Visualization helps to analyze a large amount of data very quickly. Decisions can be based on a large amount of data because visualization has helped to distill it into something meaningful. More data also helps back up decisions. Situational awareness is a prime tool to help in decision support.

- *Communicate information:* Graphical representations of data are more effective as a means of communication than textual log files. A story can be told more efficiently, and the time to understand a picture is a fraction of the time that it takes to understand the textual data. Images are great for telling a story. Try to put a comic into textual form. It just doesn't do the trick.

- *Increase efficiency:* Instead of wading through thousands of lines of textual log data, it is much more efficient to graph certain properties of the data to see trends and outliers. The time it takes to analyze the log files is drastically cut down. This frees up people's time and allows them to think about the patterns and relationships found in the data. It also speeds up the detection of and response to new developments. Fewer people are needed to deal with more data.

- *Inspire:* Images inspire. While visually analyzing some of the datasets for this book, I got inspired many times to try out a new visualization, a new approach of viewing the same data. Sometimes these inspirations are dead ends. A lot of times, however, they lead to new findings and help better understand the data at hand.

If data visualization has all of these benefits, we should explore what visualization can do for security.

SECURITY VISUALIZATION

The field of **security visualization** is very young. To date, only a limited amount of work has been done in this area. Given the huge amount of data needed to analyze security problems, visualization seems to be the right approach:

- The ever-growing amount of data collected in IT environments asks for new methods and tools to deal with them.

- Event and log analysis is becoming one of the main tools for security analysts to investigate and comprehend the state of their networks, hosts, applications, and business processes. All these tasks deal with an amazing amount of data that needs to be analyzed.

- Regulatory compliance is asking for regular log analysis. Analysts need better and more efficient tools to execute the task.

- The crime landscape is shifting. Attacks are moving up the network stack. Network-based attacks are not the prime source of security problems anymore. The attacks today are moving into the application layer: Web 2.0, instant messenger attacks, fraud, information theft, and crime-ware are just some examples of new types of attacks that generate a load of data to be collected and analyzed. Beware! Applications are really chatty and generate a lot of data.

- Today, the attacks that you really need to protect yourself from are targeted. You are not going to be a random victim. The attackers know who they are coming for. You need to be prepared, and you have to proactively analyze your log files. Attackers will not set off your alarms.

Because of the vast amount of log data that needs to be analyzed, classic security tools, such as firewalls and intrusion detection systems, have over time added reporting capabilities and dashboards that are making use of charts and graphics. Most of the time, these displays are used to communicate information to the user. They are not interactive tools that support data exploration. In addition, most of these visual displays are fairly basic and, in most cases, an afterthought. Security products are not yet designed with visualization in mind. However, this situation is slowly improving. Companies are starting to realize that visualization is a competitive advantage for them and that user tasks are significantly simplified with visual aids.

The problem with these tools is that they are specialized. They visualize only the information collected or generated by that specific solution. We need to visualize information from multiple tools and for use-cases that are not supported by these tools. Novel methods are needed to conduct log and security data analysis.

SECURITY VISUALIZATION'S DICHOTOMY

Most tools available for security visualization are victims of a phenomenon that I call the **dichotomy of security visualization.**

Most security visualization tools are written by security people who do not know much about visualization theory and human-computer interaction; the rest are written by visualization people who do not know much about computer security and adjacent technical fields, such as operating systems or networking. Therefore, tools lack one of two important aspects: either the security domain knowledge and accuracy or the visual efficiency.

Complete security visualization expertise requires knowledge of two worlds: the security world and the visualization world. The security world consists of bits and bytes, of exploits and security policies, of risk and compliance mandates. It is absolutely necessary to know these concepts to build a tool that is easy to use and effective for security experts, but also to be technically accurate. The knowledge of the visualization world encompasses visual perception and human-interface design. These two aspects are necessary to build a usable tool. We have all seen what happens when security experts build visualization tools. Three-dimensional pie charts, shades on bar charts, and illegible legends often result. I am sure you have seen the opposite, too, where a beautiful program was developed, but unfortunately it was completely useless because it was developed for one specific use-case that has nothing to do with real-world applications and problems that security professionals are facing.

There should not be a gap or a dichotomy between these two disciplines. We have to make sure they grow together. We have to work toward a security visualization community that has expertise in both areas. I do not want to claim that this book bridges the gap between security and visualization completely. However, I do attempt to show both worlds. By choosing a use-case-driven approach for most of the discussions in this book, I hope to keep the discussions on a level that stimulates the thinking about the problems in both fields: security and visualization.

VISUALIZATION THEORY

Most readers of this book are going to have a more technical background in computer security than in visualization. Therefore, in an attempt to bridge the gap in the dichotomy of security visualization, I will delve into visualization theory for just a little bit to help most readers better understand why some displays are so easy to read, whereas others are just horrible and do not seem to serve their purpose of quickly communicating information and letting the user interactively explore it.

After reading these sections about visualization theory, you will by no means be a visualization expert. Entire books cover the topic. I want to provide you with a basic overview and some concepts that are I hope you find useful in your future journey through security visualization. I encourage you to read more about these topics and pick up one of these books:

- *Information Visualization: Perception for Design,* by Colin Ware (San Francisco: Morgan Kaufmann Publishers, 2004).
  This book provides a great overview of visualization theory.
- *Information Graphics: A Comprehensive Illustrated Reference,* by Robert L. Harris (New York & Oxford: Oxford University Press, 1999).
  A great reference book for terminology and concepts concerned with visualization.

- *Envisioning Information* (Cheshire, CT: Graphics Press, 1990).
  Visual Explanations (Cheshire, CT: Graphics Press, 1997).
  The Visual Display of Quantitative Information (Cheshire, CT: Graphics Press, 2001).
  Beautiful Evidence (Cheshire, CT: Graphics Press, 2006).
  These four books by Edward R. Tufte provide great information about visualization that covers everything from visualization history to simple design principles for graphs.

The first and most important topic for visualizing data is visual perception.

PERCEPTION

The human visual system has its own rules. We can easily see patterns presented in certain ways, but if they are presented incorrectly, they become invisible. If we can understand how perception works, our knowledge can be translated into rules for displaying information. Following perception-based rules, we can present our data in such a way that the important and informative patterns stand out. If we disobey the rules, our data will be incomprehensible or misleading. What is the best way of visualizing data? What choice of color best supports the communication of properties we are interested in? Does shape and placement help improve perception? A fair amount of research has been done in this area. Two of the people who are instrumental in the field of modern visual perception are Edward Tufte[4] and Jacques Bertin.[5] They are not the ones who historically created the field of visual perception, but they greatly helped introduce a broader public to some of these visual principles.

When we look at an image, some elements are detected immediately by the human visual system. No conscious attention is required to notice them. These elements are decorated with so-called **pre-attentive visual properties.** Visual properties are all the different ways of encoding data, such as shape, color, orientation, and so forth. Some visual properties require the viewer to serially process an image or a visual representation of data to notice them and interpret them. Pre-attentive properties pop out. They catch a viewer's attention immediately. A famous example used to illustrate pre-attentive processing is shown in Figure 1-2. The leftmost illustration makes it really hard to find the eights. The rightmost side uses color to make the eights visually different. You can see them immediately.

---

[4] www.edwardtufte.com

[5] http://portal.acm.org/citation.cfm?id=1095597

```
18240987120097 | 18240987120097
90723098273093 | 90723098273093
08023497293694 | 08023497293694
24702394628346 | 24702394628346
```

Figure 1-2   How many eights are in this sequence of numbers? The leftmost illustration requires you to serially scan all the numbers. On the rightmost side, the eights are colored differently, which directly addresses a human's pre-attentive capabilities.

Visual properties that are pre-attentive can be grouped into four groups[6]: **form, color, position,** and **motion.** Each of these four groups consists of a number of visual attributes. For example, form consists of **orientation, size,** and **shape** that can be used to emphasize information. Color uses two attributes: **hue** and **intensity.** Figure 1-3 shows a few more examples of pre-attentive visual attributes. It illustrates how pre-attentive attributes can be used to make information display more effective. The important information in an image should use these attributes, such that a viewer sees the important information immediately, instead of having to serially parse the images.

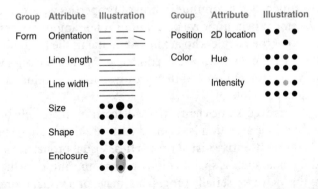

Figure 1-3   A list of pre-attentive visual attributes, illustrating how they can help emphasize information in a graphical display

If more than just a single dimension needs to be encoded in a display, multiple pre-attentive attributes can be combined. The issue is, however, that not all attributes mix

---

6   For a more in-depth discussion of pre-attentive visual properties, see *Information Visualization: Perception for Design*, by Colin Ware (San Francisco: Morgan Kaufman Publishers, 2004).

well with each other. The human brain cannot easily process some combinations. Attributes that work well together are called **separable dimensions,** and ones that do not work together are called **integral dimensions.**

If a display uses two integral dimensions to encode two different data dimensions at the same time, a human perceives them holistically. Figure 1-4 shows an example. The example of two integral dimensions is shown on the left side of the image. The ovals are using width and height and integral dimensions to encode information. It is hard to separate the width and height of the ellipses. It takes almost serial processing to analyze the image and decode it. The right side of Figure 1-4 shows two separable dimensions: color and position. Separable dimensions enable the viewer to quickly separate the different visual elements into multiple classes. You can immediately separate the gray circles from the black ones and the group of circles on the top left from the ones on the bottom right.

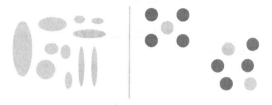

Figure 1-4   The leftmost example shows a graph that uses two integral attributes, width and height, to encode information. The graph on the right uses separable attributes, color and position, to do the same.

Perception is just one visual property that we need to be aware of when creating powerful visual displays. Let's take a look at two principles for creating expressive and effective graphs. After exploring the two principles, we will explore some more graph design principles that we should use to generate graphical representations of data.

EXPRESSIVE AND EFFECTIVE GRAPHS

Generating graphs that are easy to understand and comprehend involves the two important principles of expressiveness and effectiveness. Not following these principles will result in graphs that are either confusing or simply wrong.

clearly. *Reduce nondata ink.* It is a simple principle, but it is very powerful. Figure 1-6 shows how a graph can look before and after applying the principles of reducing non-data ink. The right side of the figure shows the same data as on the left side, but in a way that is much more legible.

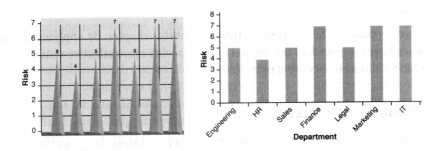

Figure 1-6   An example illustrating the data to ink-ratio and how reducing the ratio helps improve the legibility of a graph

Distinct Attributes

We briefly touched on the topic of perception in the preceding section. One perceptual principle relates to the number of different attributes used to encode information. If you have to display multiple data dimensions in the same graph, make sure not to exceed five distinct attributes to encode them. For example, if you are using shapes, do not use more than five shapes. If you are using hue (or color), keep the number of distinct colors low. Although the human visual system can identify many different colors, our short-term memory cannot retain more than about eight of them for a simple image.

Gestalt Principles

To reduce search time for viewers of a graph and to help them detect patterns and recognize important pieces of information, a school of psychology called **Gestalt theory**[8] is often consulted. Gestalt principles are a set of visual characteristics. They can be used to highlight data, tie data together, or separate it. The six Gestalt principles are presented in the following list and illustrated in Figure 1-7:

- *Proximity:* Objects grouped together in close proximity are perceived as a unit. Based on the location, clusters and outliers can be identified.

---

[8] Contrary to a few visualization books that I have read, *Gestalt* is not the German word for pattern. Gestalt is hard to translate. It is a word for the silhouette, the form, the body, or the looks of a thing.

- *Closure:* Humans tend to perceive objects that are almost a closed form (such as an interrupted circle) as the full form. If you were to cover this line of text halfway, you would still be able to guess the words. This principle can be used to eliminate bounding boxes around graphs. A lot of charts do not need the bounding box; the human visual system "simulates" it implicitly.

- *Similarity:* Be it color, shape, orientation, or size, we tend to group similar-looking elements together. We can use this principle to encode the same data dimensions across multiple displays. If you are using the color red to encode malicious IP addresses in all of your graphs, there is a connection that the visual system makes automatically.

- *Continuity:* Elements that are aligned are perceived as a unit. Nobody would interpret every little line in a dashed line as its own data element. The individual lines make up a dashed line. We should remember this phenomenon when we draw tables of data. The grid lines are not necessary; just arranging the items is enough.

- *Enclosure:* Enclosing data points with a bounding box, or putting them inside some shape, groups those elements together. We can use this principle to highlight data elements in our graphs.

- *Connection:* Connecting elements groups them together. This is the basis for link graphs. They are a great way to display relationships in data. They make use of the "connection" principle.

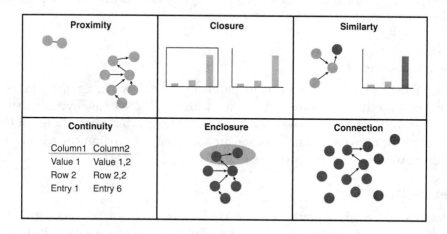

Figure 1-7 Illustration of the six Gestalt principles. Each of the six images illustrates one of the Gestalt principles. They show how each of the principles can be used to highlight data, tie data together, and separate it.

Emphasize Exceptions

A piece of advice for generating graphical displays is to *emphasize exceptions*. For example, use the color red to highlight important or exceptional areas in your graphs. By following this advice, you will refrain from overusing visual attributes that overload graphs. Stick to the basics, and make sure your graphs communicate what you want them to communicate.

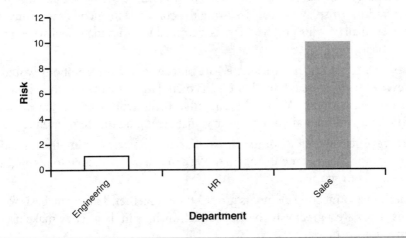

Figure 1-8   This bar chart illustrates the principle of highlighting exceptions. The risk in the sales department is the highest, and this is the only bar that is colored.

Show Comparisons

A powerful method of showing and highlighting important data in a graph is to compare graphs. Instead of just showing the graph with the data to be analyzed, also show a graph that shows "normal" behavior or shows the same data, but from a different time (see Figure 1-9). The viewer can then compare the two graphs to immediately identify anomalies, exceptions, or simply differences.

Annotate Data

Graphs without legends or graphs without axis labels or units are not very useful. The only time when this is acceptable is when you want the viewer to qualitatively understand the data and the exact units of measure or the exact data is not important. Even in those cases, however, a little bit of text is needed to convey what data is visualized and what the viewer is looking at. In some cases, the annotations can come in the form of a figure caption or a text bubble in the graph (see Figure 1-10). Annotate as much as needed, but not more. You do not want the graphs to be overloaded with annotations that distract from the real data.

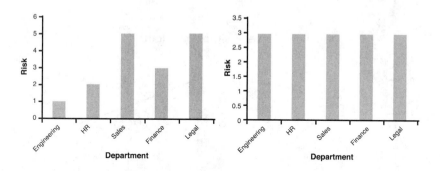

Figure 1-9   Two bar charts. The left chart shows normal behavior. The right side shows a graph of current data. Comparing the two graphs shows immediately that the current data does not look normal.

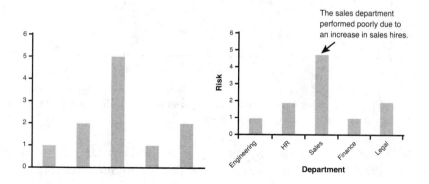

Figure 1-10   The left side bar chart does not contain any annotations. It is impossible for a user to know what the data represents. The right side uses axis labels, as well as text to annotate the outlier in the chart.

Show Causality

Whenever possible, make sure that the graphs do not only show that something is wrong or that there seems to be an "exception." Make sure that the viewers have a way to identify the root cause through the graph. This is not always possible in a single graph. In those cases, it might make sense to show a second graph that can be used to identify the root cause. This principle helps you to utilize graphs to make decisions and act upon findings (see Figure 1-11). A lot of visualizations are great about identifying interesting areas in graphs and help identify outliers but they do not help to take action. Have you ever asked yourself, "So what?" This is generally the case for graphs where root causes are not shown.

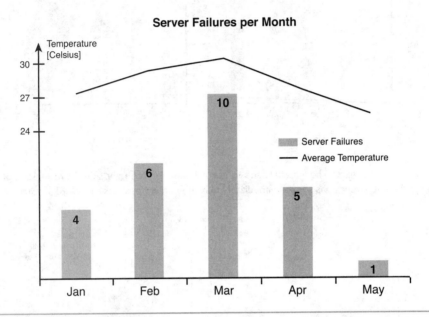

Figure 1-11 This chart illustrates how causality can be shown in a chart. The number of servers failing per month is related to the temperature in the datacenter.

By applying all the previously discussed principles, you will generate not just visually pleasing graphs and data visualizations, but also ones that are simple to read and ones that communicate information effectively.

INFORMATION SEEKING MANTRA

In a paper from 1996,[9] Ben Shneiderman introduced the **information seeking mantra** that defines the best way to gain insight from data. Imagine you have a large amount of data that needs to be displayed. For others to understand the data, they need to understand the overall nature of the data—they need an overview. Based on the overview, the

---

[9] "The Eyes Have It: A Task by Data Type Taxonomy for Information Visualization," by Ben Shneiderman, IEEE Symposium on Visual Languages, 1996.

viewer then wants to explore areas of the data (i.e., the graph) that look interesting. The viewer might want to exclude certain data by applying filters. And finally, after some exploration, the viewer arrives at a part of the data that looks interesting. To completely understand this data, viewers need a way to see the original, underlying data. In other words, they need the details that make up the graph. With the original data and the insights into the data gained through the graphical representation, a viewer can then make an informed and contextual statement about the data analyzed.

The information seeking mantra summarizes this process as follows:

Overview first, zoom and filter, then details on-demand.

We revisit the information seeking mantra in a later chapter, where I extend it to support some of the special needs we have in security visualization.

SUMMARY

Applying visualization to the field of computer security requires knowledge of two different disciplines: security and visualization. Although most people who are trying to visualize security data have knowledge of the data itself and what it means, they do not necessarily understand visualization. This chapter is meant to help those people especially to acquire some knowledge in the field of visualization. It provides a short introduction to some visualization principles and theories. It touched on a lot of principles and should motivate you to learn more about the field. However, the visualization principles will be enough to guide us through the rest of this book. It is a distilled set of principles that are crucial for generating effective security visualizations.

This chapter first discussed generic visualization and then explained why visualization is an important aspect of data analysis, exploration, and reporting. The bulk of this chapter addressed graph design principles. The principles discussed are tailored toward an audience that has to apply visualization to practical computer security use-cases. This chapter ended with a discussion of the information seeking mantra, a principle that every visualization tool should follow.

2

Data Sources

Visualization cannot happen without data or information. Therefore, before we can start talking about graphs and visualization, we have to talk about data. We need to create an understanding of the data sources that we have available. What data sources do we need to look at for security visualization? If we do not intimately understand each of the data sources that we use for visualization, we cannot generate meaningful graphs.

I start this chapter with a quick introduction to important terminology. This introduction leads into a short discussion about data. The concept of **time-series data** is one that I address first. Time-series data is very central to security visualization. The other type of data I discuss is static data or configuration data. I continue with a brief discussion about how we have to transform the data to make it useful for visualization. This is going to be only a very short discussion, but is extended and presented in much more detail in Chapter 5, "Visual Security Analysis." This section also covers a couple of challenges and problems associated with security data sources.

The remainder of the chapter is organized such that I am discussing important security data sources by going through the networking stack. Figure 2-1 shows the data sources that I discuss in this chapter, based on a network layer model. I am starting from the bottom with network captures and move up the stack one by one discussing the data sources.

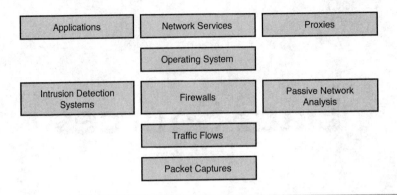

Figure 2-1   Network stack, indicating the data sources discussed in this chapter

The list of data sources I discuss in this chapter is not at all complete. Many more sources in your environment are useful for security visualization. This discussion should give you a good starting point for understanding these data sources and for understanding all the other data sources you might encounter.

Make sure you go through this chapter to be ready for the next one, where I actually start talking about visualization.

TERMINOLOGY

Before I start talking about data sources, we should agree on the usage of some key terms. The definitions are slight modifications of the ones that the Common Event Expression (CEE) standard published.[1] I start with the concept of an **event**:

> An event is an observable situation or modification within an environment that occurs over a period of time. An event may be a specific state or a state change of a system.

An event can be described or recorded. An individual record is often called a **log entry**:

> A log entry is a single record involving details from one or more events. A log entry is sometimes referred to as an event log, event record, alert, alarm, log message, log record, or audit record.

---

[1] Common Event Expression white paper, http://cee.mitre.org, 2007.

Finally, the collection of multiple log entries is called a **log**:

> A log is the collection of one or more log entries typically written to a local log file, a database, or sent across the network to a server. A log may also be referred to as a log file, an audit log, or an audit trail.

Throughout this book, I use the term event fairly loosely. A lot of people call a log entry an event. In cases where the colloquial user would refer to a log entry as an event, I do too.

With these definitions we can now move on to take a look at security data, the actual data we need for visualization.

SECURITY DATA

Everything that I show you in this book is based on security data. What is security data? From where do you get this data? These are questions we have to answer before we can do any visualization. We need to understand the data we are working with.

Security data is all the data that can help us with security analysis, investigations, reporting, or monitoring. Security data is not a distinct class of data. Records from sources such as networking devices (i.e., network flows or routing information), transaction records from financial systems, DHCP logs, and so on are all security data if they help us solve a security problem or answer a security question.

We can separate security data into two broad categories: time-series and static data. **Time-series** data is all data that can be attributed to a point in time. Log records fall into this category. Each record generally has a timestamp associated with it, identifying the time the activity was logged. Note that it is not necessarily true that the timestamp identifies the exact time an event (i.e., the physical manifestation of an activity) occurred. In certain cases, the recorded timestamp is the time when the log record was written. **Static** data is information that has no inherent time associated with it (files or documents, for example). Also, any kind of information about the machines in your environment or information about users can be considered static information. In certain cases, you can utilize static information as time-series data. For example, configuration files can be associated with a point in time by utilizing their last modification time.

One of the challenges of working with static files is that they span multiple lines. Processing this data is significantly harder than working with, for example, single-line log records. Why is this? It has to do with **parsing** of your data. Parsing is the process of taking a log record and identifying the individual parts in it. For example, assume you are given a firewall log entry. To generate a statistic over the most active machines, you need to extract that source address from the entry. This process is called parsing. You will find more on parsing in Chapter 4, "From Data to Graphs." It is significantly harder to parse a multiline record or a file because the information is not contained in a single line and information is context sensitive. It matters, for example, in what part of a configuration file a certain statement shows up. The parser therefore has to keep state, which complicates its design. As an example, take a vulnerability scan recorded as an XML file. If you want to do any analysis of vulnerabilities per host, you need to identify the place in the file where the host information is stored, and then relative to that find the vulnerabilities for the host and stitch that information together. The information is not contained in a single, easy-to-process entry.

For visualization tools to work with our data, we have to convert it to specific formats that the tools understand. Most of them do not contain built-in parsers that can be used to directly read the log files. Chapter 9, "Data Visualization Tools," discusses a few common formats used by visualization tools. To use your own data with those tools, you must transform your log files into these formats. The reason that many tools require different types of inputs is that each tool requires a slightly different set of information to operate.

It does not help that there is no currently established common format for writing log records. Parsers are needed for each and every log source to transform the data into the specific format that the visualization tool uses. There have been attempts in the past to standardize log records (for example, the Intrusion Detection Message Exchange Format [IDMEF]).[2] Unfortunately all of those attempts have failed. A new effort was started by MITRE at the beginning of 2007. It is called Common Event Expression (CEE).[3] The standard is still in its early stages. No specific log formats have been published. Some proposals have been submitted to the discussion mailing list,[4] but so far, nothing has been formally accepted. Hopefully, CEE, which is heavily influenced by industry and academic entities, is defining a widely accepted standard and will eliminate the need to write parsers for hundreds of different log formats. Visualization of security data would definitely benefit from such a development.

COMMON PROBLEMS

During your journey through analyzing log files and visualizing security data, you will come across a couple of problems. It is important to be aware of them. The first and most important one that you will most likely encounter is incomplete information. The

---

[2] http://xml.coverpages.org/idmef.html

[3] We wanted to call it CEX, but unfortunately, that was rejected by MITRE.

[4] www.nabble.com/CEE-Log-Event-Standard-f30667.html

second problem that you will find when you analyze network layer data is something that I call the source/destination confusion.

INCOMPLETE INFORMATION

Incomplete information can be a fairly significant problem in data visualization and log analysis. There are four levels of missing information:

- Missing log files or meta data
- Missing log records
- Incomplete log records
- Nonsynchronized time

It is fairly common that you are asked to conduct an investigation and you are given a set of log files. You start analyzing the logs, and you find something of interest. However, you can only get so far because you are missing the other logs to put the complete story together. This happens to me a lot when I analyze firewall log files. I find something interesting. However, I don't have any packet captures or operating system log files to get further details about the traffic. Log management is the answer to this problem. You need to make sure that all the necessary log files are collected at any time. You have to think about the use-cases ahead of time. Often, defining the use-cases dictates specifically how the logging architecture and processes need to be laid out.

Individual missing log records are a frustrating case, too. It is likely another case of incomplete logging architecture and processes. You need to make sure to not only define what devices you need logs from, but also what types of logs you need from them. A lot of devices are configurable and let the user define the types of logs recorded. Debug logs are hardly ever collected by default.

You might have all the log records that you need to fulfill your use-cases. You start visualizing some of the data only to realize that the log records do not have all the data you need. A number of applications enable the user to configure what information is being logged in the individual log records. For example, Internet Information Server (IIS) has an option whereby the user can define which fields to log. Make sure that these configurations are logging sufficient information for the purposes of your analysis. For example, if you are trying to see which machines are communicating with each other, their IP addresses need to be recorded.

Probably the most annoying situation is when you need some specific information, but there is no way to configure the applications or devices to actually log them. This phenomenon is one that I see a lot. The CEE[5] standard is therefore working on a set of logging recommendations that vendors should apply when they are implementing their logging capabilities. Unfortunately, nothing is published on this topic at this point. The only thing you can do to solve the problem of missing information in your log files is to contact the vendor of that piece of software or device to request an enhancement for the next version. Do not hesitate to do so. The vendors are generally open to suggestions in this area. Help the greater community by making these requests!

Finally, the way timestamps are recorded in log files is very important. When collecting data from systems in different time zones, the log records have to indicate the time zone. In addition, make sure that time granularity is sufficient enough. In some cases, log records have to record time with a precision of milliseconds. For example, financial transactions are very time sensitive, and differences of milliseconds can make a significant difference in how they are interpreted or the effects they have. But not only is the format in which the time is recorded important, so is the order in which events happen. The analysis of logs from distributed systems therefore requires time between machines to be synchronized. Without this synchronization, it is impossible to determine in what order two events occurred.

SOURCE/DESTINATION CONFUSION

The term **source/destination confusion** is one that I coined. To my surprise, I have not found anything in the literature that talks about this phenomenon. The problem is fairly common, however. Assume you are recording network traffic. Here are two packets from an HTTP connection, recorded by tcpdump. (See the next section, "Packet Captures," for more information about tcpdump.)

```
18:46:27.849292 IP 192.168.0.1.39559 > 127.0.0.1.80: S
1440554803:1440554803(0) win 32767
18:46:27.849389 IP 172.0.0.1.80 > 192.168.0.1.39559: S
1448343500:1448343500(0) ack 1440554804 win 32767
```

I connected to my loopback interface to access the Web server that is running on my laptop. If I use a simple parser to extract the source and destination IP addresses, I end up with a graph that looks like the one in Figure 2-2.

---

[5] http://cee.mitre.org

Figure 2-2 Simple graph that shows the concept of the source/destination confusion

You can see that there are two arrows present. One points from 192.168.0.1 to 127.0.0.1; the other one points in the other direction. However, the connection was only from 192.168.0.1 to 127.0.0.1, and no connection was opened the other way around! This happens because the parser mechanically extracted the source addresses as the first IP in the log, without trying to understand which packets were flowing from the client to the server and vice versa. To solve this problem, we need a more intelligent parser that keeps track of the individual client and server pairs.[6] This problem is additionally complicated by the fact that the parser falls out of sync. This can happen because of dropped or missed packets. In those cases, the parser does not know which of the communication endpoints is the source and which one is the destination. If you do not take care of source destination confusion in your visualization projects, you will generate graphs that look completely wrong, and you will not be able to make much sense out of them. Firewall and traffic log analysis is going to be especially complicated if you do not take the source/destination confusion into account.

PACKET CAPTURES

I am starting the discussion of data sources at the very bottom of the network stack. A network packet is physically received by the network interface. From there, it is passed to the operating system. The network driver in the operating system is responsible for decoding the information and extracting the link-layer headers (e.g., the Ethernet header). From there, the packet is analyzed layer by layer to pass it up in the network stack from one protocol handler to the next. Packet captures are recorded right when the network packet is handed from the network interface to the operating system.

There are multiple benefits to this approach as opposed to intercepting a packet higher up in the network stack. First of all, we get all the data the host sees. There is no layer in the path that could filter or discard anything. We get the complete packet,

---

[6] AfterGlow (http://afterglow.sourceforge.net) ships with such a parser; it can be found in the parser directory and is called tcpdump2csv.pl.

including the entire payload. The biggest disadvantage is that no higher-layer intelligence is applied to the traffic to interpret it. This means that we will not know, based on looking at the network traffic, how the destined application interpreted the packet. We can only make an educated guess. The second disadvantage is that the amount of data can be very large, especially if we collect traffic at a chokepoint in the network.

Various tools can be used to collect network traffic. The two most common ones are *Wireshark*[7] and *tcpdump*.[8] These tools listen on the network interface and display the traffic. Both tools take the raw network traffic and analyze the entire packet to decode the individual network protocols. They then display the individual header options and fields in a more or less human-readable form rather than the original binary format. Wireshark provides a graphical user interface to explore the network packets. It also ships with a command-line tool called *tshark*. Tcpdump is a command-line-only tool. Although Wireshark protocol-decoding capabilities are slightly better than the ones of tcpdump, I find myself using tcpdump more often.

Commonly, network traffic needs to be recorded for later analysis. The most common format for packet captures is the PCAP format. Most sniffers (or network traffic analysis tools) can read this binary format.

When using tcpdump, remember a couple of important things:

- Change the default capture length from 68 to 0. This will capture the entire packet and not just the first 68 bytes, which is generally enough to read the Ethernet, IP, and TCP/UDP headers. A lot of times you want more than just that. The command to execute is `tcpdump -s 0`.
- Disable name resolution to make the capture faster. The parameter to use is `tcpdump -nn`. This will turn off host, as well as port resolution.
- Make your output nonbuffered. This means that tcpdump will output the data on the console as soon as network traffic is recorded, instead of waiting for its internal buffer to fill up. This can be done by running `tcpdump -l`.

What is the actual data contained in packet captures that is of interest for visualization and analysis? The following list shows the typical types of information that you can extract from packet captures and their meaning:

- *Timestamp* ❶: The time the packet was recorded.
- *IP addresses* ❷: The addresses show the communication endpoints that generated the traffic.

---

[7] www.wireshark.org

[8] www.tcpdump.org

- *Ports* ❸: Network ports help identify what service is used on the network.
- *TCP flags* ❹: The flags can be used to verify what stage a connection is in. Often, looking at the combination of flags can identify simple attacks on the transport layer.
- *Ethernet addresses* ❺: Ethernet addresses reveal the setup of the local network.
- *Packet size* ❻: Packet size indicates the total size of the packet that was transmitted.

A sample packet capture, recorded with tcpdump, looks like this:

```
❶18:57:35.926420 ❺00:0f:1f:57:f9:ef > ❺00:50:f2:cd:ce:04,
ethertype IPv4 (0x0800), length ❻62: ❷192.168.2.38. ❸445 >
❷192.168.2.37. ❸4467: ❹S 2672924111:2672924111(0) ❹ack
1052151846 win 64240 <mss 1460,nop,nop,sackOK>
```

Sometimes it is interesting to dig deeper into the packets and extract some other fields. This is especially true when analyzing higher-level protocols inside the TCP packets. You could potentially even extract user names. Wireshark, for example, extracts user names from instant messenger traffic. Be careful when you are doing your visualizations based on network traffic. You will run into the source/destination confusion that I mentioned earlier.

For traffic analysis, I tend to use tshark rather than tcpdump because of its more advanced protocol analysis. There are a fair number of application layer protocols, such as instant messenger protocols, which are interpreted, as you can see in this sample capture:

```
0.000000  192.168.0.3 -> 255.255.255.255 UDP Source port: 4905
Destination port: 4905

1.561313 192.168.0.12 -> 207.46.108.72 MSNMS XFR 13 SB

1.595912 207.46.108.72 -> 192.168.0.12 MSNMS XFR 13 SB
207.46.27.163:1863 CKI 11999922.22226123.33471199

1.596378 192.168.0.12 -> 207.46.108.72 TCP 51830 > 1863 [ACK] Seq=11
Ack=62 Win=65535 Len=0 TSV=614503137 TSER=8828236

1.968203 192.168.0.12 -> 207.46.27.163 TCP 52055 > 1863 [SYN] Seq=0
Len=0 MSS=1460 WS=3 TSV=614503140 TSER=0
```

```
2.003898 207.46.27.163 -> 192.168.0.12 TCP 1863 > 52055 [SYN, ACK] Seq=0
Ack=1 Win=16384 Len=0 MSS=1460 WS=0 TSV=0 TSER=0

2.003980 192.168.0.12 -> 207.46.27.163 TCP 52055 > 1863 [ACK] Seq=1
Ack=1 Win=524280 Len=0 TSV=614503141 TSER=0

2.004403 192.168.0.12 -> 207.46.27.163 MSNMS USR 1 xxxxxxx@hotmail.com
1111111111.77777777.6666699

2.992735 192.168.0.12 -> 207.46.27.163 MSNMS [TCP Retransmission] USR 1
xxxxxxx@hotmail.com 1111111111.77777777.6666699
```

As you can see in this example, tshark explicitly calls out the users communicating over instant messenger. Tcpdump does not contain that level of information.

Network captures prove useful for a lot of network-level analysis. However, as soon as applications need to be analyzed, the packet captures do not provide the necessary application logic to reproduce application behavior. In those cases, you should consider other sources.

TRAFFIC FLOWS

One layer above packet captures in the data stack we find traffic flows. By moving up the stack, we lose some of the information that was available on lower levels. Traffic flows are captured on routers or switches, which operate at Layer 4 (transport layer) in the network stack. This means that we don't have any application layer information available. It is primarily routers that record traffic flows. However, sometimes people set up hosts to do the same. The different router vendors designed their own protocol or format to record traffic flows. Cisco calls it NetFlow,[9] the IETF task force standardized the concept of NetFlow as IPFIX,[10] and yet another version of traffic flows is sFlow,[11] a.k.a. RFC 3176, and the version of traffic flows that Juniper supports is called cFlow.[12] All the formats are fairly similar. They mainly differ in the transport used to get the flows from the

---

[9] www.cisco.com/go/netflow

[10] www.ietf.org/html.charters/ipfix-charter.html

[11] www.sflow.org

[12] www.caida.org/tools/measurement/cflowd

routers to a central collector. Any one of the flow protocols can be used to collect traffic information and analyze it. Traffic flows record the following attributes:

- *Timestamp* ❶: The time the flow was recorded.
- *IP addresses* ❷: The addresses representing the endpoints of the observed communications.
- *Ports* ❸: Network ports help identify the services that were used in the observed communications.
- *Layer 3 protocol* ❹: The protocol used on the network layer. Generally, this will be IP.
- *Class of service:* The priority assigned to the flow.
- *Network interfaces* ❺: The network interfaces that the traffic enters, respectively leaves the device.
- *Autonomous systems (ASes):* In some cases, the AS[13] of the endpoints of the observed communication can be recorded.
- Next hop: The Layer 3 address of the next hop to which the traffic is forwarded.
- Number of bytes ❻ *and packets* ❼: The size and number of Layer 3 packets in the flow.
- *TCP flags:* Accumulation of TCP flags observed in the flow.

Routers can generally be instrumented to record most of this information. It is not always possible to collect all of it. Mainly it is the AS, the next hop, and the TCP flags that are not always available. A sample record, collected with nfdump (see the sidebar for more information about nfdump), looks like this:

```
❶2005-10-22 23:02:53.967  0.000   ❹TCP  ❷10.0.0.2: ❸40060 0>
❷10.0.0.1: ❸23    ❼1    ❻60   1    ❺0    ❺1
```

You might realize that there is some interesting new information that we did not get from packet captures, namely the AS, the next hop of a packet's path through the network, and the number of packets in a flow. Each router decides, based on its routing table, what interface and next hop to forward a packet to. This information can prove useful when you are trying to plot network traffic paths and to understand the general network topology.

---

[13] For more information about autonomous systems and core routing technology, such as BGP, have a look at www.cisco.com/univercd/cc/td/doc/cisintwk/ito_doc/bgp.htm.

Note that we are not getting any information beyond some of the key Layer 3 and Layer 4 data. Neither application data nor any sort of extended Layer 3 and Layer 4 information is collected. This could be a challenge in your analyses. Also note that, due to the sheer volume of traffic flows, it is not always practical to keep all of them. In addition, in some cases, because of high utilization, the reporting device will not record traffic flows. Most routers turn off traffic captures in favor of actually routing packets when under load.

COLLECTING TRAFFIC FLOWS

You can collect traffic flows directly on a host, rather than a router, with a variety of tools. Argus, available at www.qosient.com/argus, is an example of such a tool. Run the following command to collect traffic flows from the machine's Ethernet interface (eth0) and store it in the file file.argus:

```
argus –i eth0 –w file.argus
```

Another way to collect traffic flows is to first collect packet captures and then convert them into traffic flows with, for example, Argus:[14]

```
argus -r file.pcap -w file.argus
```

Looking at the records that this command generated with the ra command that is part of the Argus distribution yields the following flow records:

```
$ ra -r file.argus -n
05-14-06 11:06:38 e  icmp 10.69.69.13     -> 10.69.69.20    4  600  URP
05-14-06 11:06:43 e  llc  0:9:43:e0:7d:b8 -> 1:0:c:cc:cc:cc 1  376  INT
05-14-06 11:06:58 eI udp  10.69.69.20     -> 10.69.69.13.53 2  156  INT
```

Generally, I do not generate traffic flows from packet captures but instead instruct my routers to send NetFlow directly to a central location. To enable NetFlow on a Cisco router, use the following commands:

```
interface Ethernet0/0
  ip route-cache flow
ip flow-export version 5
ip flow-export destination 192.168.0.1 8888
```

---

[14] Note that you need to install the Argus server and not just the Argus client to execute the argus command.

NETFLOW VERSION 9

You can configure your router to export NetFlow version 9[15] records, instead of version 5. You can use version 9 of NetFlow to record more data about flows, which is sometimes useful. To configure NetFlow 9 on your Cisco router, use the following commands:

```
interface Ethernet0/0
  ip route-cache flow
ip flow-export destination 192.168.0.1 8888
ip flow-export version 9 bgp-nexthop
ip flow-capture vlan-id
```

This not only enables NetFlow 9 on Ethernet0/0, but also instructs the router to add the bgp-nexthop and vlan-id fields in the output. These fields are available only in version 9 and higher. NetFlow 9 is very different from version 5 on various levels. For example, the transport is template based, which makes it more scalable. From a traffic record perspective, version 9 has a wide variety of new fields available that can be recorded (for example, Multiprotocol Label Switching [MPLS]-related information). Furthermore, starting with NetFlow 8, the export of data from aggregation caches is possible.

Aggregation caches allow the user to summarize NetFlow data on the router before it is exported to a NetFlow collector. Instead of exporting every single flow, aggregate statistics are exported. This improves performance on routers, and it reduces the bandwidth required to transfer the records.

Here is an example that shows how to configure NetFlow to record aggregation information:

```
ip flow-aggregation cache destination-prefix
  cache entries 2048
  export destination 192.168.0.1 991
  export version 9
  exit
interface Ethernet0/0
  ip flow egress
```

---

[15] www.cisco.com/en/US/products/ps6645/products_ios_protocol_option_home.html

This example defines aggregates based on the destination IP addresses and their prefixes. A sample output looks like this:

```
Dst If   Dst Prefix   Msk  AS  Flows  Pkts  B/Pk
Null     0.0.0.0      /0   0   5      13    52
Et0/0.1  172.16.6.0   /24  0   1      1     56
Et1/0.1  172.16.7.0   /24  0   3      31K   1314
Et0/0.1  172.16.1.0   /24  0   16     104K  1398
Et1/0.1  172.16.10.0  /24  0   9      99K   1412
```

You can find more information about NetFlow aggregation at www.cisco.com/en/US/docs/ios/12_4/netflow/configuration/guide/onf_ccg.html.

Note that Argus does not support NetFlow 9 yet. Should you get a blank screen when collecting NetFlow with Argus, that's why. Nfdump, on the other hand, deals just fine with version 9.

Replace Ethernet0/0 with the interface on which you want to enable NetFlow accounting, and change 192.168.0.1 to be the machine that is collecting the NetFlows. The set of commands enables NetFlow 5, the version supported by most routers and which contains the record details discussed previously. Various tools enable you to collect the NetFlows generated by the routers.[16] The challenge with collection is that you will be collecting multiple flow records for the same connection. There will be duplicate flow records, even if you are collecting network flows from only a single source. In the case of longstanding connections, NetFlow will periodically report the current status of that connection. Therefore, you have to **de-duplicate** and **stitch** the records back together. Various tools can help with this task. One tool that I use to do this type of processing is ragator from Argus.

Argus ships with a number of tools that help generate, process, and analyze traffic flows. Other tools are better at collecting NetFlow data on a large scale, such as nfdump (see sidebar). However, Argus ships a great collection of tools to analyze NetFlow data:

- ragator merges matching flow records together.
- racluster merges flow records based on custom criteria.
- ranonymize anonymizes flow records.

---

[16] See, for example, www.cert.org/netsa.

The following section shows how these tools enable you to work with traffic-flow data.

NFDUMP

Nfdump (http://nfdump.sourceforge.net) is another tool that enables you to collect NetFlow data. It is fairly similar to Argus, but with some important differences. If you are operating in a bigger environment and you want to collect NetFlow data, you should use nfdump. Argus was not built to collect NetFlow. It adds a lot of overhead and does not perform too well. Nfdump is optimized for speed and efficiency in reading NetFlow data. The data-management capabilities of nfdump are by far superior. The collected flows are automatically compressed, the files can be rotated, and they can be set to expire after a certain time. Run the following command to use nfdump to collect NetFlow on port 8888:

```
./nfcapd -w -D -p 8888
```

Then use the following command to read one of the capture files and customize the output format to write only the fields you really need. This is just an example to show how you can change the output format to include the interfaces in the output:

```
./nfdump -r /var/tmp/nfcapd.200801021115 -o "fmt:%ts %td %pr %sap -> %dap %pkt %byt %fl %out %in"
```

Sample output generated with this command looks like this:

Date flow start	Duration	Proto	Src IP Addr:Port	Dst IP Addr:Port	Packets	Bytes	Flows	Output	Input
2005-10-22	23:02:00.859	0.000 ICMP	10.0.0.2:0	0>	10.0.0.1:3.3	1	176	1	0	1
2005-10-22	23:02:53.967	0.000 TCP	0.0.0.2:40060	0>	10.0.0.1:23	1	60	1	0	1

AGGREGATING TRAFFIC FLOWS

A sample use of ragator, to aggregate flow records, looks like this:

```
ragator -r file.argus -nn -A -s +dur -s +sttl -s +dttl
```

This aggregates all the flows in the Argus capture file (file.argus) and outputs the flow information. The parameters enable application-level byte counts and add duration, as well as TTL fields, to the output. Here is some sample output generated by the preceding command:

```
04-12-08 16:16:27.554609  tcp   64.127.105.60.993    <?>   192.168.0.10.51087 3   0
159  0   TIM  60.010402   57   0
04-12-08 16:16:33.616371  udp  208.201.224.11.53     ->    192.168.0.10.52233 1   0
86   0   INT   0.000000   59   0
04-12-08 16:16:33.630215  udp  208.201.224.11.53     ->    192.168.0.10.52234 1   0
93   0   INT   0.000000   59   0
```

CLUSTERING TRAFFIC FLOWS

To summarize traffic flows, you can use the Argus racluster command. A sample application is the following:

```
racluster -r file.argus -m saddr daddr dport -c, -s saddr daddr - 'tcp and dst port 22'
```

This invokes the racluster command, which clusters flows based on the attributes given by the -m parameter. In this case, racluster aggregates or clusters all the connections and their ports. The output shows only the source and destination address (-s). The flows are filtered to show only TCP connections to port 22 (tcp and dst port 22). The -c parameter is a new one in version 3 of the Argus tools. It defines what output separator to use (i.e., what character is used to separate individual fields). The default is tabulators, but you can change it to a comma to generate CSV output.

The preceding command might look wrong because not all the fields that were clustered on are also used in the output. You would assume that the -s parameter should also use dport as an argument to show the destination port. There is a reason for not doing so. By using the command as is, there is going to be an output record for every port that was used. If multiple ports were used on the same connection, this will result in duplicate output records. You can then count how many times each connections was recorded and determine from that how many distinct ports were used by that connection.

ANONYMIZING TRAFFIC FLOWS

Another handy utility provided by the latest version of Argus is ranonymize. A sample invocation is as follows:

```
ranonymize -r file.argus -w - | ra -r - ..
```

This instructs `ranonymize` to read the flow file `file.argus` and anonymize the records. The output is then passed on to another Argus command, `ra` in this example. The `ra` command is used to read the records from the anonymization command and then display the output on the console. You can configure `ranonymize` to anonymize any number of the following flow attributes:

- Network addresses
- Protocol-specific port numbers
- Timestamps
- TCP sequence numbers
- IP identifiers
- Record sequence numbers

When anonymizing, for example, the network addresses, the subnets are kept intact. Otherwise, the entire flow file would not make sense anymore.

As you can probably imagine, traffic flows can be used for a lot of use-cases. Visualizing them can help you wade through the insane amount of data that is generally collected.

FIREWALLS

Firewalls operate on Layer 4 of the network stack. Some newer generations operate on Layer 7 and apply application inspection, deep content inspection, or protocol analysis. Different vendors call this different things, although technically they are all the same. I discuss the application layer functionality in the next section when I cover intrusion detection and prevention systems.

When reduced to the traditional functionality, firewalls generate log entries very similar to traffic flows. The only difference is the addition of information about whether a packet was passed through the firewall or was blocked. The common fields a firewall record contains, therefore, include the following:

- *Timestamp* ❶: The time the connection was recorded.
- *IP addresses* ❷: The addresses representing the endpoints of the blocked or passed communication.
- *Ports* ❸: Network ports help identify the services that were used in the communication.

- *Translated IP addresses (and ports):* In some cases, when Network Address Translation (NAT) or Port Address Translation (PAT) is applied, the firewall will also log the translated addresses and, in even fewer cases, the translated port numbers.
- *Ethernet addresses:* The Layer 2 addresses (Ethernet addresses) reveal the previous and the next router that handles the traffic for this communication.
- *Network interface* ❹: The network interface through which the packet was processed. Sometimes the firewall log also indicates what direction (in or out) the packet was flowing.
- *Packet size* ❺: The number of bytes in the packet.
- *Rule or ACL number* ❻: The rule number responsible for passing or blocking this packet. Unfortunately this information is not always present.
- *Action* ❼: An indication whether the packet was blocked or passed.

The following sample firewall log contains most of these fields:

```
❶Oct 13 20:00:05.680894 rule ❻57/0(match): ❼pass in on ❹xl1:
❷195.141.69.45. ❸1030 > ❷217.12.4.104. ❸53: ❺7040 [1au]
A? mx1.mail.yahoo.com. (47) (DF)

Oct 13 20:00:05.760437 rule 179/0(match): pass in on xl1:
195.141.69.44.54700 > 64.156.215.5.25: S 462887145:462887145(0) win
32768 <mss 1460,nop,wscale 0,nop,nop,timestamp 3931103936 0> (DF)

Oct 13 20:00:10.095829 rule 197/0(match): block in on xl0: 66.140.98.85
> 195.141.69.47: icmp: echo request
```

As you can see in the example output, in addition to the fields discussed, the firewall (an OpenBSD's pf firewall) logged a few additional pieces of information that other firewalls do not log (TCP flags, for example). It also did some protocol analysis to show a slightly decoded DNS packet (see first line).

Analyzing firewall log files can be very frustrating. Be aware of the following challenges:

- Make sure logging is turned on and set to an appropriate logging level. This is the hardest problem you will face. How much logging is enough? If you can, log all blocked and passed connections. A lot of times, this is not feasible because of the large number of connections passing through the firewall. Come up with the use-cases that you need to cover and define your logging strategy accordingly.

- For which interface and in what direction on that interface is logging turned on? With the most flexible firewalls, you have four places to enable logging: on the inbound interface coming in, on the outbound interface going out, or on both interfaces in the opposite direction (see Figure 2-3). Depending on the setup, you might end up with redundant or duplicate log entries. De-duplication is not easy! Make sure your logging policy is sound such that you are not collecting duplicate log entries.

- Missing information in log records can be another challenge. For example, **iptables** is notorious for not even having a standard field that defines whether a packet was passed or blocked.[17] You need to use the `--log-prefix` to explicitly add a note to the log record that indicates a block or a pass. Other firewalls expose similar problems.

- Layer 4 firewalls do not log any higher-layer information, such as application data. This can make log analysis especially hard because the application context is missing. Just think of the case where Web traffic is analyzed. You will never see the URL that was used.

- Although most firewalls are fairly good at logging connection information (i.e., blocked and passed packets), they are horrible at logging updates to their ruleset. A fair number of firewalls do not log rule changes at all. The others do not log exactly what has changed. This makes it really hard to verify and audit firewall rule changes. You might need some other mechanism to address this problem.

- Firewalls often do not log logins to the box, changes to the general configuration, and so forth. This can be a challenge for change management.

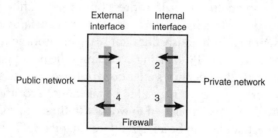

Figure 2-3 Firewall schematic showing two firewall interfaces and four places where logging could be applied: 1 is inbound on the external interface, 2 is inbound on the internal interface, 3 is outbound on the internal interface, and 4 is outbound on the external interface.

---

[17] Based on the iptables architecture, this makes sense to a certain degree, but I still do not understand why the target chain is not recorded in the logs.

INTRUSION DETECTION AND PREVENTION SYSTEMS

Hardly any IT infrastructure is operated without intrusion detection or prevention systems. A defense in-depth approach suggests that you not just filter traffic or deploy other prevention mechanisms but that you also implement detection capabilities. Dedicated detection capabilities are available (for example, in intrusion detection systems [IDSs]). IDSs come in two forms: host based (HIDS) and network based (NIDS). HIDS are deployed on the end system itself. They monitor process behavior, user activities, and network activity from the host's perspective. NIDS are listening on the network. They can be either inline or operated as a sniffer. For the purpose of this discussion, I focus on NIDS, although a lot of the discussion applies directly to HIDS, too. In addition, I talk mostly about NIDS and not network-based intrusion prevention systems (NIPS). The difference is that a NIDS detects only violations, whereas a NIPS can take immediate action and mitigate the problem by blocking the offending network traffic. Again, all the concepts we discuss here apply one to one.

A NIDS employs two different types of detection methods: signature and anomaly based. **Signature-based** approaches use a rule or signature set that defines patterns corresponding to known attacks or misuse patterns. They can be simple string-matching expressions and increase in complexity to difficult state transitions. **Anomaly-based** systems try to establish a normal baseline of the objects being monitored. Statistically significant deviations from this normal behavior are then flagged as possible violations or anomalies.

One of the biggest challenges with NIDSs is the vast number of false positives they generate. Unlike all the data sources we have seen so far, we cannot always trust the alerts a NIDS emits. Two possible solutions help address this problem: filtering or prioritizing events. Filtering is based on black lists, where certain values are known false positives and are filtered out. This approach obviously does not scale. Environments change and the black list needs to change with it. Prioritizing events uses the paradigm of letting events of interest bubble up to get the operator's attention. Getting prioritization correct is not an easy task. Many different parameters need to be taken into account. Later in this book, I show how visualization can be used to work with these approaches to reduce the number of NIDS events that have to be analyzed (see Chapter 5, "Visual Security Analysis").

A typical intrusion detection event carries the following information in an alert (or a log record):

- *Timestamp* ❶: The time the violation was recorded.
- *IP addresses* ❷ : The addresses representing the endpoints of the observed communications. The source is the potential attacker and the target the victim.

- *Ports* ❸: Network ports help identify the services that were used in the observed attack.
- *Priority* ❹: A numeric value assigned by the IDS to rate the importance of the generated alert or the severity of the observed communication (i.e., attack). Each IDS uses different scales to record this property, which makes cross-correlation of IDSs hard.
- *Signature* ❺: The precise rule that was matched. The attack/behavior observed.
- *Protocol fields* ❻: TCP/IP packet fields of the observed communication. This helps identify some of the attack properties.
- *Vulnerability* ❼: The vulnerability associated with the observed behavior, indicating the type of attack attempted.

Note again that NIDS logs generally do not contain any normal or legitimate behavior. NIDSs are used to flag abuses or violations. This reduces the number of use-cases that we can use NIDS logs for. It also means that we often need other information aside from NIDS alerts to reproduce how a certain attack was executed and assess the impact.

NIDSs are not very good at logging. Most of them do not log when a new set of signatures was applied or when the signature set was changed. This information is crucial for change management. In addition, hardly any NIDS has a notion of a **signature confidence.** Some of the signatures are written very tightly, meaning that the potential of false positives is really minimal. It is important to have this piece of information so as to not spend a lot of time trying to prove that the alert is a false positive. Alerts triggered by a signature with low confidence can be given a lower priority, and we can look for more evidence to either confirm or deny the reported attack or violation.

By the virtue of NIDSs working on the lower network layers, their alerts do not contain any application layer information. **User names** are among the useful information missing in NIDS alerts. Without the user who executed an attack or committed a violation, we can only associate the activity with an IP address, a machine. It would be much more useful to assign an attack to an actual user rather than just a machine. This is part of a bigger problem that will occupy us later in this book.

Collecting IDS alerts is not always as simple as reading from a syslog feed. Syslog is fairly restricted with regard to how much data it can carry. Only 1,024 bytes can be carried by most syslog implementations. IDS alerts generally need to carry more information. This has led the IDS vendors to invent all kinds of proprietary transmission protocols. To collect IDS alerts, you might have to implement a special network receiver, or it might be necessary to read the IDS alerts directly from the IDS's databases. In other cases, IDSs store the events in files, which makes it slightly easier to read the alerts.

Snort[18] has various ways to collect NIDS logs. One of them is to write an "alert" log. A sample alert record follows:

```
[**] [❺1:1768:2] ❺WEB-IIS header field buffer overflow attempt [**]
[Classification: Web Application Attack] [Priority: ❹1]
❶12/05-13:42:46.138639 ❷217.118.195.58: ❸2525 ->
❷13.144.137.82: ❸32949
❻TCP TTL:64 TOS:0x0 ID:58929 IpLen:20 DgmLen:951 DF
***AP*** Seq: 0x3A86174F  Ack: 0x2527838A  Win: 0x16A0  TcpLen: 32
TCP Options (3) => NOP NOP TS: 2898391430 22834846
[Xref => ❼CVE-2003-0242]
```

The first line records the signature that was triggered. The information following shows the priority and a categorization of the alert. Following that is the time the alert was recorded, as well as the involved entities (IP addresses). The following three lines list a set of TCP and IP packet fields that might be of interest in further investigating the attack. The last line ties the alert to a vulnerability, generally linking to a CVE[19] entry.

Some NIDSs provide a capability to not just record an alert when an attack or violation is observed, but to also record the network packets associated with the attack. This capability can prove useful for weeding out false positives by verifying the alert against the actual traffic. Emails, for example, are prone to triggering all kinds of IDS signatures. In Snort, you can use the tag modifier[20] on a signature to record the packets associated with the alert.

So far, I have ignored the topic of network-based intrusion prevention systems (NIPSs) and Layer 7 firewalls. I have talked only about detection. The reason is that these systems are not that different from NIDSs. Instead of just generating an alarm for potential attacks, a NIPS or a Layer 7 firewall can actually block a communication. Therefore, the NIPS signatures need to be written very tightly, with a very low rate of false positives. Otherwise, you are going to block legitimate traffic, which will have a negative impact on the availability of your services. The log files of these devices look fairly similar to NIDSs. In addition to all the fields of an IDS, an IPS also records whether a communication was blocked.

---

[18] www.snort.org

[19] The Common Vulnerability Enumeration (CVE) is the quasi standard for cataloging vulnerabilities. You can find it at http://cve.mitre.org.

[20] You can find more information about how to use the tag modifier on Snort signatures at www.snort.org/docs/snort_htmanuals/htmanual_280/node320.html.

- *Hostname* ❷: The host that logged the record. When forwarding syslog records, an additional hostname is added for the machine that forwarded the record. However, only a maximum of two hostnames is supported.
- *Process* ❸ *and process ID* ❹: The logging process and its ID.

The remainder of a syslog message is free text. This is the reason that parsing syslog messages is such a complicated and elaborate effort. Here are a couple of log entries that illustrate the problem:

```
❶Nov 12 14:54:11 ❷dbhost ❸sshd[❹24053]: Bad protocol version
identification 'Big-Brother-Monitor-1.9i' from ::ffff:10.1.222.7
Nov 12 14:57:15 dbhost sshd[24066]: Invalid user rgibbons from
::ffff:10.1.222.130
Nov 12 14:57:16 dbhost sshd[24066]: Failed none for invalid user
rgibbonslke from ::ffff:10.1.222.130 port 4832 ssh2
Nov 12 14:57:24 dbhost sshd[24068]: Accepted password for user2 from
::ffff:10.1.222.130 port 4833 ssh2
Nov 12 15:18:24 Macintosh-6 sudo[34774]: raffaelmarty : TTY=ttys002 ;
PWD=/private/var/audit ; USER=root ; COMMAND=/usr/sbin/praudit
20071225050142.20071225220015
```

There is not one parser that could be used to analyze all the different syslog records. To address this problem, some standardization efforts are underway to try to create some guidelines for applications to follow. For more information, have a look at the CEE effort, which you can find at http://cee.mitre.org.

On Windows, logging is slightly more involved. A lot of people forward event log information from Windows to a syslog host. A number of available tools, such as Snare,[22] Kiwi Syslog,[23] and NTsyslog,[24] enable you to do this. Unfortunately, the log files collected this way are fairly cryptic, and not necessarily all the information from the original Windows event is preserved. A sample Windows log collected through Snare looks like this:

```
<14>Dec 10 10:42:19 winhost MSWinEventLog      1      Security
3193    Sat Nov 17 04:01:52 2007        540    Security     netbackup
```

---

[22] www.intersectalliance.com/projects/SnareWindows/

[23] www.kiwisyslog.com

[24] http://ntsyslog.sourceforge.net

```
User    Success Audit   NAS-1   Logon/Logoff Successful Network Logon:
User Name: netbackup     Domain: IT      Logon ID: (0x0,0x15362E)
Logon Type: 3    Logon Process: NtLmSsp       Authentication Package:
NTLM     Workstation Name: \\192.168.222.5     Logon GUID: -      Caller
User Name: -     Caller Domain: -     CallerLogon ID: -      Caller
Process ID: -     Transited Services: -     Source Network Address:
192.168.222.5     Source Port: 0        5
```

Fairly cryptic, isn't it? Some numbers are floating around without a label, making it impossible to determine what they mean without knowing the format's definition. Nevertheless, this is better than nothing.

A better approach to log management on Windows is to use the Windows Management Instrumentation Command (WMIC).[25] This command enables you to query a huge range of information about remote or local systems. The following command, for example gathers all the log entries from the system log and stores that information in CSV format in the file log.csv:

```
WMIC NTEVENT where LogFile='System' get /format:csv > log.csv
```

A sample entry from the log.csv file looks like this:

```
Node,Category,CategoryString,ComputerName,Data,EventCode,EventIdentifier
,EventType,InsertionStrings,Logfile,Message,RecordNumber,SourceName,Time
Generated,TimeWritten,Type,User
RAM,0,,RAM,,63,-2147483585,2,{OffProv12;Root\MSAPPS12},Application,A
provider, OffProv12, has been registered in the WMI namespace,
Root\MSAPPS12, to use the LocalSystem account.  This account is
privileged and the provider may cause a security violation if it does
not correctly impersonate user
requests.,1064,WinMgmt,20071129212944.000000-480,20071129212944.000000-
480,warning,NT AUTHORITY\SYSTEM
RAM,0,,RAM,,63,-2147483585,2,{OffProv12;Root\MSAPPS12},Application,A
provider, OffProv12, has been registered in the WMI namespace,
Root\MSAPPS12, to use the LocalSystem account.  This account is
privileged and the provider may cause a security violation if it does
not correctly impersonate user
requests.,1063,WinMgmt,20071129212944.000000-480,20071129212944.000000-
480,warning,NT AUTHORITY\SYSTEM
```

---

[25] http://technet.microsoft.com/en-us/library/bb742610.aspx

This makes the Windows event log nicely accessible. You can tune the query to get exactly the information needed. The only drawback is that the WMIC command needs to be executed on a regular basis to get new events. No mode enables you to continuously poll the logs.

Recently, the Samba project started working on a library that enables Linux hosts to remotely query Windows event logs via the WMI mechanism.[26] The Linux libraries are available at http://dev.zenoss.org/svn/trunk/inst/externallibs/. The Read Me contained in this tarball has detailed instructions on how to build the source code, even for MAC environments. It also explains in detail how to execute the commands to remotely collect information from your Windows systems.

OPERATING SYSTEM STATE INFORMATION

Additional OS information can be gained from the OS state. Each OS ships with tools that make state information available to the user. State information is different from configuration information, which is the setup of the OS. We discuss configuration information later in this chapter. Tools available in UNIX to gather OS state information include the following:

- *netstat:* Displays network status, including all types of networking-related information, such as open sockets, network interface statistics, and so on.
- *iostat:* Reports input/output statistics for CPUs and disks.
- *vmstat:* Reports memory statistics.
- *lsof:* Outputs a list of all open file descriptors and the processes using them.
- *top:* Shows a list of running processes along with process statistics. Information such as memory utilization, runtime, process ID, parent process ID, and so on is shown for each process on the system.
- *ps:* Displays status for each process running on the system. The output contains information about the process ID, the current state, the process owner, the command that initiated the process, and so forth.

Windows ships with some of the same tools, such as netstat or tasklist. In addition, add-ons exist that you can use to inspect other types of information. A great collection of tools is available at http://technet.microsoft.com/en-us/sysinternals/default.aspx. In addition, you can also use the WMIC command to retrieve information from hosts. For

---

[26] For more information about WMI, check http://www.microsoft.com/whdc/system/pnppwr/wmi/.

example, to remotely fetch information about running processes, formatted in CSV, you can use the following command:

```
WMIC /NODE:"ram" process GET Caption, CommandLine /format:csv.xsl
```

The output looks like that listed here. The node identifies the machine from which the information was collected, Caption is the name of the process and CommandLine shows exactly what command was executed to start the process:

```
Node,Caption,CommandLine
RAM,System Idle Process,
RAM,smss.exe,\SystemRoot\System32\smss.exe
RAM,winlogon.exe,winlogon.exe
```

The same can be done for many other pieces of information on these machines (for example, the running services or memory information).

Network devices make static information available, too. You can use various techniques to gather the output of network-device-related commands. For some of the data, SNMP is the only way to get to it. Under UNIX, you can use a toolkit called Net-SNMP[27] to access SNMP information on remote devices. For example, the following command enables you to retrieve the number of CRC errors on the interfaces of a Cisco router:

```
snmpwalk -v 1 -c public 192.168.99.1 .1.3.6.1.4.1.9.2.1.57
```

This command assumes that the SNMP community string is configured to be `public` and the router is at `192.168.99.1`. The information queried by the command is located at node `.1.3.6.1.4.1.9.2.1.57`. SNMP organizes information in a tree-like structure. Every node of the tree represents a specific piece of information that can be read or written. The structure of the tree is referred to as the Management Information Base (MIB) (see Figure 2-4). Read from left to right, the object identifier (OID) `.1.3.6.1.4.1.9.2.1.57` identifies what branch to take at each node in the tree. At the root, choose number 1. Then choose number 3, and so on. The path in the preceding sample query takes us to a Cisco sub-branch that holds the CRC errors on router interfaces.

---

[27] http://net-snmp.sourceforge.net

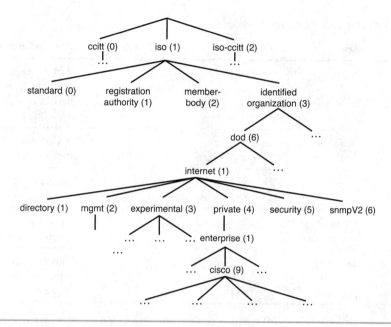

Figure 2-4 MIB structure

You need to execute an SNMP WALK and not a simple GET to get the CRC errors for router interfaces, because there might be multiple interfaces in your network device. The WALK returns the CRC errors for all the interfaces (not just one interface). Table 2-1 lists commands that enable you to gather state information on different platforms. The table also shows what information (i.e., data fields) is returned in the output.

Table 2-1 Gathering State Information

Platform	Use	Command	Information in Output
Cisco router/ switch	ARP cache	`sh arp`	MAC address, IP address, interface
Cisco router/ switch	CPU load	`snmpwalk .1.3.6.1.4.1.9.9.109.1.1.1.1.5`[28]	The overall CPU busy percentage in the last 5-minute period

continues

---

[28] A great tool to search the Cisco MIBs is located at http://tools.cisco.com/Support/SNMP/do/BrowseOID.do.

Table 2-1   Gathering State Information *(continued)*

Platform	Use	Command	Information in Output
Cisco router/switch	Interface	`sh interface`	Interface, packet statistics, error rates, interface type, interface configurations, and so on
Cisco router/switch	Failed packet deliveries	`sh int | inc (errors|line prot)`	Interface, packet errors, interface statistics
		`snmpwalk 1.3.6.1.4.1.9.2.2.1.1.12`	Number of CRC errors for each interface
Operating system	Open network connections	`netstat -na`	Protocol, local address, foreign address, state
Operating system	Listening network sockets	`netstat -nlp`[29]	Protocol, local address, foreign address, state, process
Operating system	ARP cache	`arp -an`	MAC address, IP address, interface
UNIX	CPU/disk load	`iostat`	us % of CPU time in user mode sy % of CPU time in system mode id % of cpu time in idle mode KB/t Kilobytes per transfer tps Transfers per second MB/s Megabytes per second
UNIX	Interface statistics	`netstat -i -I <interface>`	Interface, MTU, MAC address, input/output -packets, and errors
Windows	Running processes	`tasklist`	Process name, process ID, session name, memory usage

---

[29] The –p option to show the listening process is not supported on all platforms.

Table 2-1 summarizes some of the commands available on operating systems and network devices that return state information. Unfortunately, none of this information is collected in any kind of log file that can be read. It can be useful to know the open network ports on a machine over a period of time, either for statistical purposes or for investigations. CPU utilization is an example where statistical information is interesting. Deviations and anomalies can be seen easily and action taken. Another example is the list of running processes on a machine. Knowing the running processes at any time can be invaluable for analyzing a security incident. In a proactive scenario, knowing which processes were running at specific points in time might help reveal some anomaly that can be linked to a security incident. You have to set up a process that runs these tools and then captures the output. The difficulty is that you must extract certain information from this output to do the desired analysis. I do not detail how such an implementation looks.[30]

OPERATING SYSTEM LOG PROBLEMS

The main problem with OS logs—Windows or Linux—is the unstructured nature of the log files and the various ways logs are recorded. In Linux, we have syslog, which generates a completely unstructured log file. Writing parsers for it is really hard. You cannot write the parser for a message until you have seen it at least once in your logs. In the case of Windows, there is a tool called Log Parser[31] that you can use on the command line to access Windows log files. However, getting your query syntax right with the tool is not easy and requires some knowledge of the different types of log messages that Windows can generate. Furthermore, services on Windows (e.g., DNS or DHCP) are using log files to log their activity. To be correct, some messages are still logged via the event log, but not all of them. This can be fairly challenging, especially because all the logs are kept in a different format and location. I know that in case of Windows, Microsoft is working on a new log format or even a logging infrastructure, which is based on XML. I am not sure that will solve a lot of problems, but it is an attempt to streamline some of the logging in Windows.

No matter what the operating system, they all are conservative about writing log records. Enabling file auditing, for example, requires special libraries under Linux and some configuration under Windows. Certain activity is really hard to get logged, if it is

---

[30] A system that is freely downloadable and deals well with log files and output from these types of tools is Splunk (www.splunk.com).

[31] www.microsoft.com/technet/scriptcenter/tools/logparser/default.mspx

possible at all. It is frustrating that special libraries are needed to get logs for certain activity. My favorite example is a password change on a Linux system. You need to use a special PAM library to log password changes.[32] The library is not shipped by default.

As soon as you start working with log files from different systems, you will run into namespace collisions. For example, two people can have the same user name on different machines. The main issue you want to solve with user names is the attribution of an activity back to a human person. If each person is assigned a globally unique user name, you can achieve that. However, reality is different. The same user on different machines can belong to two different people. There is also the problem of local versus domain accounts. A login by the Administrator account could be from the local or the domain account. How do you differentiate them? Hopefully, the log file is explicit enough to do so. What about users with multiple accounts? How do you correlate their activities? I do not know exactly how many different user accounts I have on different machines. There are quite a few. Without knowing what all users belong to me, it will not be possible to build a comprehensive picture of my activities. Do your users share their logins? This is yet another problem that can throw analysis off. Do you have any service accounts enabled on your systems (users like test, for example). Who owns them? Who is account-able for these activities? And finally, if you allow direct root or Administrator logins to your machines, you have no idea who was actually behind that activity. You need to make sure that root cannot log in directly, but the user has to log in with his or her user first and can then either change to root or execute commands with something like sudo. That way you can attribute information back to individual people.

A last problem around OS logs I want to mention has to do with correlating network-based logs with OS logs. Operating systems are really bad about recording IP addresses. For activity caused by a network connection, they will barely ever log IP addresses. How do you correlate these log entries with network activity? You can use the destination address from the network log and use it to get all the logs from that machine. However, if you have multiple sources connecting to that machine, how do you know which connec-tion is responsible for what OS log entry? This is a hard problem. The only solution for you as a user is to regularly dump the socket states of a machine via netstat, for example. This will allow you to stitch the OS and network logs together. The more elegant solu-tion is to fix OS logging, but that's not so easy (see Figure 2-5).

---

[32] Snare (www.intersectalliance.com/projects/Snare/) can also be used to achieve logging of password changes.

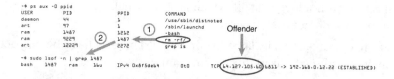

Figure 2-5 To uncover who is responsible for a certain activity on a host, the following steps are necessary: 1) Use the list of processes to identify the user's command. Most likely, the user's command was executed in an interactive shell. To uncover the shell's process ID, find the process' parent ID. 2) Use a list of open sockets to associate the process with a socket that in turn identifies the remote entity's IP address.

APPLICATIONS

Traditionally, log analysis has been applied to the lower layers in the network model. Application logs have not received a lot of attention. However, a large number of use-cases can be addressed only by looking at application log files (fraud detection, for example).

What are some interesting data fields that an application log can contain? Here are a few that you might find in specific log files:

- *User name:* The user who executed the action
- *Status:* The application status that resulted from the action
- *URL:* The Web request or URL that was requested
- *Database query:* The exact query executed on the database

You will encounter many more application-specific fields. These fields can be very interesting and useful for log analysis. However, a number of problems are associated with the data fields in the application logs themselves:

- A lot of application log records can be interpreted only in the realm of the application. If you do not understand the application well enough, you will likely not be able to make sense out of a lot of the records.
- The application log formats are all over the place. There are no standards, whether you are considering their syntax or the transport mechanism. Be prepared to freshen up your XML skills and dust off your Perl books.
- A lot of application log records are missing essential information. This is especially true for us log analysts who are not using the application logs in isolation, but want to correlate them with other data sources; we need more information. The worst case

is when activity is not logged at all, which is fairly usual. I am sure you have seen applications that do not even have a log file.

- Application logs can get really large. Be prepared. This also has a big impact on visualization. We need methods to display large amounts of data.

- Privacy concerns are yet another problem with application logs. Suddenly you are not just looking at IP addresses but names of actual persons. You see financial transactions, patient histories, exact purchases, email messages, and so forth. From a privacy perspective, who should be able to see these records? A number of laws and regulations address this issue. Without going into depth on this topic, let me just say, beware; it might not be legal to look at these type of records.

Addressing the first concern from the preceding list, one important fact you should keep in mind is that you do not have to understand all the fields in a log record to visualize it. Often, you can apply some generic heuristics and methods and let the application owners interpret the graphs. All the other issues associated with application log files are definitely limiting, but application logs are immensely useful for a lot of analysis use-cases.

In the following sections, I briefly discuss a couple of applications. I start with Web proxies and mail logs and then close by discussing databases.

WEB PROXY

Web proxies are an interesting source for log files. Instead of just logging network connections, as with traffic flows, you can see the exact Web requests that were issued. In addition, if you set up your Web proxy such that only authenticated users can use it, you will even get information about the user who accessed the Web sites.

To get started with Web proxy log analysis, you can, for example, install a simple proxy on your laptop. I have a proxy running all the time. In Chapter 4, "From Data to Graphics," I present a step-by-step approach on how to install a proxy to then collect the logs and analyze them. In bigger settings, you might have a proxy server for all Web connections from your company network to the Internet. Proxies can be used for all kinds of purposes, including the following:

- Caching frequently visited websites to reduce bandwidth consumption and speed up website delivery
- Filtering Web requests to prevent access to "bad" sites
- Filtering malicious code in websites
- Only allowing authenticated users to access the Web

Proxy logs generally contain the following fields:

- *Timestamp* ❶: The time the packet was recorded.
- *Client address* ❷: The machine issuing the Web request.
- *Web server* ❸: The Web server from which the website was requested.
- *Request URL* ❹: The actual Web request being issued.
- *Return code* ❺: The HTTP reply status code.
- *Size* ❻: The amount of data transferred from the server to the client.
- *User name* ❼: If authentication is enabled, this is the user who issued the Web request.
- *Content type* ❽: The content type field from the HTTP header, indicating the type of Web response to expect.

Here is an example of a proxy log entry:

```
❶2007-11-18 05:10:55 ❸200.30.108.63 ❻585 ❻31
TCP_MISS_PRIVATE_ON_STOP_LIST/200 ❷220.181.34.24 ❺200 ❺200 - -
❼ntlm W5509C - 0 GET HTTP/1.1 -
❹http://code.qihoo.com/ad_bcast/html_show.js?a=2183&b=1003&p=2001&nt=
&w =760&h=102&m=169221 - [b8]"text/html" "Mozilla/4.0 (compatible; MSIE
6.0; Windows NT 5.1; .NET CLR 1.1.4322; InfoPath.1)" -
```

As you can probably imagine from looking at this log entry, proxy logs are a great source for all sorts of analyses. They are not just useful for business intelligence, where you would analyze them for the most popular sites, but are also useful from a security perspective for detecting Trojan horses and other types of malicious code and activities. There are a few problems associated with proxy logs, but fortunately, proxy logs generally contain all the information necessary to do meaningful analysis and correlation with other sources. Often, some information is not included in the standard log output, but it is a matter of correctly configuring the log output to include the additional data (not that you just can't get it).

One of the problems that you will encounter when analyzing proxy logs is parsing the URL. Often, it is better to break the URL into its components such as the hostname, the file accessed on the server (or the page), and the parameters passed to the page. The parameters are especially cumbersome and, as the preceding example illustrates, are often cryptic. I don't think you would be able to tell me what all the parameters mean by looking at them. If you are dealing with POST requests, an additional problem is that the parameters are not passed as a URL parameter but inside of the HTTP request, which is not logged. This might taint your analysis, so watch out for that.

The number of log entries is another problem that you face when visualizing proxy logs. Remember, you will not just get one proxy entry for every Web page you open. Each Web page generates multiple entries, one for each file accessed: style sheets, images, and frame elements. This can result in a fair number of entries per page accessed. Depending on the type of analysis you are interested in, you will have to somehow aggregate all of these entries.

MAIL

Email servers are another representative of applications that can benefit from visualization. A significant amount of research has been done on social network analysis.[33] By analyzing relationships between users, you can derive social cliques and use the information for information leak protection. You can find more on the topic of information leak prevention in Chapter 8, "Insider Threat."

Email logs come in two broad categories. The first category of logs stems from mail transfer agents (MTAs). MTAs are responsible for accepting and delivering email. They are doing the job of sending email from one server to another. The second category is made up of mail stores that can be accessed via POP or IMAP. I do not focus on the POP or IMAP logs. They are fairly straightforward and contain information about who accessed their mailboxes at what time and which emails were read. These logs contain no information about the emails themselves.

An MTA log generally contains the following information:

- *Timestamp* ❶: The time the email was processed.
- Sender ❷ *and recipient* ❸: The sender and recipient email addresses involved in the communication.
- *Subject:* In some cases, the subject of the email message is stored. This is not always the case.
- *Relay* ❹: Either the mail server that handed the email to this mail server or the next mail server that will receive this email.
- *Size* ❺: The total size of the email message.

---

[33] A great overview of social network analysis is provided in this talk: http://videolectures.net/kdd07_kleinberg_cisnd/.

- *Number of recipients* **❻**: Number of recipients of this email.
- *Delay* **❼**: The time spent between receiving the email and delivering it.
- *Status* **❽**: Indication of that status of this email. Was it successfully delivered, did it get deferred, was it rejected, and so forth.
- *Message ID* **❾**: Globally unique ID associated with this email.

Sendmail[34] is a popular MTA. Here are some sample logs that Sendmail generates for the delivery of an email:

```
❶Jun 11 04:09:30 linux2 sm-mta[19407]: k5B25Rux019397:
from=<❷moder@burncompany.com>, size=❺3555, class=0, nrcpts=❻ 1,
msgid=<❾000001c68cf8$2bc42250$e7d4a8c0@mvu82>, proto=SMTP, daemon=MTA,
relay=❹host62-225.pool8711.interbusiness.it [87.11.225.62]
Jun 11 04:05:33 linux2 sm-mta[19401]: k5B25Rux019397:
to=<❸ram@cryptojail.net>, ctladdr=<ram@cryptojail.net> (0/0),
delay=❼00:00:06, xdelay= ❼00:00:00, mailer=local, pri=294718, dsn=2.0.0,
stat=❽Sent
```

You can see that an email was received from moder@burncompany.com by ram@cryptojail.net. Additional useful information contained in the log entries includes the relay that sent the email and the status of the message. Implicitly, you can derive from these log entries that the server that accepted the email is the mail exchange (MX) for cryptojail.net. This means the mail server is responsible for the cryptojail.net domain, and it will store mail on the server such that the user can retrieve it later. It will not forward it to another server.

You might have identified one of the problems with Sendmail through this example: Each email generates at least two log entries. The first entry identifies who was sending the email, and the second one shows the recipient. The two log messages are linked by the message identifier, which is the 14-digit string right before the email addresses (k5B25Rux019397). Note that in some cases you will find more than just two entries for the same message ID. For example, if an email could not be delivered upon first attempt, the server writes a log entry and keeps retrying. Each retry generates a new log entry. This definitely complicates analysis.

The next problem with email logs, not just with the ones from Sendmail, is that emails sent to multiple recipients record a list of recipients in the to field. You have to be aware of this to correctly handle that case in your parser and later for visualization; instead of generating one single node, you have to generate multiple nodes!

---

[34] http://www.sendmail.org/

A few pieces of information not available in Sendmail are the subject of an email and whether an email contained an attachment. If there was an attachment, it would be interesting to know the file name and file type. Other MTAs, such as Exchange, have the capability to log the subject and indicate whether an attachment was included in the email. With Sendmail, you could use a heuristic that if a certain message size was exceeded; it had to contain an attachment. I have not seen an email server that completely parses an email to extract the attachment filename and file type. It would be significant work for an email agent to do so. If you need this functionality, have a look at a commercial information leak prevention tool, such as Vontu, Reconnex, or Vormetrics.

If you are looking for a quick solution to parse Sendmail logs without building your own parser that reassembles the "to" and "from" log entries, you can use the Perl script available at http://secviz.org/?q=node/8. A remaining problem is that you have to split up multiple recipients yourself. This parser does not do that for you.

DATABASES

The last type of application that I discuss here is databases. By default, databases are very quiet. They do not log much information. However, almost every database has different logging mechanisms that can be turned on. By default, databases log startups, shutdowns, errors, and in some cases, logins. This information is certainly interesting for diagnostic purposes. The really interesting information, however, is stored in so-called audit records or logs. Most databases support audit logs into which each database query can be recorded. Information contained in these records includes the following:

- *Timestamp* ❶: The time the packet was recorded
- *Database command* ❷: The exact command (e.g., SELECT statement) that was executed against the database
- Database user ❸: The effective user who executed the statement
- Status ❹: The outcome of the command executed

Some databases also enable logging of this additional information:

- *Operating system user* ❺: The operating system user who connected to the database to execute the command
- *Source address* ❻: The network address of the machine from which the command was executed

Audit records can be configured to record any statement executed against the database. (e.g., SELECT, INSERT, ALTER TABLE, or GRANT). This enables you to very granularly monitor the data in the database and how it is changed. A sample database record from a Microsoft SQL Server looks like this:

```
0         ❶11/11/2007 17:02:53    11/11/2007 17:02:53    0.009   0.009
5.000     ❻172.16.36.57    172.16.20.70    3066  1433    0       0
192       389     1       1       0.000   -       ❸-      -       -
EM006     ❺PubAnonymous   PUB     ❷17     ❹5703   0
Warning::Changed database context to 'mycorp'. , Changed language
setting to us_english.       -       0       ❷Login:PubAnonymous@3066 mycorp  386
```

A lot more information is contained here than I outlined above. Most fields have to do with the data transferred and the exact connection information. Although database audit records are a great source of information for tracking data, there are a few challenges associated with these logs files. First and foremost is the performance impact that auditing has on databases. Each record that has to be written consumes processing power on the database. It is therefore not advisable to enable full auditing on a database. Generally, one would audit only a subset of all activity (for example, deletion of information, access of system tables, and all activity on really critical database tables). Most databases enable granular configurations to support this.

The next problem is the sheer amount of data generated by database audit logs. If you log every SELECT statement, you will end up with a lot of information that you need to aggregate intelligently to visualize it. Another problem with the audit records is the way the queries are logged. Visualizing database logs (as you will see in Chapter 7, "Compliance"), often requires that we break down the queries to figure out which exact database tables have been accessed. Parsing a SQL query statement to extract this information is by no means a simple task. It would help a lot if the database would log separate fields for the database tables that were accessed by a specific command.

You will encounter yet another challenge when you try to interpret some of the queries that the database logged. If you are not the database administrator and you have both intimate knowledge of the database structure (i.e., the tables) and of your database query language (not just pure SQL-92), you might not be able to make sense of the queries. It is therefore crucial that you are working with your database team to analyze the log files.

CONFIGURATIONS

A last category of data sources for visualization is configurations, which differ from system stats. It is often interesting to know what the configuration of a system is. Log files do not record configurations. They log state changes. Collecting the configuration of a system, either on a regular basis or ad hoc, when needed, can add necessary additional information. Table 2-3 shows a summary of commands and use-cases for this type of information.

Table 2-3 Gathering Configuration Information

Platform	Use	Command	Information in Output
Cisco router	Current ACLs	`sh access-lists`	ACL number, action, protocol, IP addresses, protocol, logging?
Cisco router/switch	Running configuration	`sh run`	Complete running configuration of the network device.
Cisco router	Routing information	`sh ip route`	Default gateway, networks, interface, gateway.
Operating system	Routing tables	`netstat -rn`	Default gateway, networks, interface, gateway.
Windows	Scheduled Jobs	`WMIC JOB list`	Command, scheduled time, owner.
Windows	List of users	`WMIC USERACCOUNT`	Account type, user name, password policies, SID.
Windows	Service status	`sc queryex`	Service name, type, and state.

NAVIGATING CISCO IOS

Cisco routers and switches are administered via a command-line interface. You can either telnet into the router or use SSH to access it, depending on whether SSH is enabled. After successful login, the command interface allows you to query some nonsensitive information. However, at this point, no configuration is allowed. To get into privileged execution mode, where the router can be configured, you need to enter the `enable` command. You should be asked for a password, and then you have free access to configure the router and query for any type of information.

At this point, you can use the show command to query all kinds of information about the system. For example, the show running command reveals the entire network device's configuration. By typing show and then entering a question mark, you will see a list of available subcommands that can be used to query more information.

To configure the device, you need to enter configure terminal. This puts you into configuration mode. From here, there are again multiple areas that can be configured. By typing a question mark, again, the commands that are available at this stage are displayed. If you want to configure an interface, you use the command, interface Ethernet0/0. Now all the configurations for the Ethernet0/0 interface are available. We can, for example, change its IP address: ip address 192.168.155.2 255.255.255.0 Use Ctrl-Z to get back out of the interface configuration. Depending on the feature set of the network device, a slightly different set of commands is available.

Another way to gather configuration information is to log in to the device and retrieve the configuration via the execution of a command (e.g., sh config). This is useful in cases where you need to gather information on an ad hoc basis (for example, to troubleshoot an issue on a machine). The problem with this approach is that you can look at only the present state and not at historic values. It is often necessary to record historic configurations.

The following is an example of how ad hoc information can be collected from a remote Windows machine called ram. The command gathers information about the OS that is running:

```
WMIC /NODE:"ram" OS GET Caption,CSDVersion,CSName
```

The result coming back then looks something like this:

```
Caption                          CSDVersion      CSName
Microsoft Windows XP Professional   Service Pack 2   RAM
```

Storing configuration information as that above is somewhat of a challenge. You need a way to store multiline output collected at short time intervals. Files are not really suited for this. Files are great for storing single-record information. Storing the output of a command such as sh running is not just ugly but also really hard to parse and analyze later on. One solution is to use a database with a really large text field that can hold the output. Another solution is to use a tool such as Splunk[35] that can capture not just log files but also configuration files and output from commands. By treating the data as time-series data, the user can then operate on the data as if it is a single record in a file, diff recorded data, generate statistics, and so on.

All in all, configuration data adds a significant and important piece to the complete picture of activity in a networked environment.

SUMMARY

This chapter has taken us through the world of data sources. Data is the basis for any visualization. Without data, there is no visualization. The chapter started with a definition of some common terms in the log analysis world that are also important for visualization. I then defined security data. This set the stage for the rest of the book, which is concerned with security data visualization. The chapter continued by outlining two very common problems in the log analysis space: incomplete information in log entries and the source destination confusion.

The main part of this chapter covered a sample set of data sources. It started out with a discussion of packet captures, and then went on to traffic flows, firewall logs, intrusion detection and prevention logs, and passive network analysis. Following all of these network-based data sources was a discussion of operating system logs and static operating system information, which is often forgotten in discussions about log analysis. The chapter closed with a look at application log files. The field of application log files is huge, and it is impossible to even capture a small portion of the existing application log files. I therefore concentrated on a generic introduction and three common examples of application logs: Web proxies, mail, and databases.

With an understanding of all of these data sources, we are now ready to move on and have a look at how this data can be visualized.

---

[35] www.splunk.com

Visually Representing Data

Choosing a visualization technique to generate an image of your data is not a trivial task. Should you use a bar chart or a line chart? Or is a scatter plot better suited? I address these questions in this chapter and also discuss for each of the graphs their drawbacks and benefits. In addition, for each of the graphs, I discuss what type of data it represents best.

Once you know what data you want to analyze and what information is encoded in the data, you need to decide how to visually represent the data. Many types of graphs can be used to visualize data. Each graph has its own features and is suited for a specific analysis scenario. Some graphs are great at visualizing large amounts of data; others are better suited for highlighting slight variations and trends.

This chapter introduces the following graphs, which I use throughout the rest of this book:

- Simple charts
  - Pie charts
  - Bar charts
  - Line charts
- Stacked charts
  - Stacked pie charts
  - Stacked bar charts
  - Stacked line charts

- Histograms
- Box plots
- Scatter plots
- Parallel coordinates
- Link graphs
- Maps
- Treemaps

Each of these graphs has different capabilities and emphasizes specific aspects of the data. The graphs facilitate the analysis of the **distribution** of values in a single dimension or the **relationship** between two or more dimensions in the data. If I talk about a **dimension** in a dataset, I am referring to a column—a field. In the field of data analysis or statistics, it might be referred to as a variable or a feature. Examples include such things as the source IP address or the target port of a log or data entry.

I begin with some general discussion of graph properties before turning to specific charts and graphs. The chapter ends by addressing how to determine what graph to use in particular circumstances.

GRAPH PROPERTIES

Graphs use a two-dimensional plane, such as a computer display or a sheet of paper, to represent data. Even though the data is represented in a two-dimensional plane, this does not mean that graphs are limited to displaying only two data dimensions. Some graphs, as you will see, represent only one data dimension, whereas others can display many more than just two. In addition to the spatial dimensions of a graph, you can use other visual elements to encode additional data dimensions.

DATA TYPES

Graphs need data that they can display. Data has an associated data type. There are four types commonly discussed: **categorical, ordinal, interval** and **ratio.** Data types are important for graphing data. Depending on the data type, a different set of visualizations can be used to represent the data. For example, you cannot use a scatter plot to sensibly visualize categorical data.

Categorical data is data that has as values two or more categories. Such data dimensions are also called **discrete** or **nominal.** There is no intrinsic ordering to the categories.

The TCP flags (ACK, RST, FIN, SYN, PSH, URG, and so on) constitute a categorical dimension. There is no intrinsic ordering to the TCP flags. The action field in a firewall log is also a categorical variable having two values (block and pass), and again, there is no agreed upon way to order these, so the action field is a nominal data type. IP addresses and port numbers are categorical values, too.

If categorical values have an order defined, they are called **ordinal.** For example, the severity of an event, with the values low, medium, high, makes up a set of an ordinal values. Only one sorting order makes sense for these values. Nobody would say that medium is larger than high. On the other hand, the difference between low and medium is not known to be exactly the same difference as that between medium and high. This is another characteristic of ordinal data.

Another type of data is referred to as **interval.** Interval data can be measured on a continuum or a scale. The data has no breaks or gaps, and the differences between adjacent values are always the same (i.e., the difference between 6 and 7 on an interval scale is the same as the difference between 9 and 10). Sometimes this kind of continuous data is called **numeric** data. A lot of fields in log files constitute interval data: TCP sequence numbers, packet sizes, and so forth. Interval data is said to lack a true zero point. That is, it is difficult or impossible to talk about absence of the dimension.

Ratio data fields are ones that have the full expressiveness of real numbers. The use of a ratio scale implies a true zero value. (It is possible to consider absence of the thing measured.) File size might fit the bill here as an example.

Interval and ratio data types are sometimes jointly referred to as **continuous.** Mathematically speaking, interval and ratio data can have most all mathematical operations applied to them. That is, they can be multiplied, divided, squared, and so on. You can calculate means, standard deviations, and the like for such data.

As soon as you have multiple data dimensions, you will find that people distinguish between **primary variables** (also generally referred to as **independent variables**) and **dependent variables**. The dependent variable is the data dimension that you observe to see how it changes when a change is made to the primary variable. The new value of the dependent variable is thought to be caused by (or in some way dependent on) the value of the primary variable. I use this a little later to distinguish the two variables plotted in a chart. The primary variable is generally plotted on the x-axis, and the dependent variable is drawn on the y-axis.

The data types are important for choosing the right graph. Depending on what type of data you need to visualize, you need to use a certain type of graph. You will see during the discussion of the different graphs which data types the graphs are best suited for.

COLOR

Color can be used in graphs not only to affect their aesthetics but also to represent an additional dimension. One of the problems with color is that similar colors are hard to distinguish. Hence, the represented values are not easily accessible. Because of this, color is mostly used to display a small set of categorical values. Legends are needed to decode them and map them back to individual values, unless you use some culturally accepted color assignments. For example, you might use red to represent bad or green to represent good. When using these colors without a legend, make sure the color assignments are contextually obvious. In general, dimensions with only a small number of distinct values are well suited to be encoded by color. It is fairly easy for the reader to remember the mappings and interpret the graph. As soon as the number of values mapped to colors gets too high, the user becomes confused and has a hard time identifying what the underlying, categorical values represent. Colors have another interesting property; they are quite well suited to representing continuous ranges. Different color ranges (e.g., rainbow or grayscale) can be mapped to value ranges (see Figure 3-1).

Color should not be used for aesthetics! Colors should be used to add meaning to a graph. Try to use bright colors to highlight information and grab the viewer's attention. A tool that helps with choosing colors for a graph is ColorBrewer.[1] It is a Web tool for selecting and listing specs for color schemes that you can then use in your graphs. It even offers a color-blind safe version to help choosing colors that can be distinguished by people with color-blindness. Keep in mind when you are choosing color for your images that quite a significant number of people are color-blind.[2]

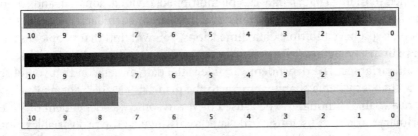

Figure 3-1   Different color assignments. The first two are continuous ranges, where every real number between zero and ten can get a slightly different color. The third color range is a discrete or categorical mapping where only four colors are possible. (This figure appears in the full-color insert located in the middle of the book.)

---

[1]   http://www.personal.psu.edu/cab38/ColorBrewer/ColorBrewer.html

[2]   More on color-blindness can be found at http://en.wikipedia.org/wiki/Color_blindness.

SIZE, SHAPE, AND ORIENTATION

Another way of representing additional dimensions of data, instead of using color, is to use **size, shape,** and **orientation.** Using size to encode a value has problems similar to those of color; it is generally not possible to tell the exact value from looking at a certain sized point. However, relative relationships can be highlighted very well. Shapes are generally used to represent a small number of categorical values, such as the transport protocol or operating system type. Orientation is not commonly used, but can be yet another way of adding another data dimension to your graphs.

Coloring the nodes is generally a better way to represent an additional dimension of data. Similar to color, shapes can be used to represent certain dimensions; instead of using simple dots, you can use boxes, ovals, stars, and so on to encode specific values.

CHART AXES

Chart axes help the viewer identify the values of data points. Labels and check marks are used to associate the data points with a specific value. It is common to refer to the vertical axis as the y-axis. The horizontal axis is called the x-axis. In three-dimensional charts, the vertical axis is generally the y-axis. Which of the two other axes is designated x or y varies depending on the application. Good practice calls out the unit of measurement that is used for the labels along an axis.

Keep in mind three important display methods for drawing chart axes:

- If the x-axis labels are hard to read, it sometimes helps to rotate the entire graph by 90 degrees (i.e., inverting the axes). That way, the labels can be written horizontally, and they become more legible.

- Axes should generally start at zero. Especially with bar charts, the y-axis should start at zero to make sure the areas of the bars are proportional to the values they represent.

- In some cases, the spread of values to be displayed is so big that a nonlinear axis scale would be useful. Such an example is shown in Figure 3-2. The values on the top chart are not legible because the axis had to be scaled to show one very high value. The bottom chart uses a logarithmical scale. In the lower values, a higher density is used than in the higher ones. That way, the smaller values can still be identified in the graph.

The following sections explore the eight types of graphs previously listed. At the end of the chapter, we discuss and summarize which graphs are best suited for which use-cases.

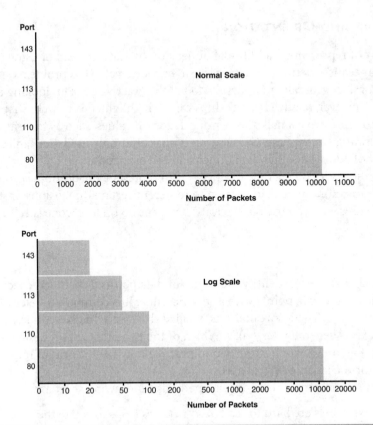

Figure 3-2   The top part of this figure shows a graph that uses a linear scale, and the bottom part of the figure encodes the same data in a graph that uses a logarithmical scale. On the logarithmical scale, the low values can be interpreted.

SIMPLE CHARTS

The best known and easiest way to visualize data is through **charts.** Charts come in a variety of forms: **pies, bars, line charts,** and **3D bar charts.** These charts are generally used to visualize a single dimension of your data, with the exception of 3D bar charts, which can present two dimensions. These basic charts are all available in ubiquitous software programs such as Excel or OpenOffice.

The question of when to use what type of chart is central to this chapter. While introducing the individual charts in the following sections, I also discuss when the charts can and should be applied. In addition, at the end of the chapter, I summarize all the charts and other graphs again and show when you should be using which one (refer to Table 3-1).

PIE CHART

The chart that you are probably most familiar with is the **pie chart.** The pie chart is also the one visual that is abused the most. Every sales dashboard that I have seen uses pie charts for some data representation. However, the pie chart is hardly ever the right chart to use. There are better ways (better graphs) to represent the same data. Bar charts are often better suited to basic visualization needs.

Pie charts are best used to compare values of a dimension as proportions or percentages of a whole. The data should be categorical. You might be able to use a pie chart for continuous values, but only if not too many possible values have to be represented. This is a general drawback of pie charts. They can visualize only a small number of different values. As soon as too many different values need to be represented, the chart becomes illegible.

The example in Figure 3-3 shows a pie chart in which only three different values are used. It is almost impossible to derive absolute values for the individual data values. However, it is fairly simple to see that the amount of traffic on the outside was 50 percent of the total. Good practice is to add labels to the pie chart that call out the exact values.

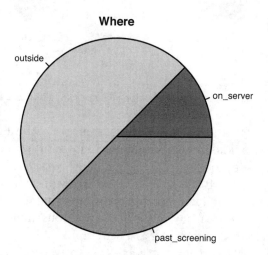

Figure 3-3 A sample pie chart used to compare values of a dimension as proportions or percentages of a whole.

BAR CHART

In its most generic form, a bar chart presents a visual representation of the count of individual values of a data dimension. Figure 3-4 shows an example bar chart in which the data dimension is the destination address and the chart represents the count per destination address.

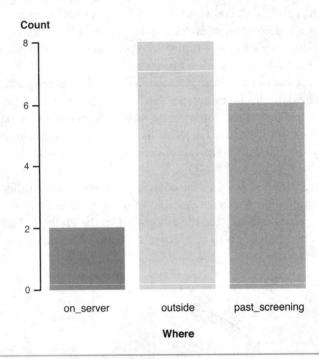

Figure 3-4 This chart shows the count of destination addresses visualized as a bar chart.

Bar charts are used to show the frequency of occurrence of each value of a dimension. They are intuitive and obvious, making it easy to compare the number of cases or records at each value just by looking at the height of the bars. The bar chart operates primarily on categorical data. It is not meant to be used with dimensions having continuous values or many values. It does not represent the continuous nature of such a data dimension; and when there are many values to a continuous dimension, it can be difficult if not impossible to read or interpret as a bar graph.

Whenever possible, make sure that the y-axis (i.e., the vertical axis) of your bar charts starts at zero. Anything else is confusing and makes comparison of individual graphs, or even bars in a single graph, difficult.

In addition to using a **count** function, which simply counts the number of times a certain value was seen, you can use other functions, such as **sum, average,** or **ratio.** All of these functions take a second dimension to apply the function. Figure 3-5 shows an example in which the same bar chart as in Figure 3-4 is used, but this time it is not the count that is shown but the average of bytes transferred for that IP address.

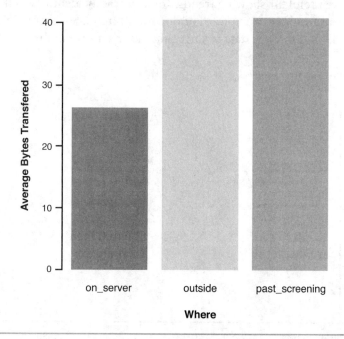

Figure 3-5   This bar chart shows the average number of bytes transferred per destination address.

The additional data dimension needs to be numeric. Otherwise, it is not possible to calculate a sum or an average. This might mean that you have to preprocess your data and make numeric values out of one of your dimensions. For example, if you have a dimension that calls out the priority or severity of an event as a discrete value (high, medium, low) you have to preprocess that data and convert it to numeric values. Another possibility for non-numeric dimensions is to define a **distinct** function. The chart would then plot the number of distinct values it saw for a certain x-value.

LINE CHART

If the data dimension you want to visualize is interval level, you can use a line chart rather than a bar chart. Although you could still use the bar chart for this type of data, a line chart is a little better suited. It explicitly represents the idea that adjacent values compose a continuum by connecting them. Like bar charts, in their simplest form line charts are used to show the frequency of occurrence of each value of an ordinal dimension (see Figure 3-6). As with the other chart types, instead of just using frequency, you can use any other aggregation function, such as average or sum.

Line charts are useful for showing trends. You can readily identify whether a time-based data dimension shows an upward or downward trend. Sometimes neither is the case, and you will find that the data is fairly random in nature (not related to time).

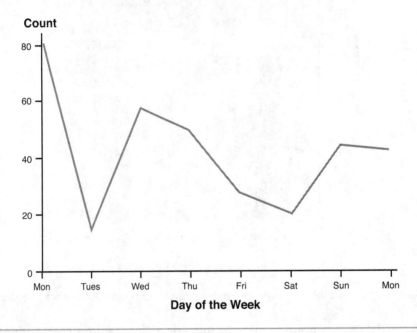

Figure 3-6   This line chart is used to show the frequency of occurrences of each value of a dimension. The line chart shows the number of logins seen over the period of a week.

3D BAR CHARTS

If you need to represent two categorical data dimensions simultaneously, you can use a **3D bar chart.** Instead of using the x-axis to plot your data dimension and then the y-axis to show the count of each of the values, you can use an additional data dimension to be represented as the y-axis. The z-axis is then used to plot the count. Figure 3-7 shows an example of what I am describing. For each day of the week, the graph shows the number of connections for each of the three machines plotted on the y-axis.

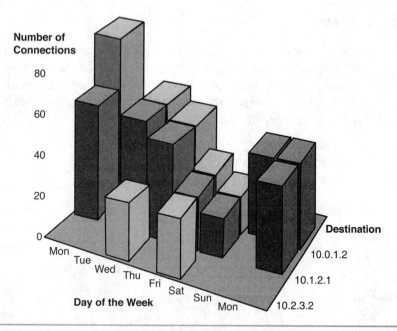

Figure 3-7   3D bar chart, used to represent frequency of occurrence of values of two or more dimensions.

The same as for bar charts, the main axes need to represent categorical values for the main axes. Try not to use 3D charts very often. They suffer from a lot of problems that 3D graphs exhibit generally. Occlusion is one of them. This is the phenomenon where some of the bars in the front hide the ones in the back, making it impossible to read those values. For example, in Figure 3-7, the bars on Tuesday for 10.1.2.1 and 10.0.1.2 are hidden behind others. It also shows that it can be difficult to match bar height precisely with the scale. There are better ways to represent this type of data, as discussed later.

STACKED CHARTS

Adding an additional data dimension to simple charts results in stacked charts. Generally, the problem with stacked charts is that an additional data dimension is forced to fit onto what is an inherently simple chart. This mostly ends up resulting in a confusing chart that is hard to read and has a lot of disadvantages. Almost all stacked charts can be drawn in better types of graphs, such as multidimensional versions of simpler graphs.

STACKED PIE CHART

An additional data dimension can be mapped into a pie chart to make it into a **stacked pie chart.** The individual slices are subdivided by the additional data dimension. Figure 3-8 shows a stacked pie chart that visualizes the distribution of protocols used. In addition, it shows how the protocols were distributed among the target machines by subdividing the slices of different gray shades.

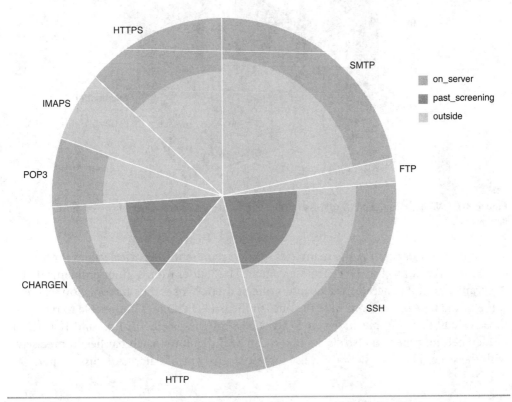

Figure 3-8   A stacked pie chart. Instead of showing only one data dimension, the distribution of protocols, the chart subdivides the individual slices and shows what destination address used which protocol.

Stacked pie charts are deceptive. The outer portions of the pie chart appear to be larger than the inner ones, even if they represent the same number of values. Therefore, a good practice is to label the individual pie slices (i.e., sectors) with their respective percentage or proportion.

STACKED BAR CHART

A variation on the basic bar chart is the **stacked bar chart** (see Figure 3-9). Compared to a regular bar chart, stacked bars use an additional dimension to subdivide the individual bars. Figure 3-9, for example, shows for one destination address the distribution of protocols used. Plotting multiple stacked bar charts in one graph makes these charts a tool to compare data (bottom part of Figure 3-9). You can see how multiple machines get hit with different distributions of protocols. It can be hard to judge the exact heights of a bar in a stacked bar chart, or compare the heights of two bars. If exactitude or comparisons are of primary importance, consider a line chart or a stacked line chart instead.

Be careful with stacked bar charts. They can be deceiving. Take a look at Figure 3-9 again. What amount of FTP traffic was 10.0.0.1 producing? Is it about 20 packets, or is it 100 packets? Contrary to, for example, stacked line charts, the values are not cumulative. In other words, the amount of FTP traffic was 20 packets and not 100 packets. The FTP traffic is represented by the area between 80 and 100 packets in the chart. Your readers might not be aware of this, and you should explicitly call this out.

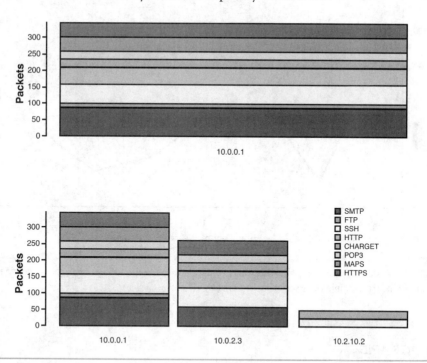

Figure 3-9 The top portion of the figure shows a simple stacked bar chart. It shows the network protocols used by one machine. The bottom part shows the same data, but for three machines. This makes it easy to compare the three machines to each other.

STACKED LINE CHART

In much the same way that an additional data dimension can be represented in a bar chart by subdividing the bars, you can modify a line chart to display multiple data series rather than just one. Figure 3-10 shows a **stacked line chart.** It displays data for not only one destination address but for three of them at once. This helps to compare the three destination addresses and how they performed over the time frame given (7 days). The same principles apply here as for regular line charts: The data mapped to the x-axis should be ordinal, and the y-axis should be a function that maps the data to a continuous (i.e., numeric) range.

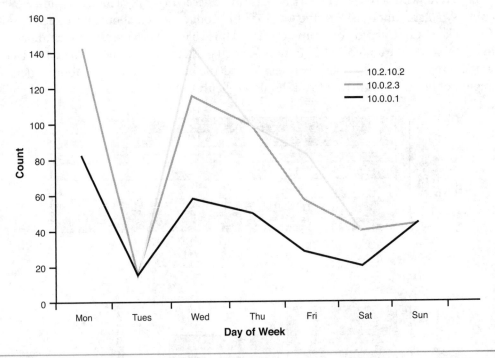

Figure 3-10   A stacked line chart showing multiple data dimensions. This chart has the advantage that the viewer can compare multiple data series in one chart.

HISTOGRAMS

Histograms show the distribution of data (i.e., the frequency of the individual data values). They look very much like bar charts. However, they are particularly well suited to continuous data, whereas bar charts are not.

When a data dimension has hundreds or even thousand of values, they can be grouped (also called binned or bucketed), and the frequency counts for the values in those groups can be represented in the histogram. Each bar represents a group of contiguous values rather than a single value.

Histograms are great for detecting patterns such as spikes (or gaps) in activities. However, they often summarize data significantly and therefore are not always suited to communicating other properties such as the individual data values.

Figure 3-11 shows a histogram of login attempts over the period of a day. Because time is a continuous data type, the histogram summarizes the data into hourly groups or buckets. The histogram nicely shows that the working hours of this organization are 9 a.m. to 5.p.m., with some people starting a little earlier and some people working a bit later. The interesting part, however, is that a spike in logins occurs at 6 a.m. It is not clear

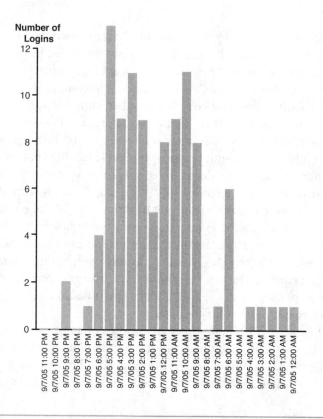

Figure 3-11 A histogram showing logins to machines over the past day. At 6 a.m., there is a spike of logins to a series of different machines, which seems slightly odd.

what these logins are and why so many people would log in to all those machines in the early-morning hours. It could be that there is a simple explanation, such as a board meeting that requires people to finish some work before the board meeting is held later that day. However, based on the access pattern of these machines, this activity is out of the norm. Although this type of behavior can be detected with histograms, it also shows the limitations of this type of chart. In this histogram, it is impossible to pinpoint the exact time when something happened. If a different time resolution were used for the binning of values (for example, a minute), we would be able to do this. However, the number of bars would explode. There are always trade-offs. If we use color to encode the types of servers accessed, more analysis is possible. For example, an interesting read from the chart would be to see the distribution of types of servers accessed.

Box Plots

Comparing values is often done by looking at the average of a data dimension. For example, if you are interested in the number of bytes transferred by your firewall, you will probably collect the data and then see what the average connection size was. Maybe you are going to break that number down by protocol to compare what the average packet size was for each of the protocols. The problem with this approach is that you are losing a lot of information. An average or mean is referred to in statistics as an indicator of **central tendency.** Other indicators of central tendency are the median and the mode. They do give you information about the most **typical** value. But that ignores the rest of the values. In other words, a mean does not tell you anything about the how the data is **distributed.** Were there a lot of large packets? What was the smallest packet? These are questions that you want to answer with a plot of the average size of packets per protocol. This is where box plots are useful. Figure 3-12 shows how a box plot is constructed. The top and bottom whiskers indicate the maximum and minimum values for that data value. The line inside of the box indicates the median,[3] which is the centermost element in the data. It is not equal to the mean or the average. The gray box shows which values fall in the center 50 percent of all the data points. This gives you a feeling for the distribution of the values and not just for the average.

Take a look at Figure 3-13, which shows an example of a box plot of firewall packet sizes, broken up by protocol. Each protocol gets an individual box plot. Be careful reading this graph. The y-axis is shown in logarithmical scale. I had to do this because of the maximum values, which are very large compared to all the other statistical properties.

---

[3]   The median of a list of numbers can be found by arranging all the numbers from lowest value to highest value and picking the middle one.

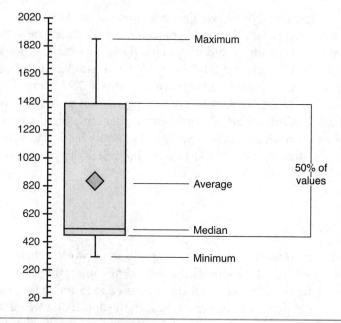

Figure 3-12   Explanation of a box plot symbol.

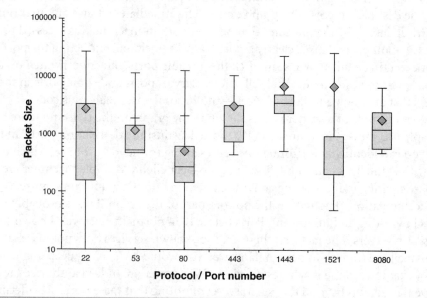

Figure 3-13   Box plot of firewall packet sizes broken up per protocol.

With a linear scale, you could barely see the boxes themselves. This also indicates an interesting property of this data. The averages seem to be all about the same, with a small variance. However, the maximum, and the general packet size distributions, is fairly large. What seems interesting is that DNS (port 53) has a compact distribution of packet sizes. This is not surprising because the maximum size of a DNS packet is limited for UDP communication. TCP DNS packets can be bigger, but it seems that we are not dealing with any of those. Also note another interesting phenomenon. It seems like the traffic on port 8080, which is generally associated with HTTP proxies, is encrypted. It does not have the distribution that port 80 (HTTP) shows, but resembles more closely what is seen for port 443 (HTTPS).

SCATTER PLOTS

One of the most utilized and best understood graphs in network security is the **scatter plot.** Scatter plots are used to visualize either ordinal or continuous data. They are not suited for nominal data. Scatter plots can either be used to examine how two data dimensions relate or to detect clusters and trends in the data. For a two-dimensional scatter plot, two dimensions of the input data are chosen and assigned to the x- and y-axis, respectively. This spans a two-dimensional plane, where every point is defined by a pair of input fields. Figure 3-14 shows two examples where the destination IP is plotted against the destination port. The graph on the left immediately draws our attention to the "vertical line." The line indicates that one destination machine was accessed on multiple destination ports. This is clearly a port scan! The person conducting the port scan was not executing a full-blown scan of all the possible ports, but concentrated on the most important ones—mainly the well-known service ports and some ports in the high numbers that are known to host services—and in some cases malicious code.

Another example of a scatter plot is shown in the graph on the right in Figure 3-14. The graph also shows the destination IPs plotted against the destination ports. In this graph, you can identify a horizontal line representing traffic to port 6348, which is associated with Gnutella, a commonly used peer-to-peer client. Multiple machines are apparently participating in file-sharing activities. Looking into the graph some more, you can see an accumulation of activity at the bottom part of the graph. This is probably not quite as interesting and important. Ports below 1024 normally host well-known services, such as Web servers. The fact that these are well-known services does not necessarily mean that all the traffic was benign. However, you would have to dig deeper and verify that. For example, all the machines offering a Web server are indeed authorized to do so. To move the analysis beyond the general level of noting that these ports are offering services, you must investigate whether the traffic itself carries benign traffic and not attacks on a certain protocol. This analysis is easiest if additional data sources, such as Web server logs, are available.

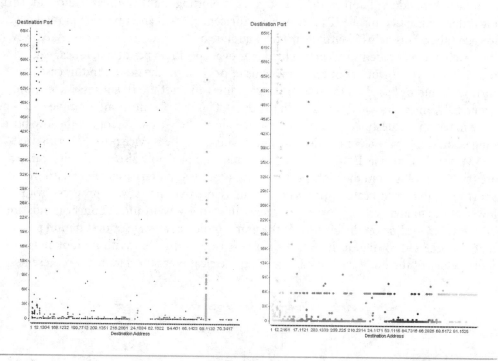

Figure 3-14 This graph shows two scatter plots. Both of them plot the destination port against the destination address. On the left side, a vertical scan can be seen; on the right, a horizontal scan dominates the graph.

To display more than two dimensions in a 2D scatter plot, you can use color, shape, and size to represent additional data. Color, shape, and size were already discussed in the section "Graph Properties." The same benefits and limitations identified in that discussion apply here.

If you plot the time on the x-axis, you get a chart that is sometimes referred to as a **time table.** Time tables are useful for identifying trends over time. They help identify either sequences of behavior or gaps in such. It is not just horizontal trends (trends over time) that are of interest but also vertical ones. Vertical lines indicate behavior distributed over multiple values of the y-axis. For example, if the y-axis spans IP addresses, a vertical line indicates activity at a specific point in time, associated with a set of IP addresses. Another difference compared to scatter plots is that the y-axis can be nominal data. It does not have to be ordinal or continuous. This can be fairly interesting if you, for example, plot the behavior for different users over time.

It is important to note that the sorting of the y-axis is important for identifying patterns! A lot of times, sorting based on the values of the y-axis is not the only and best approach. What does that mean? Assume you are plotting the IP addresses and your sorting criterion is based on the IPs themselves. Adjacent IPs will end up being plotted next to each other. This helps identify scans over a range of contiguous IP addresses. However, if we were trying to identify a certain behavior over specific types of machines (e.g., all the Web servers), it would not result in a cluster or "line" in the graph. In this case, the sorting should be based on the role of the machines and not the IP addresses (or more generically, an additional dimension in the data). Figure 3-15 shows an example of a time table in which the destination ports are plotted along the y-axis. On top, in the low-port range, you can see an accumulation of values. These are the service ports, offering well-known services, such as DNS. What is interesting, and probably also a little bit strange, are the values plotted in the high-port ranges. Some clear patterns show here. All the short vertical lines indicate some sort of a scan. (Note that they always progress from lower values to higher values over time, never the other way around.) Longer trends are visible, too. One line on the bottom of the graph indicates a range of destination ports that was accessed contiguously over the entire period of the plot. Without looking at more details of the underlying data, it is not quite clear what the data really represents.

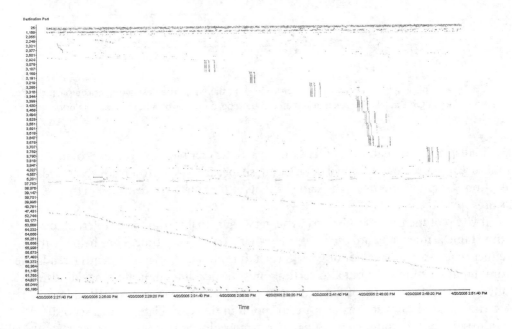

Figure 3-15   This graph shows a scatter plot where the x-axis represents time. In this particular time table, the y-axis shows destination ports. Multiple time-based patterns are visible in the graph.

PARALLEL COORDINATES

Often, we want to simultaneously visualize more than two or three dimensions of our data. In 1985, A. Inselberg published an article in *The Visual Computer* titled "The Plane with Parallel Coordinates." The article describes how **parallel coordinates** can be used to visualize many dimensions in one graph. Figure 3-16 shows a sample of a parallel coordinate graph.

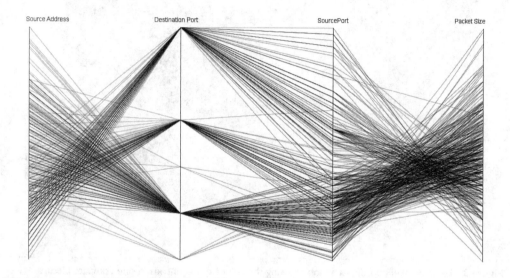

Figure 3-16   A simple parallel coordinate graph

The axes in the graph represent individual dimensions or fields of the dataset. The values of the different dimensions are plotted along each of the vertical axes. A data entry is represented as a line from left to right, connecting each of the values in adjacent axes.

Parallel coordinates are mainly used to examine how multiple dimensions relate to each other. You can, for example, see in Figure 3-17 how the asset role is related to both the source address and the destination addresses. It seems that every asset role has exactly one machine associated with it. By rearranging the individual axes so that they become neighbors with another dimension, you ease the analysis of the relationship between specific data dimensions. Allowing the user to interactively change the axes order is useful to this analysis. If a lot of data is mapped into a parallel coordinate display, the rearrangement of axes can help reduce the visual clutter. Any tool that supports parallel coordinates should therefore allow the user to change the order of the axes.

Another interesting property is that the value space for all the dimensions can be displayed in a compact way. Clusters and gaps are thus quickly identified.

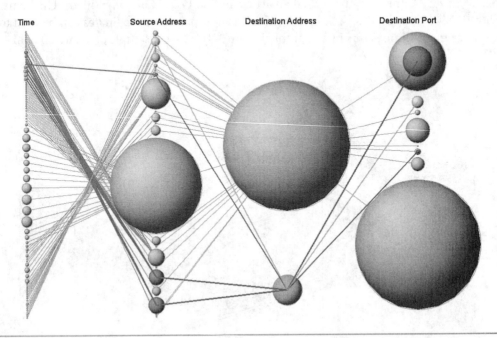

Figure 3-17 A parallel coordinate graph showing thousands of log entries in one compact picture. Bubble sizes are proportional to the number of times an entry shows up for a specific data dimension. One target machine was selected in the graph, resulting in a set of colored edges and bubbles to indicate all the traffic targeting this one machine. (This figure appears in the full-color insert located in the middle of the book.)

Selected target

Parallel coordinates greatly benefit from interactivity. As Figure 3-17 shows, the selection of a value in one axis, a specific destination IP address in this case, propagates through the graph to highlight the events using the selected address. In this parallel coordinate graph, **bubbles** indicate the distribution of values in a single dimensions. They are a good tool to indicate relative frequencies in the data.

The biggest advantage of parallel coordinates compared to all the other charts discussed so far is the multidimensional aspect. You can visualize not only two or three dimensions and analyze the relationships between them, but it is also possible to simultaneously analyze relationships between more than three dimensions. Color can be used to help emphasize one of the dimensions of the data. The connecting lines between the dimensions will inherit the color from one dimension. Thus, the data of one dimension can be tracked across the other dimensions, and relationships are easier to spot. Figure 3-17 uses the asset role to determine the color, making it easy to see the role of the targeted machine across all the dimensions.

One of the disadvantages of parallel coordinates is the possibility to clutter a display with too much data. Another is that if the data is uniformly distributed among the individual dimensions, you will see a filled area with no clearly visible patterns. Probably even more important is the fact that parallel coordinates are not as well known as other techniques (and therefore) people require some time to understand them. The rearrangement of axes can be especially crucial to show patterns, and it requires some experience to see how axes should be arranged.

LINK GRAPHS

Visualizing relationships in security data is a fairly common use-case. The most common example is probably the visualization of communications in a log file to see what the machines are that are interacting with each other. There are dozens of more examples— as you will see throughout this book—of interesting relationships among data dimensions. The best-suited graph for visualizing relationships of this type is the **link graph.** People familiar with graph theory know this type of graph very well. A link graph consists of nodes and edges connecting the nodes. A directed link graph uses arrows to define a direction between two nodes. For example, in a firewall log file, we are interested in making a distinction between source and destination addresses. Arrows can be used to make this distinction. Link graphs are sometimes called by other names: semantic graphs, relationship graphs, event graphs, network maps, or link maps.

As just mentioned, link graphs are useful for visualizing communication patterns. Figure 3-18 shows an example of source and destination addresses involved in communications on a network. In one picture, it shows all the machines involved in network traffic and whether they contacted a machine or were contacted by a machine. It seems like the internal machines are utilizing the 10.0.0.0/8 address space. Some of them communicate only with other internal machines, whereas others are communicating with machines on the Internet, and some others are being contacted by external machines.

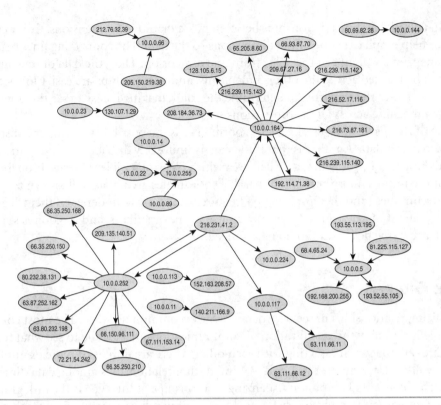

Figure 3-18   A simple link graph showing machines involved in communications on a network.

Instead of showing only two dimensions, like the source and destination addresses in Figure 3-18, a third node can be introduced between the two existing ones. Figure 3-19 shows how such a configuration would look and introduces a naming schema for the nodes to directly address them. There is a **source node,** a **predicate node,** and a **target node.**

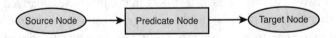

Figure 3-19   A nomenclature for the graph nodes showing a source, predicate, and target node.

The method of adding a third node can be used to annotate the connections with further information, such as the type of communication. Figure 3-20 shows exactly this. You can see that not only are the communicating entities shown, but the type of communication is identified by the **predicate** node.

The graph can be read in various ways. If you are interested in the communicating machines, you start by reading the source or destination nodes (ovals). If you are interested in the type of traffic (for example, email versus DNS), however, you would start with the predicate nodes (rectangles). Looking at Figure 3-20, it is easy to find machines that are accessing shared folders on Windows machines by looking at the cluster on the top right of the graph. Machines browsing the Web are shown on the left side of the graph.

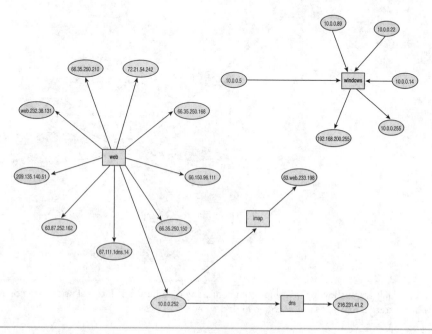

Figure 3-20 A three-node configuration visualizing the traffic between source and destination machines with an additional predicate node that identifies the type of communication

Encoding additional data dimensions in a link graph can be done by using **color, shape,** and **edge thickness.** One interesting way of color-coding IP address nodes is to color internal addresses—ones that are assigned to the machines to be protected—with one color and all the other nodes with another color. This helps to immediately identify internal communications versus ones involving external machines. Figure 3-21 shows this idea, where we own the 111.0.0.0/8 address space. All these address nodes are colored in dark gray, and the external addresses are colored in bright gray. We can immediately see that only one internal machine is talking to other internal machines. All the other machines are being contacted by external machines. In addition, two connections show increased activity, indicated by the thicker edges.

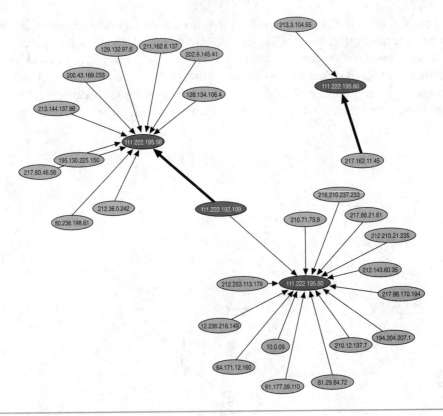

Figure 3-21   Link graph showing machines communicating on a network. Internal nodes are colored in light gray, and external machines are encoded in dark gray.

One of the biggest challenges in generating link graphs is the **layout** or arrangement of nodes in a graph. In graph theory, the problem is formulated as this: Given a set of nodes with a set of edges (relations), calculate the position of the nodes and the connection to be drawn for each edge. One of the criteria for a well laid-out graph is that edges are nonoverlapping and similar nodes are grouped together. Overlapping edges make it hard to read a graph. Multiple algorithms exist to lay out the nodes, each using a different approach to arrive at an optimal node placement. I refer the interested reader to a paper written by Ivan Herman et al., called "Graph Visualization and Navigation in Information Visualization: a Survey." Figure 3-22, Figure 3-23, and Figure 3-24 show how three different layout algorithms arrange the same set of nodes. All three graphs display the same underlying data; only the layout algorithm has been changed!

Figure 3-22 uses a circular approach for placing the nodes. In simplified terms, the algorithm works such that it analyzes the connectivity structure of the nodes and arranges clusters it finds as separate circles. The circles themselves are created by placing the nodes of the cluster on concentric circles.

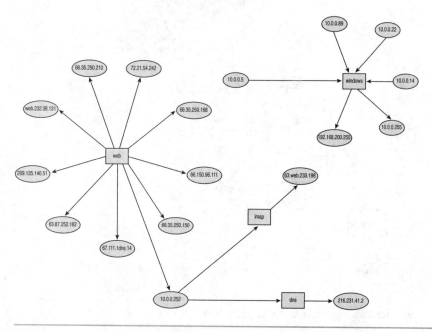

Figure 3-22   This is the first of three graphs that display the same data. Each graph uses a different layout algorithm to lay out the nodes. This graph uses a circular layout algorithm.

Another layout option is shown in Figure 3-23, where you see the same data; this time using a "spring"-based layout algorithm. The approach is to use a spring model (see "An Algorithm for Drawing General Undirected Graphs," by Kamada and Kawai, *Information Processing Letters* 31:1, April 1989). The edges between nodes are treated as springs. When you place a new edge in the graph, the graph seeks equilibrium. That means that the nodes it is being attached to move closer to each other. However, the old edges that were already attached to the nodes pull the new nodes back.

Figure 3-24 shows the same data again, this time using another heuristic to lay out the nodes: a hierarchical layout. Hierarchical layouts place the nodes in a tree. Figure 3-24 shows how the same nodes that are shown in Figure 3-22 and Figure 3-23 are drawn by a hierarchical layout. Hierarchical layouts are best suited for data that does not create very wide trees, meaning that no nodes have a lot of neighbors. Otherwise, the graphs will end up very flat and illegible.

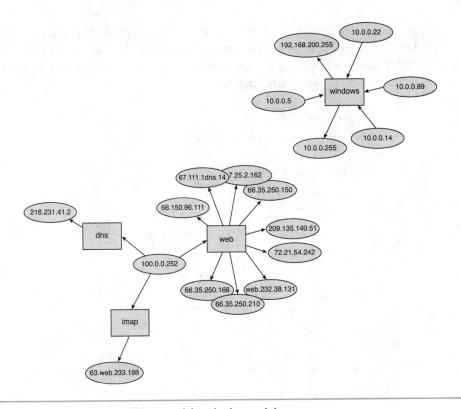

Figure 3-23   This graph uses a spring model to do the graph layout.

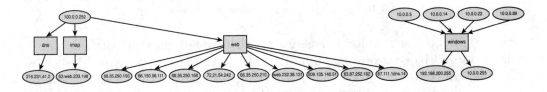

Figure 3-24   This graph uses a hierarchical layout algorithm to place the nodes.

Probably the biggest limitation of link graphs is the number of nodes that can be visualized simultaneously. Too many nodes will make the graph illegible. However, a lot of times it is necessary to visualize hundreds or thousands of nodes. A solution to this problem is to combine nodes into groups and represent them as one individual node. This is also known as **aggregation.** The disadvantage of aggregation is that information is lost. Intelligent aggregation is nevertheless a good trade-off for visualizing thousands of nodes. I use the term *intelligent aggregation*. That means nothing more than trying to identify nodes for which we are not interested in the exact value, but the mere presence of such a type. Assume you are visualizing IP addresses as one of the nodes. A lot of times you are not really interested in the very specific value of a node, but it suffices to know what subnet the node belongs to. In that case, you can aggregate your nodes based on either Class C, B, or A masks. Figure 3-25 shows a sample graph. The leftmost side shows all the individual nodes. The rightmost side shows what happens if all the nodes are aggregated per Class A network. Comparing these two graphs, you can see that quite a bit of detail is missing in the new graph. For certain analysis tasks, however, this is sufficient.

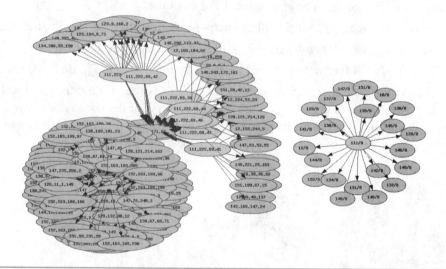

Figure 3-25   This graph shows a simple graph in which the source nodes are aggregated by their Class A membership.

MAPS

Some of the dimensions in our data have a close relationship to a physical location. IP addresses, for example, are associated with machines, which have a physical location. Various degrees of granularity can be applied to map addresses to countries, cities, buildings, desks, and so forth. Visually communicating location is often an effective way of analyzing data. Maps are just a general bucket for graphs that display data relative to their physical location. You can use world maps, city maps, building plans, and even rack layouts to plot data atop them.

When using maps to plot data, you have to make two decisions:

- What data dimensions determine the location? For example
  - The source address only, as shown in Figure 3-26.
  - The source and destination address, as in Figure 3-27.
  - The reporting device's location, as in Figure 3-28.
- How is the data going to be represented? For example
  - Encode data with color inside of the map—a choropleth map (see Figure 3-26).
  - Use a link graph that connects the entities in the graph (see Figure 3-27).
  - Draw a chart at the corresponding location on the map (see Figure 3-28).

Often, this type of mapping requires some data preprocessing. Adding the geo-location for IP addresses is one example. If you are going to map your data onto, for example, a building plan, you must include the coordinates relative to the building plan in your data.

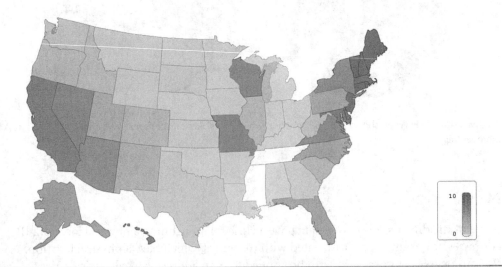

Figure 3-26   Data is mapped onto a map of the United States. Color is used to encode the severity of an alert. The darker the color, the more severe the alert represented.

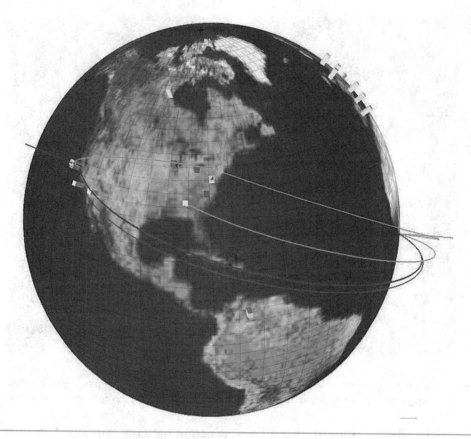

Figure 3-27 A globe where event information is encoded as links between the source and destination location. Color on edges is used to express the severity of the event reported. (This figure appears in the full-color insert located in the middle of the book.)

Maps are useful for examining spatially distributed data. For example, if you are interested in where people are located when they access your services, the originator's IP address can be mapped to a location on the globe and then plotted on a world map. Figure 3-28 shows another example where you have a distributed network and sensors deployed in geographically disparate locations. You can now map the number and priority of events on a map based on the location of the sensors. This type of mapping helps to immediately identify which branch office, site, or network segment has the most problems and which ones are running smoothly. Maps are a great example of graphics that are used for situational-awareness displays, which we discuss a little later in this book. Maps are also a great tool to communicate information to nontechnical people. They are easy to understand.

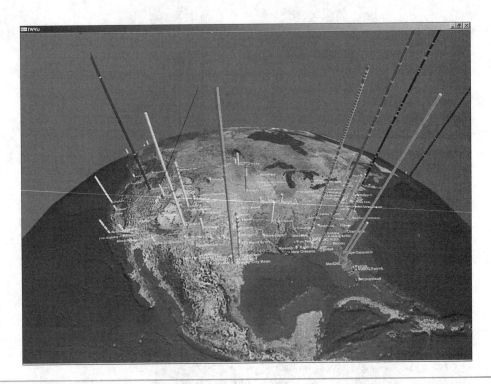

Figure 3-28   A globe where the events are mapped to the location from which they were reported. Stacked cubes are used to represent each event. Color coding indicates the severity of the event reported.

Maps are often overused. It is not always the best way to display information. For example, if your goal is to show relationships between machines and not their geographical location, you should use a link graph. One of the main problems with maps is data density. Suppose you are mapping IP addresses to a map. In some areas, there will be a lot of data points, such as in metropolitan areas (e.g., in Manhattan). In other areas, the density will be sparse, such as in Montana. This relative density results in large areas of the graph that get wasted and others that have a very high data density, making it hard to decode values.

TREEMAPS

Treemaps are another alternative for visualizing multidimensional, hierarchical data. Even though they were invented during the 1990s,[4] the computer security community

---

[4] http://www.cs.umd.edu/hcil/treemap-history

has not really caught on to using them for analyzing data. Almost certainly, treemaps will be seen more often in the future, as soon as people realize how easy it is to analyze their security data with treemaps.

Treemaps provide a visual representation of hierarchical structures in data. Hierarchical or tree structures are created by piecing together multiple data dimensions (for example, by taking the action, the source IP address, and the destination IP address). If we were to take the following log file and arranged it in a tree, we would end up with a tree structure as shown in Figure 3-29:

```
Feb 18 13:39:26.454036 rule 47/0(match): pass in on xl0:
211.71.102.170.2063 > 212.254.109.27 [Financial System]
Feb 18 13:39:26.889746 rule 71/0(match): block in on xl0:
192.27.249.139.63270 > 212.254.109.27 [Financial System]
Feb 18 13:39:27.046530 rule 47/0(match): pass in on xl0:
192.27.249.139.63271 > 212.254.110.10 [Financial System]
Feb 18 13:39:27.277447 rule 71/0(match): block in on xl0:
192.27.249.139.63277 > 212.254.110.99 [Mail Server]
Feb 18 13:39:27.278849 rule 71/0(match): block in on xl0:
192.27.249.139.63278 > 212.254.110.97 [Mail Server]
```

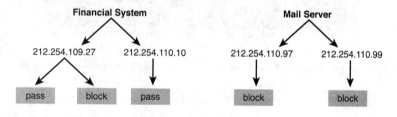

Figure 3-29   A tree structure, displaying the log file as a tree.

Treemaps use size and color to encode specific properties of the leaf nodes (the gray nodes in Figure 3-29)—the destination IP addresses in our case. Leaf nodes in a tree are ones that have no further children. The root node is the one at the very top of the tree. Treemaps are useful when comparing nodes and subtrees at varying depths in the tree to find patterns and exceptions.

Figure 3-30 shows how the log file is mapped to a treemap. The size of the individual boxes is determined by the number of times a certain block or pass occurred targeting one of our machines. For color coding, I chose to use dark gray for blocked traffic and light gray for passed traffic. Any other dimension could have been chosen to assign the color. By choosing the action, I can readily show which traffic was blocked and which traffic actually passed the firewall.

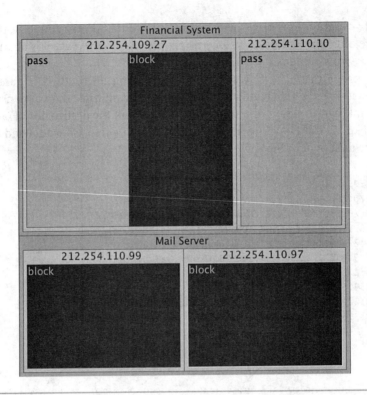

Figure 3-30   A treemap that provides a visual representation of the simple log example discussed earlier.

In Figure 3-30, you can see that two financial systems are monitored. For one of them, half of the connections that were attempted were blocked. The other financial system had no traffic blocked by the firewall. The other systems protected by this firewall are two mail servers. No traffic was being passed through the firewall that was targeted at either of the mail servers. This visualization gives the user a quick overview of which types of systems are being protected by the firewall and which systems the firewall had to block traffic for. Various use-cases can be addressed by this view. It could be used for troubleshooting purposes by, for example, checking whether certain systems are being blocked by the firewall or for gaining an overview of which systems get hit with the most traffic that the firewall has to block. It is possible to reconfigure the hierarchy of the treemap to highlight other properties of the data.

Figure 3-31 shows an example where a lot of data, approximately 10,000 records, was mapped into a treemap. This figure really shows the strength of treemaps—that a large amount of data can be mapped into a single graph. You can quickly identify the sources and the destination ports they accessed. Color in this case indicates whether the traffic was blocked or passed by the firewall. Immediately, you can see that traffic for some ports got blocked for almost all the traffic, while other traffic was let through.

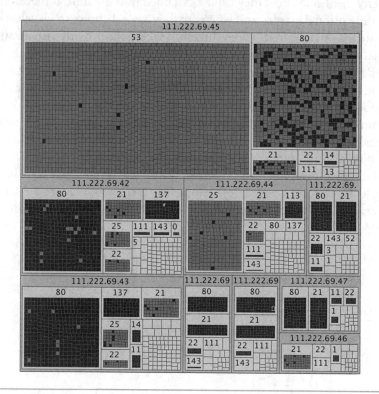

Figure 3-31 This treemap encodes approximately 10,000 records in a small space.

Treemaps have unique properties that turn out to be advantages over other types of graphs. The first advantage is that treemaps can show relationships based on hierarchies. It is easy to compare different data dimensions with each other. Second, treemaps are great at visualizing more than just three dimensions. With color and size, it is especially possible to visualize multiple data dimensions simultaneously. The third advantage is that clusters are easily detectable. You will see how all of these advantages play out during various use-cases later in this book.

THREE-DIMENSIONAL VIEWS

So far, we have focused largely on two-dimensional graphs. When I discussed 3D bar charts, I briefly mentioned how they can be extended into the third dimension. Are there other three-dimensional graphs, and when are they a good choice to visualize data?

Let me state the obvious first. Three-dimensional graphs provide visualization of an additional data dimension as compared to two-dimensional ones. You would think that this makes them great tools to visualize data. Let's think about this for a second. We might be able to use three data dimensions and plot them in, for example, a three-dimensional scatter plot. To look at the scatter plot, however, we have to project it down to the two-dimensional screen or the two-dimensional paper printout. We really lose one of the dimensions. Hand in hand with this problem go two phenomena that often show up in three-dimensional graphs: **disorientation** and **occlusion.**

Disorientation happens when you try to identify some of the exact coordinates of values in a graph. An example where this is happening is shown in Figure 3-32. Beyond identifying exact coordinates, can we even tell in what general area points are located? It is hard to do so!

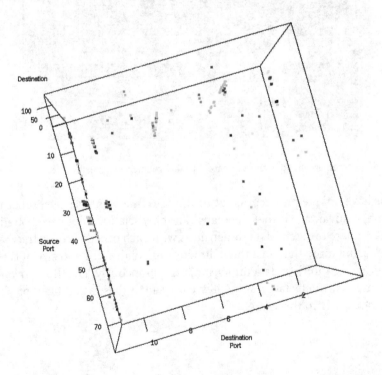

Figure 3-32   A sample three-dimensional graph that suffers from both disorientation and occlusion.

Figure 3-32 shows occlusion, too. Some of the data points hide others. This example adds to the general observation that three-dimensional graphs are often hard to read and interpret.

One way to address the problems of occlusion and disorientation in three-dimensional graphs, at least where the graph is available through a computer, is to make the displays **interactive.** Whereas two-dimensional graphs simply benefit from interaction, three-dimensional graphs actually lose a lot of their value if interaction is *not* available. Letting the user rotate, zoom, and pan the view is essential for making the graphs usable. If on top of that there is a capability that identifies the coordinates of data points when a cursor hovers over them, we can address some of the disorientation problems.

THREE-DIMENSIONAL SCATTER PLOTS

Most of the graphs we have discussed so far can't be extended into a third data dimension. Pie charts and histograms are two examples. There is no real way to extend these with a third data dimension. Although we can make the graphs more visually appealing by using three-dimensional pies and shading and texturing, this is not what we understand by three-dimensional graphs. We want to be able to visualize an additional data dimension. Treemaps and parallel coordinates already provide more than two dimensions. We don't have to think about extending these by an additional dimension.

Scatter plots can be extended into three-dimensional space. The advantage over two-dimensional plots is the capability to simultaneously compare three data dimensions, instead of just two. Figure 3-33 shows an example of a firewall log, where the x-axis is the source IP, the y-axis is the destination address, and the z-axis represents the destination port. It shows a very clear dark line in the top right of the figure. When we try to identify—which is not easy—what this is, it seems that one source is generating many connections to one individual destination on a sequence of ports. It is not easy to identify what is happening because **disorientation** sets in. Are we really seeing a port scan or are multiple sources hitting a single destination port on one machine? This would be the case if the dark sequence were in a plane parallel to the "source" axis.

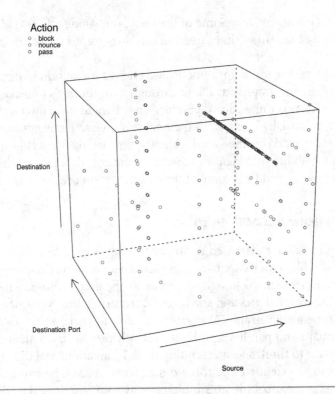

Figure 3-33   A three-dimensional scatter plot visualizing firewall data. The x-axis shows the source address, the y-axis is the destination port, and the z-axis is the destination address. The color of the nodes is encoded by the action the firewall took.

A solution to the problem of occlusion is to show not only the three-dimensional graph, but simultaneously show the two-dimensional projections (see Figure 3-34). This helps a great deal with disorientation and occlusion and helps identify the individual values represented by the scatter plot.

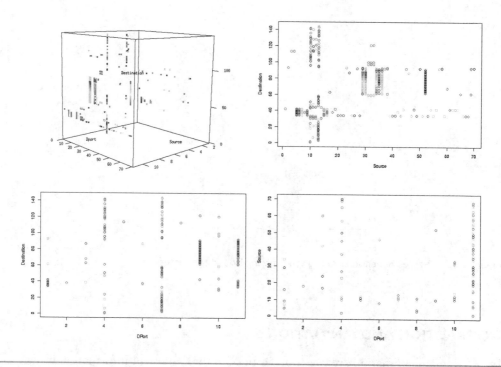

Figure 3-34 A three-dimensional graph along with the three projections. Including the projection helps identify values in the otherwise hard-to-read three-dimensional view.

THREE-DIMENSIONAL LINK GRAPHS

Three-dimensional link graphs are an extension of the planar link graphs that we have discussed. The results of such graphs can be visually impressive, as shown in Figure 3-35. The analytic value of these graphs is questionable. It is generally harder to see shapes and trends in the data than it is in two dimensions. Unless the graph is interactive, the three-dimensional benefits really get lost.

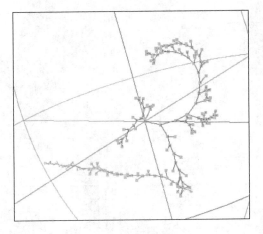

Figure 3-35   A three-dimensional link graph suffering from disorientation

INTERACTION AND ANIMATION

Interaction and animation are two topics crucial in the context of information visualization. Interactive graphs enable you to explore the data instead of just looking at a static image. Similar to interaction, animation adds another element to a visual display. Instead of a single static image, an animated visualization can show how the underlying data develops over time.

Instead of manually having to generate a series of graphs, starting with the overview and then focusing on a specific area of the data with incremental detail, you can generate one graph and either let the user interact with it to get to the desired details or use animation to move through the data along a predefined path. The meaning of a path can be very generic: It could be a literal path achieved by panning through the graph, or a time factor could be used to see the changes of a graph over time.

INTERACTION

While discussing three-dimensional graphs, we saw that the full potential of these graphs can be unleashed through an interactive user interface. Merely displaying the data in 3D does not add much benefit. However, as soon as we can make the graph interactive and let the user navigate through the data, the three-dimensional aspect has a lot of benefits.

The main advantage is that objects are distributed not only along two axes, but a third coordinate can be used to represent a certain property. That way, we have three degrees of freedom that we can use to navigate a graph, not only two.

In the literature, you will often find the term **dynamic query.** Instead of using static queries, you can interactively formulate your query and get immediate feedback. A static query example is this: Suppose you are writing a SQL statement that retrieves a certain piece of data from a database. The query is fixed. You decide what you want to see, and then you issue the query. A dynamic query lets you look at the overall data in a graph, and then you define a query, usually through some kind of user interface, such as sliders or by selecting certain areas in the graph. The interesting part is that the feedback to your query is in real time. You get the new graph right away, and you can refine or change your query again until you find the data or view that you are interested in.

Unfortunately, not too many open source visualization tools make use of interactive user interfaces or support dynamic queries. Chapter 9, "Data Visualization Tools," discusses open source visualization tools and identifies whether each tool has an interactive component.

ANIMATION

If you string a sequence of individual images together, you create an animation or a movie. Generating animated sequences of graphs is not a trivial task and is therefore a tool not often used in security data visualization. If done correctly, it can be a great additional tool to help you understand your security data. Animation in some ways is a means of incorporating an additional dimension into the visualization process. The animation of data over time is one example of a technique or a technology that helps you to understand how certain constellations of data are formed and how relationships come about over time.

A problem with animated displays is stability. The more items in the graph change, the harder it gets for a user to track and find the regions to which they should attend. I use link graphs to discuss this problem. The other graphs have similar problems, and similar solutions can be applied to those graphs. Take a look at Figure 3-36. It shows two consecutive snapshots from a link graph animation. The layout of the graph has rearranged the nodes so much that it is really hard to track nodes from the first graph and map them to the second graph. Imagine how annoying this gets if you have a snapshot like this every few seconds. For this reason, the change between the individual images needs to be minimal. Gradual progress is easy to follow, whereas radical changes will confuse and annoy the viewer.

The pretty obvious solution to this problem is to keep the layout as static as possible. There are indeed link graph layout algorithms that can help with this. Tools that are using animation should make use of these types of layout algorithms. One such layout algorithm for link graphs is the Fruchterman and Reingold algorithm.[5] As an input to the algorithm, not only do you have to provide the new nodes that should be drawn, but also the position of the nodes, if they existed in the previous picture. The algorithm then makes sure that the nodes from the previous graph are placed at the old positions (or at least fairly close to those). This method stabilizes the nodes and guarantees a smooth animation.

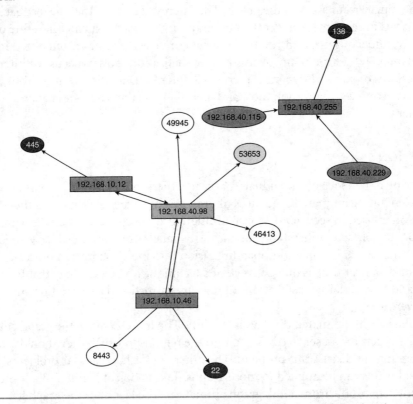

Figure 3-36   Two images out of an animation sequence. The problem of instability makes the graphs hard to compare.

---

[5] http://cs.ubc.ca/rr/proceedings/spe91-95/spe/vol21/issue11/spe060tf.pdf

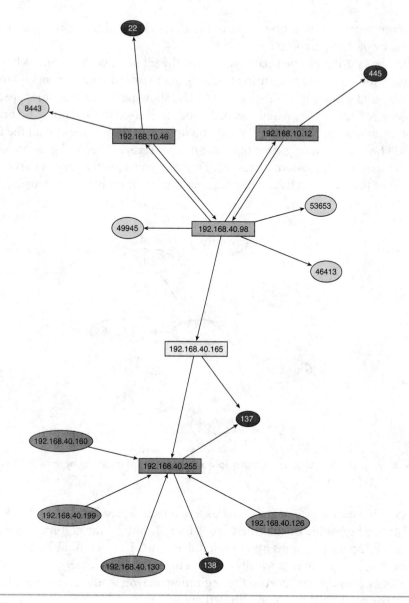

Figure 3-36b

A second technique for making an animated graph more legible and helping the user track changes is to slowly fade out old nodes over time. This way, old nodes will not suddenly disappear from one graph to the next one. In addition, this technique draws visually pleasing graphs.

Yet another solution can be used if you know the set of values up front. What does that mean? Suppose you are capturing traffic going to one of your networks—maybe your DMZ—and you want to visualize the traffic, showing which machines are accessing your servers. You know the possible set of IP addresses used in this subnet before you start looking at any packet captures. What you do now is draw nodes for all the IP addresses. The nodes can be grayed out, as shown in Figure 3-37. The grey nodes are not currently active, only the colored ones are. This way, you keep the graphs fairly static, and you allow the viewer to track progress over time without having to reorient for every image.

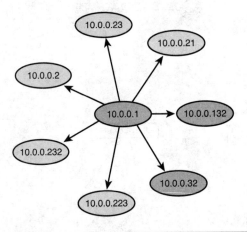

Figure 3-37   A snapshot of an animation that solves the problem of instability by drawing the nodes a priori and graying them out.

You get even better results by combining different techniques. Draw the set of known nodes from the beginning on and then use fading to animate the graphs. These techniques can be applied to graphs other than link graphs. The technique of drawing all the nodes from the beginning is especially useful. Think about bar charts. If you did not draw the set of possible values from the beginning on, you would always see one single bar (the active one). This is of fairly limited use.

CHOOSING THE RIGHT GRAPH

We have discussed a variety of different graphs in this chapter. While looking at the individual graphs, we discussed sample use-cases to see how they can be applied. The big challenge you will face when you start to visualize your own data is to choose the right graph for your purposes and data. I provide two tools to make your process of choosing the right graph a little easier. The first tool is Table 3-1, which summarizes all the graphs discussed in this chapter. For each of the graphs, the table summarizes the following information:

- The number of data dimensions that can be visualized
- The maximum number of data values that can reasonably be displayed in such a graph
- The data type best suited to the graph type
- The basic use-case scenario
- A sample, security-related application
- An example graph to illustrate the use of the graph

The basic data dimensions do not take into account all the additional ways of using color or shape to encode additional dimensions.

The second tool I want to put into your hands is a flow chart (see Figure 3-38) that will help you decide what graph to use for the data you are trying to visualize. The right choice of graph depends not only on the type of data you are visualizing, but also on the objective you are trying to meet. Both of these data points are taken into account in the following flow chart.

Before you start to work with the flow chart, make sure you are clear on two points about your data (to enable proper decision making in the chart):

- How many dimensions do you want to visualize? Make sure you have all the dimensions you need, but omit the ones you don't need. This might sound obvious; in many cases, however, you can omit some data without compromising the goal you are after. Unnecessary data only overloads your graph and makes it harder to interpret.
- What is it that you want to gain from visualizing your data? What is your objective? Do you just want to see counts of things for a single dimension? Are you trying to see a relationship between two dimensions? What is it that you want to know?

Table 3-1   Chart Types

Visualization Technique	Data Dimensions	Maximum Number of Data Values	Data Type	Use-Case	Example Application	Example Chart
Pie chart	1	~10	Categorical	Use to compare values of a dimension as proportions or percentages of the whole.	Proportion of application protocols.	
Bar chart	1	~50	Categorical	Use to show the frequency of the values of a dimension or the output of an aggregation function. Each bar represents a value. The height of the bar represents the frequency count of the value.	Number of bytes transferred per machine.	
Line chart	1	~50	Ordinal, interval	Use to show the frequency of the values of a dimension or the output of an aggregation function. The height of data points in the chart indicates the counts. The data points are connected by lines to help display patterns or trends.	Number of blocked connections per day.	

Visualization Technique	Data Dimensions	Maximum Number of Data Values	Data Type	Use-Case	Example Application	Example Chart
Stacked pie	2	~10 times 5	Categorical	Use to compare values of two dimension as proportions or percentages of each whole.	Based on the role of machines, identify the percentage of protocols used to connect to the machines.	
Stacked bar	2	~50 times 5	Categorical	Use to show the frequency of values or the output of an aggregation function for two dimensions. The chart represents one dimension as the bars. The second dimension is represented as subdivisions in the bars.	For each destination port, identify the role of the machines involved in the traffic. The role is determined by the protocols the machine was using.	
Stacked line	2	~50 times 10	Ordinal or interval for each of the data series	Use to show the frequency of values or the output of an aggregation function for multiple dimensions.	Number of attacks per day across multiple locations.	

continues

Table 3-1 Chart Types (continued)

Visualization Technique	Data Dimensions	Maximum Number of Data Values	Data Type	Use-Case	Example Application	Example Chart
Histogram	1	~50	Ordinal or continuous	Use to indicate the shape of the distribution of values.	Distribution of number of logins over period of a day.	
Box plot	2	~10	Continuous, categorical	Use to show distribution of values. The categorical dimension can be used to split into multiple box plots for comparison.	Distribution of packet size in traffic.	
Scatter plot	2 or 3	Thousands for each dimension.	Continuous, continuous	Use to examine how two data dimensions relate or to detect clusters and trends in the data.	Show communication patterns of machines by plotting the endpoints along with the destination ports they accessed.	
Parallel coordinates Compare relative frequency per dimension and relationships across dimensions.	n	Thousands for each dimension. Up to 20 dimensions.	Any	Use for visualizing multidimensional data in a single plot.	Analyzing firewall rulesets to show for each rule what traffic is affected.	

Visualization Technique	Data Dimensions	Maximum Number of Data Values	Data Type	Use-Case	Example Application	Example Chart
Link graph	2 or 3	Without aggregation: 1000	Any, any	Use for visualizing relationships among values of one dimension and across multiple dimensions.	Identify the impact and extent of a compromise by visualizing communications of the compromised machine after the attack.	
Map	1	100	Coordinates, any	Use to display data relative to a physical location.	Number of trouble tickets per state.	
Treemap	n	10,000	Categorical, any	Use to visualize hierarchical structures in data. Enable comparison of multiple dimensions at once.	Assess risk by visualizing severities and criticalities of vulnerabilities per machine.	

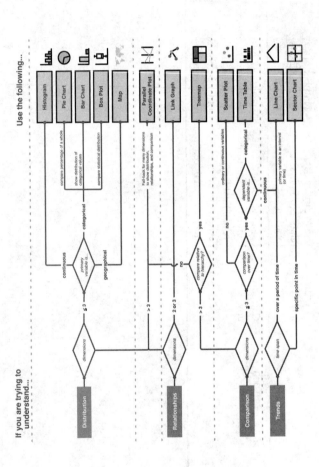

Figure 3-38 Flow chart that simplifies the process of choosing the right graph for the data to be visualized and use-case pursued.

Consider these few comments about the diagram in Figure 3-38:

- You will not find a **stacked pie chart** in the diagram. I do not think they are particularly useful. For the sake of simplicity, I eliminated them from the diagram.
- There is also no **stacked line chart** in the diagram. You use them whenever you have multiple (not more than ten) data series that have the same data types and you need to compare them. They are useful, but they are a straightforward extension of the single dimension case. So, they also are not included so as to keep the table a little simpler.
- You will find that time is shown in only one single decision branch. This does not mean that data with time can be applied only there. You can treat time as continuous variables.

A similar approach for choosing the right graphs is taken by ChartChooser, which you can find at http://chartchooser.juiceanalytics.com. The interactive website lets you explore graph types based on what use you intend for the graphs. You choose your uses for the graphs, and the tool displays the appropriate graphs. After you have selected a chart you want to use, you are presented with the option to download an Excel or PowerPoint template to put the graph to work.

CHALLENGES

This chapter has given you some tools to choose the right graph for your data and the problem you are trying to solve. Keep in mind, however, that even the right graph is not going to magically answer all your questions about a particular dataset. There are multiple challenges associated with using the right graphs and visualizing your data.

The first and most important challenge when displaying data is the source data itself. Garbage in, garbage out. A graph merely provides a visualization of the data at hand. If the data does not contain certain information, there is no way for a graph to display it. Make sure the data you visualize contains the information you need. If you know that many of the data entries are irrelevant, filter them out. Do not burden your graphing algorithms with unnecessary data. On the other hand, if there is more information that could be useful for displaying your data, make sure that data is available and included!

The second challenge is deciding the amount of information to visualize in a single graph. Suppose you are drawing a link graph and you try to display a hundred thousand individual nodes. This is too much data, and the resulting image will not show anything useful. We are facing a resolution problem. A possible solution might be to further process the dataset and build aggregates of individual events that can then be displayed as one node. Aggregation is a very interesting problem in graphical data processing. More and more products are also trying to employ aggregation techniques to help users analyze and interpret datasets.

The third problem, which mainly pertains to link graphs and parallel coordinates, is the arrangements or layout of nodes in a graph or the axis of a parallel coordinate plot, respectively. We discussed this problem briefly when we discussed link graphs. A layout algorithm is the process of distributing nodes over the graph such that the edges have minimal overlap. Ideally, the algorithm also draws nodes that belong together in proximity. This is an incredibly hard problem to solve. Especially if you have a large number of nodes to display, it might require a significant amount of time to optimize parameters of the layout algorithm to come up with a good graph. We run into some optimization problems later in this book and then discuss some ways to solve them.

To address these problems or challenges, two approaches generally help to address the issues at hand. The first one is to use multiple linked views to display different aspects of the same data. Adding interactivity to the visuals is the second tool. In the case of multiple visuals, if they are linked, interactivity is an enormously useful tool to explore data. Figure 3-39 shows an example of linked visuals. The selection of a value in one of the visuals reflects the selection of the other ones.

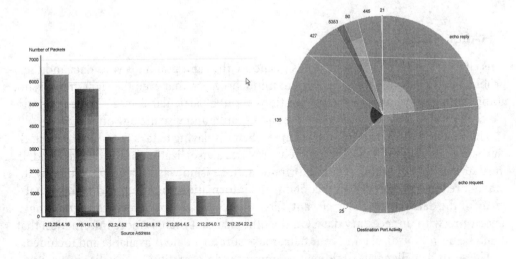

Figure 3-39   Two graphs linked together to improve interactivity. Some values selected in the first graph propagate the selection to the second graph. Each destination port is encoded with a separate color. The bar chart on the left, therefore, also shows how the destination ports are distributed among the selected source addresses. (This figure appears in the full-color insert located in the middle of the book.)

SUMMARY

This chapter has taken us on a journey through the world of graphs. The discussion started with different graph properties, such as color, size, and shape, and how you can use them to visualize additional data dimensions in a graph. I then dove into the different types of charts. I covered the kind of data they visualize, the type of information provide, and some of their limitations. There are more graph types than just charts. We looked at histograms and box plots as two more graphs that can be used to visualize one-dimensional data. After that, I introduced some graphs that enable you to visualize more than one data dimension (scatter plots, for example). And when you need to visualize more than two dimensions, there are also graphs that are well suited for that, such as parallel coordinates, link graphs, and treemaps. The discussion of three-dimensional views showed some of the challenges associated with those graphs. To help address the issues of occlusion and distortion in three-dimensional charts, we saw how to apply interaction and animation to counter those problems.

The core part of this chapter is the summary of all the graph types and their properties. The summary was followed by a discussion of when you use which chart. When is it appropriate to use a bar chart? When do you use a line chart as opposed to a pie chart? I presented a graph decision process that helps you decide what type of graph to use for the problem and data at hand.

We are now ready to move on and take a look at how you go from data to graph.

From Data to Graphs

The previous chapters discussed the building blocks of visualization. We discussed some of the most common data sources. The discussion showed what kind of information the log files contain and what the differences are between the different data sources. We then looked at graphical representations of data. The graph selection process then helped choosing the right graph for the data and use-case at hand.

This chapter brings the previous ones together and shows the steps involved in successfully transforming textual data into graphical representations. It introduces a process that helps you to systematically define your problem, choose the data needed, transform the data, and finally arrive at a graphical representation of your problem. You also see that this is generally an iterative process. When you generate a first graph, you may realize that your data is not sufficient to solve your problem. Or you might experience things the other way around. You may find that your problem was not stated correctly in the context of your data. Through an iterative process, you come to find the right representation for your problem.

INFORMATION VISUALIZATION PROCESS

Visualization of data is not always a straightforward process. It is important that the problem or objective is very clear to start with. After the problem has been clearly identified, various decisions must be made. Color assignment, for example, is one choice to make, and the choice of the right graph for the data and problem at hand is another.

To increase the chances of generating a useful graph that addresses the objective and helps solve the problem, I introduce an **information visualization process.**

The process I am introducing is inspired by the InfoVis Diagram[1] developed by Yuri Engelhardt and Juan C. Dursteler. Figure 4-1 illustrates the six steps of the information visualization process. Starting from the left, the problem needs to be identified first. Based on the problem statement, specific data sources are needed to answer the questions posed in the problem statement. After the data has been identified, various processing steps are applied to eventually arrive at a graphical representation. This process is the same for any type of data analysis and is not specific to a security use-case. The process is security specific in the decisions that are made along the process.

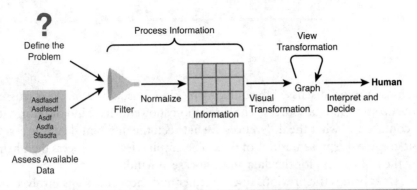

Figure 4-1   Information visualization process diagram illustrating the six steps necessary to generate a graph.

Table 4-1 summarizes the six data analysis steps and provides a short explanation of each step.

Table 4-1   The Six Steps of the Information Visualization Process

Step	Explanations
1. Define the problem.	What is it that you are interested in? What questions need to be answered by the graph that you are about to generate?
2. Assess available data.	What data is available? What logs files do you have that could help answer the problem(s) stated in Step 1. Is there additional data that is needed apart from log files? For example, is there a mapping from IP addresses to geographic locations?

---

[1]   www.infovis.net/printMag.php?num=187&lang=2

Step	Explanations
3. Process information.	The log files need to be parsed and probably filtered to extract the necessary information.
4. Visual transformation.	What graph properties are needed? How are color, size, and shape used in the graph?
5. View transformation.	The graph generated in the previous step can be viewed in different ways. View transformations scale, translate, zoom, and clip the graph to focus on the important parts.
6. Interpret and decide.	Now that the final graph has been generated, what is the answer to the initial problem? Have you addressed all the objectives?

The six steps in Table 4-1 and the brief explanations are in need of some more explication. I address each of the steps in the following sections. Each section contains a sidebar where I lead you through an example to show you how the current step is applied to a sample problem.

STEP 1: DEFINE THE PROBLEM

In many organizations, the salespeople are told not to sell features but solutions. The same can be said about visualization. Visualization should never be data driven. Visualization should be use-case driven. What is it that you need to understand, communicate, or explore? What do you expect to see? What would you like to see? This is why the very first step in the information visualization process is about defining the problem.

CIRCUMVENTING A WEB PROXY

On my laptop, I am running a proxy server to filter all my Web traffic and remove advertisements, unnecessary scripts, and cookies. In addition to filtering Web traffic, I am forwarding certain Web traffic to an encrypted anonymization network. The forwarded traffic is generally for Web pages that do not offer secure Web connections while requiring me to log in. I do not like the idea of my user names and passwords being transmitted unencrypted. I also do this to circumvent curious minds. For example, there is the 16-year-old hacker at the coffee shop trying to sniff the traffic while I am using the public wireless network or the system administrator at my work who is practicing his windump skills. To make sure that none of my "sensitive" Web traffic is transmitted in plain text, I want to analyze my log files and detect instances where my proxy was not running or was circumvented.

I am using Privoxy[2] as my proxy server in concert with Tor[3] to provide the necessary secure connections that prevent someone from sniffing my Web surfing activities. The setup looks such that my Web browser connects to Privoxy, which in turn uses Tor to encrypt some of my plain-text Web traffic.

You will frequently run into two problems when attempting to visualize log files. The first one is when you analyze a log file for a system that you have not seen before. You might not even understand the meaning of all the fields in the log. In a lot of cases, it is not necessary to understand all the fields in the logs to achieve the objective. If you encounter such a case, make sure that you understand the objective very well. For example, you might be given a transaction log from some enterprise resource planning (ERP) system that uses all kinds of strange transaction codes and such. If your objective was merely to identify the users involved in these transactions and the user name was one of the fields of the transaction log, you would not have to understand any of the other information to report over the user names.

You might encounter the second problem even with easy-to-understand log files. For example, assume that you have to analyze a firewall log file. This time you are asked to find anomalies. It is unlikely that you will find anomalies by blindly generating graphs. Try to identify what exactly you are looking for. Are you trying to find anomalous ports accessed on your internal network? Are you interested in anomalous connection patterns? Try to define as many cases as you can and use visualization to verify and analyze them. Along the way, you will likely find some other anomalies that you had not thought of before.

STEP 2: ASSESS AVAILABLE DATA

The next logical step after you have defined your problem is to find out what type of data you need to potentially answer the questions posed. I am being careful with my last sentence. There is no guarantee that you will answer the question from your problem

---

[2]   www.privoxy.org

[3]   http://tor.eff.org

statement with the data and graphs you are going to generate. In some cases, you will be left in the dark, and you might have to reside to other methods to address your problem. But let's assume you can solve the problem. What pieces of data do you need? For example, to figure out what types of attacks are hitting your company, you need the IDS logs from the NIDS deployed outside of your border firewall. The firewall logs will not work in this case. They will not tell you what attacks were issued. If you also want to know what geographical region was executing those attacks, you need a way to map IP addresses to geographic locations, unless the IDS already includes this information in its log files.

PROXY LOGS

To detect Web traffic that is not secured, meaning traffic not using the proxy server or the anonymizer, I analyze the logs from the proxy as well as those from the anonymizer. I use Privoxy as the proxy server. I am running it with the default logging options, which means that a log entry is generated for each GET/POST and CONNECT request. The only change I made to the default configuration was to redirect specific pages to Tor, the anonymizer. The main purpose for this is not necessarily to anonymize the connection but to encrypt it on the local network. The following line has to be added to Privoxy to forward connections to raffy.ch and secdev.org to Tor:

```
config:forward-socks4a .raffy.ch localhost:9050
config:forward-socks4a .secdev.org localhost:9050
```

This forwards traffic to the Tor server running locally on port 9050.

Next we have to set up Tor to do the necessary logging. By default, Tor does not log the connections it establishes. With the following entries in the *torrc* configuration file, you can change that and enable logging:

```
# turns on logging of requested host names
SafeLogging 0
# sets the log level to informational which
# enables connection logging
Log info file /var/log/tor/info.log
```

What type of data do we have available now? We know every time someone uses the proxy to make a Web request. However, we are blind to connections that simply don't use the proxy. We need some additional data source to tell us about that. I have yet another program running on my laptop to do exactly that. I am using *tcpspy*[4], which is a tool that logs all TCP and UDP connections made on my laptop, whether incoming or outgoing. To enable additional logging, I pass the -p parameter to tcpspy when it is launched. On my Ubuntu installation, I simply changed the /etc/default/tcpspy file to read:

```
OPTIONS=-p
```

This logs the filename of the executable that created/accepted the connection, in addition to all the other connection information.

With these three log files, tcpspy, Tor, and Privoxy, we have all the information we need to detect unsecure connections made from my laptop.

STEP 3: PROCESS INFORMATION

At this point, we know what the problem is that we are trying to solve and we have identified and collected all the data necessary to do so. However, the data is not in the right format to go ahead and use visualization tools to generate graphical representations. We have to process the data first and bring it into the right format. In other words, we want to transform the data into information. What do I mean by that? If you are not familiar with a specific log file, you might not understand all the data contained in it. Transforming the data into information adds **meta data** to the fields that explains the meaning or semantics of the data. This transformation process is also called **parsing.**

The basic idea of a parser is that it takes a raw log file and extracts the individual fields from it. Another way to think about the problem is the following: Assume you have a log file and you want to insert the data from the log file into a database. The database has a set of predefined columns: source address, destination address, destination port, event name, user name, and so on. The process of processing the raw log file into a SQL query that inserts the individual pieces into the database is what parsing does.

---

[4]   http://directory.fsf.org/project/tcpspy/

For example, Table 4-2 shows how the following data from a firewall log can be parsed into its components:

```
Feb 18 13:39:32.155972 rule 71/0(match): block in on xl0: 195.27.249.139.63310 >
10.0.0.3.80: S 103382362:103382362(0) win 32768 <mss 1460,nop,wscale
0,nop,nop,timestamp 24086 0> (DF)
```

Table 4-2 Parsing a Firewall Log Entry into Components (Only a subset of all of the components is displayed.)

Component	Data
Date	Feb 18 13:39:32.155972
Rule	71/0
Action	Block
Interface	xl0

The meta data that was introduced is, for example, where xl0 is the Interface. By simply looking at the log entry, this is not obvious at all, especially if you have never used a BSD system or seen a PF firewall log entry.

Parsers for various types of log files are available on the Internet. For example, the Security Visualization portal, http://secviz.org, has a subsection where parsers are available for various log formats, such as Snort alert logs, PF firewall logs, tcpdump, Sendmail, and so forth. Commercial parsers are also available to help you with this process. For example, all the security information management (SIM) or enterprise security management (ESM) tools do exactly that.

I said earlier that you do not necessarily have to understand all the fields of a log entry. What you do need to understand is the fields in the log file that express the properties that you are interested in. This sounds very theoretical, but it is actually straightforward. Consider the example firewall log entry from before. If you are interested in the fields that represent communication patterns, the endpoints involved in the traffic, you have to understand only the IP addresses in this log entry. Keep this in mind when you are looking at a log file that seems really, really complicated! On the other hand, if you are looking for anomalies in the maximum segment size, you must understand more about the inner workings of TCP and where to find that information in the log entry.

ADDING ADDITIONAL DATA

After parsing the information, you might have to augment it with some additional data as discussed in the previous section. Such additional data includes things such as geographic locations, DNS hostnames, or asset roles. Think about this as an additional column in your database. Having this additional information will enable you to not only understand the log records a bit easier, but it also helps in making graphs simpler to read and analyze.

A lot of logs contain the IP address of machines involved in certain activity and not their **DNS hostnames.** Often, the data is easier to interpret if DNS names are used for IP addresses. If you are attempting to resolve the IP addresses and use the DNS names instead, make sure you have access to the correct DNS servers. For example, if you have private address spaces (RFC 1918 addresses), only your DNS server will correctly resolve those IP addresses. Any other DNS would likely not even know those addresses. Also watch out for Web traffic. If you are recording network traffic (for example, you are using the NetFlow protocol), you will not be able to identify the virtual host that the client was accessing. What the NetFlow results will tell you is only the Web server's IP address, and you can resolve that to the primary DNS hostname. However, various virtual websites can be hosted on one machine, and you will not be able to derive that information from Layer 4 information alone.

It is sometimes interesting to not just know the logical location of a computer (the IP addresses) but also its geographic location. You can find this information on many different sites on the Internet. Libraries for your favorite programming language are also available. For example, in Perl you can use Geo::IPfree.[5] I show in the next section how you can make use of this library to map IPs to geographic locations. It is important to know that this information might be out of date or, in cases where the IP addresses belong to the government, they might all point to one single spot on the globe, although the machines using these addresses are spread all over the world. So, use this data with caution.

Additional data includes the role of machines. Especially if you are analyzing log files from your network, it helps to flag the IP addresses with their machine's role. Possible roles include finance, development, Web server, mail server, desktop, and so on. Using these attributes along with the IP addresses or hostnames often helps a lot when interpreting graphs. Figure 4-2 shows an example in which the roles of the machines are encoded in the graph.

---

[5]   http://search.cpan.org/~gmpassos/Geo-IPfree-0.2/

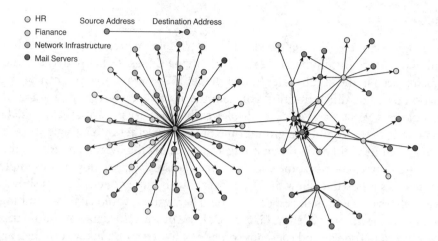

Figure 4-2 A visualization example in which additional data was used to augment the original firewall log file with information about the machines. The link graph uses color to encode the role of the machines.

Parsing and adding additional data is used to prepare the data and transform it into information, but it also enables us to more easily extract individual fields from a log entry. As mentioned earlier, depending on the use-case, different data fields are needed.

Be careful when applying additional data. Some additional data is time sensitive. For example, an IP address that resolves to a certain DNS name today might resolve to another one tomorrow if that domain has been moved. It therefore might be useful to cache the additional information at the time the original data is collected. Also remember that a DNS lookup may alert an attacker. If we resolve an IP address, the authoritative DNS server is going to receive our query. If the attacker operates the DNS server, he now knows that we performed a lookup on his address, telling him to apply extra care or start obfuscating his origin.

FILTERING LOG ENTRIES

Similar to selecting fields from a single log entry, we need to select the relevant entries from the source data. By identifying our objectives in the first step, we made an implicit choice about which log entries we are interested in. It is not always necessary to visualize the entire log file; it is often sufficient to visualize a specific subset of log entries that fulfill a certain criterion. In other words, we need to select the information from the log file that can express the properties we are interested in. For example, if we are interested in analyzing traffic targeting our Web servers, we have to extract those log entries from the log files, removing everything else.

Be careful when filtering log entries. Filtered information is lost information.

AGGREGATION

Often, aggregation is another step needed to prepare data. Aggregation involves the summarization of data points in the interest of simplifying things so that patterns in the data can be better seen in the graph. Later in this chapter, I show you how you can aggregate information based on different fields. For example, if you are aggregating a graph based on port numbers, you are not going to display each and every port number as a data value or a node in the graph. You group some of them together into a single value. This helps remove clutter, while still maintaining and revealing the overall patterns in the data.

Time-based aggregation is somewhat of a special case of aggregation. For example, a diagram that is supposed to show the count over time is quite useless if it just shows each instance of the events and their respective time. The y values would all be 1, resulting in a straight line, as shown on the left in Figure 4-3. If we process the data and summarize the events for a certain time period (perhaps something like every hour), we can then aggregate the counts over each hour and display a data point that represents the aggregate count. This will result in a trend line, as shown on the right in Figure 4-3. It might be even simpler to aggregate across the whole day and just show a single date for each day on the x-axis. The resolution for the data depends on the data and the goal of the analysis.

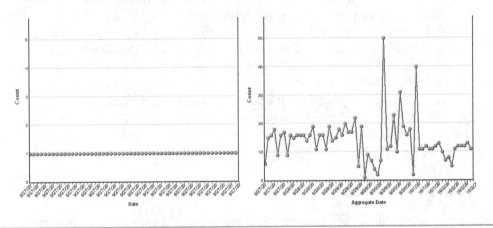

Figure 4-3   Sample graph showing how aggregation is sometimes needed to translate events into a meaningful graph. The leftmost graph shows the result without aggregation. The graph on the right uses aggregation.

If we are looking at something other than the count on the y-axis, for example, the number of bytes transferred, we have to be careful as well. The samples, the number of bytes transferred, have to be collected in regular intervals to guarantee equidistant placing on the x-axis. Otherwise, the trend in the graph is going to be distorted. Suppose, for example, that you collect data points for each day in January and then weekly ones for the rest of the year. The graph would be very misleading, with a much higher granularity toward the left of the graph. If the January samples were also aggregated per week, however, the graph would then correctly display the collected samples. Make sure all your data is in the same unit of analysis.

DATA PROCESSING CHALLENGES

A couple of problems or challenges are associated with data processing. The first one has to do with adding additional data to log entries. Assume you are using the machine's role as an additional data field. With a high probability, we would end up with some machines that were tagged with more than one role. For example, we might want to classify a machine as both a development server and also as a machine storing intellectual property. Now think of our parsing effort as a database table again. We only have one field that lets us classify the machine. However, we need two. Well, nothing simpler than that, we are just going to add yet another column to the database and store the second role in it. But, when you will stop adding columns? How many columns do you need for asset roles? And then, as you will see in the next few sections, how do you map all the fields to your graph? One possible solution uses the most important role only. Another slightly better solution defines a better classification schema that removes ambiguities. Instead of lumping, for example, the importance of the machines into the "role" as well, the two concepts can be modeled as their own fields: role and importance.

A second problem that is much more important than the previous one is how the semantics of fields in a log entry can change. This is a problem that we will run into a little later when we visualize data from sources suffering from this problem, such as tcpdump. To illustrate the problem, let's look at a truncated log entry generated by tcpdump:

```
07:37:13.874735 IP 206.132.26.82.22 > 192.168.2.212.49653: S 2271769079:2271769079(0)
```

To extract the source address from this entry, we could use the following awk command:

```
awk '{print $3}'
```

This command extracts the third token from the log entry, where a token is defined as a set of characters separated by white spaces. If we were to count how many times each source address is contained in a log file to then generate a bar chart, we would just run the entire log file through the awk command and generate the chart from that. What will happen if we do that? Let's look at the very next log entry from the same communication captured by tcpdump:

```
07:37:13.874773 IP 192.168.2.212.49653 > 206.132.26.82.22: . ack 1
```

Do you see what just happened? Instead of finding the source address at the third position, we now find the destination address of the first log entry there. This would totally taint our analysis. If we were to write a parser for this, we would have to teach it to invert the source and destination for all the responses. The tcpdump parser provided by AfterGlow has heuristics built in to deal with these issues and output the parsed results in the correct way.

This is not an isolated example where a source/destination confusion happens. Many firewall log entries have that same problem, which we have to account for.

If every product that logs information conformed to a common standard that defined what had to be logged and how the log entries had to look, we would not need to deal with all of these issues. At the least our time spent on parsing and dealing with anomalies in application logs could be spent on more important issues. Fortunately, some people are working on these issues. Common Event Expression (CEE)[6] is one of the efforts. Hopefully, the fruits of this effort will soon result in easier log data processing.

PREPARING LAPTOP LOG FILES

It is time to have a look at the log files and extract the pertinent information. The first log is from Privoxy. With the log level set to informational, I get quite a lot of entries that are not of interest. For my purposes, it is enough to focus on the *requests* entries. A sample entry looks like this:

```
May 09 17:57:07 Privoxy(b7dd4b90) Request:
www.fish.com/inbox.aspx?SID=x2cemzvhj2fbgyzmzmpp3u55&Guid=399013
```

For the purpose of visualizing which websites I accessed, I need only the hostname part of the log entry. I use the following command to extract the hostname and translate it into an IP address:[7]

---

[6] http://cee.mitre.org

[7] The details of the commands are discussed in the end of this chapter.

```
grep Request privoxy.log | sed -e 's/.*Request: //'
-e 's#[/:].*##' | uniq | perl -M'IO::Socket' -n
-e 'chomp; printf"%s,%s\n",$_,
join(".",unpack("C4",gethostbyname($_)));'
```

This results in a CSV file with hostnames in the first column and the corresponding IP addresses in the second column.

Next I am interested in the Tor logs. The Tor logs turn out to be very chatty when it comes to Tor's internal operation and very sparse with regard to logging connection data. I assume this is due to the anonymization and privacy considerations of the application. This is an example of a log entry that I am interested in:

```
May 09 17:57:07.327 [info] addressmap_rewrite(): Addressmap: rewriting
'www.hotmail.com' to '208.172.13.254'
```

Parsing this entry is fairly simple. I am interested in the address fields only:

```
grep rewriting tor.log |
sed -e "s/.*'\(.*\)' to '\(.*\)'/\1,\2/"
```

Finally, we are left with the tcpspy logs. Here is a sample log entry:

```
May  9 13:40:26 ram-laptop tcpspy[5198]: connect: proc (unknown), user privoxy,
local 192.168.81.135:52337, remote 81.92.97.244:www
```

The log file will contain a lot of additional entries that I am not interested in. The following is the command to extract all Web connections and parse out the source address, the destination address, and the destination service, as well as the user who made the request:

```
grep "tcpspy.*connect.*\(http\(s\)\?\|www\)" tcpspy.log |
awk '{printf("%s%s,%s\n",$10,$12,$14)}'|
sed -e 's/,$//' -e 's/:/,/'
```

This took care of filtering the log files and extracting the pertinent information from them. We are ready to start visualizing.

STEP 4: VISUAL TRANSFORMATION

The output from the previous steps are parsed log entries that contain all the information we need for visualization. This includes things such as asset role mappings, geographic locations, or DNS hostnames. The parsed output should be available in a comma-separated format, a CSV file. CSV makes it simple to further process and work with the data. The next step in our process is mapping the data into some visual structure that produces a graphic representation. The transformations that make this possible are called **visual transformations.** For example, a three-column input file can be transformed into a 3D scatter plot, using each of the input data fields as one of the graph dimensions. The same input data could also be used to produce a 2D scatter plot with the third input field representing size or color of the data points.

DATA MAPPING

The first decision you have to make is what data dimension is the primary one. This is the dimension you want to analyze or on which you want to compare the distribution of the data on the other dimensions. If multiple data dimensions turn out to be important, it will influence what type of graph you are going to choose to represent the data. Various charts are indifferent to assigning a preference to a data dimension: link graphs, scatter plots, and parallel coordinates. For all the other graph types, you must decide which data dimension to use as the main focus. Once you decide on the primary dimension or realize that all the data dimensions can be treated the same way, you need to identify whether all the data dimensions need to be explicitly displayed or whether there are certain ones you want to use for graph attributes, such as size, color, and shape. Only now are you ready to choose a type of graph, with the main data dimensions leading you to your graph decision process. Fortunately, we have already discussed this process in Chapter 3, "Visually Representing Data." It is time to take out that **Graph Decision Process** sheet and put it to work.

Assuming we have three data dimensions and we want to visualize relationships, we would choose a link graph as the visualization vehicle. We have to further decide in what order we want the nodes to be drawn. Figures 4-4 through 4-6 show what happens if we change the order of drawing the nodes.

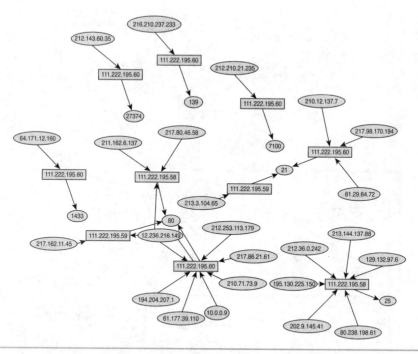

Figure 4-4 Graph using a configuration of source address, destination address, destination port.

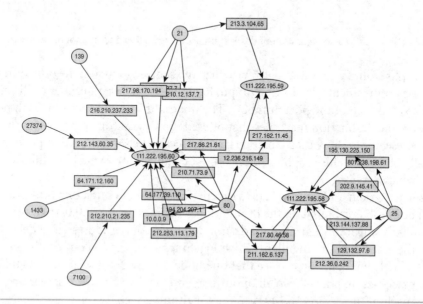

Figure 4-5 Graph using a configuration of destination port, source address, destination address.

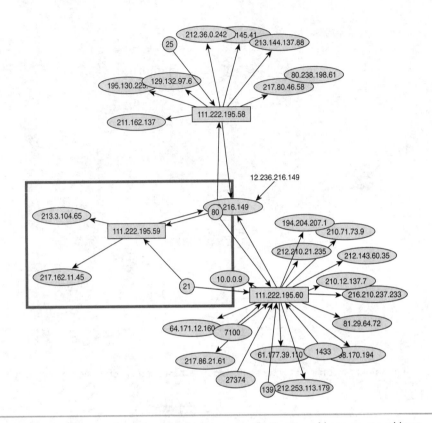

Figure 4-6 Graph using a configuration of destination port, destination address, source address.

All the graphs from Figures 4-4 to 4-6 visualize the same log entries; the only difference is the node arrangements. In the first graph, Figure 4-4, you see a number of disjointed clusters around each of the port numbers. The nodes directly connected to each port number are the destination machines that offered the service (or in the case of this firewall log, these nodes show that someone tried to access the service on that port and was potentially blocked). This graph enables you to quickly identify which machines are offering which services.

The second graph, in Figure 4-5, uses exactly the same data but a different order of nodes. The graph is centered on the destination machines (111.222.0.0/16 in this case). As a result of using a configuration of destination port, source address, and destination address, the graph helps to highlight which machines are accessing our destinations. If you look closely enough, you can see that one node, 12.236.216.149, accessed all of our internal machines on port 80. Do all of our machines really run a Web server on port 80, or is the machine at 12.236.216.149 probing for running Web servers?

The last graph, the one in Figure 4-6, focuses on the destination ports again. Following the port numbers, you can identify which machines are offering a service and which machines are accessing it. However, this graph has an information presentation problem. Focus on the area in the graph highlighted in the rectangle. It is not possible to clearly reconstruct the original log entries from the graph, and it is not clear which of the two source machines was accessing ports 80 and 21 on the destination (111.222.195.59). It could be that they both were, but it is also possible that each source machine accessed one of the ports. The point of this figure is to show that not all graph configurations can be used for the same purpose. Whereas this graph works well to identify which services are offered by which machines, it is not suited to identifying exactly which sources were using which services on the destination machines.

An important initial decision when considering your node configuration is whether you require two or three nodes. Generally, this decision is based on the previous step in which you decide the exact information that you need to see in the graph. If you want to see the machines involved in a communication and the services they are using to communicate, you need three nodes: one showing the source address, one for the destination address, and one for the service (i.e., the destination port). We have seen that exact configuration in Figure 4-4.

Time spent on the visual transformation or data mapping is time well spent. It is one of the most important steps and can help significantly in generating useful graphs. Table 4-3 shows a few configurations for firewall log files and describes the problems that different types of graphs help to highlight.

Table 4-3   Configurations for Firewall Log Files Identifying What Problems They Can Highlight

Use-Case	Source Node	Event Node	Destination Node
Port scan identification.	Source address	Destination address	Destination port
Horizontal machine scans.	Source address	None	Destination address
Horizontal scans on the same port.	Source address	Destination port	Destination address
Finding machines for which certain traffic was blocked and for which other traffic was allowed through. Are they probing the firewall?	Source address	Action	Destination port
Which machines that access a specific service (destination port) and are they allowed to do so?	Destination port	Source address	Action

To visualize more than three dimensions, but also to make a graph more readable, different attributes can be used. I discuss the use of size, shape, and color to enrich graphs.

LOOKING AT WEB CONNECTIONS FROM MY LAPTOP

Our journey so far was fairly boring. All we looked at was log files. It is time to generate some pretty pictures. The starting point is the tcpspy logs. Figure 4-7 shows a link graph of all the Web traffic originating from my laptop.

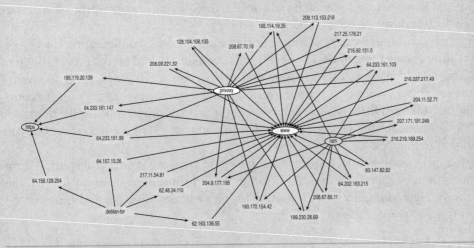

Figure 4-7   Link graph of Web traffic originating from my laptop.

I am using a configuration of *User name > Web server > Service* to generate the link graph in Figure 4-7. The graph looks fairly boring and does not directly identify any pertinent information. I want to try and replace the IP addresses with hostnames from the proxy logs. This will help understanding what machines I surfed to. Instead of IP addresses, we see DNS names of the systems. Figure 4-8 shows this result.

The data for the graph was generated by merging the Privoxy log with the tcpspy log. The command used for this is the following:[8]

```
merge_logs.pl privoxy.csv tcpspy.csv -o
```

---

[8]   The `merge_logs.pl` command is part of AfterGlow, which can be found at http://afterglow.sourceforge.net.

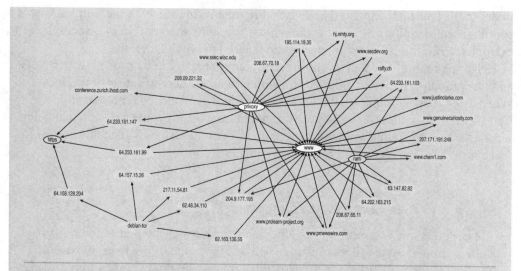

Figure 4-8   Web traffic link graph where IP addresses were replaced with hostnames.

The following couple of sample lines result from this command:

```
193.170.154.42,www,privoxy,www.prolearn-project.org
130.236.132.241,www,privoxy
```

In a perfect world, the output of the merge command would show all the hosts accessed by the Privoxy user resolved to a host name, as shown in the first line above. Unfortunately, there are all kinds of cases where no entry is available in privoxy.csv to map the IP address to a hostname (the second line above). One of the reasons could be that instead of browsing to a website by entering the DNS name, I browsed to some sites by directly using an IP address (e.g., http://216.92.151.5).

SIZE AND SHAPE

The use of size means different things for different graph types. For charts, size is an integral part of the graph. Bar charts, for example, use height to represent a specific count. Pie charts use area to represent proportions. Line charts also use height to indicate counts. For scatter plots and link graphs, size can be applied to the points or nodes in the graph. I already discussed some of the drawbacks of using size to represent a data dimension. Size really only lends itself to relative comparison. This is not at all to say that size cannot be useful! Treemaps rely heavily on size to convey information. The leaf nodes of the data hierarchy need a value that represents their size. In the simplest case, a count is used to indicate how many times a specific value was seen. In more complex examples, an additional data dimension can be used to provide the size.

Height represent frequency counts in histograms. Shapes can be used in scatter plots and link graphs to represent a dimension with a small number of categorical values. When using shapes, numeric data dimensions cannot generally be represented. Categorical values, however, if they are limited in number, are quite well suited to being represented by different shapes. A legend that decodes the shapes is generally needed to make sure the graph can be interpreted correctly.

SHAPE AND SIZE INCREASE LEGIBILITY

Size is a great way to communicate how many times a specific item showed up. If an item showed up ten times, the node will be bigger than if the item showed up only two times. This let's quickly parse the graph to find nodes and communications that occurred most frequently. In addition to size, I want to use shape to distinguish between the different node types (source, event, and target node). The result of applying both shape and size is illustrated in Figure 4-9.

The property file used to generate Figure 4-9 with AfterGlow (see Chapter 9, "Data Visualization Tools") is the following:

```
maxnodesize=1;
size.source=$sourceCount{$sourceName};
size.event=$eventCount{$eventName};
size=0.5
sum.source=0;
shape.target=triangle
```

These properties control the size of the source and the event node, as well as the shape of the target nodes:

- The size of the source and event node is based on the number of times the source node showed up.
- The target node size is going to default to 0.5 based on the catchall statement.
- The `maxnodesize` parameter defines that a node can have a maximum size of 1 and the node sizes are scaled to that.

- By defining `sum.source=0`, we tell AfterGlow to not sum up the individual values for each of the sources, but to take the last value that it encounters. The last node inspected is used to determine the size.

- The last property assigns `triangles` as the target node shape. The default is to use boxes for source and target nodes and circles for the event nodes. This is why you see three different shapes in the figure, but only one assignment in the configuration file.

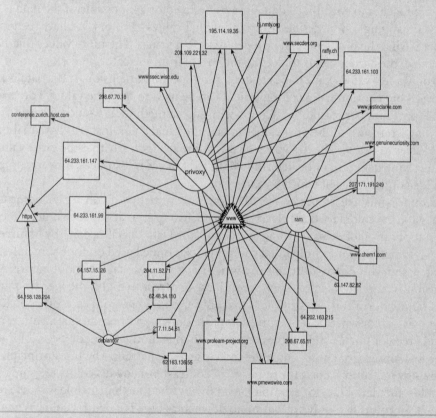

Figure 4-9   Web traffic link graph that uses shape and size to encode further information.

The graph now encodes not just which machines were accessed but also how many times. Larger nodes are machines that were frequented more often than others.

COLOR

Just like shape, color is another method to encode information in a graph. Color can be used for two purposes. First, it can be used to differentiate various parts of a graph. For example, if one node in a graph is colored red, and all the other nodes are green, the red node obviously represents completely different information than all the green nodes. The second use for color is to encode additional information. In network graphs, where nodes represent IP addresses or machines, color is often used to encode the types of machines and whether they are located on the internal network or are external. Two different approaches to encoding a data dimension in color are possible. If the data is categorical, a mapping can be defined from individual values to colors. We have seen in Chapter 3 what the problems can be when mapping values. The more values that have to be encoded, the harder it gets to decode the values from the color. Therefore, color works best if only a few values have to be encoded for a specific dimension. If the data is not categorical but continuous, a color gradient can be used to map the values. For example, the TCP port numbers could be encoded with such a method. It would be hard to define a mapping from each of the port values to an individual color. Instead, a gradual mapping is easier to define. The drawback of this approach is clearly that the exact value of the underlying data cannot be determined. In a lot of cases it suffices, however, to get a rough idea of the range of which a value is in.

A common mistake is poor choice of color. Make sure that if you are encoding categorical data, the colors used are clearly distinguishable. A great paper that talks about the correct application of color is "Choosing Colors for Data Visualization," by Maureen Stone.[9] Assigning color to individual components is done based on four principles.

First, **assign color according to function.** This is what we talked about before. A data dimension is mapped to color. Then second, use **contrast to highlight** specific data points. Think of contrast as two colors that are very different from each other. Figure 4-10 shows a color wheel. Contrasting colors are drawn on opposite sides. For example, red and green or purple and yellow contrast with one another. Do not use a color such as purple to contrast from blue. Those are too close to each other. The third principle is to **use analogy to group.** This is the opposite of contrast. Analogous colors are similar (light blue and dark blue, for example). And finally, the fourth principle is to **use red as an action color.** Red draws attention to it, whereas blue is a neutral color. When

---

[9] www.perceptualedge.com/articles/b-eye/choosing_colors.pdf

choosing colors, always keep in mind that some people are color-blind and cannot distinguish certain colors; most of them have trouble differentiating green and red. To choose good colors, you can use ColorBrewer.[10]

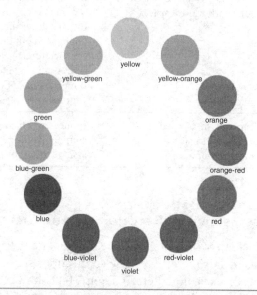

Figure 4-10   Color wheel helping to identify contrasting and analogous colors. (This figure appears in the full-color insert located in the middle of the book.)

Table 4-4 shows a few examples of how you can use color to encode information in security or network related graphs.

Table 4-4   Different Use-Cases for Utilizing Color to Encode Data in Graphs

Data Used for Color	Application in Graph	Objective Addressed
Criticality of internal machines	Color the internal machines according to their criticality. For example, ask yourself whether your company would lose money if this system stopped running.	Helps identify the critical machines immediately. It also encodes how critical the targeted machine is.
Spyware port numbers	Use a dominant color to highlight spyware ports.	Helps immediately identify machines that are using common spyware ports, potentially identifying infected machines.

continues

---

[10] www.personal.psu.edu/cab38/ColorBrewer/ColorBrewer.html

Table 4-4   Different Use-Cases for Utilizing Color to Encode Data in Graphs *(continued)*

Data Used for Color	Application in Graph	Objective Addressed
Dark address space	Highlight IP addresses residing in the dark address space.	IP addresses in the dark address space should never be used by any machine. The Internet governing association, IANA,[11] has not handed out these IP addresses to anyone yet; therefore, the presence of these addresses in log files is a warning sign that someone is spoofing addresses to access your network.
Acceptable use policy	Translate the acceptable use policy into a color configuration.	Immediately flags policy violations, eliminating the need to thoroughly analyze the graph to identify them.

COLOR INCREASES LEGIBILITY BEYOND SIZE AND SHAPE

A graph should immediately communicate the state of affairs to the viewer. If "critical" connections bypass the proxy, those connections should show up in red. All other connections can be colored green. Figure 4-11 shows the results of this. The AfterGlow configuration for this is fairly simple and uses the user name to define the color.
The color configuration is as follows:

```
color="orange" if ($fields[0] ne "privoxy")
color="white"
```

In addition to coloring unsecure Web access in white, we can incorporate the Tor log to color connections that are using Tor in red:

```
variable=open(TOR,"tor.csv"); @tor=<TOR>; close(TOR);
color="red" if (grep(/^\Q$fields[1]\E$/,@tor))
color="orange" if ($fields[0] ne "privoxy")
color="white"
```

---

[11] www.iana.org/assignments/ipv4-address-space

Figure 4-11 shows the graph with this cofiguration. It shows two connections that were secured and anonymized by Tor. Color encodes this information directly into the graph, which makes it easy to identify those connections.

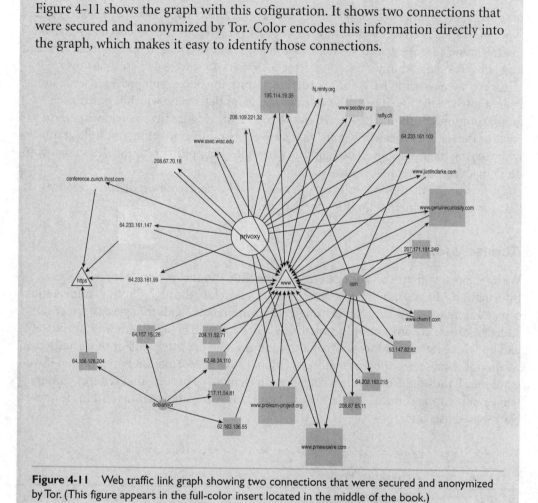

Figure 4-11   Web traffic link graph showing two connections that were secured and anonymized by Tor. (This figure appears in the full-color insert located in the middle of the book.)

STEP 5: VIEW TRANSFORMATION

In Step 4, we produced a first visual representation of our data. If we were careful and made good choices for what to display and how to display it, we already have a graph that we can use. Most of the time, this is not the case. Very commonly, we end up with too many nodes, too many bars, or too many slices in the pie chart. Occasionally, we will realize that the graph we chose to represent the data is not suited for the data. Ideally, the tool we use to generate the graph lets us modify our choices of color, shape, size, graph type, and so on. Even if this is not the case, we can still restart the process and iteratively use the knowledge we gained. Sometimes it is sufficient to zoom in on a specific area and highlight that data. At other times, we have to go back to square one and start over.

Even if we have to go back and regenerate graphs, the first graph provides some initial insight into the log file. It provides context and helps determine which log entries or graph components should be filtered out to highlight and identify the really interesting parts of the log file. This is generally an iterative process of generating multiple graphs with varying filters. However, be cautious when filtering nodes or log entries so that you don't inadvertently remove critical data.

One common method to reduce clutter is to filter data. However, filtering removes data for good. Another method is **aggregation.**

AGGREGATION

We have already discussed aggregation to some extent in the section "Step 3: Process Information." To address the problem of information loss through filtering, information can be summarized rather than eliminated. Common data fields for aggregation are IP addresses. If we are, for example, visualizing a firewall or IDS log file, we will most likely end up with a lot of IP addresses that are somewhere in the Internet. For those addresses, we do not always need the exact address. Often, enough information remains even if we combine all those addresses into a single graph element (a process that reduces clutter while maintaining context). Table 4-5 lists common aggregation configurations for network-based use-cases.

Table 4-5   Graph Aggregation Configurations Along with Their Application Domain

Data Type	Aggregation Property	Use-Case
IP address	Summarize IP addresses based on their subnets. Depending on the size of the net mask that is applied, the reduction can be controlled. A Class A aggregation results in a bigger reduction than a Class B aggregation.	Especially in network logs, there are a lot of different source addresses. In these cases, it is not necessary to know the exact source address from the log file; it suffices to know from which network a connection was initiated.
IP address	Aggregate all the "external" nodes (for example, all the IP addresses that are not owned by your organization).	If knowing which external machine was involved in the activity is not important, it is often enough to aggregate all those data points into one single "external" value.

Data Type	Aggregation Property	Use-Case
IP address	Aggregate by the role of machines, such as mail, Web, DNS, and so on.	Often, it is interesting to see how a certain set of servers is behaving. A DNS server being contacted on port 80 might signal a problem.
Port number	Summarize the ports higher than 1024 into one single node.	Ports higher than 1024 are generally not used for services (although there are exceptions, such as 1521, which is used by Oracle, or 5432, which is used by PostgreSQL). As an alternative, well-known and used ports could be aggregated into a single node.
Port number	Use a list of port numbers to aggregate related ports, For example, aggregate spyware ports or ports that are known to carry protocols that are not encrypted.	Knowing the exact port number involved is often not important; what is important is knowing which machines were accessing the ports. Aggregating the port numbers helps reduce clutter while still allowing you to identify the machines using those ports.

AGGREGATING NODES IN PROXY LOGS

A candidate for summarizing nodes is the event node. An interesting way of summarizing is to show only top-level domains rather than both top-level and second-level domains. This can be achieved with the following configuration in AfterGlow:

```
cluster.event=regex_replace(".*?\\.(.*\\..*)")
   if ($fields[1] !~ /\d+$/)
cluster.event=regex_replace("^(\\d\+)\\.\\d+")."/8"
   if ($fields[1] =~ /\d+$/)
```

This configuration takes the label of the event nodes and uses a regular expression to extract the part of the domain name after the second to last period. This is where the top-level domain name starts. It applies this replacement only if the field itself is not an IP address, which is encoded in the if statement. The second statement aggregates IP addresses based on the Class A net block that the IP address belongs to. Figure 4-12 shows the result after applying this aggregation.

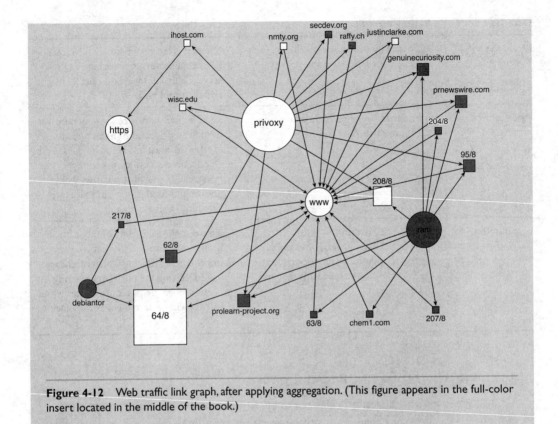

Figure 4-12   Web traffic link graph, after applying aggregation. (This figure appears in the full-color insert located in the middle of the book.)

STEP 6: INTERPRET AND DECIDE

Step 5 potentially resulted in multiple graphs to focus the graph on the relevant data. The final graph is the one that, we hope, can now be used to satisfy our initial objectives. This might seem to be the easiest step in the entire process, to read the final graph. However, it often turns out to be not so trivial. Have a look at Figure 4-13, which shows an extract of a graph. How would you interpret this?

Let me give you a tip. The numbers are ports, and they were obtained from a firewall log file by parsing out the destination port field. Does this look like a port scan to you? It did to me, when I first read the graph. But look again. Why would someone scan these ports? Isn't that strange?

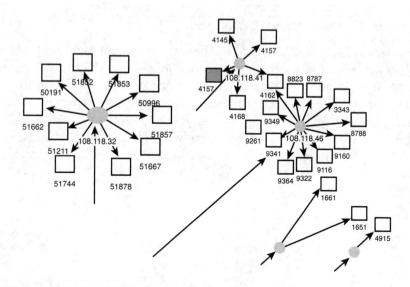

Figure 4-13 An extract of a graph that is easily misinterpreted.

Now what really happened here? It is not uncommon that somewhere during the data analysis process, generally in the parser, the source and destination of an event get confused. Why would that happen? Remember the source/destination confusion I talked about a little earlier? That's exactly what you see here. Even commercial products have this problem.

So, be careful when looking at graphs, and verify things to make sure that what you are looking at is really what you think it is.

A method that often proves useful when analyzing and interpreting graphs is the comparison against other graphs. These graphs can either be ones that have been generated over the same type of data but at a previous point in time or it can be a reference graph for that type of visualization. If you know that a graph should always display a certain pattern and it suddenly does not show up anymore, you just found an anomaly. For the analyst, this is especially easy because he does not need to completely understand the underlying data to spot anomalies and noteworthy changes in the data.

Let's assume your graph is displaying what you think it should display. Now that you interpreted the graph and you understand what the underlying log file presented, you should go back to the problem definition. What were you looking for? Why did you generate the graph? Based on the problem and the graph in front of you, you should now be able to make an informed decision about how to solve your problem or at least be able to answer the question you had when you started the process.

ANALYZING LAPTOP PROXY LOGS

Looking back at Figure 4-12, I would not be surprised if you were fairly confused. I certainly was when I first started interpreting the results. What is going on in this graph? My first question was why was there traffic from the user debian-tor, which should be the Tor daemon, to certain machines on port 80 (or www)? I would expect all the traffic from Tor to be SSL encrypted. I found the answer to this question when I started to look a bit closer at what Tor is doing. Tor uses a set of proxy servers in the Internet that it uses to send the Web requests to. Figure 4-14 illustrates that.

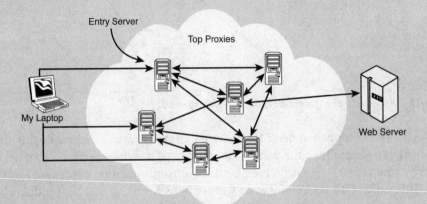

Figure 4-14   Tor uses a network of proxy servers to conceal our Web traffic.

The next important piece of information is that the Tor proxies use port 9030 to communicate among each other. My laptop also uses port 9030 to communicate into the network via one of the entry servers. What are the other connections by debian-tor on port 80, though? It turns out these are control connections between my laptop and the entry servers, and they don't have anything to do with actual Web traffic being passed around.

Another important fact about connections in the Tor network is that they are long-lived and they are being reused by many Web requests. This means that not every Web request will show up as a separate connection in tcpspy!

What all this really means is that we should filter out the debian-tor connections on port 80 (www). They do not add any important information for our purposes.

The next thing in Figure 4-13 that draws attention is that the user ram, as well as privoxy, is requesting websites. All the connections directly made by the user ram are circumventing the proxy server, and they should not show up. To do damage control, the graph helps me identify which servers I was accessing without using a proxy. It also lets me verify that I did not connect to any of the critical sites (in dark gray) without encrypting my connection through Tor.

Continuing to analyze Figure 4-12, I see some more things that are odd. I thought that all the connections to sensitive sites were encrypted. At first glance, everything looks fine, and my connections to raffy.ch and secdev.org are indeed encrypted. But what are all these IP addresses that were not replaced with host-names? Investigating this issue some more, I found out that some Web pages have embedded components, such as Java scripts, which are linked into the main pages by using an IP address in the URL and not a hostname. These are exactly those artifacts. What this means is that I need to be careful when defining which pages have to use the Tor network to also include all those cases where the IP address is used directly to access the sensitive sites! After I had done that, I came up with the graph shown in Figure 4-15. Note that the debian-tor connections are gone, as is the link between ram and the 195/8 node, which was one of those IP addresses that I had to explicitly include in my configuration to encrypt the traffic.

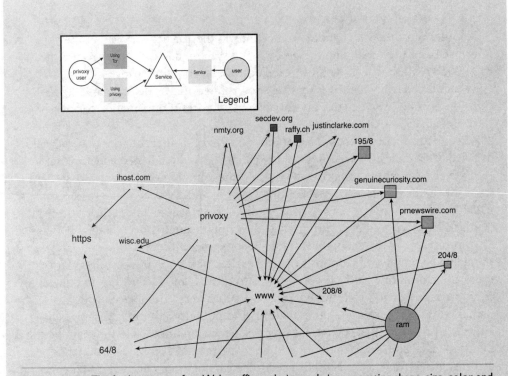

Figure 4-15 The final instance of my Web traffic analysis graph, incorporating shape, size, color, and aggregation. (This figure appears in the full-color insert located in the middle of the book.)

TOOLS FOR DATA PROCESSING

During the information visualization process, I used various tools and techniques to process information. In this section, I talk about some useful and common tools that I use to prepare log files for visualization. Most of these tools are not necessary, and you can do all the preparation by hand. However, the manual approach is going to take you a long time, and so it is well worth taking the time to understand the basics of the tools I introduce here. This is especially true if you want to automate some of your data analysis processes at some point.

EXCEL, OPENOFFICE, AND TEXT EDITORS

Data preprocessing does not necessarily have to be done through some kind of programming. It can be done with a simple text editor. You can use Notepad to modify the log files and extract the information you need for later visualization. Just a step up from doing data preprocessing manually is the use of a tool such as Microsoft Excel or OpenOffice spreadsheets. If you are really savvy with Excel, you might even be able to automate some of your processing. However, most of the data processing that we need for log analysis is not supported in Excel and is fairly hard to automate. Excel also has a limitation of handling only 65,535 rows, which is generally not enough when dealing with log files.

An alternative that I find myself using quite often is VIM,[12] a VI clone. I like using UNIX commands to process Comma Separated Value (CSV) files, and by using VI, I can use UNIX tools to do exactly that while still having the flexibility of a text editor. For example, to call awk out of VI, you use the following VI command:

```
:%!awk -F, '{printf"\%s,\%s",$2,$1}'
```

This command inverts the first and the second column of a two-column CSV file inside of VIM.

REGULAR EXPRESSIONS

If you are not familiar with regular expressions, you should definitely learn them or brush up and try to understand at least the basics of how a regular expression, or regex for short, works. Various tutorials are available on the Internet. One of my personal favorites is www.regular-expressions.info. It offers a quick start and a reference guide for those quirks that you can never remember. In the following discussion, I assume that you have a basic understanding of regular expressions; I do not introduce all the basic concepts.

I want to add one word of caution here. Using regular expressions, you will fairly quickly run into the topic of greedy versus nongreedy matching. I have to admit, it happens to me all the time. What is the greedy business all about? A greedy match is a match where the regular expression tries to consume as many characters as it possibly can while

---

[12] www.vim.org

still satisfying the rest of the regular expression. Let's assume we have the following log entry:

```
Apr 17 08:22:27 rmarty kernel: Output IN= OUT=vmnet8 SRC=192.168.170.1
DST=192.168.170.255 LEN=258 TOS=0x00 PREC=0x00 TTL=64 ID=0 DF PROTO=UDP SPT=138
DPT=138 LEN=238
```

We want to extract the output interface from this log entry. The first attempt would probably be something like this:

```
perl -pe 's/.*(OUT=.*) .*/\1/'
```

More or less surprisingly, this does not give us the right output, but instead it extracts all of the following:

```
OUT=vmnet8 SRC=192.168.170.1 DST=192.168.170.255 LEN=258 TOS=0x00 PREC=0x00 TTL=64
```

The correct way of extracting the interface is to use a nongreedy match for the interface name:

```
perl -pe 's/.*(OUT=.*?) .*/\1/'
```

This command correctly extracts the interface: OUT=vmnet8. So, be careful to avoid unwanted greedy matches!

UNIX TOOLS

UNIX, or Linux for that matter, comes with a set of very powerful and usually fairly simple-to-use tools that are of great assistance when dealing with log processing. The tools I am using here are also available for Microsoft Windows. One commonly used package for Windows is cygwin.[13] Another one is UNIX Utils,[14] which provides tools such as grep, sed, and awk. Let's take a look at each of these three tools separately and see how they can help us with processing log files.

---

[13] http://cygwin.org

[14] http://unxutils.sourceforge.net

grep

Probably the simplest UNIX utility when it comes to data processing is grep. When used on a file, it extracts the entries that match the search condition given as an argument:

```
grep "connection:" logfile.log
```

The preceding command will look through the file *logfile.log* and extract all the lines that mention the connection: string. All the other lines will not be shown. The inverse can be done by using the following command:

```
grep -v "connection:" logfile.log
```

This command excludes all the lines that do not contain the string from the log file. Instead of just using simple strings, you can use regular expressions to extract lines that match a more complex pattern. grep is generally used to filter entire log entries and does not modify individual log entries. However, you could use the -o parameter to extract portions of a log entry, which sometimes proves very helpful.

awk

If you need to parse log entries or reformat them, awk is one candidate tool. Whenever a log file has a simple structure—or in other words, a specific separator can be used to break a log entry into multiple chunks—awk is the tool you want to use. What do I mean by that? Assume you have the following types of log entries:

```
May 9 13:40:26 ram-laptop tcpspy[5198]: connect: proc (unknown), user privoxy, local
192.168.81.135:52337, remote 81.92.97.244:www
```

One way to extract specific fields is to use a full-blown parser or a regular expression. However, we can very simply use awk to extract, for example, all the users from the log entry:

```
awk '{print $10}' logfile.log
```

This simple command prints the tenth token. By default, awk uses any number of white spaces (spaces or tabs) as separators for the tokens. You can use the dollar notation to reference specific fields to operate on. The first token is denoted by $1. The next one is $2, and so on.

Another sample use for awk is if you have a CSV file and you want to rearrange its columns. The first column should really be swapped with the second one. What you need to do is first change the field separator to be a comma rather than white spaces. You can do this with the -F parameter. Here is the command to swap the first column with the second one:

```
awk -F, '{printf"%s,%s,%s\n",$2,$1,$3}' logfile.log
```

The command assumes that you have a CSV file with three columns. You get the idea. A slightly different way of doing the same thing is the following:

```
awk -F, -v OFS=, '{tmp=$1; $1=$2; $2=tmp; print}'
```

This changes the output field separator (OFS) to a comma, and then simply switches the first and second column around before printing the record again. There are various other uses for awk, but these are the two you will most likely be using.

sed

Another tool that I use fairly often is sed. Whenever a log entry does not have a simple structure and I cannot identify a simple separator such that I could use awk, I use sed. With sed, I can specify a regular expression to extract the pieces of the log entry that I am interested in:

```
sed -e 's/.*Request: //' -e 's#[/:].*##' logfile.log
```

This is a fairly complex example already. But let's break it down into pieces and see what it does. There are two separate commands that both start with the -e parameter. Following the parameter, you find a regular expression. The first one just removes the entire beginning of the line up to and including the part of the log entry where it says Request:. In short, it gets rid off the header part. The second command looks somewhat more complicated, but it really is not. What you have to know here is that the first character following the s command is used as the separator for the substitute command. In the first command, I was using a forward slash. In this example, I use a hash sign (#).

Why? Because if I use a forward slash, I have to escape all the forward slashes in the following regular expression, and I want to avoid that. The regex of the second command identifies instances where there is a slash or a colon followed by any number of characters, and it will remove all of that. Here is the original log entry followed by the output after the sed command was applied:

```
May 09 19:33:10 Privoxy(b45d6b90) Request: sb.google.com/safebrowsing

sb.google.com
```

In essence, the command extracts domain names from proxy logs.

PERL

Instead of using UNIX tools, you could also use a scripting language, such as Perl. I use Perl for a lot of things, such as augmenting log entries with geographic information or doing DNS lookups. You should be aware of three simple cases when using command-line Perl to process log entries. The first case is essentially a grep alternative:

```
perl -ne 'print if (/^1/)' file.txt
```

This command looks for all the entries in the file that start with a 1. The next use is a substitute for sed:

```
perl -pe 's/^ +//' phonelist.txt
```

This command eliminates all the spaces at the beginning of a line. And finally, another command where you could use sed to extract individual parts of a log entry looks like this:

```
perl -pe 's/.*(IN=\S+).*/\1/'
```

This command extracts all the inbound interfaces in an IP tables log file.

Two somewhat more complex examples of useful Perl scripts are adding geographic locations for IP addresses and the reverse lookup of IP addresses in DNS to use the hostname rather than the IP address for graphing purposes. Both of these data mapping examples can be implemented with simple Perl one-liners.

Let's assume we have the following log file, already formatted in a comma-separated form:

```
10/13/2005 20:25:54.032145,62.245.243.139,195.131.61.44,2071,135
```

We want to get the country of the source address (the first IP address in the log file) and add that at the end of the log file:

```
cat log.csv | perl -M'Geo::IPfree' -lnaF/,/ -e
'($country,$country_name)=LookUp($F[1]); print "$_,$country_name "'
```

This one line produces the following output:

```
10/13/2005 20:25:54.032145,62.245.243.139,195.131.61.44,2071,135,Europe
```

Let's take a closer look at that command. Most important, I am using a Perl module to do the country lookup. The library you need is *Geo::IPfree*, which you can find on CPAN.[15] To use a library in Perl, you have to use the -M option to load it. Following that, I am using an -n switch to create a loop through the input lines. Every line that is passed to Perl will be passed through the command specified after the -e switch. The other two parameters, -aF/,/, instruct Perl to split each input line, using a comma as a delimiter. The result of the split is assigned to the array @F. The command itself uses the Geo library's Lookup() function with the second column of the input as an argument, which happens to be the source IP address from our input logs. Using chomp, I am stripping new line characters from the original input line so that we can add the $country_name at the end of the line.

In a similar fashion, we can either add or substitute IP addresses with their corresponding hostnames. The command for that looks similar to the Geo lookup:

```
cat log.csv | perl -M'Socket' -naF/,/ -e
'$F[1]=gethostbyaddr(inet_aton($F[1]),AF_INET)||$F[1]; $,=",";
print @F'
```

This time, I am substituting the second column with the hostname of the IP address, instead of appending the hostname to the end of the line. The function to look up the

---

[15] http://search.cpan.org/~gmpassos/Geo-IPfree-0.2/

DNS host name for an IP address is called `gethostbyaddr`, and it is provided by the Socket library. I am using a couple of interesting things in this command. The first one is that I am resolving the hostname, and I make sure that if it is empty, I am printing the original IP address, rather than an empty string. That way, if an IP cannot be resolved, it will just stay in the log entry. The other thing I am using is $, which lets me change the output separator. If I were not setting the output separator to be a comma, the following print command would print all the elements from the array one after the other, without any separating character. However, I would like to have a comma-separated file again, so setting the separator to a comma will do the trick.

PARSERS

If you check Webster for a definition of **parser,** the following will come up:

> A computer program that breaks down text into recognized strings of characters for further analysis.

In our environment, this translates to taking a complex log entry and reducing it to smaller, easier-to-process components. For example, a firewall log file can be parsed into its components: source address, destination address, source port, rule number, and so on. We have used this idea throughout this chapter to extract pieces from the log files that we wanted to graph. The proxy example used simple UNIX commands to do the parsing. This is not necessarily the most efficient way to go about getting to the point of log visualization. It is much easier to reuse a parser that someone else wrote. This is especially true if an application uses various different types of log entries. You can find a lot of parsers on the Internet. One of the best places is secviz.org under the topic of "parser exchange."

As an example, let's look at the Sendmail parser. Sendmail logs are annoying if you want to graph email communications. The problem is that Sendmail logs two separate entries for every email, one for the sender and one for the recipient. Here is an example:

```
Jul 24 21:01:16 rmarty sendmail[17072]: j6P41Gqt017072:
from=<root@localhost.localdomain>, size=650, class=0, nrcpts=1,
Jul 24 21:01:16 rmarty sendmail[17073]: j6P41Gqt017072: to=raffy@raffy.ch,
ctladdr=<root@localhost.localdomain> (0/0), delay=00:00:00, xdelay=00:00:00,
mailer=local, pri=30881, dsn=2.0.0, stat=Sent
```

As you can see, the first entry shows the sender piece of the email, and the second one shows the recipient information. To generate a graph from these log entries, we have to merge the two entries. Two entries in the log belong together if they have the same message ID (j6P41Gqt017072). Instead of building some complex way of parsing these messages and doing the match up, we can just reuse the Sendmail parser from secviz.org[16] as follows:

```
cat /var/log/maillog | sendmail_parser.pl "sender recipient"
```

The output from this command is a CSV file that consists of sender-recipient pairs. It is now fairly simple to graph this information.

If you are in the fortunate position of operating a security information management (SIM) tool in your environment, you can probably make use of the parsing from those tools to generate parsed output. These tools rely heavily on parsing and generally come with a fair amount of device support. The only capability you need from the SIM is to export events into a simple format (CSV, for example).

OTHER TOOLS

Doing log analysis, I find myself writing a lot of little tools to make my life easier. I am trying to share my work so that people do not have to reinvent the wheel and can help me improve my tools. You can find all of my tools as part of the AfterGlow project at http://afterglow.sourceforge.net. If you download a recent version, the tools are located under src/perl/loganalysis, as well as src/perl/parsers. Have fun browsing through them.

SUMMARY

This chapter has taken us through some more of the background we need to tackle our visualization projects. I introduced an information visualization process that consists of six steps. The process starts out by defining the problem that needs to be solved. To solve the problem identified, certain data sources need to be available. In some cases, additional data must be collected. The next step is to process the information and filter it down to the necessary data. Using visual transformations, the data is then mapped into a graph. Various decisions need to be made at this point. Those decisions include not just what type of graph to use but also how to utilize color, shape, and size to best communicate the data properties. In the next step, view transformations can be applied to do a

---

[16] www.secviz.org/?q=node/8#comment-2

final tweak of what exact part of the data the graph should show. This generally incorporates the process of aggregating certain groups of values into one single cluster. And finally, the graph needs to be interpreted and vetted against the original objective.

The remainder of the chapter showed various simple tricks concerned with how to work with log files. Two of the more interesting applications were doing DNS lookups on the command line and doing IP address location lookups.

With all this information and a new process in our tool box, we can now proceed to look at the topic of **visual security analysis,** which is the topic of the next chapter.

Visual Security Analysis

The beginning of this book introduced all the building blocks necessary to generate graphs from security-related data. I have discussed some of the data sources that you will encounter while analyzing security data. The discussion showed what information each of the sources records and what some of the missing information is. I discussed the different graphs and how to most effectively apply them to your problems, and after that I introduced the information visualization process, which guides you through the steps necessary to generate meaningful visual representations of your data. As the last step of the information visualization process, I briefly touched on the analysis and interpretation of the graphs generated.

This chapter elaborates on that concept and shows different ways of analyzing security data using visual approaches. I separate the topic of graph analysis into three main categories:

- Reporting
- Historical analysis
- Real-time monitoring

Reporting is about communicating and displaying data. Historical analysis covers various aspects of analyzing data collected in the past. The motivations and use-cases are manifold. They range from communicating information to investigate an incident (or other type of problem) to analyzing the data to comprehend the underlying data and situations reported. We discuss the topic of **historical analysis** by separating it into three subcategories:

- Time-series visualization
- Correlation graphs
- Interactive analysis
- Forensic analysis

After looking at historical analysis, we follow up with **real-time monitoring,** which, in the context of visualization, heavily uses the concept of **dashboards.** I discuss some of the main criteria for building effective dashboards for communicating security data. A topic closely related to dashboards is **situational awareness.** I discuss the importance of real-time insight into key security-relevant areas and how it can be used to drive decisions and react to, or proactively address, upcoming problems.

Each of the four historical analysis sections focuses on **analysis.** This material is not about how specific sets of data can be represented in a graph; we have already discussed that in the beginning of the book. Here the focus is on how to represent different sets of data to analyze and compare them. What are some of the common ways of analyzing security data? In some cases, we will see that the analysis requirement will influence how to create visualizations of the individual datasets, creating a closed loop with the graph-generation process.

REPORTING

One of the most often used techniques to communicate and display data is the **report.** Reports are not the prime example for showing the advantages of visualization. However, visualization in the form of graphs is a commonly used tool to improve the effectiveness of reports. Reports are a great tool for communicating and summarizing information. Reporting ranges from status reports, which show, for example, the type of network traffic the firewall blocked during the past seven days to compliance reports used to prove that certain IT controls are in place and operating.

A report can consist of just text, a simple graph, a combination of a graph and text, or a collection of graphs with optional text. A report based only on text is not something I discuss here. This book is concerned with visual communication of information and not textual encoding. One of the key properties of a report is that it focuses on past information. Reports are generated ad hoc, when needed, or on a scheduled basis. For example, I am using a weekly report to see the amount of blocked traffic per protocol that targeted my laptop. The report is emailed to me so that I get a feeling for what the attack landscape looked like during the past week. Instead of using textual information, I am using graphs to summarize the data visually. Figure 5-1 shows an example of such a report.

The prevalent data source for reports is a database. The advantage of having the data in a database—over, for example, a file—is that SQL can be used to process the data before the report is generated. Operations such as filtering, aggregating, and sorting are therefore easy to apply. In some cases, reports can be generated directly from log files, which I did for the report in Figure 5-1. However, this might require some more manual data processing. The one type of data source that is not well suited to reporting is real-time feeds. Reports are static in nature and represent a snapshot in time. In contrast to reports, dashboards are designed to deal with real-time data. More about dashboards a little later. Apart from the real-time data sources, most other data sources are well suited to reporting.

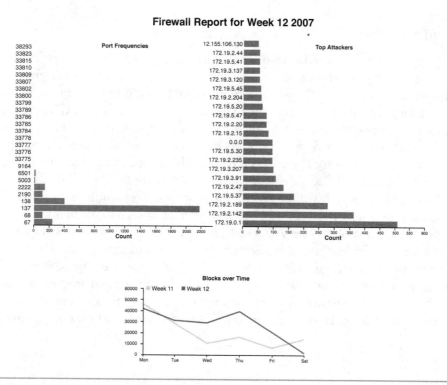

Figure 5-1   A sample report of traffic targeting my laptop. The charts show protocol distributions, the top attackers, and the number of blocked traffic incidents over the past seven days.

The goal of a report is to communicate information. The audience should be able to read the report and understand immediately what is shown. It should not be the case that additional information or explanations are needed to understand a report. Therefore, graphs that are complicated by nature are not well suited to reports. Simple graphs are preferable. That is why bar charts and line charts are great candidates for inclusion in reports. Sometimes scatter plots or time tables can be used, too. All the other graphs, such as link graphs, treemaps, parallel coordinates, and all three dimensional graphs, generally need more explanation or the capability for the user to interact with the graph to make it effective and useful. Bar charts and line charts are by far the most familiar graphs. Everybody has seen them used for many different data visualizations. There are, as always, exceptions to the rule. In addition to choosing the right graph to visualize your data, make sure that you apply the graph design principles with regard to size, color, shape, data-ink ratio,[1] and so on to make sure the graphs are easy to read.

REPORTING TOOLS

Tools to generate reports can be divided into three main categories. The first category consists of security reporting solutions, such as security information management (SIM) and log management tools. These solutions are capable of not just generating reports, but also taking care of all the processing to get the data into a report, such as collection, normalization, storage, and so forth. These tools focus on security events and generally ship with a set of predefined reports for specific reporting use-cases. Unfortunately, most of these tools are not cheap. Those SIM tools available as open source are limited in their capabilities and generally lack adequate support for data feeds.

The second category consists of general-purpose reporting solutions. Microsoft Excel and OpenOffice spreadsheets, Crystal Reports, Advizor, and gnuplot fall into this category. These tools do not deal with data collection. In addition, these types of tools are not built for security data and therefore might not offer some of the functionality necessary. For example, functions to format or process IP addresses are generally not available. However, these tools offer a great variety of graphic capabilities and are generally easy to use and operate. Other drawbacks that you might find annoying fairly quickly are that they operate on static data and that the generation of a new report cannot be automated.

---

[1] Edward Tufte talks about the data-ink ratio, which is defined as the amount of ink essential to communicate the information divided by the total amount of ink actually used in the chart. The "extra ink" is used to elaborate or decorate the graph but is not necessary for communicating the data information. See also Chapter 1, "Visualization."

The third category consists of programming libraries. There are dozens of such libraries, both commercially available and open source. Most libraries support the common programming languages, such as Java, PHP, and Perl. In Chapter 9, "Data Visualization Tools," I discuss some of the open source libraries that can be used to generate reports. One of the libraries I use fairly often is *ChartDirector*, which is available at www.advsofteng.com. The great benefit of libraries is that you can script the generation of reports and embed them into your own tools. This makes libraries the most flexible tool for report generation. You might pay for the flexibility because of the learning curve associated with working with the library and building the coding framework to use it.

ISSUES AND PROBLEMS

What are some of the problems or issues to watch out for when generating reports? One ubiquitous challenge is that too much data is available. It is important to filter and aggregate the data meaningfully and then apply the right graph type to represent the data. Doing so will help prevent cluttered graphs and make sure large amounts of data are dealt with efficiently. A point that I cannot stress enough about the entire world of visualization is that we have to keep the audience in mind with every decision we make. Who is going to look at the graph? A technically savvy person? A business person? If I generate a report for myself, I don't have to add much meta data for me to correctly interpret the graph. After all, I have been the one generating the report. I should know what is in it. However, if I were going to generate that same report for someone else, I would likely have to add some meta information so that the other person could understand the report.

REPORTING MACHINE ACCESS—AN EXAMPLE

Let's take a look at two sample charts that are frequently used to report machine access. Figure 5-2 shows a user login report where the number of logins is indicated for each user. The horizontal bars, rather than the normal vertical ones, helps keep the labels legible. Especially for long labels, this solution yields better results. The information for this type of graph can be collected from operating system or application logs. It would not hurt to even combine those two types of logs (operating system and application) into one single chart. The chart gives you insight into the behavior of the most active users, as well as the general user population accessing machines. Many things can be identified easily with this chart. For example, you might want to look out for direct **root** access. Good security practice is that root should never directly access a machine; instead, sudo or su should be used to execute commands that require root privileges. Also look for users who show an abnormally high login count. Pay attention in particular to the dark portion of the bars encoding the failed logins; they should not be too long. You should be alarmed if the number of failed logins is almost 50 percent compared to the total number of logins, as is the case for a couple of users in Figure 5-2. Why would there be so many failed logins? Depending on your exact setup and the machines or applications for which you are collecting login information, you might want to look out for other things. It might even make sense to configure the graph to highlight some of those instances with a special color (for example, the root logins, as shown in Figure 5-2).

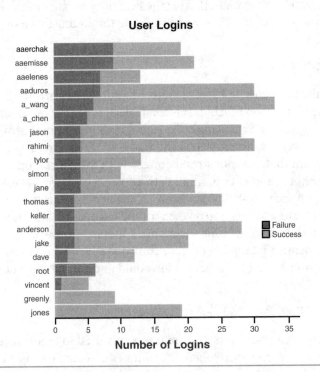

Figure 5-2   A sample report showing the number of logins per user. The chart also encodes whether the logins were successful and where they failed.

GENERATING BAR CHARTS

Bar charts are easy to generate with, for example, Microsoft Excel or a similar tool. You could also use ChartDirector (see Chapter 9) to write a script that can automate the process of generating a bar chart.

To generate a bar chart that shows the number of successful and failed logins per user (see Figure 5-2), we need to first collect the operating system logs that show login activity. On Linux, you find the logins in /var/log/messages or /var/log/auth.log. A successful login looks like this:

```
May 18 13:56:14 splunker sshd[4359]: Accepted publickey for rmarty from
76.191.199.139 port 33617 ssh2
```

A sample failed login looks like this:

```
May 18 21:00:02 raffy sshd[4484]: Failed password for
raffy from 127.0.0.1 port 50679 ssh2
```

You then use a regular expression to extract the user names from these records:

```
cat auth.log | perl -ne 'if(/sshd\[.*for.*from/) {
s/.*(Failed|Accepted).*for (?:invalid user )?(\w+)
from.*/\1,\2/; print;}'
```

The Perl command first looks for only SSH logins and then extracts whether the login succeeded or failed, along with the user name. The output of the preceding command looks like this:

```
Failed,cvsuser
Failed,cvsuser1
Failed,mana
Accepted,mysql
```

To generate a bar chart from this data, either load the data into Excel or write a Perl script that utilizes ChartDirector to do so. An example Perl script that shows how to use ChartDirector for a slightly different use-cases is shown later in this chapter.

Continuing with login information, in some cases you are not interested in the distribution of logins based on users, but you need to know the distribution per machine. This is shown in Figure 5-3. The chart encodes failed logins with black bars, and the bars are sorted to show the most failed logins on top. The second bar from the top clearly sticks out. Why is the percentage of failed versus successful logins for this machine about 90 percent? This is probably a case worth investigating.

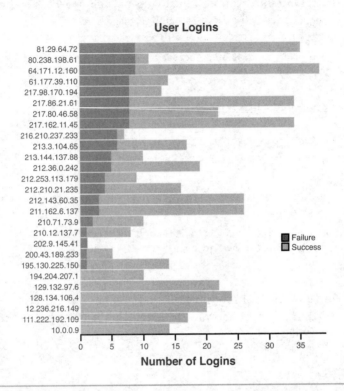

Figure 5-3   A sample report showing the number of logins to various machines. The chart uses color to encode whether the login succeeded or failed.

These reports are great tools to communicate among different teams. Security analysts frequently deal with log files and are comfortable with textual log data: syslog, packet captures, and so on. Using these logs to communicate with other teams, such as the operations team, is not very efficient. You will quickly realize that the operators are generally not keen on even trying to understand the log files you send them. Using graphical reports instead can work wonders. I know of an example where the security team used to hand log files to the operations people whenever a worm-infected machine was found, with little effect. The operators took their time trying to understand what the log files documented, and in a lot of cases returned them with a note that they were not able to find the problem. Upon the introduction of graphical reports, requests to clean worm-infected machines were handled in record time. People understood the reports. It is easy to make claims in a graphical report that even management understands without further explanation. Figure 5-4 shows a sample graph that illustrates this scenario.

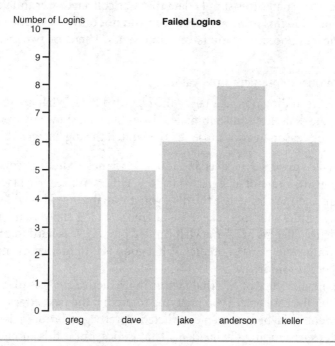

Figure 5-4 A sample graph showing the number of failed logins to various machines per user.

During the analysis of the last three charts, you might have felt an urge to compare the logins to an earlier state. How do the logins of this week compare to the ones of last week? This is where historical analysis, which I discuss in the next section, comes into play.

HISTORICAL ANALYSIS

Historical analysis can be categorized into four main areas: time-series visualization, correlation graphs, interactive analysis, and forensic analysis.

TIME-SERIES VISUALIZATION

In the preceding section, I mentioned that it is often useful to compare present data with past data. An entire branch of statistics is concerned with **time-series analysis,** which is the analysis of data that was collected over time. For our purposes, it is not necessary to discuss those statistical principles. This section focuses on how visualization can help analyze time-series data.

What is time-series data? It is simply data that was collected over time. For example, if you are recording all logins to your systems and you not only record the username but also the time the login occurred, you have a time series. There are two goals in time-series analysis:

- Develop a model to predict future values.
- Gain an understanding of and analyze the recorded data. What are the variances in time? Does the data show any anomalies? Does the data show any trends? What is the underlying reason or root cause that generated the log entry?

Predictive analysis is always controversial. You have to make sure that you are in a closed system where you are aware of all external factors. Otherwise, external factors suddenly start showing up and may influence the data you are analyzing. This will skew your analysis, and the results will not make sense anymore. In log analysis, the use-cases surrounding predictive analysis are somewhat limited anyway. It is hard to come up with measures that you would want to predict. What good is it to predict the number of failed logins that will occur tomorrow?

To illustrate the influence of external factors in predictive analysis of computer security data, consider the case where you are tying to predict the next attack. You have data about past incidents. Maybe you even conducted a pretty good root-cause analysis and collected log files surrounding the incident. That is nice, but is this enough to actually predict the next attack? Did you really think of all the data points you have to consider, such as the machine's vulnerabilities, the possible attack paths, misconfigurations of the systems, and so forth. How do you take all these factors into account for your predictive model? I am not saying that you could not do it. I am saying that it is hard and you have to be extremely careful when doing so to not forget any of the important factors. I am not going to further discuss this problem, but instead focus on the other part of time-series analysis: understanding the recorded data.

I review five methods to analyze past data: **time tables, multiple-graph snapshots, trend lines, moving-average charts,** and **sector graphs.** These methods are not generally used for statistical time-series analysis. Most of the time, some other statistical method is used, but I discovered that these methods lend themselves quite well to analyzing logs files.

Time Tables

One of the graph types introduced in Chapter 3, "Visually Representing Data," was the time table. This type of graph is inherently meant for time-series visualization and lends itself nicely to analyzing and identifying three scenarios:

- Gaps in activities
- Periodicity of activities
- Temporal relationships

An example that shows all three—gaps, periodic behavior, and temporal relationships—is shown in Figure 5-5. The graph plots activity for a set of different target ports. The top series shows port 445 activity. Port 445 is used for all kinds of Microsoft Windows services, such as share access and Active Directory queries. Two clear gaps can be identified in the first half of the graph. Without knowing more about the dataset, it is hard to determine why there are such significant gaps. If this data was collected on a desktop, it could show that the desktop was idle for a while. Maybe the user stepped away for a break. If this was a server that should be under fairly constant load, these gaps might be a bad sign.

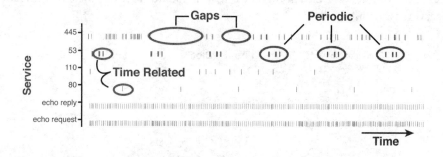

Figure 5-5   Timetable graph showing periodic behavior, as well as gaps in behavior, and time-related activity.

The next data series shows port 53, DNS-related traffic. This looks like a fairly interesting pattern. First thing to note is the periodicity. Six clusters repeat themselves. Internal to the clusters, there seem to be three groups. Note that the markers are fairly thick, representing more than just one event. What could this be? DNS is an interesting protocol. Normally, a client is configured with multiple DNS servers. If the first server on the list does not respond, the second is contacted; if the second one also fails to answer, the third in the list is being used. Only then will the DNS resolver return an error. Three servers do not always have to be configured. A lot of clients are configured with just one DNS server. The DNS traffic in Figure 5-5 could be representing such a scenario where the first two DNS servers fail to answer. This would also explain the multiple marks for each of the three groups. DNS tries three times for each server before giving up. Assuming this is the right interpretation, this also explains the temporal relationship with the port 80 traffic. After every DNS clusters, there is consistent activity on port 80.

This could indicate that the last DNS lookup was successful and thereafter a Web session was initiated.

I could not find an open source visualization tool that would generate a graph similar to the one in Figure 5-5. I therefore used a commercial tool, Advizor, which offers a graph called a timetable.

Multiple-Graph Snapshots

Probably the most straightforward approach to analyzing data over time is to take snapshots at different points in time and then compare them. With some graph types, it is even possible to combine data series of different time frames in a single graph. For example, with line charts, separate lines can be used for different aspects of the data. Figure 5-6 shows an example where each line represents a different server. In this example, there are three servers, and at regular intervals the number of blocked connections to those servers is counted.

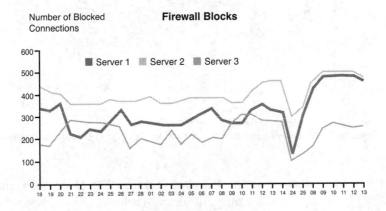

Figure 5-6   Comparing values over time can be done using multiple data series in a single chart; for example, a line chart can be used to do it, as shown in this figure.

When using multiple charts to compare data over time, make sure you are following these quite obvious principles. Figures 5-7 through 5-10 show, for each principle, how things look if the principle is not followed.

1. Compare the same data types: apples with apples. For example, do not try to compare different data, such as failed logins last week with successful logins this week (see Figure 5-7).

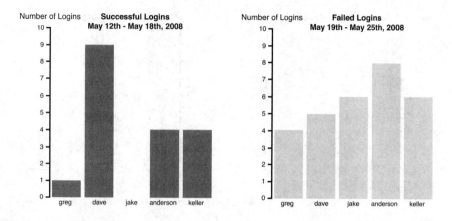

Figure 5-7   Compare the same data types: apples with apples. You would not compare failed logins with successful logins.

2. Compare the same exact values. For example, when monitoring logins, you should keep the same usernames on the graph, even if they have null values. Comparing disjoint sets of usernames is neither efficient nor very useful (see Figure 5-8).

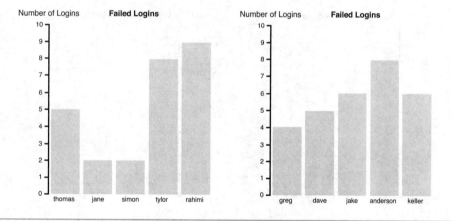

Figure 5-8   Compare the same exact values. You would not compare across disjoint sets of users.

3. Compare the values in the same way. Do not sort the charts by the values of the dependent variable, and especially do not do it for one of the charts and not the other(s). Use the same sort of value of the variable for each instance being compared (see Figure 5-9).

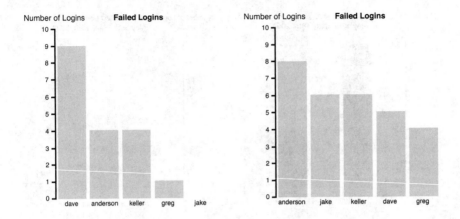

Figure 5-9   Compare the values in the same way. Use the same sorting. You would not sort by the values of the dependent variable in one instance and not the other.

4. Use the same scale on all the graphs. If one graph uses a scale from 1 to 100 and the other from 1 to 10, a bar filling up 100 percent means completely different things (see Figure 5-10).

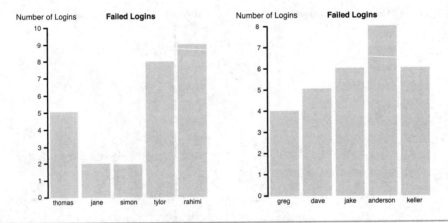

Figure 5-10   Use the same scale on all the graphs.

Figure 5-11 shows an example with three graphs showing user activity at three different points in time. Note how all the four principles are being used. All graphs compare successful logins over the same period of time, a week. They use the same usernames for each of the graphs, although some users failed to log in during specific weeks. The values of the variables appear in the same order, and the scale is kept the same.

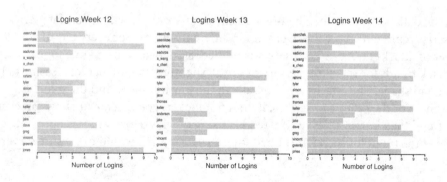

Figure 5-11 Three snapshots of successful logins at three different points in time. The four principles for point-in-time comparison are being followed.

As you can see in Figure 5-11, all the logins have increased over time, except for aaemisse. This could be a significant sign. On the other hand, this person might have been on vacation.

Figure 5-11 uses a bar chart to compare values over time. Some other charts are fairly well suited for this type of analysis too, whereas others are horrible candidates. Link graphs are probably the graphs least suited for analysis using snapshots over time. The problem with link graphs is that the layout significantly changes even if the underlying data is fairly similar. This results in graphs that look completely different even though the data might be almost the same. Some layout algorithms try to take care of this problem, but I am not aware of any tool that would leverage them.

Treemaps are tricky, too. To make them easy to compare with each other, you need to make sure that the data hierarchy is fairly stable. They are most valuable if the data hierarchy is staying completely stable and just the color is changed. With varying degrees of success, you can also try to change the size of the individual boxes, but it makes comparing multiple treemaps significantly harder.

What about scatter plots? Well, they are actually quite well suited for comparison with each other. The same is true for parallel coordinates. However, for scatter plots it is important to keep the axes the same; and in the case of parallel coordinates, it is important not to overload the graphs. In general, parallel coordinates are better suited for interactive analysis than static snapshots. In some cases, they work really well for static analysis, such as in cases where the dataset is fairly specific.

Trend Lines

Almost in the realm of predicting future values is the determination of a trend line for a data dimension. What is a trend line? A trend line indicates the general direction, or the trend, the data takes over time. Figure 5-12 shows an example with three data series. Each series represents the same data but for different servers. For every day of a week, the number of attacks targeting each server is plotted, along with a trend line for each server. The attack trends for the different servers are all slightly different. Server 3 seems to be in pretty good shape. The attacks are generally in the low numbers, and the trend is decreasing. For the other two servers, it does not look as good. Server 1 shows an even worse trend than server 2. Server 2's trend is rising quickly. However, it is not rising as quickly as the trend for server 1. If I had to prioritize work, I would make sure server 1 is secure!

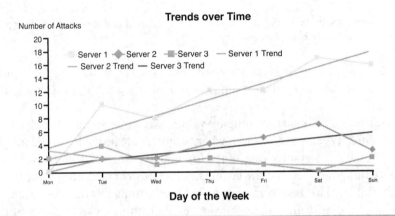

Figure 5-12   A line chart of activity over time. Three datasets are shown. Each refers to a different server that was targeted with attacks. Each of the datasets has its trend line plotted in the graph.

NOTE

Graphing software typically uses a statistical technique called regression analysis to find a linear trend line. Regression analysis finds a line through the data points that minimizes the average squared distance between each of the data points and their corresponding point on the line. This is also referred to as least squares regression.

You might be able to make a prediction, also called an extrapolation, of what the data will look in the future, based on a trend line. In Figure 5-12, you would extend the trend line to the right and see where it ends up for future points in time. The values you end up with would quite certainly not be exact. It is likely that the predicted value would not be the same as the actual value. However, it represents a best guess or an educated guess as to what the actual value would be. There is also the possibility that the trend is going to change over time, depending on external factors, such as changes in usage patterns, firewall rules that change, and so on. Essentially, be careful when you are making future predictions. On the other hand, your prediction based off of the trend line is better than a "seat of the pants" prediction (that is, one that is not data based).

CREATING TREND GRAPHS

To generate a trend graph like the one in Figure 5-12, I use ChartDirector. I wrote a little tool that you can find in the AfterGlow distribution that plots line charts with corresponding trend lines. The input for the script needs to be in CSV format. The first column is the x-axis label, and the following columns each encode an individual data series. An example looks like this:

```
Mon,10,1
Tue,12,2
Wed,14,10
Thu,1,20
Fri,2,40
Sat,0,10
Sun,2,2
```

The weekdays are the labels on the x-axis, and the two following columns encode two data series that will be plotted. If you save this data in a file, you can then run the trendline.pl tool that uses ChartDirector to generate a trend graph:

```
cat data.csv | ./trendline.pl -t "The Title" -a
```

The -t switch is used to define a title for the graph, and the -a switch instructs the trendline script to draw a trend line.

Any graph type other than line charts is not well-suited for trend analysis. One of the dimensions needs to be time. The other data dimension can be used for one of two possibilities. The first possibility is any categorical variable in your log: target ports, users, the originating network where a connection came from, or IDS signature name. Count the number of occurrences for a given time period and compare that value over time. The second possibility is to use a continuous variable or data dimension, such as the total number of bytes or packets transferred. Especially for network flow data, these are useful metrics.

A fairly interesting analysis that can be gained from a trend line is a feeling for how anomalous your events are. The distance between each of the data points to their trend is a measure of their anomaly. If you find a point that is very far away (also often referred to as **outlier**), you have found a significantly anomalous event that might be worth investigating. Be careful with this analysis, however. The data dimension you are investigating needs to have a relationship with time before you can claim any particular data points are anomalies. If your data points appear to be spread randomly, the data dimension under investigation is not likely to have any relationship to time.

You can also make use of a **confidence band** to summarize the size of the errors or distances between the individual points and their trend, as shown in Figure 5-13. If the value of interest falls within the confidence band, you agree to disregard the deviation from the baseline. If not, you can call it an outlier. This is just a visual tool to aid in detecting anomalous entries.

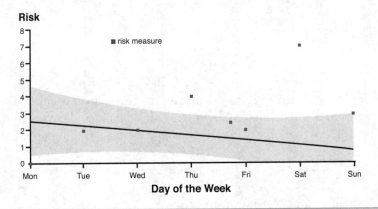

Figure 5-13 A trend line with a confidence band indicates the baseline that is used to plot new values against. If the new values leave the confidence band, they are labeled as anomalous.

GRAPHING CONFIDENCE BANDS

A confidence band summarizes the size of the errors between individual data points and their trend. A 95 percent confidence band, for example, implies a 95 percent chance that the true regression line fits within the confidence bands. I am using a ChartDirector script to graph data with a confidence band. Below is some sample code you can use to plot a line chart with a confidence band. The code assumes that you have a file with one data point per line. The data has to be sorted. Each data row is plotted one after another, assuming an increasing x-coordinate. Here is the code:

```perl
#!/usr/bin/perl
use perlchartdir;
use strict;

my @label; my @data;
# read input data.
my $index=0;
while (<>) {
  chomp;
  push @label,$index++;
  push @data,$_;
}
# prepare the chart
my $c = new XYChart(600, 300);
$c->setPlotArea(45, 45, 500, 200, 0xffffff, -1,
  0xffffff, $perlchartdir::Transparent,
  $perlchartdir::Transparent);
$c->xAxis()->setLabels(\@label);
$c->addScatterLayer(\@label,\@data);

my $lineLayer = $c->addTrendLayer(\@data, 0x444444);
$lineLayer->setLineWidth(1);
$lineLayer->addConfidenceBand(0.95, 0x80666666);
# generate the chart
$c->makeChart("confidenceband.png");
```

Trend Line Graphing Example

Let's walk through a simple example of how to generate a time series graph from iptables log files. I am interested in an analysis of all the blocked outgoing traffic. To do so, I will use a line graph for the last four days of blocked iptables traffic. The graph shows the traffic distributed over 24 hours and does so for each day as an individual data series. The result is shown in Figure 5-14. But let's start at the beginning by looking at an iptables log entry:

```
May 25 20:24:27 ram-laptop kernel: [ 2060.704000] BLOCK any out: IN= OUT=eth1
SRC=192.168.0.15 DST=85.176.211.186 LEN=135 TOS=0x00 PREC=0x00 TTL=64 ID=0 DF
PROTO=UDP SPT=9384 DPT=11302 LEN=115 UID=1000
```

To generate the desired graph, we need the date and the hour from this entry. All other information we can disregard for now. To extract this information, I use the following command:

```
sed -e 's/^... \(..\) \(..\):.*/\1,\2/' iptables.log | uniq -c |
awk '{printf("%s,%s\n",$2,$1)}' | sort -r
```

The output looks something like this:

```
24,10,1484
24,11,2952
24,14,105
25,20,471
26,02,255
```

The first column is the date, the second one the hour of the day, and the third one indicates how many packets the firewall blocked during that hour. To graph this in a line chart, I use following Perl code that utilizes the ChartDirector library to draw the graph in Figure 5-14:

```
1   #!/usr/bin/perl
2   use perlchartdir;

3   # The labels for the x-axis, which is the hour of the day
4   my $labels = ["0" .. "24"];

5   # reading input
6   my $i=0;
```

```
7   while (<>) {
8     chomp;
9     # input needs to have three columns: Day,Hour of Day,Count
10    split/,/;
11    if ($current ne $_[0]) {$current=$_[0]; $i++;}
12    # @data is a day x hour matrix, which contains the count as
13    # the entry.
14    $data[$i-1][$_[1]]=$_[2];
15  }

16  # Generate a line chart and set all the properties
17  my $c = new XYChart(600, 300);
18  $c->setPlotArea(55, 45, 500, 200, 0xffffff, -1, 0xffffff,
       $perlchartdir::Transparent, $perlchartdir::Transparent);
19  # The x-axis labels, which are the hours of the day.
20  $c->xAxis()->setLabels($labels);
21  $c->addLegend(50, 30, 0, "arialbd.ttf", 9)
       ->setBackground($perlchartdir::Transparent);
22  my $layer = $c->addLineLayer2();

23  # Iterate through the days
24  for $i ( 1 .. $#data+1) {
25    $aref = $data[$i];
26    # Making sure no NULL values are present, otherwise
27    # Chartdirector is going to seg-fault
28    for $j ( 0 .. $#{$aref} ) {
29      if (!$data[$i][$j]) {$data[$i][$j]=0};
30    }
31    # Use a grayscale palette to color the graph.
32    my $color = $i * (0x100 / ($#data + 1));
33    $color=($color*0x10000+$color*0x100+$color);
34    # Add a new dataset for each day
35    $layer->addDataSet($aref, $color, "Day ".$i);
36  }

37  # Output the graph
38  $c->makeChart("firewall.png");
```

To run the script and generate the graph, save it as **firewall.pl** and execute it with cat out.csv | ./firewall.pl. The output is going to be an image called firewall.png. Make sure you install the ChartDirector libraries before you execute the script. The Perl code itself is not too difficult. It basically takes the CSV input, splits it into multiple columns (line 10), and creates a two-dimensional array (@data), which is later used for graphing. The code on lines 17 to 21 prepares the graph with axis labels and so forth.

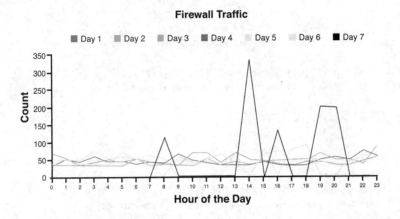

Figure 5-14   A sample report generated with the firewall.pl script, showing firewall events over 24 hours, split into individual series by day.

The final step is to go through each row of the data array, make sure there are no NULL values (lines 28 to 30), and then plot the value as a line in the graph. The color computation (lines 31 to 33) is somewhat fancy. I wanted to use grayscale colors for the graph. The two code lines for the color assignment make sure that each line gets a unique gray tone.

Figure 5-14 shows firewall activity for six consecutive days. The traffic is plotted over a 24-hour period. We can see that for most days, the traffic volume is fairly constant over the day. However, day 1 shows a completely different pattern. It shows spikes at 8 in the morning, at 2 p.m., at 4 p.m., and between 7 p.m. and 8 p.m. This seems a bit strange. Why would there be no traffic for certain times, and why are there huge spikes? Was there maybe some kind of infrastructure outage that would explain this phenomenon? This is worth investigating, especially because all the other days show regular behavior.

If you are interested in pursing these ideas some more with statistical methods, have a look at the next section, where I discus **moving averages.**

Moving-Average Charts

Trend lines are only one way to look at how your time-series data is evolving over time. Another method that is commonly used in stock price analysis is a **moving-average analysis.**[2] A moving average helps to smooth data values. Smoothing data values has the effect that individual outliers show up as less extreme. They are adjusted in terms of the

---

[2]   More on moving average analysis of stock prices can be found at http://stockcharts.com/school/doku.php?id=chart_school:technical_indicators:moving_averages.

rest of the data. It therefore makes it easier to spot trends. This is especially useful for volatile measures (that is, measures that change a lot over time).

How (and more important, why) would you look at moving averages? They are useful for analyzing trends of various measures and are an alternative to trend lines. Moving averages are more precise, and the analysis methods I show you here can prove useful in decision making based on time-series data.

As a decision maker, you need to know when exactly to make a decision based on a set of measures. You can try to look at a trend line, but the trend line is too generic. It does not react well to change. If you are the holder of a certain stock, you want to know when to sell. When monitoring attacks targeting your network, by either looking at firewall logs or intrusion detection logs, you need to know when the number of attacks starts deviating too much from the normal amount so that you know to start investigating and addressing a potential problem. I show you ways to make that decision.

MONITORING RISK TO DRIVE DECISIONS

One application of moving averages is to monitor risk associated with the number of unpatched machines on a network. Based on the risk readings, we can manage resource allocations to mitigate the exposures. Unfortunately, the budget for patching machines is limited, and we need to know when to make an investment in patching and when to take resources away from the patching efforts. We also want to use the risk measures to guide strategic investments in new security measures that can help contain the risk if a high watermark is crossed.
I am loosely defining risk in this context as follows:

> The **total risk,** due to unpatched machines, is the sum of risk over all machines. The risk of an individual machine is the sum of the exposure for each of the vulnerabilities of that machine multiplied by the business value of that machine.

This risk changes over time. It increases when new vulnerabilities are discovered, new machines and applications are introduced to the network that are not fully patched, and when reconfigurations happen. The risk decreases when patches are deployed, machines are removed from the network, operating systems are upgraded, and when machines are consolidated.

We can use this risk metric as a trigger for various actions:

- If the risk *increases*, we institute new countermeasures to reduce or mitigate it. Sample countermeasures are hiring new resources, training people, and purchasing new solutions.
- If the risk *decreases*, we can potentially reallocate resources away from patching machines.

We could use absolute risk thresholds to trigger these actions. Huge fluctuations in an observed metric trigger the thresholds constantly and are therefore a challenge to deal with. We need a more strategic trigger. If we add 20 new servers that are not completely patched, we would likely increase the risk significantly and trigger an action. However, a couple of days later, these machines will be patched, and we might trigger a low threshold. This continues constantly, and we are reacting to every change. This is where we are going to rely on moving averages to help us smooth some of the spikes.

Simple Moving Average

A moving average is computed by taking the average of data values over the last n values, where n defines the period for the moving average. For example, a 5-day moving average is computed by adding the values for the past 5 days and then dividing the total by 5. This is repeated for every data value. This process smoothes individual outliers and shows a trend in the data. The result of this procedure is illustrated by analyzing the risk associated with unpatched systems in a large network (see sidebar). A graph showing the risk of unpatched machines is shown in Figure 5-15. The figure shows the actual data values along with their moving average. You can see that moving averages are **lagging** indicators. They are always "behind" the actual data values.

By defining a high and a low threshold, we can determine when an activity has to be triggered. You can see in Figure 5-15 that for the moving average the spikes are smoothed and thresholds are less likely to be crossed as compared to the raw data, unless there is a real trend in the data. Crossover points of the data line and the moving average line mark a potential decision point. When the moving average crosses the data line, the data is significantly moving against the moving average, and therefore breaking away from the norm.

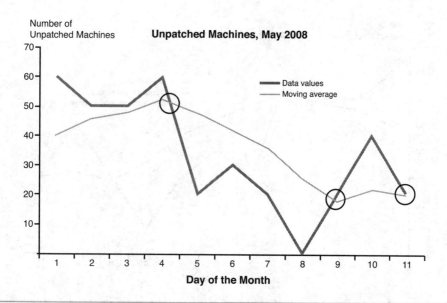

Figure 5-15 Example of applying a simple moving average to see the risk associated with unpatched machines. The three crossover points indicate a change in trend development.

Advanced Moving Averages

The issue with moving averages is that the lag is significant. Various methods help address this problem. For example, **exponential moving averages**[3] (EMA) are used to reduce lag by applying more weight to recent values relative to older values. The result of calculating an EMA on the data is shown in Figure 5-16.

Instead of EMAs, which address the problem of lag, we can also use a dual moving average analysis, where two moving averages of different time periods are used. The crossover points indicate upward trends when the shorter period moving average moves above the longer term moving average; it indicates a downward trend otherwise.

You might realize that this type of comparison is still fairly poor for the given data. There are three decision points. The second and third one seem to be not well placed. Just because there was one value that was higher on May 10 does not necessarily mean that things have changed for good. We need a better method than the simple moving average to reduce the number of decision points.

---

[3] For more information about exponential moving averages, have a look at http://en.wikipedia.org/wiki/Moving_average.

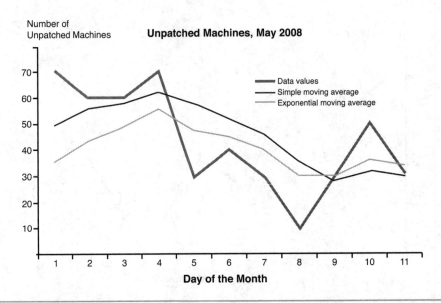

Figure 5-16   Example of an exponential moving average, compared to its simple moving average.

A more sophisticated analysis can be done by using a moving-average convergence/divergence analysis (MACD). It addresses some of the shortcomings of the simplistic methods I introduced earlier. It takes two moving averages, one over a longer period of time and one over a shorter period of time, and computes a measure based on the difference of the two. I borrowed this analysis from stock analysts.[4] A sample MACD chart is shown in The challenge is to come up with a good time period for the two moving averages. The period depends on your use-case and your data. The shorter the period, the quicker you are prompted to make a decision. The longer the period, the less reactive the analysis is to local spikes. To give current values more weight than older ones, an EMA can be used for both of the moving averages.

Figure 5-17 was generated with Excel, by calculating the individual values for each of the EMAs and then plotting them in the graph. I do not discuss the MACD analysis and the chart in Figure 5-17 any further. Some people say that the analysis is pure voodoo. It is difficult to define the right time periods for the EMAs. Changing them can significantly change the location of the decision points. Each application has its own optimal values that need to be determined.

---

[4] A great explanation of the MACD in stock analysis can be found at http://stockcharts.com/school/doku.php?id=chart_school:technical_indicators:moving_average_conve.

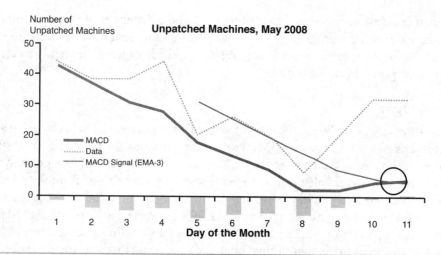

Figure 5-17 MACD chart with a 5- and 10-day EMA. The thick black line is the MACD line, computed by subtracting the 5-day EMA from the 10-day EMA. The 3-day EMA is plotted as the gray line, and the histogram at the bottom shows the difference between the MACD and the 5-day EMA. The histogram is positive when MACD is above its 3-day EMA and negative when MACD is below its 3-day EMA. A signal is generated when MACD signal crosses the MACD.

Applying Moving Averages

Here are some rough guidelines for when to use moving average analysis and when not to:

- Use moving average analysis to get information about trends and changes in trends.
- If you deal with data values that do not show a general trend—the data seems fairly chaotic—moving-average analysis is not very well suited.
- The moving-average time period is a parameter that needs to be carefully chosen. The smaller the time period, the more the moving average becomes reactionary. This means that you are reacting to the data more quickly and you are dealing with the problem of "false positives."
- Do not use this type of analysis for measures that can uniquely be associated with "good" or "bad." For example, a risk of 10 is "bad," and a risk of 1 is "good." You do not need moving averages to tell you when to react to the risk development. You can define a risk of 6 or higher as noteworthy.

Or positively formulated:

- Use moving-average analysis for measures that do not have set boundaries. For example, the number of packets blocked by your firewall is a measure that has no boundaries. You do not know what a good or a bad value is. However, you want to know about significant changes.

Often, it is useful and necessary to capture the trend behavior at the present point in time. Whereas moving average charts show you the development of your metric over a longer period of time, you can use sector graphs to quickly capture the trend at a certain point in time, generally in the present.

Sector Graphs

An interesting way of analyzing the current state of a time-series dataset is by using a sector graph. The *New York Times* uses this type of graph to show the performance of stocks or markets.[5] The idea of the chart is simple. You take a time-series and fix a point in time that you want to analyze. Calculate the percentage change of the value from the point in time you chose to the value a day ago. Then do the same for the value you chose and its value a week ago. Assume you get a 5 percent change since the day before and a −10 percent change compared to a week ago. These two values now define a point in a coordinate system. Plot the point there. Repeat this for all the time series that you are interested in. By looking at the sector graph, you will get a comparison between all the series.

Instead of choosing a day and a week as the time periods, you can take any other time period that you are interested in. What is of importance is where a point for a time series is going to land in the coordinate system. If the point lands in the upper-right quadrant, for example, you are dealing with a series that has performed well over both periods of time. If the point lies in the bottom-right quadrant, you are dealing with a series that has done well over the short period, but not so good over the long period. It's an improving series. Analogous statements can be made for the lagging and slipping quadrants.

Instead of just drawing simple data points in the quadrants, you can use color and size to encode additional information about the time series. Color, for example, can be used to distinguish between the different series.

An example of how to use a sector chart is given in Chapter 7, "Compliance." There the chart is used to show the development of risk in different departments.

Figure 5-18 shows an example of a sector chart that was generated with Microsoft Excel. The exact steps of generating this graph can be found in Chapter 7. Figure 5-18 shows two data points. The values encode the number of incidents recorded for the Finance and the Engineering departments. The current number of incidents in the Engineering department is 25. The data point is located on the top right, which means that the incidents in the Engineering department have constantly been rising. This is a concern. The finance department shows a current number of 14 incidents. The data point lies in the bottom-left quadrant, which indicates that a constant decrease of incidents has been recorded. This is a good sign.

---

[5] www.nytimes.com/packages/html/business/20060402_SECTOR_GRAPHIC/index.html

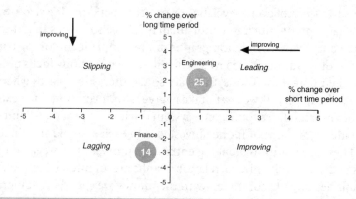

Figure 5-18 Sector chart with explanations of what it means when data points are drawn in the specific quadrants.

CORRELATION GRAPHS

Correlation graphs can be used, like time-series analysis, to analyze data by assessing the extent to which two continuous data dimensions are related. In other words, you want to know for values in one data dimension, do the values of the other data dimension correspond in some orderly fashion? There are two ways to use a correlation graph to analyze log data. Either two data dimensions of the same log file are correlated with each other or the same data dimensions are correlated for different log files. A correlation graph of two data dimensions of the same log entry is used to show how one dimension is related to another. For security log files, this is not very interesting. Different fields from the same log file are not correlated, unless it is already inherently obvious. For example, the event name and the target port are generally correlated. The target port determines the service that is accessed and therefore dictates the set of functionalities it offers. This set of functionalities is then generally expressed in the event name.

Correlation in this context works only with continuous or ordinal data. This already eliminates a lot of data dimensions such as IP addresses and port numbers. Although they could be considered continuous data, in most of the cases they should be treated as values of a nominal variable. There is no inherent ordering that would say that port 1521 is worth more or more important than port 80. It is just a coincidence that Oracle runs on a port that is higher than 80. So what are the data fields that make sense for correlation graphs? Well, they are very limited: Asset criticality is one, for example. This is generally an additional data field that is not contained in the log files, but here you can clearly make a statement about an order. What are some other fields? Traffic volumes, such as bytes or packets transferred, event severities or priorities, and the file size are all continuous variables. That is pretty much it. Unfortunately. This also means that there is not much reason to actually use correlation graphs in this simple form for log correlation.

If we are expanding our narrow view a little bit and we shift our focus away from only log entries and their data dimensions, there are some interesting places where correlation graphs can be applied. What if we try to take aggregate information—for example, the total number of vulnerabilities found on a system during the past day—and correlate that number with the amount of money invested into each system for vulnerability remediation? These are not individual log entries anymore, but aggregated numbers for vulnerabilities and cost. Suddenly, correlation graphs are an interesting tool. Is the number of vulnerabilities directly correlated with the money we spend on vulnerability management? We hope it is negatively correlated, meaning that the number of vulnerabilities goes down if the money invested in vulnerability management is increased.

A somewhat more complex example is shown in Figure 5-19, where a **correlation matrix** is drawn. I took four data dimensions that were measured in regular intervals. The matrix shows the correlations between each of the four data dimension. The figure shows the individual correlation graphs, where the data points from two dimensions are presented in a scatter plot. Each of the graphs also contains their trend line and the correlation coefficient of the two dimensions. When looking at the trend line, you have to manually inspect the pattern of the data points. Do they run from the bottom-left corner to the top-right corner as in a positive correlation? Do they run from the top-left corner down toward the right-bottom corner as in a negative correlation? How close is each data point to the trend line itself? The closer to the line, the stronger the correlation. If they are randomly dispersed all over the place and do not group around the line, there is no correlation. This is the case in all the graphs in the first column of Figure 5-19. This means that the number of incidents is not related to any of the other data dimensions: Employee Hours, Personnel, or Cost. On the other hand, these three data dimensions are somewhat correlated with Employee Hours and Personnel, showing a strong correlation.

The **correlation coefficients** shown in each of the graphs are mathematical indices expressing the extent to which two data dimensions are linearly related.[6] The closer to 1 (or −1) the correlation coefficient is, the stronger the relationship.

How do we read the correlation matrix in Figure 5-19? You can clearly see a trend in the data points for Employee Hours and Personnel. They group nicely around the trend line. To a lesser extent this is true for Employee Hours and Cost and Personnel and Cost. Second, have a look at the correlation coefficients. They make a statement about whether

---

[6]   You can find more information about the correlation coefficient at http://en.wikipedia.org/wiki/Correlation.

the data dimensions are linearly related. Again, you will find that our two data dimensions of Employee Hours and Personnel are showing a fairly high value, which means that they are strongly linearly related. If one increases, the other will, too. That just makes sense; the more personnel who respond to an incident, the more hours will be burned. It seems interesting that the cost is not more strongly related to the employee hours. There must be some other factor that heavily influences cost. It could be something like there is considerable variability in the payscale of the personnel. It also seems interesting that the number of incidents is not related to any of the other data dimensions. I would have expected that the more incidents, the more expensive it would be to address them—but perhaps once personnel are called to respond to one incident they stay around and address further incidents. It would take some investigating to nail down these other influences on the data.

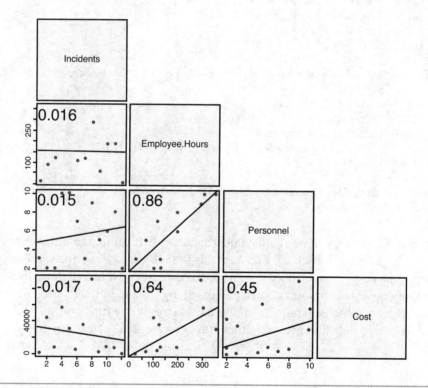

Figure 5-19 Correlation matrix showing the relationships among multiple data dimensions. It shows how the security investment (Cost), hours spent on security-related projects (Employee Hours), and the number of incidents, as well as personnel needed to clean up an incident, are related to each other. The number indicates the strength of the correlation between the two data fields.

GENERATING A CORRELATION GRAPH

To generate the correlation graph in Figure 5-19, you can used R (see Chapter 9). The following is a sample R script that reads data from a CSV file and then generates a correlation graph:

```
1  Dataset <- read.table("data.csv", header=TRUE,
   sep=",", na.strings="NA", dec=".", strip.white=TRUE)
2  panel.cor <- function(x, y, digits=2, prefix="", cex.cor) {
3    usr <- par("usr"); on.exit(par(usr))
4    par(usr = c(0, 1, 0, 1))
5    r <- abs(cor(x, y))
6    txt <- format(c(r, 0.123456789), digits=digits)[1]
7    txt <- paste(prefix, txt, sep="")
8    cex <- 1.5/strwidth(txt)
9    text(0.5, 0.5, txt, cex = cex * 0.4)
10 }
11 panel.myfitline <- function(x, y, digits=2, prefix="", cex.cor, ...) {
12   usr <- par("usr")
13   reg <- coef(lm(y [td] x))
14   abline(coef=reg,untf=F)
15   panel.smooth(x,y,col.smooth=0)
16 }
17 par(cex.axis=2)
18 par(pch=20)
20 pairs(Dataset, lower.panel=panel.myfitline, upper.panel=panel.cor, cex=2,
   cex.labels=2)
```

To run this script, you need a data file (data.csv) that contains a number of data series to be compared. Each column contains the values for a specific variable (for example, the cost). The script first reads the data in line 1. It then defines two functions (panel.cor in lines 2 to 10 and panel.myfitline in lines 11 to 16). The functions are used to generate the individual squares in the final output. The command in line 20 puts the pieces together and generates the correlation graph.

INTERACTIVE ANALYSIS

So far, we have used static images or graphs to represent data. Once the input data was prepared, we defined the graph properties, such as color, shape, and size, and used it to generate the graph. During the definition process, we generally do not know how the graph will turn out. Is the color selection really the optimal one for the data at hand? Is there a better data dimension to represent size? Could we focus the graph on a smaller dataset to better represent the interesting parts of our data? What we are missing is a feedback loop that gives us the possibility to interactively change the graphs instead of backtracking to make different choices.

In the Introduction to this book, I mentioned the information seeking mantra: Overview first, zoom and filter, then details on-demand. I am going to extend this mantra to include an additional step:

1. Overview first.
2. Change graph attributes.
3. Zoom and filter.
4. Then details on-demand.

The second and third steps can be repeated in any order. Why the additional step? You could choose the graph properties before generating the first graph. However, this is one of the disadvantages of static graphs. You do not generally know how the graph will look before you have generated a first example. Looking at a first instance of a graph significantly helps to make a choice for the other graph attributes. It is also useful to change the graph attributes, such as color, on demand to highlight different portions of the data. After some of the attributes have been adapted and a better understanding of the data has been developed, a zoom and filter operation becomes much easier and effective.

The second and third steps of the new information seeking mantra are called **dynamic query** in the visualization world. A dynamic query continuously updates the data filtered from the database and visualizes it. It works instantly within a few milliseconds as users adjust sliders or select buttons to form simple queries or to find patterns or exceptions. Dynamic queries have some interesting properties:

- *Show data context:* How do data entries look that are similar to the result, but do not satisfy the query? Conventional queries only show the exact result, whereas dynamic queries can also display data that is similar to the result. This is often a useful thing to know to understand the data better.

- *Dynamic exploration:* Investigations, such as "what if" analysis, are intuitively possible.

- *Interactive exploration:* User-interface support, such as sliders, can be used to change the value of a variable interactively.

- *Attribute exploration:* The data of a single data dimension can be analyzed and explored interactively.

These aspects are all covered by dynamic queries. Keep in mind dynamic queries are a type of user interface. Behind the scenes, systems that support dynamic queries need a way to query the underlying data stores. This is often done through conventional query languages such as SQL.

Dynamic queries are unfortunately not supported by many tools. Most of the ones that exist are in the commercial space. Second, if you have used one of those tools, you know that the amount of data you can explore is fairly limited and is generally a factor of the amount of memory you have available. To support efficient dynamic queries, those tools need to load all the data into memory. Make sure that for large amounts of data you limit the scope of individual queries and work on a sample before you expand your view to the entire dataset.

A second interface concept that supports data exploration is the use of **linked views.** Each type of graph has its strengths when it comes to communicating data properties. You read about these properties in Chapter 3, "Visually Representing Data." To explore data, it is often useful to apply multiple different graphs to see various properties simultaneously. Using a display composed of multiple types of graphs can satisfy this need. To make this view even more useful, it should enable user interaction (i.e., support dynamic queries). The individual graphs need to be linked, such that a selection in one graph propagates to the other ones. This is an incredibly powerful tool for interactive data analysis.

The different types of graphs support different analysis use-cases. Bar charts, for example, are suited for attribute exploration. They are good filtering tools, too. **Attribute exploration** is a method used to analyze a single data dimension. What are the values the dimension assumes? How are the values distributed? Do some values show up more than others? Are there outliers and clusters of values? All these questions can be answered with a simple bar chart showing the frequency of each of the data values. Figure 5-20 shows an example with two linked bar charts, illustrating the concepts of attribute exploration and linked views. The bar chart on the left shows the count of users in the log file. Most activity was executed by the privoxy user. The rightmost side shows the ports used. Only two ports show up, www and https, indicating that we are dealing with Web connections. As the bar chart on the right shows, only about an eighth of connections were secured, meaning that they used HTTPS. On the rightmost bar chart, the secure connections (https) are selected. This selection propagates to the linked bar chart on the left side. We can now see that most secure connections were executed by the privoxy user, followed by ram and debian-tor. Root executed no secure connections at all. Why? Is this a problem? This simple example shows how a bar chart can be used for attribute exploration to show both secure and insecure connections by user.

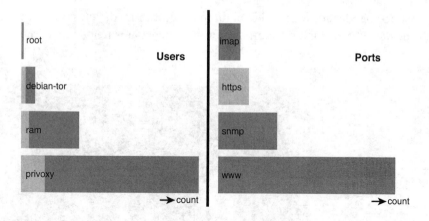

Figure 5-20 Linked bar charts, illustrating the concepts of attribute exploration and linked views. The left side shows the number of log records that contained each of the users. The right side shows the protocol associated with the users' activities. The https protocol bar on the right side is selected, and the selection is propagated to the linked bar chart on the left side, showing that most of the HTTPS connections were executed by privoxy, some by ram, and the rest by debian-tor.

What are some other charts and their role in interactive analysis and linked views? Scatter plots, for example, are a good tool to detect clusters of behavior. We have discussed this in depth already. Using scatter plots simultaneously with other linked views has a few distinct advantages. Interactivity adds the capability to detect clusters interactively and explore the data by selecting the values. This immediately reflects in the other graphs and shows what the clusters consist of. The other chart types, such as line charts, pie charts, parallel coordinates, and so on, can all be used in a similar fashion to represent data. I have already discussed the strengths and applications of all of these charts. All the benefits outlined for scatter plots apply to the other types of graphs, too. Linked views significantly improve the data-exploration process.

Not only selections can be propagated among graphs, but also the choice of color. Each of the graphs can use the same color encoding. This is yet another way that linked views are useful. Instead of using a separate graph to analyze a specific data dimension, that dimension can be used to define the color for the other graphs.

A great tool for interactive data analysis is the freely available **ggobi.** A detailed discussion of the tool appears in Chapter 9. Figure 5-21 shows a screen shot of ggobi, giving you an impression of how an interactive analysis looks. Note how the different graph types are used to highlight specific data properties. In addition to the graphs themselves, color is used to encode an additional data dimension. It immediately communicates the values of the data dimension and shows how this dimension is related to all the others.

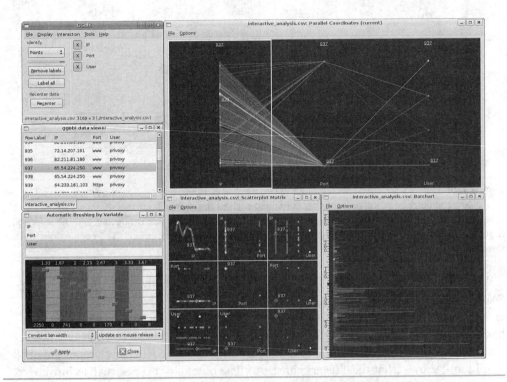

Figure 5-21 An interactive analysis executed with ggobi. Multiple views of the same data simplify the analysis by showing multiple data dimensions at the same time. Color is used to highlight specific entries, and brushing can be used to interact with the data.

The screen in Figure 5-21 is divided into two parts. The left side shows settings for the graphs and a window into the underlying data—the data viewer. The bottom part shows the configuration of the color bins. By moving the sliders, you can interactively change the color assignments for the three data variables that are visualized. The right side of the screen shows three different views into the data. By analyzing all three views, we get a feeling for all the data dimensions. We can see which machines are using which ports and which users are associated with that traffic through the parallel coordinates. We can identify how the data dimensions are correlated, if at all, by using the scatter plot matrix, and the bar chart can be used to see the distribution of the IP address values. Selecting data values in one graph propagates the selection through the other graphs. This supports the interactive analysis of the data.

FORENSIC ANALYSIS

All the concepts discussed in this chapter to this point were methods of analyzing data. How do we put all of these methods and concepts to work to tackle a real problem: the forensic analysis of a dataset unknown to the analyst? Forensic analysis can be split into three use-cases:

- Data exploration to find attacks, without knowing whether attacks are present
- Data exploration to uncover the extent and exact path of an attack
- Documentation of an incident

The second and third use-cases should be integral parts of the incident response (IR) process. Visualization not only helps speed up and facilitate the process of analyzing data, it is also a powerful tool for documenting an incident. I am not going into detail about how your IR process can be enhanced to use visual tools because IR processes differ slightly from company to company. However, given an understanding of the last two use-cases, it is a natural extension to include visualization in your own IR process.

Finding Attacks

Trying to uncover attacks through log analysis is not an easy task. This is especially true if there are no hints or you have no particular reason to be suspicious. It is much like trying to find the proverbial needle in a haystack. Visualization should play a key role in this detection process. We can learn from the visualization world about how to approach the problem. We have come across the **information seeking mantra** a couple of times already. We will see that it has its place in forensic log analysis, too. The first analysis step according to the information seeking mantra is to gain an overview. Before we can do anything with a log file, we have to understand the big picture. If the log is from a network that we already know, it is much easier, and we can probably skip the overview step of the analysis process. However, the more information we have about a log and its data, the better. We should try to find information about the contents of the log file from wherever we can. Information such as that which can be gathered from people who operate the networks we are about to analyze or system administrators responsible for the machines whose logs we have can help provide needed context. They can all help us interpret the logs much more easily and help us understand some of the oddities that we will run into during the analysis process.

All the principles discussed earlier around interactive analysis are useful to achieving an efficiently conducted forensic log analysis. Many questions about the log files can be easily answered with dynamic queries. For example, what services is machine A using? Nothing easier than that. Generate a linked view with two bar charts. The first bar chart shows the source addresses, and the second one the target ports. Select machine A in the first chart and have a look at the linked selection in the target port bar chart. Find something interesting? Follow it and explore the data, one click after the other.

Unfortunately, there is no simple recipe for forensic log analysis that is independent of the type of log file to analyze. Each type of log file requires specific analysis steps. For certain types of logs, however, there are commonalities in the analysis process. I will introduce an analysis process that tries to exploit these commonalities.

The complete process for forensic log analysis is shown in Figure 5-22.

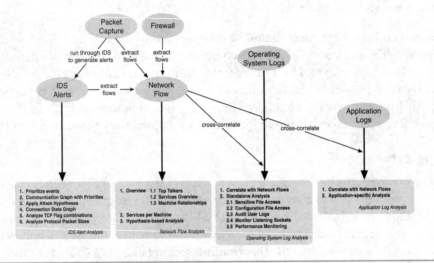

Figure 5-22   Forensic analysis process summary diagram. Ovals represent data sources, and the boxes contain the individual analysis processes.

The analysis process differs significantly depending on the type of log file that is analyzed. If it is a network-based log—anything from packet captures to network-based IDS logs—certain analysis steps apply. If a host-based log has to be analyzed, either on the operating system level or even on the application level, different analysis steps are necessary.

For the discussion of the forensic analysis process, I break the process up into different phases based on the diagram in Figure 5-22, and will therefore start with network flow data.

Network Flow Data

Network flow records are a great tool for gaining an overview of a forensic situation. Keep in mind that network flow data can be derived from other log types, such as packet captures, and in some cases firewall log files, and sometimes even from NIDS logs. I discussed this in depth in Chapter 2, "Data Sources." We first need to gain an initial understanding of the network traffic that we are analyzing. Here are the graphs we will generate:

1. Top Talkers (source and destination)
2. Top Services
3. Communication Graph

We start by generating some overview graphs to see the hosts and their roles in the network. Use a bar chart to show the frequency of connections seen for both source and destination addresses. Sort the charts by the connection frequencies to see the top "talkers" on the network. If you have data about machine's roles, use it as color in the chart. Make sure you are focusing on the most important roles so as to not overload the charts with color. Do the same for the destination ports. Use the machine's role as the colors again.

So far, the graphs do not reveal relationships between machines. You could use an interactive tool to explore the relationships by selecting different machines in the bar charts and simultaneously monitoring the change in the other charts, but there is a better solution. Use a link graph that displays the source and destination addresses in a communication graph.

You could use the amount of traffic to encode the thickness of the edges between the machines. You can measure the amount of traffic in either bytes, packets, or as number of passed packets, and so on. There are no limits to your creativity. If you use firewall logs to begin with, color the edges based on whether traffic was blocked or passed. If packets are passed and blocked, use yet another color.

Figure 5-23 shows all four graphs for a sample firewall log. I decided to show only the top 15 sources and destinations. Otherwise, the bar charts would be illegible. The same was done for the services. To match the data in the bar charts, the link graph shows only traffic between the top 15 addresses, too. The link graph colors machines that are managed by us in light gray. All other machines are dark gray. Also note that the edges (i.e., arrows) are colored based on whether the traffic was blocked. Dark edges indicate blocked traffic.

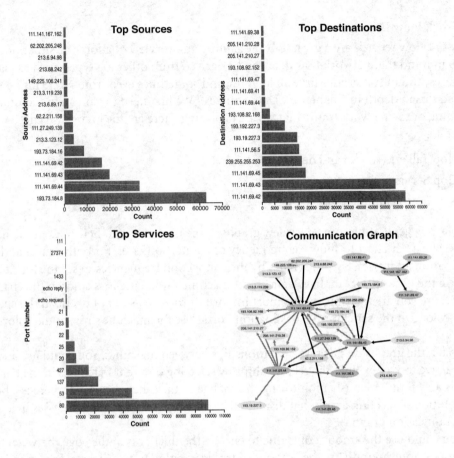

Figure 5-23   Gain an overview of the traffic in the log file. Who are the top talkers, what are the services accessed, and what is the relationship between these machines?

This gives us a first overview of what the log file is about. To explore in further detail how the graphs were generated, check the sidebar.

GENERATING A TRAFFIC OVERVIEW GRAPH

To generate the graphs in Figure 5-23, I used a pf log from my OpenBSD firewall. The first step in analyzing the pf log file is to convert it from pcap into some textual format. This can be done with tcpdump, which comes with OpenBSD.[7] Reading the log is done with

```
tcpdump -i pflog0 -nn > pf.log
```

Now you need AfterGlow (see Chapter 9), more specifically the pf parser shipped with AfterGlow. The script is located in src/perl/parsers/pf2csv.pl. Further, you need ChartDirector (again, see Chapter 9) and the bar.pl tool shipped with AfterGlow. It is located in src/perl/charts/bar.pl. That's it. When you have all these components, run the following command to generate a bar chart of the source addresses:

```
cat pf.log | pf2csv.pl "sip" | bar.pl -f source.png -n 15 -t "Source Addresses"
-p > sources.list
```

The command first extracts the source addresses (sip) from the log file. Then the bar chart is generated for the top 15 entries and saved as source.png. The -p switch is used to print the top 15 entries to the console. I am saving them for later use in a file called sources.list. You will see in a minute why. You repeat the same command for the destination addresses (dip). Don't forget to save the top 15 entries as destinations.list. Then do the same for services (dport). Almost done; we just need the link graph now. This gets interesting. The challenge is to graph only the top 15 hosts. How do we filter all the others out? AfterGlow does not provide an explicit capability to do this. However, by using a combination of the following command and properties file, we can achieve this:

```
cat pf.log | pf2csv.pl "sip dip action" | afterglow.pl -t -c graph.properties
```

Note the action in the list of fields to extract from the pf log. Why do we need this field if we graph only the sources and destinations? Remember, I colored the edges

---

[7] Do not try to read those files with other versions of tcpdump; you will not be able to read them. OpenBSD uses a proprietary, extended pcap format to store the pf logs.

between the hosts based on the action field—hence the field in the data. To show only the first two columns (sip and dip) in the link graph, we use the -t switch when running AfterGlow. By feeding it three columns, the third column can be used in the property file to control the color for the edges!

To show only the top 15 hosts, you have to create a property file like this:

```
variable=open(SRC,"sources.list"); @src=<SRC>
variable=open(DST,"destinations.list"); @dst=<DST>

color="darkgray" if (grep(/$fields[0]/,@src) &&
  (grep(/$fields[1]/,@dst)) && (field() = ~ /^111/))
color="gray" if (grep(/$fields[0]/,@src) &&
  (grep(/$fields[1]/,@dst)))
color="invisible"

color.edge="green" if ($fields[2] eq "pass")
color.edge="red"
```

I am using two commands to start with. First, I read the sources.list file into the array @src. The same is done for the destination addresses. The variable property is used to specify arbitrary Perl code that is executed when AfterGlow is started. After that, I color the machines on the list of top 15 sources (i.e., addresses on the sources.list), as well as the destinations on the destination.list in gray. The source addresses are accessible by using the $fields[0] field. I am defining two different shades of gray to distinguish between internal nodes and external nodes. The internal nodes I identify by looking at IP addresses that start with 111. All nodes that did not get a color assigned are going to be filtered out by giving them an invisible color. Finally, the edge color is defined by the third column, which is not plotted as a node, but we can still access its value. If the field's value is pass, we use a gray edge; otherwise, the edge is black.

For more information about AfterGlow, have a look at Chapter 9.

Instead of using pf logs, the same graphs could have been generated with traffic flows, for example, from Argus (see Chapter 2). Assuming your source is a pcap file, the commands are as follows. First you need to convert the pcap into an Argus file, which essentially extracts the relevant information that represents the network flows:

```
argus -r file.pcap -w file.argus
```

Now you can run the ra tool suite on the Argus file to extract the information you need. This is the command to generate the bar charts from the network flows:

```
ra -n -s saddr -r file.argus | bar.pl -f source.png -n 15 -t
"Source Addresses" -p > sources.list
```

You cannot use rahosts to do this because it does not output the number of times the host showed up. You might want to consider using ragator rather than ra to aggregate the flows and not just show raw flows. See Chapter 2 for more information about this.

To generate the link graph of communicating hosts, you use the following:

```
ragator -n -s saddr daddr -r file.argus --ip
| awk '{printf("%s,%s\n",$1,$2)}'
| afterglow.pl -t -c graph.properties
```

The use of awk converts the tab-delimited output into a CSV-delimited output that AfterGlow can understand. In addition, I filtered for only IP traffic, which gets rid of MAC addresses in the output. If you want them back, just remove that part in the command. In graph properties, you can take out the edge color assignment because there is no information about passed and blocked packets as in the firewall case. The rest of the property file can stay the same. Voilà, you have the same graphs, generated based on Argus data.

Using the graphs we generated, we should now try to figure out whether we have found any visible anomalies. Questions we can try to answer include the following:

- Is there a source or destination host that sticks out? Is there a host that generates the majority of traffic? Why is that? Is it a gateway that possibly even does Network Address Translation (NAT)? This would explain why it shows up so much.
- Is a certain service used a lot? Is that expected? If TFTP is the service used the most, for example, something is probably wrong.
- Are there services that were not expected? Is Telnet running on some systems instead of SSH?
- Are some machines communicating with each other that should not be?

Fairly quickly, after answering all these questions, you will want to know which services each machine is offering. To best visualize this information, use a treemap, as shown in Figure 5-24. Treemaps are well suited to encode a lot of information in a small area. They allow us to easily analyze the distribution of protocols in the network traffic.

Figure 5-24   Treemap showing the machines on the network along with the services they are being accessed on.

We can easily see that there is one machine, .42, that gets most of the traffic on port 80. The other machines are so small that they seem to be hidden. Therefore, I generated a second graph of the same traffic, this time filtering out machine .42. Figure 5-25 shows the result. Now we can see all the machines and the ports they were accessed on. In the case of visualizing a firewall log, we could use different colors to reflect whether the traffic was blocked or passed.

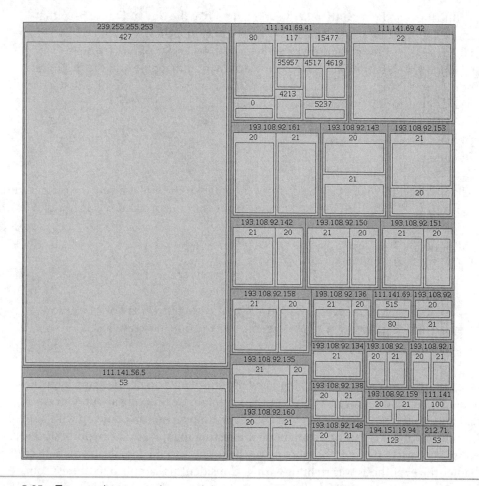

Figure 5-25 Treemap showing machines and their services. This time the dominant machine is filtered to show all other machines.

Figure 5-25 shows that a lot of machines were targeted with FTP. The next step is to verify whether these connections were indeed successful, and if so, whether those machines were meant to have FTP running? You can verify this by either looking at the raw packet captures or executing a port scan of those machines.

VISUALIZING NETWORK TRAFFIC IN A TREEMAP

Traffic logs can be used to generate a treemap like the one in Figure 5-25 that shows the machines and the services targeted. Here is how you take a log from a UNIX iptables firewall and prepare the data to be visualized in Treemap (see Chapter 9). We have to first extract the destination machine and the destination port from the log records and then format the output as a TM3 file. First, enter the header lines for the file and save this as services.tm3:

```
COUNT      Machine     Service
INTEGER    STRING      INTEGER
```

Then, extract the necessary fields from the iptables log and convert the output into tab-separated records. Then append the records to the previously generated file:

```
cat iptables.log | perl -pe 's/.*DST=([^ ]*).*
DPT=(\d+).*/\1,\2/g' | sort | uniq -c
| perl -pe 's/^\s*//, s/[, ]/    /g' >> services.tm3
```

Open this data in Treemap and visualize it with a hierarchy of Machine > Service, which generates a treemap similar to the one in Figure 5-25.

From here, the next step in analyzing network flow data is to define some **hypothesis** about the data and then verify the data against them. By thinking about your environment and what types of activities you could encounter, you can come up with a set of assumptions about what traffic might be interesting to look at. The hypothesis does not necessarily have to be true. By applying the hypothesis to the log file, it will help confirm whether the hypothesis was right or wrong. Consider this sample hypothesis: You are trying to uncover worm attacks by saying that a worm-infected machine will contact a lot of other machines and generate extensive communication patterns that will be readily visible in communication graphs.

Various other graphs can be used to analyze network flow data in more detail and find possible attacks. The generic analysis steps did not necessarily uncover attacks. Most of the times it is the application of a hypothesis that will help uncover anomalies and, possibly, attacks. In Chapter 6, "Perimeter Threat," I present some hypotheses that help, for example, uncover DoS attacks or worms. To be honest, detecting these two cases is not rocket science because the volume of traffic involved in both of these attacks is quite significant. Again, other use-cases depend specifically on the data and use-cases that are of interest. Here I gave an introduction and a starting point for your quest. You can find more use-cases involving network flows in Chapter 6, where I show an example of how to monitor network usage policies to uncover unwanted behavior.

Table 5-1 shows the individual analysis steps that you can use to analyze network flow data. If you collected packet captures and not just network flows, you can use an additional step to analyze your data. Run your packet captures through an intrusion detection system to see whether it finds any attacks. To do so with Snort, run the following command:

```
snort -l /var/log/snort -c /etc/snort.conf -U -A full -r <pcap_file>
```

This command writes the Snort log file into /var/log/snort/alert. The additional IDS events generally uncover a significant amount of additional data. The next section shows how to deal with all this information.

Table 5-1 Summary of Network Flow Data Analysis Steps

Step	Details
1. Gain an overview.	Analyze: • Top talkers • Services overview • Machine relationships
2. Analyze overview graphs.	Can you find any anomalies in the previous graphs? Verify the top talkers, services, relationships, and so on.
3. What services are target machines offering?	Generate a treemap that shows the services per machine.
4. Verify services running on machines.	Are there any machines that should not be offering certain services? Analyze the previous graph, keeping your network configuration in mind. A DNS server should probably not expose a Web server, either.
5. Hypothesis-based analysis.	Come up with various hypotheses for analyzing your network flows.

Intrusion Detection Data

What can we do with network-based intrusion detection data? The difference from the data we have discussed before is that NIDS data shows only a subset of all connections, namely those that violated some policy or triggered a signature. The only thing we can do to figure out which machines are present on the network and what their roles are is to treat the limited information in the IDS logs as network flow data. This is definitely not a complete picture, but it at least shows the machines that triggered IDS alerts in relationship to each other. However, we can do more interesting and important things with IDS logs.

IDS logs can, to a certain degree, be leveraged to prioritize and assess machines and connections. How hard has a target machine been hit? How "bad" is a source machine? How malicious is a connection? To do so, we need to define a **prioritization schema.** The higher the priority, the worse the event. I am assuming a scale of 0 to 10, where 10 is a highly critical event. As a starting point for calculating the priority of an event, we are using the priority assigned by the IDS, sometimes called the severity. We might have to normalize the numbers to be in the range from 0 to 10, which in some cases requires the conversion from categorical values, such as High, Medium, and Low to numeric values. Unfortunately there is no standard among IDSs to use the same ranges for assigning a priority to events. Some use scales from 0 to 100, others use categorical values. Based on this initial score, four external factors are applied to skew the score:

- The **criticality** *of the target machine:* This requires that every target machine is classified based on its criticality to the business. Machines that contain company confidential information should be rated higher than test machines.

- **History** *of the sources:* Keep a list of machines that were seen attacking or scanning your network. Machines that have scanned your network before will get a higher score. Ones that have attacked machines on your network will also get a higher score.

- **Chance of success***:* Is the port indicated in the event open on the target machine? Often, IDSs report attacks that did not have a chance to succeed (for example, because the target port was not open). If the target port was not open, lower the priority score.

- **Vulnerability** *status:* Is the vulnerability that the attack was trying to exploit exposed and present on the target machine? If it was not present, lower the priority score.

To validate the last two points, you might need a vulnerability scan of the target machines. If those two conditions are false, you can drastically decrease the priority of your event. The attempted attack does not have the potential to significantly harm you. This type of event prioritization is something that security information management (SIM) solutions are using to calculate priorities for events and help get everyone focused on the important ones. You can also use other factors to rate an event. Depending on your environment, you might want to consider doing so.

Now that you have a priority for each event, you can first assign this to each event and then plot them atop your already existing communication graphs. The figure shows only priority 9 and 10 events so as to not overload the graph. In addition, for the priority 9 events, all the external nodes, machines that are not situated on our network, are aggregated to a single "External" node. For the priority 10 events, I show the exact address for the node. These configuration decisions are simply measures taken to prevent overloading of the graph and to keep it legible.

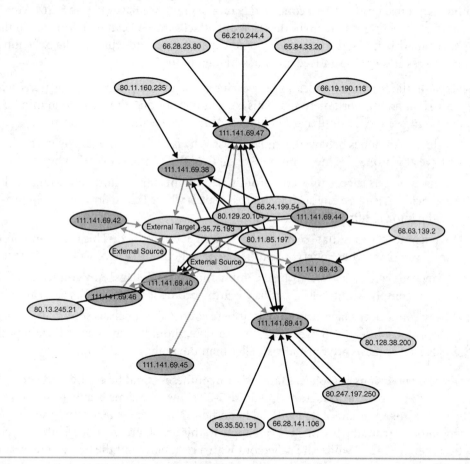

Figure 5-26 A network communication graph generated from network flow data. In addition to the network flows, IDS data is used to color the edges with the corresponding priorities.

The edges (i.e., arrows) are colored based on the priority. The darker the edge, the higher the priority. If a link was seen multiple times, the maximum of the individual priorities was used to choose a color for the edge.

If you are fortunate enough to have NIDS logs and network flows, you can execute numerous interesting analysis tasks. The following discussion assumes that you have both types of logs available. Some of the analysis also works if you have only NIDS logs.

What are the next steps to take after we have a graph that helps prioritize individual connections, such as the one in Figure 5-26? We should look at the graph and analyze it. What are the things we can identify that might hint at a problem or a potential attack? There are many things to look for, and some of them might require us to generate some additional graphs. For now, let's concentrate on the graph we have (Figure 5-26). We should start by defining some hypotheses about attacks that we can then look for in the graph. What are some of the things we would expect to see, and what are the questions we need to ask if there was indeed an attack hidden in the logs?

1. Based on the scoring of nodes and the exclusion of all low-priority connections, what are serious and important events? This is an important question to keep in mind. At this point, we should think hard before we dismiss a specific communication.

2. Do clusters of nodes behave in similar ways? Why is that? Do the targets in that cluster have any properties in common? Are there outliers in the cluster? Why?

3. If a machine gets successfully compromised, it might start to initiate sessions back to the attacker. Are there any such instances? This is where traffic flows can help provide the information about new sessions.

4. Do machines try to initiate sessions that never get established? This is common for scanning activity where ports are probed to see whether a service will answer back.

5. Do any connections show a strange combination of TCP flags? Any connection that does not comply with the RFCs, thus violating protocol specifications, is a candidate.

6. Do any connections have an anomalous byte count? This analysis should be done on a per protocol level. DNS over UDP, for example, should always have a certain packet size. HTTP requests are normally smaller than the replies. And so on.

This list is by no means complete. Many other hypotheses could be established and checked for. For now, the link graph in Figure 5-27 shows the same graph as in Figure 5-26, but this time it is annotated with all hypotheses that were true for this graph. The only hypotheses from the list that we can apply to this graph are the one identifying clusters of target machines, which are called out with a rectangle, and the one where we are looking for outgoing connections, possibly identifying infected or compromised machines. All those cases are called out with a small circle.

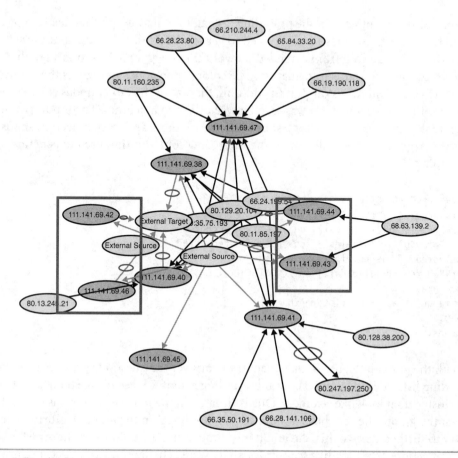

Figure 5-27   Attack analysis graph with callouts that mark the attack hypotheses.

There seem to be two clusters of two machines each that have similar behavior. These machines very likely have a similar role in the network. Based on the fact that the clusters are small, it will not be spectacularly interesting to analyze the clusters anymore. If they were bigger, we should figure out what the exact IDS events were that targeted these machines. It seems more interesting to investigate the connections going to the outside. There is one particular instance that is called out with a big oval that seems interesting. The IDS observed an attack of highest priority targeting an internal machine. In addition, the IDS picked up another high-priority event that went back to the attacking machine. This is strange. Why would the internal machine trigger another high-priority event backout? This is definitely an instance that should be investigated!

Some of the hypotheses in the preceding list call for a new graph that needs to be generated to answer those questions. We need to get some additional data about the sessions, which we can gain from extended network flows. Figure 5-28 shows a graph that includes connection status information. The color of the nodes represents the connection status based on Argus output. In addition, the size of the target nodes encodes the number of times a connection was seen between the two machines. The input used to generate the graph is to extract the source, the destination, and the connection status from the Argus logs. The following is the AfterGlow configuration used to generate the graph:

```
color="gray" if ($fields[2] eq "RST")     # reset
color="gray20" if ($fields[2] eq "TIM")   # timeout
color="gray30" if ($fields[2] eq "ACC")   # accepted
color="gray50" if ($fields[2] eq "REQ")   # requested
# connected, finished, initial, closed
color="white" if ($fields[2] =~ /(CON|FIN|INT|CLO)/)
color="gray50"
size.target=$targetCount{$targetName}
size=0.5
maxnodesize=1
```

With the graph in Figure 5-28, we can try to answer the questions 4 and 5 from the preceding list. Does the graph show any scanning activity? It seems like there are at least two clusters that look like scanners. One is situated in the middle, and one is on the left side of the graph They are both annotated as thick circles in the graph. Unfortunately, if we try to further analyze this, the graph is of limited use. I would like to know whether the connections that look like scanning activity were actually successful. Because multiple connections are overlaid in one node, however, the source node's color encodes the connection state of just one connection. It does not communicate the status for each of the connections, and the target nodes are too small to actually see the color on the nodes. To address this, we need to generate another graph and filter the original data to only show those nodes. The result is shown in Figure 5-29.

To confirm the hypothesis that the two nodes in question are really scanners, we have to look at the connection status. The upper-left machine shows a lot of connections in the INT or REQ state, meaning that only a connection request was seen and never an established connection. Very likely, this is some machine that is scanning. On the other hand, the machine on the lower right seems to have only established connections. Most likely this is not a case of a scanner.

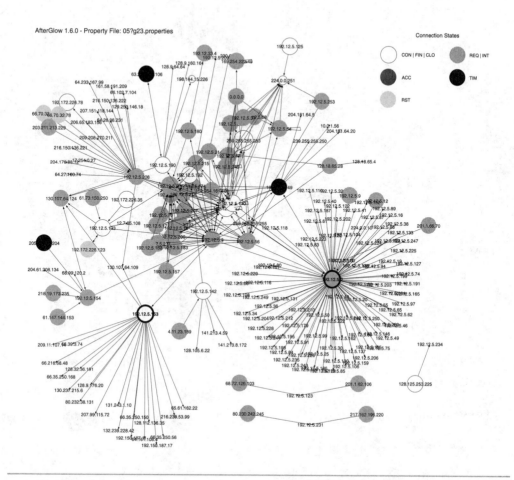

Figure 5-28 Attack analysis graph encoding the connection states and the number of times connections were seen between the machines.

The good news is that all the connections the scanner (upper-left machine) attempted were unsuccessful. The part that causes concern is that there are some machines that are attempting to connect to the scanner machine. We should verify whether those connections were successful to assess the impact. It is not quite clear, without knowing the role of this machine, why other machines are trying to contact it.

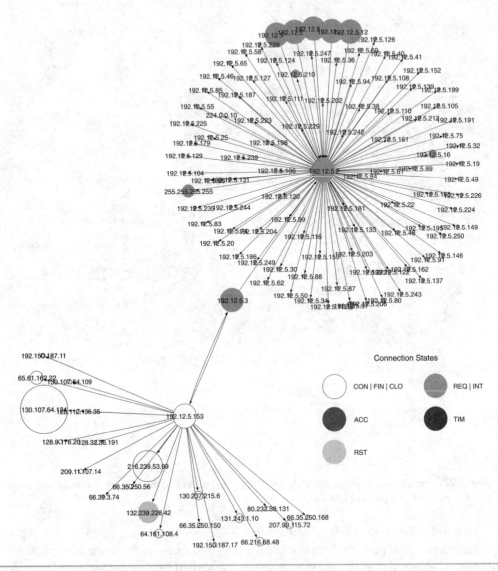

Figure 5-29   Zoom of the attack analysis graph, which only shows potential scanners.

What are some other things that we can identify in the original graph (refer to Figure 5-28)? The fifth hypothesis asked whether there were strange combinations of

TCP flags in a session. This requires generating a graph that shows all the TCP flags for a session. With Argus, this is fairly simple. The following command will accomplish this:

```
ragator -nn -s saddr daddr dport bytes status -Z b -A -r log.argus - ip
```

The ragator command merges matching flow records in the Argus log (log.argus) and outputs the result on the console. The -Z b switch instructs Argus to output the individual flags of a session. Here is a sample output listing:

```
192.12.5.173     130.107.64.124.53          31      189      CON
192.12.5.173     192.172.226.123.443        652     3100     FSRPA_FSPA
```

The first record indicates that a connection was established, indicated by the CON flag. The termination of the session was not yet seen in the time frame observed. The second entry shows the summary of multiple sessions of which some were terminated with regular FINs, while some of the connections were terminated with a RST, hence the R in the output. Both outputs are absolutely normal and will commonly show up. A way to visualize this type of information is to use the packet counts as sizes for the source and target nodes and use the status flags to drive the color. This is similar to what we have been doing in the previous graphs. I leave it to the reader as an exercise to generate this graph and analyze it.

The sixth hypothesis is about analyzing packet sizes for different protocols. Each protocol has characteristic packet sizes. A DNS request, for example, should always be fairly small. If you see large packets as DNS requests, something is wrong. To analyze packet sizes, I am going to use a box plot. Figure 5-30 shows how the sizes of both requests and responses are distributed for each destination port shown in the log file. Note that the x-axis is displayed using a logarithmic scale. This helps to display the packet sizes, because a lot of the packets are fairly small and a few of them are really large. The side-by-side display of request and response sizes enables the comparison of individual services. You will need quite a bit of experience to interpret this graph. What are the packet sizes for all the protocols used on your network? How do requests and responses compare? To analyze the graph, apply heuristics. For example, HTTP (port 80) should have fairly small request sizes. If you see a lot of large requests, it probably means that unwanted data is being transferred in HTTP requests. On the other hand, HTTP responses are probably fairly large. As shown in Figure 5-30, this is exactly the case.

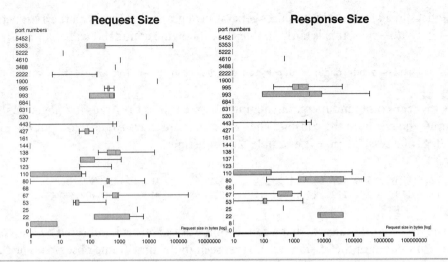

Figure 5-30   Box plot showing protocol size distribution for requests and responses of different protocols.

GENERATING A PACKET-SIZE BOX PLOT

The box plot in Figure 5-30 was generated by using ChartDirector and the `boxplot` script from AfterGlow.[8] The data to drive the plot stems from an Argus traffic capture. To graph that data, we first extract the correct fields from the data. To do so, use the following command:

```
ragator -nn -s dport bytes status -z -A -r cap.argus
- ip | awk -v OFS=, '{print $1,$2}' > out.csv
```

We need the service (`dport`), the bytes transferred (`bytes`), and the status of the connection (`status`) from the capture. We just need IP traffic, because all the other traffic does not offer services. To generate a box plot of this information, use the following command:

```
cat out.csv | boxplot.pl -f service.png -n 6000 -l
```

This command generates a box plot of all the port numbers that are smaller than 6000. It also makes use of a log scale for on the x-axis to accommodate for protocols that have large packets sizes. This way we can see the smaller packet sizes more clearly.

---

[8] http://afterglow.sf.net

Operating System Log

The analysis of operating system log files yields some interesting use-cases and possibilities to further provide the insights necessary to find attacks. Operating system logs can be used in two cases: either to correlate them with other log sources or on their own. The first case is to use them to provide additional intelligence for network-based logs. For example, if an IDS reports a DoS attack against a service on a machine, the operating system logs can be used to verify whether that service indeed terminated and the DoS attack was successful. The other use-case for operating system logs is to use them on their own. By looking for interesting entries in the OS logs, you can often identify attacks, too. However, finding attacks with only OS logs is not always easy. As discussed in Chapter 2, not that many types of events are recorded in OS logs, and attacks are not specifically identified in OS logs.

How can an OS log be correlated with a network-based log, such as network flows? There are many ways to do so. The general idea is always that you either confirm or deny some activity that was discovered in the network-based data (especially when dealing with IDS events) or the OS logs are used to complete the picture and give more context. Often, this reveals interesting new information that the network-based logs alone would not reveal.

Correlating OS with network-based logs raises the challenge of "gluing" the two logs together. This is done through the IP addresses in the network logs. We need to combine the OS logs from a machine with the corresponding network-based log entries mentioning that specific machine. Let's look at an example to illustrate this process. The case I discuss shows network-flow data with SSH connections targeting one of our machines. A sample entry looks like this:

```
05-25-04 11:27:34.854651  *   tcp    192.168.90.100.58841  ?>
192.4.181.64.ssh    149    172    14702    54360    CON
```

The flow shows that there was an SSH connection from 192.168.90.100 to 192.4.181.64. In the OS logs of the target machine (192.4.181.64), we can find a log entry generated by SSH, indicating a successful login:

```
May 25 11:27:35 ram-laptop sshd[16746]: Accepted password for root from
192.168.90.100 port 58841 ssh2
```

In addition, we have to make sure that the times of the log entries match. This is where it is important to have synchronized clocks! Figure 5-31 shows a graph where all network traces from SSH connections are shown. In addition, the SSH entries from the OS log are included in the graph. The benefit of looking at both traces is that we get a more complete picture. The network traces show all the SSH activity from all the hosts. In addition to that information, the OS log provides information from an operating system perspective. The OS logs contain the user that logged in and not just from which machine the login originated. This information can be useful. The example in Figure 5-31 utilizes the OS logs to show which users accessed our server (192.4.181.64). The graph helps identify one machine, 192.168.90.100, which was used to log in to our server. The network traces help complete the picture to show all the SSH connections the originator machine attempted.

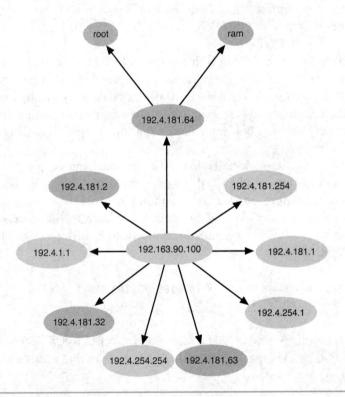

Figure 5-31   SSH activity, shown from both the network and the operating system perspective. This picture reveals that our critical server (192.4.181.64) is not the only machine this user accessed.

Why did the source machine in Figure 5-31 attempt to connect to all these other machines? And worse, the login to the critical server was successful. It seems that the user account was compromised and the person behind all this activity, the one controlling the originator, should be investigated.

OS logs do not necessarily have to be correlated with network traces. Even by themselves, they provide a lot of value. In some cases, these use-cases need special configurations of the operating system to enable the necessary level of logging to record these instances. The following are some use-cases that OS log files can be used with:

- *Monitor file access* of sensitive documents: To enable file auditing, have a look at Chapter 2. This can reveal users poking around in files that they have no reason to look at. Also, graph the number of files an individual user accesses, possibly even across multiple machines. This often reveals users who are snooping around.[9]

- *Monitor file access* of configuration files: Chapter 2 shows how to set up file auditing. Configure all configuration files to be audited. Make sure there is a justification for every configuration change on your machines. Ideally, there is a capability to correlate configuration changes with trouble tickets that document the change and show the proper authorization.

- *Audit user logins*: Look for logins per machine. Who are the users accessing machines? Graph the total number of logins per user. Do some users show suspicious numbers of logins?

- *Monitor listening sockets*: Every new open port showing up on a machine needs to be investigated. There needs to be a good reason why a server suddenly starts listening on a new port. Again, you will hope that a trouble ticket justifies the new service. If not, why does a machine suddenly offer a new service?

- *Monitor performance-related parameters*: By looking at CPU load, memory utilization, free disk space, and so on, you can not only detect performance degradations or machines that are starting to run at their limit, but performance related measures sometimes reveal interesting security-related issues. If a server is generally dormant during the night and suddenly shows a lot of activity, this might be a sign of an intrusion.

OS logs can prove useful in many more use-cases. This list serves merely as an inspiration. Visualization is powerful; through it, changes in behavior are easy to detect.

Application Logs

Going up the network stack, after the operating system we arrive at the application layer. There are many interesting use-cases where visualization is of great help in this space.

---

[9] The monitoring of file access would have revealed that Gary Min of Dupont was accessing thousands of documents, and an embarrassing insider crime case could have been prevented. See Chapter 8 for a discussion of this case.

The big difference from the previous discussion is that there are no generic use-cases. Instead, every application, depending on its logic, has its own unique analysis approaches. The following are some sample classes of applications that I briefly address to outline visualization use-cases:

- Network infrastructure services, such as DNS and DHCP
- Network services, such as proxy servers, Web servers, and email servers
- Applications, such as databases, financial applications, and customer relationship management software

It would be instructive to consider many more classes of applications, but I picked these classes of applications because they can be correlated with network flows. I cover more application-based use-cases later in this book. Fraud is an interesting topic in the realm of application log analysis. I discuss the topic of fraud in Chapter 8, "Insider Threat."

The classes of applications listed here can all be used to visualize and detect problems in the application itself. DNS, for example, can be used to find unauthorized zone transfers. Again, I do not discuss these application-specific use-cases here, but pick them up later, for example in Chapter 6. What I am interested in, for the moment, is how application logs can help with some of the analyses we have done earlier. For example, can DHCP logs be used to facilitate or improve the analysis of network-based logs?

We can use many network infrastructure services such as DNS and DHCP to improve our network data visualizations. How can we use DNS logs? Well, DNS is about mapping host names to IP addresses and vice versa. Why would we use that information for visualization? One could argue that to resolve IP addresses into host names, you could just do a DNS lookup at the time the graph is generated. That would certainly work. However, we have to be clear about what exactly we are doing. We are resolving an IP address at a different point in time, and more important, we are probably resolving it with a different DNS server than the one that was used in the original network where the logs were captured. Imagine a network where a private address space is used. The DNS server for that network will be able to resolve the private IP addresses to a host name. If you try to resolve those addresses with a different DNS server, the IP will not resolve to the same host name. This is the reason we should use DNS logs to improve our analysis.

DHCP logs represent a similar source of data. They give us a way to map IP addresses to MAC addresses, or actual physical machines. MAC addresses are globally unique and therefore identify a machine uniquely. This can be useful in an environment where DHCP is being used. At the time of visualization, the IP address showing in the graph would most likely not be the same machine anymore as the one that was generating the activity. Ideally, you would also have an asset inventory at hand, which maps MAC addresses of machines to their owners. That way you have the capability to not just identify a specific machine responsible for a specific activity, but you could also identify a person responsible for the given machine. Applying all this data to a problem is fairly straightforward. The data can be used as a lookup table and is utilized to replace the IP addresses in the original logs.

How can we use network services, such as Web or mail servers, to aid in our analyses? Again, for this discussion, I am not interested in specific use-cases for these types of logs. Those are discussed in the Chapter 6. For the purposes of this analysis, I am interested in what additional information these logs can provide. Let's start with proxy logs. There are multiple types of proxies. Some are merely relays. The ones that I am interested in are proxies that require users to authenticate themselves. The logs from those proxies enable us to map IP addresses to users! This is incredibly interesting. Instead of identifying a machine that was causing mischief, we can now identify user names that are responsible for some activity, and we hope this will translate to actual humans. Note that this is not necessarily an easy task!

Do other network service logs result in similar benefits? The answer, as usual, is "it depends." All services that require a user login are potential candidates. We need to look for log entries that tie the user login to his or her IP address. ipop3d is a POP daemon that logs every session with a user name and client address from where the session was initiated:

```
Jun 12 09:32:03 linux2 ipop3d[31496]: Login user=bhatt host=PPP-
192.65.200.249.dialup.fake.net.in [192.65.200.249] nmsgs=0/0
```

If we extract the user and the user's IP address, we have an association of user to machine again. Other services provide similar log entries that help associate users with machines. With some logs, it is possible to associate a machine not just with a login but also with an email address. Fairly obvious, mail servers are candidates for this. One of them is Sendmail. Be careful with mail server logs. They are among the worst logs I have ever seen. Instead of logging on a session level, mail servers often log on an application logic level. For example, Sendmail logs a message as soon as the server gets an email that has to be delivered. At that point, Sendmail logs that it got a message from a certain email address. It does not yet log to whom the messages was addressed. Only after the email is ready to be delivered will it log that information. This makes it incredibly hard for us. We have to manually stitch those messages together. Mail processors generate even worse logs, logging every individual step during the mail processing and always logging just a piece of the complete information that we would need for visualization.

The only class of information that we have not looked at yet is desktop applications. The challenge with desktop applications is that they do not allow logins over the network. Therefore, the log files do not contain IP addresses that we could use to correlate the information with network traffic. One possible use of application logs is to use them to gain more information about users and their roles. We will run into various problems trying to do that, however. Assuming that the user names are the same among applications and network services, we can try to look for events related to the same user's activities and glean information from the application log entries. Most likely, however, the flow is the other way around. You will have to use application logs as the base and augment the information with network layer information. This will enable you to correlate activity in applications with the origin of that activity. This can help to verify what other activities a certain user is involved in. Is someone executing a certain transaction on an application while at the same time using a network service? An example application is the supervision of financial traders. If they are placing a trade shortly after receiving a call via Skype or an instant message from a machine outside of the corporate network, it is possible that they got a tip from a third party.

The graph in Figure 5-32 shows what a simple, fake scenario could look like. The left part of the graph shows all instant messenger traffic. You can clearly see that the traders are communicating with each other. However, one machine seems to be an outlier. It looks like an instant message originated from the gateway address. This could indicate that an external message was received. This might be important to know. This by itself might indicate a policy violation. To see whether this is really something to investigate, we need the IP address to do an owner association. In addition, we want to see the trades themselves. Some example trades are shown in the figure. We see the user who posted the trade, the accounts involved, and the amount transferred. The rightmost graph in Figure 5-32 shows a graph where all this information is merged together. The IM traffic is plotted but with the nodes changed to the machine's owner rather than the IP addresses. In addition, the nodes are colored based on the transaction volume that each of the users traded. The darker the node, the more money was traded. We can see that the user who received an instant message from an external address was not the one posting the biggest trade. In addition to this graph, it would be interesting to see a timetable that shows the timing sequence of how the trades relate to the instant messages. I leave it to you to imagine what such a graph would look like.

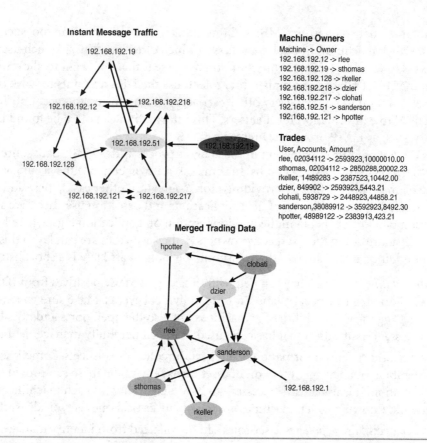

Instant Message Traffic

192.168.192.19

192.168.192.12   192.168.192.218

192.168.192.51   192.168.192.19

192.168.192.128

192.168.192.121   192.168.192.217

Machine Owners
Machine -> Owner
192.168.192.12 -> rlee
192.168.192.19 -> sthomas
192.168.192.128 -> rkeller
192.168.192.218 -> dzier
192.168.192.217 -> clohati
192.168.192.51 -> sanderson
192.168.192.121 -> hpotter

Trades
User, Accounts, Amount
rlee, 02034112 -> 2593923,10000010.00
sthomas, 02034112 -> 2850288,20002.23
rkeller, 14t89283 -> 2387523,10442.00
dzier, 849902 -> 2593923,5443.21
clohati, 5938729 -> 2448923,44858.21
sanderson,38089912 -> 3592923,8492.30
hpotter, 48989122 -> 2383913,423.21

Merged Trading Data

hpotter

clobati

dzier

rlee

sanderson

sthomas

rkeller   192.168.192.1

Figure 5-32 An example where an application log was correlated with network behavior based on the user names in the log files.

Additional Data Sources

A number of data sources are not covered in the process I just outlined. This does not mean that they are less useful. On the contrary, they could provide some significant insight into the behavior the logs recorded. Additional data comes not only from devices that generate real-time log files, but also from completely different sources, such as statically updated spreadsheets. Information such as the role of machines on the network is often managed in spreadsheets. Only a few networks that I have seen are actually documented in a configuration management database (CMDB) or in an asset management tool. This is unfortunate because it would make our analyses much easier if we had access to up-to-date data from CMBDs. Other information is important, too, such as policies. Which machines should have access to which other machines? Which user roles have access to which machines? One common use-case is that you want to allow only users in the DBA (database administrator) role to use the DBA accounts to work on the database. You want to prevent every other user account from using this account. To do so, you need role information for the users. This information can often be found in a directory, such as LDAP or Active Directory.

How do you use this information in the analysis process? Ideally, the data sources are used as overlays to the existing graphs. In some cases, it will enhance the accuracy and the ease of analyzing log files by providing more context. In other cases, these additional data sources spawn an entire set of new applications and detection use-cases. We saw one application of additional data in the previous section on application logs, where I mapped IP addresses to their respective owners. Other use-cases are similar to this. What are some additional data sources that we should be looking at? Here is a short list:

- *Vulnerability scanners:* They can help with filtering out false positives from IDSs and factor into the priority calculation for the individual events. Make sure you are not just getting the vulnerabilities for machines but also the open ports and possibly some asset classification that has been used in the vulnerability management tool.

- *Asset criticality:* This information is often captured in spreadsheets. Sometimes the vulnerability management tool or an asset management database can provide this information. It is not always necessary to have a criticality for each machine on the network. Knowing which machines are the highly critical ones is typically sufficient.

- *User roles and usage policies:* User roles can be collected from identity management stores or possibly from logs that mention role changes. This information can be useful, especially in conjunction with policy modeling. If you can define usage policies, this will enable the monitoring of user activity with regard to respective roles. Things such as engineers accessing an HR server or salespeople accessing the source code repository become fairly easy to express and monitor. Policies are not restricted to IP addresses and who can access machines. They can extend to the application layer where the definition of acceptable behavior inside of applications becomes possible.

- *Asset owners:* Generally, this type of information is found in spreadsheets. Sometimes an asset management or a CMDB is available that stores this type of information. The information is useful for mapping IP addresses to machines and perhaps even to the owners responsible for those machines.

You can use this information in multiple ways for visualization. It could be used to replace values with ones that are looked up in these sources, as we have done in Figure 5-32, where we replaced the IP addresses with the respective owner of the machines. Another way is to use them for color assignments or you could even use the owner and explicitly use it as an additional data dimension in the graph.

This concludes the discussion of the attack detection process. We have seen how we can forensically analyze log files and apply graphs to simplify the process. Unfortunately, the process does not guarantee the detection of attacks that have happened. It is merely a tool to help analyze the logs files for any suspicious signs and to uncover potential problems, or in some cases, attacks. The next section examines how to assess an attack. This is slightly different from what we have done so far. Instead of looking for the attack, the premise is that you know that there was an attack, possibly even knowing what some of the affected machines are or how the attack was executed.

Assessing an Attack

A fairly different use-case compared to detecting attacks in log files is the assessment of a successful attack. An attack can be detected in a number of ways, be that through the attack detection process or, for example, a customer who called in and reported an issue that could be as benign looking as a performance problem or a service doesn't work anymore. The assessment of the attack impact and extent is important to know what was affected and how big the loss is. It is also necessary to understand how the attacker was able to penetrate the systems and in turn how to prevent similar attacks in the future.

The following discussion applies mainly to cases where more complex attacks are executed. Typically, those attacks involve a network component. If the attack affects only one host and is executed locally on the machine, visualization of log files cannot help much in this scenario. However, if an attack is executed over the network and potentially involves multiple machines, there is a chance that visualization can help shed some light on the details of the attack, how pieces are related, and so on. I call this analysis **attack path analysis.** I would like to understand how an attacker was able to enter the network, what he touched, and so forth.

To start the process, we start with data gathering. As soon as the attack assessment process is started, we need to begin collecting pertinent log files. I hope that a variety of logs are available: network flows, intrusion detection data, firewall logs, host logs, and so on. We should extract a period of time preceding the attack. It might be enough to go back an hour. Depending on the type of attack, it is possible that not even a day is enough; instead, an entire year might have to be analyzed. When you start analyzing the attack, you will fairly quickly understand the time frame that you are interested in. Let's start with just an hour. Most likely, you will know what machine was attacked. Extract records just for this machine (or machines, if multiple ones were affected). Most likely, your problem at this point will be that you don't know what the source of the attack is. Therefore, finding the source of the attack is going to be the first analysis objective. How do you do that? It might be close to impossible if the attacker executed the attack carefully enough. However, most likely the attacker made a mistake somewhere along the line. One of those mistakes could be that the attacker tried to access services on the target machine that are not available. Another possibility of detecting an attacker is the number of interactions he had with the target machine. Use a bar chart to show how many connections each of the sources opened to the target machine. Anything abnormal there? Use some other techniques of the attack analysis process to see whether you can find anything interesting that might reveal the attacker.

After you have identified potential attackers, use this candidate set to analyze all the activity seen by these machines. Most likely, a link graph will prove useful to show the relationships between all the attack candidates and the target machine. At this point, it might prove useful to extend the analysis window and take more data into account to see what the source machines have touched over a longer period of time. This will give you a good understanding of the extent of the attack. Which machines were affected and what services were used?

Especially with the information about the services the attackers used, you can verify the host logs to see whether you find any clues about how exactly the attackers entered the systems. The goal should be to gain a clear understanding of how the attack worked, who the attackers were, and which machines were involved. And more important than that, you should have a clear understanding of what data was affected!

In the next step, you can try to design a response to this attack. There are many possibilities:

- Blocking this type of traffic on a firewall between the attackers and the target machine
- Patching the vulnerabilities on the end system that the attackers exploited
- Introducing additional levels of authentication
- Deploying automatic response capabilities to block such attacks in real time

Visualizing the attack path is probably one of the most useful tools. It can help you not just analyze and understand the attack, but it also helps communicate the attack to other teams and eventually to management. Let me summarize the individual steps again that I went through to assess the attack:

1. Get records for the affected machine.
2. Find the source of the attack by looking for strange access patterns (e.g., connections to ports that are not open, excessive number of connections, strange behavioral patterns).

3. For the sources identified to be the potential attackers, analyze all the data referencing them. Find which machines they touched.

4. Deploy countermeasures to prevent similar attacks in the future.

5. Document the attack in detail (see the next section).

It would be interesting if you had the capability to execute all these steps in near real time. Doing so, you could prevent the attacks from happening. The part about responding to the attack and putting mitigation capabilities into place especially benefits from quick turnaround times. Commercial systems are available to help with these steps.

Documenting an Incident

The last part of forensic log visualization is the documentation of an incident. The attack detection process helped us find an attack and identify it. The second part was about assessing the impact and extent of an attack. When that information is known, we generally have to document the incident and provide this information to management, possibly law enforcement; and in a lot of cases, we can use the information gathered to educate people in our organization. Only part of incident documentation can be done with log files. Often, forensic images will be taken from machines that will serve as evidence and documentation of an incident. However, the part that can be done through log files is often useful to help communicate how an attacker entered the systems and the extent of the problem.

I have already discussed a lot of the elements of incident documentation when we talked about reporting. The important things to keep in mind are two things:

- Who is the audience for the incident documentation?
- What is the best way to represent the information?

These two questions will help you make sure that the documentation meets its goals. If you are writing the documentation for your management, make sure that you show on a higher level how the attack happened. Why was the attacker able to get in? Don't go into all the gory details of the vulnerabilities that were present and the exploit code that was used. Show concepts and where more controls could have prevented the attack. If you are communicating the information to the owner of the servers that were penetrated, mention all those gory details. Help them understand how the attacker penetrated the system, but don't forget to mention how the attack could have been prevented. The system administrators will not be too interested in the network components of the attacks but instead will want to know what happened on the server itself.

It is not always the best idea to use graphs and visualization for this type of documentation. Some of the documentation is better communicated in textual form. However, if you are trying to show an attack path, how the attacker actually entered the system, a picture is still worth a lot. Show the network topology, and on top of it, how the attacker was able to come in. Link graphs are generally a great tool for this type of documentation. I could spend a lot more time on this topic, but it is not one that benefits tremendously from visualization. In sum, if you can summarize information in a graph to communicate the pertinent information with other people, do so!

REAL-TIME MONITORING AND ANALYSIS

Thus far, our focus was on forensic or historical analysis of security data. Let's shift our focus slightly and take a look at how data on systems, and applications, can be monitored in real time (or near real time, to be accurate). The focus for real-time monitoring is to understand the current state of systems and applications, and presently ongoing tasks or events of interest. These events will obviously directly impact the current state and change it consequently. To communicate these properties, the current state, as well as current events, we use **dashboards.**

DASHBOARDS

You have definitely seen and possibly used a dashboard before. Stephen Few in his book on information dashboard design[10] defines a dashboard as follows:

> A dashboard is a visual display of information needed to achieve one or more objectives which fits entirely on a single computer screen so it can be monitored at a glance.

This is a lot crammed into one sentence. However, all the individual components are important. I show you a little later how to put all the components in the definition to work. One of the key points that is not explicitly mentioned in the definition, but is implicitly covered under the topic of an objective, is the focus on building a dashboard for a specific audience. In other words, a dashboard should always have the exact use-cases and people looking at it in mind. In computer security, three main groups or types of dashboards are needed:

---

[10]   Stephen Few. Information Dashboard Design (O'Reilly, 2006) p. 34.

- *Operational:* A dashboard used to track core processes, metrics, and status. It communicates low-level information at a glance and is used for real-time monitoring. The audience is security analysts in need of accurate real-time information.
- *Tactical:* Used for tracking processes of departments, networks, states of machines, and so forth. It helps analyze exception conditions and summarizes data to analyze the root case of a problem. Managers of security operations or supervisors are often the audience for this dashboard.
- *Strategic:* A dashboard that helps monitor the execution of strategic objectives. Trend visualizations are commonly found in these dashboards. The need for real-time information is relaxed. These dashboards are used to improve coordination and collaboration, and the audience generally includes the CISO, CSO, and other executives.

No matter what type of dashboard, one of the most common and important concepts is the concept of **comparison.** It is the capability to see trends and changes over time that should attract the attention of the viewer. This does not mean that only changes should be shown in dashboards. Often, it is the fact that some measure has not changed that makes it noteworthy. Table 5-2 shows some examples of comparative measures. Also shown in the table are examples of how these measures can be used and what type of dashboard would generally employ this measure.

Table 5-2 Dashboard Comparative Measures

Measure	Example	Dashboard Type
Comparison against the same measure in the past	Number of attacks last year compared to today	Tactical/strategic
The current state of a measure	Number of exposed vulnerabilities at present	Operational/tactical/strategic
The relationship to a future target that the measure should meet	Percentage of unpatched machines	Tactical
A prediction of the measure established sometime in the past	Forecast of the cost to keep antivirus signatures current	Tactical/strategic
The relationship to a future prediction of the measure	Percent of machines updated to a new operating system this quarter	Tactical/strategic

continues

Table 5-2   Dashboard Comparative Measures *(continued)*

Measure	Example	Dashboard Type
A value reflecting the norm for this measure	Average number of failed logins per person, or the normal time ranges when people log in to their desktops, or the number of hours it takes on average to patch critical systems	Operational/tactical
Future prediction for a measure	Number of machines that need replacement in a year or the size of the user population in a month	Strategic
A different version of the same measure	How the risk posture compares to other companies in the same industry	Strategic
A related measure to compare with	Cost of running in-house security monitoring compared to the security and risk posture that would result if security monitoring were outsourced	Strategic

As can be seen from Table 5-2, most comparative measures are useful for strategic dashboards. Tactical and, especially, operational dashboards more commonly use fixed measures to convey a state of a measure. Communicating states of a measure, as opposed to a comparative expression, can be done in many different ways. However, it is not only measurement or comparison that a dashboard is used for. A dashboard can help address a number of other objectives and goals. I mentioned *aggregation* and *summarization* of information in previous chapters. This means that various heterogeneous data sources are possibly combined into one single measure. The indicators from these devices are generally summarized to represent one single value or measure that presents the big picture. A more complicated process than simple summarization is the process of *correlating* information. We have discussed correlation at length in different places throughout this book. It is one of the main methods for helping to reduce the base information into manageable pieces that help **trace** and **monitor** the state of security. These are both passive means, but dashboards are also used for active tasks such as **alerting.** The dashboard should have the capability to quickly communicate measures that are out of their norm. It should alert and help focus the attention on the most important areas.

The consumer or viewer of a dashboard is often using it to **predict** future states. As always with predictive analysis, however, you have to really understand all the factors that can change a measure and weigh them against known or possible future changes of those. How are they going to change, and how in turn are they going to change the measure?

What is of utmost importance when designing a dashboard is that it is designed for the target audience. A CISO is not interested in the same measures as a security analyst. The analyst is likely interested in much more technical and operational detail, which the CISO generally doesn't have much interest in. He or she is going to be interested in aggregate measures and higher-level metrics. As a case study, let's identify what a CISO dashboard could look like.

The CISO Dashboard

I talked to a few CISOs about what they want to see on their dashboard. Interestingly enough, I got as many different answers as I interviewed people. On the other hand, there was definitely a common theme: "Show me when my crown jewels are at risk." Every company has a different set of crown jewels. For example, for the private bank in Geneva, Switzerland, it is the list of numbered accounts along with the information as to who their owners are. The other common theme is risk management. Ideally, they would like to see how much risk their information is exposed to. However, the way to measure and display the risk differs among all the CISOs. I got the many different answers mainly because every CISO has a slightly different role and corresponding responsibilities. Some of them are fairly technical and have no problem in engaging in detailed discussions about network devices and such. Those people usually tend to want more technical details on their dashboards. In contrast, some CISOs are not technical at all. They come more from the business side. For them, a dashboard that shows TCP port numbers and such is useless. You will find all possible profiles of CISOs between the two extremes I have outlined.

A CISO's job, no matter how technical he is or what his exact job description looks like, is to keep an organization's information secure. He is generally situated more on the business side than the technical side, although most people working for him are fairly technical. This has the effect that he will need a dashboard that aggregates and translates the technical details of information security into business metrics. Terms such as *mean time to repair* (MTR), *threat,* and *exposure* will definitely play an important role. So what does the CISO's dashboard look like? What information does it convey? Before we can answer these questions, we have to think about the goal, the purpose of such a dashboard. As mentioned previously, the CISO needs a knowledge management dashboard. He needs a way to see the current state of information security in his organization. The dashboard needs to aggregate and report on some key performance indicators (KPIs) that enable him to make informed business decisions based on facts and hard numbers, not on feelings and unfounded indicators. A dashboard needs to enable the CISO to take action so that security is managed to business expectations. More and more, the security organization is not viewed as a cost center but instead as a service that has to show business value. This clearly means that the technical inputs, the technical data collected by systems and devices, need to be translated into business, policy, and compliance requirements.

The information flow should not be unidirectional. The technical indicators are not only aggregated, summarized, and reported up to the CISO's dashboard, but the flow also works the other way around. The indicators collected will (or should) result in policy adjustments, process improvements, and new IT controls. The information flow should be a learning process that helps track exceptions to then improve security architectures and policies and enable management processes to be tuned.

These requirements merely give us a high-level idea of what the CISO will be interested in. It should be clear at this point that we should not list metrics such as the number of vulnerabilities on a host or the amount of free disk space on our critical servers. These are measures that are important for operational and technical dashboards. What are some measures that a CISO would find interesting? Compliance is one of the areas. This includes compliance with regulations, such as Sarbanes-Oxley, HIPAA, PCI, and so on, but it also means compliance with company policies. Another area is strategic risk management. What is the risk landscape surrounding critical company information? How efficient is the security department? Where is potential for improvement to simplify processes and make them more effective?

An important factor to always keep in mind is that a CISO has reporting responsibilities, too. He needs to justify his budget with the finance department and the board of directors. The board in turn would like to see how well the company complies with regulations and how risk is distributed across the organization. Although IT or informational risk is only a part of the total risk, it is an important factor in the overall risk equation.

So what does a CISO's dashboard look like? Figure 5-33 shows you! Note that for the dashboard in Figure 5-33, I am not going to discuss how to calculate the individual indicators. The risk calculation, for example, is not the topic of this chapter. It is the way the data is represented that is important. On the top left, you find an indicator of the overall current status of information security. If this traffic light is red, a critical incident is currently happening. This could be that a router absolutely critical for financial trading is down. Whether this is indeed a security problem is not important at this point. Every minute such a device is down costs the company a lot of money in lost productivity. It is important to investigate the possibility of a security breach at this point. The second traffic light indicates the risk associated with the "crown jewels." This light should always be green. If it starts turning orange or even red, the crown jewels are being exposed to a significant risk. In some cases, this means that the information is being accessed anomalously. This is important if you have, for example, a recipe for a beverage that is highly confidential. It could be that the integrity is at risk for information such as chemical compositions of materials or it could be that the availability of the core customer service is not guaranteed anymore, resulting in significant monetary losses for the company. However you map the most significant risk, this traffic light should represent the state of that risk.

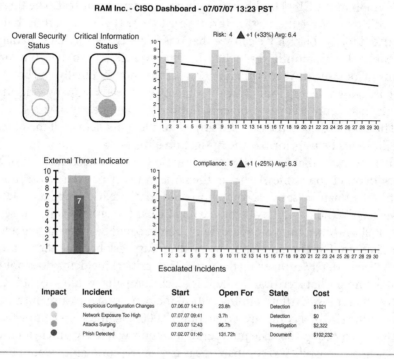

Figure 5-33   A sample dashboard for a chief information security officer.

On the top right of the dashboard, the dashboard shows how risk has developed over time. The same trend information is shown for the state of compliance. Compliance means how well the policies are implemented, assuming that the company actually has meaningful policies that also map to the regulatory mandates to which the company has to adhere, such as Sarbanes-Oxley for companies that are traded on the U.S. stock market. Again, I will not discuss how to map data into this chart. I am assuming that there is a way to map the compliance state into a number between 0 and 10, where 10 indicates perfect compliance.

An interesting way to use these two trends is to analyze the impact of external factors on the measures. For example, suppose you are running a security-awareness program. What effect does that program have on the risk exposure and the compliance behavior of your network? You will hope that the program has the effect that the risk decreases and the compliance measure increases. The nice thing about having a way to measure these indicators is that it suddenly is possible to document an impact on or an improvement in specific measures. This is incredibly useful when trying to justify investments or show how investments manifested themselves in the network.

The last graph in the CISO dashboard indicates the external threat. The three differently colored bars indicate the average threat year to date (light gray), month to date (dark gray) and today (black). We can see that this instance shows that generally there is a high threat level. This month was higher than the average year to date, but fortunately today seems to look slightly better than the rest of the month. Finally, the bottom part of the dashboard shows the top four critical problems that need companywide attention. Not all of them are pure security problems, but they do potentially have a security aspect to them. The color indicates the assessed impact of these incidents. All the other data about the incidents helps prioritize the mitigation efforts.

One other indicator that would be interesting for CISOs is a comparison of certain measures with other companies, either in the same industry or even across industries. For example, if a financial services company could compare its compliance state with other players in the industry, the outcome could be used to either justify the security budget or, if all the other companies are doing better, could be a means to get a bigger budget to catch up. The comparison is not at all an easy task because the measures need to be normalized. Merely comparing the number of critical incidents does not work. It starts with defining what a critical incident is. Each company would probably define this in a slightly different way. After defining critical incidents, the measure must be normalized based on the size of a company. Protecting 10,000 machines is a completely different endeavor than protecting 100. The number of incidents will likely differ significantly. However, having a capability to compare measures across companies would be interesting and useful.

Figure 5-33 is an example of a generic strategic dashboard. Independent of the company and its exact business, the dashboard can look the same. The definition of a tactical or operational dashboard, on the other hand, is dependent on the user of the dashboard, technical controls deployed, regulatory drivers, and so forth. I therefore refrain from defining such dashboards. If you are going to define your own dashboard, or you have a chance to influence how your own dashboard looks, here are some dashboard design principles that you might find interesting and helpful.

Dashboard Design Principles

The design of the dashboard in Figure 5-33 adheres to some simple design principles for dashboards. These design principles are universal, and all dashboards should follow them. The principles are as follows:

- *Use a single screen:* As soon as the viewer has to scroll around to see all the information, he needs to interact with the dashboard, which is not desirable and is not always possible. Just think of the case where the dashboard is projected on a wall. There is no way of interacting with the display. Furthermore, scrolling makes the user lose focus and get lost. Also, make sure that there are no more than five elements on a dashboard. Users generally find more than five elements hard to digest.

- *Show the right amount of detail:* Often, rounded numbers and values are easier to read and remember than exact values. Exact values might clutter and obfuscate important information.

- *Use simple graphs and designs:* Make the dashboard visually attractive, but without unnecessary decorations, such as backgrounds, gauges, and so on. Use visual design principles so as to not overuse color and other visual properties (see Chapter 3).

- *Use the right graphs and charts for the information at hand:* Use simple graphs and keep the variety to a minimum. The more of the same types of graphs that can be used, the simpler it is to read the dashboard. It is not just the choice of graphs but also how data is put in context and mapped to the graphs that is important. It is, for example, deceiving to start a bar chart at a value other than 0.

- *Provide enough context for the data:* Showing a number that indicates 100 attacks year to date does not communicate much. What is it compared to? Is this a lot? What is the trend? All sorts of contextual information could be added such as the data for the previous year or industry numbers.

- *Highlight important data effectively:* The most important data should be on the upper left of the dashboard. Use visualization theory to design the graphs. For example, the color red draws attention. You can use color to highlight exceptions.

These principles will ensure that a dashboard is not cluttered with unnecessary information and does not deteriorate to an expensive tool that nobody uses (because of difficulty interpreting it).

Unfortunately, I am not aware of a free tool that enables you to easily implement such a dashboard. One option is to use a library such as ChartDirector and build a dashboard from scratch. Some commercial solutions can help in this area, such as RTView from SL.[11] The problem with most of these solutions is, however, that they need quite some tuning and they do not necessarily implement all the previously listed principles.

We have touched on a few interesting topics in this section. I alluded to security metrics a lot. How do you measure security or aspects of it? To keep the focus on visual

---

[11] www.sl.com

analysis, I did not go into detail about how to measure individual components and have refrained from defining too many metrics. If interested, take a look at Andrew Jacquith's book *Security Metrics* (Addison-Wesley, 2007). It is a great book for those interested in the topic of security metrics. For in-depth discussions of dashboards and the visual design aspects of them, I can recommend Stephen Few's book *Information Dashboard Design* (O'Reilly, 2006).

SITUATIONAL AWARENESS

One topic often mentioned in the context of dashboards is **situational awareness** or **situation awareness.** The term has its origin in the military and intelligence world. It often has a connotation of real time and geographical views. However, in the end, a situational awareness view is nothing other than a dashboard. An example is shown in Figure 5-34. Here, the geographic location of intrusion detection sensors is encoded on a map. Each intrusion detection event is painted as a little square block, stacked on top of each other. Different colors are used to encode the severities of the alerts.

The graphs in a situational awareness display are near real time to provide a current situational picture. This is useful when decisions need to be made based on the actual state at the very moment. The display in Figure 5-34 helps manage a set of IDS sensors, deployed all across the United States. An analyst can quickly make decisions based on which site is currently under attack and shift his focus and attention accordingly.

When do you use these types of dashboards, and why are they useful? Have you ever been in a position to make a decision and you wished you had a view into your data to know how all your individual business areas are doing? Does your boss keep asking you about the compliance status of all the machines in Europe? Or did you have to decide where in your network you wanted to introduce a new Web service first? All these scenarios and many more are in support of a situational picture of certain aspects of your data. Situational awareness is about being able to make better decisions based on available data. If you know that currently a lot of security incidents are being investigated in your New York location and the Munich office shows absolutely no activity, it is probably smart to introduce a new Web service in Munich first.

Situational awareness screens are frequently used in command centers and projected on the wall where everyone can see them. These screens are also useful for communicating certain properties to upper management. Imagine, as another example, a traffic light type of view that indicates whether all the vital services of your business are running correctly. This can be broken down into lights that represent each individual service. Those can be further broken down to show the supporting infrastructure that enables the service to work. Again, this is all familiar turf for us. It follows the paradigm of generic dashboards.

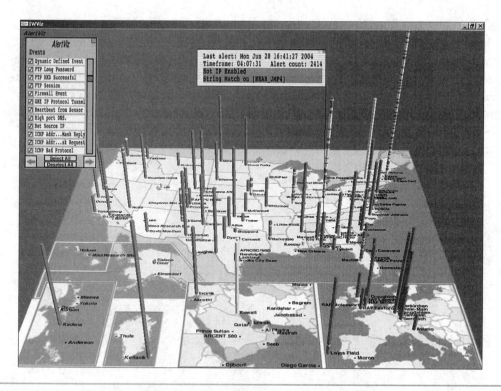

Figure 5-34   A sample situational awareness dashboard showing the distribution of intrusion detection events across sensors deployed all over the United States.

SUMMARY

This chapter showed the process of using visual methods to analyze security data. It focused on the analysis process rather than discussing the data feeds and how they can be collected or processed. We looked at two main topics of visual analysis: historical and real-time analysis. I discussed four areas of historical analysis, covering reporting, time-series visualization, interactive analysis, and forensic analysis. The discussion of these various methods has shown that there are multiple approaches to understanding log data. One powerful tool is interactive analysis of logs. The discussion introduced an extension of the information seeking mantra to include an iterative step of refining graph attributes and filters. I then discussed the forensic analysis of log data for three different use-cases: discovering attacks, attack assessment, and incident reporting. Attack detection was done using a process that should be followed to investigate log files. It helped us not just detecting attacks, but also correlating different log sources.

After the aspects of historical log analysis were covered, I shifted to the real-time use-case. The main portion of this section was covered by discussing dashboards to communicate real-time information to help consumer of the dashboards make more accurate and timely decisions. The chapter ended with a short discussion about situational awareness, which is a special case of dashboards that links the real-time data to, for the most part, geographical locations.

Perimeter Threat

The previous chapters discussed the basics for exploring the first of three major use-case areas covered in this book. This chapter on perimeter threat covers a select set of use-cases that center on analyzing data that is useful for protecting the network perimeter. This chapter's goal is to establish some tools for making perimeter protection more efficient and more fun. The chapter discusses how to protect the crown jewels from external threats.

The perimeter threat discussion hooks into the attack analysis process from Chapter 5, "Visual Security Analysis" (refer to Figure 5-22). Wherever the process mentions hypotheses, there is an opportunity for exploration, and this is what this chapter is about.

This chapter is organized by data sources. It starts with a discussion of traffic flows and a select set of use-cases based on them. The next section discusses firewall data visualization. I do not reiterate how to analyze firewall traffic logs. The discussions in Chapter 5 were extensive on this topic already. However, an interesting problem is the analysis of firewall rulesets. Can visualization help us analyze rulesets and find misconfigurations or nonsecure setups? The next topic I discuss is how IDS signatures can be tuned. I do not cover IDS data analysis. We have already discussed that topic in Chapter 5, in the context of the generic attack analysis process. The last network-level data source covered in this chapter is wireless networks. Through the extension of our networks into the wireless world, we have opened many potential holes into our corporate network. I show you how to obtain data about wireless network traffic and how to visualize it.

The discussion then shifts focus to application layer visualization. Email logs serve as an example in this area. I have some fairly interesting data that shows how to look at social networks and what they can help us identify. The analysis of vulnerability scan data ends the chapter, showing you how to analyze vulnerability data and put it into a business context.

TRAFFIC-FLOW MONITORING AND ANALYSIS

Security visualization is often performed on traffic flows. They are easy to collect and available in almost every environment. The use-cases that can be covered are fairly broad, too. First we take a look at the traffic and the uses of visualization to get an understanding of all the services and machines communicating. Although this is interesting in itself in terms of gaining an overview, we are often more interested in finding anomalies in traffic patterns. So what comes next is a section on finding anomalous behavior with traffic flows. Then we turn to how to detect worms, denial-of-service (DoS) attacks, and botnets. The last use-case for visualizing traffic flows is concerned with policy monitoring. I show how it is possible to detect people on the network who are behaving in a way that violates the corporate security policy.

SERVICE CHARACTERISTICS

The first questions people ask when confronted with a new set of traffic captures is what the communicating machines are and what the monitored topology looks like. Regular traffic flows record only the communication endpoints, which are not enough to reconstruct the network topology (see Chapter 2, "Data Sources"). However, traffic flows are great for understanding the machines communicating on a network. We can quickly generate a link graph to visualize the traffic flows between different machines. This is precisely what we did in Chapter 5.

After analyzing which machines communicate with each other, it is of interest to know which services these machines are using or offering. The first question I want to explore is whether it is possible to detect suspicious or malicious activity by looking at how different services are used. Each service must have a unique fingerprint—a way that it is used over time. For example, almost every HTTP request is preceded by a DNS lookup. The same is true for other protocols. They need to issue a DNS lookup before they can access the destination service. In addition, some protocols are used in bursts, whereas others should show a more regular behavior. For example, the Network Time Protocol (NTP) shows very regular behavior. Syslog (port 514) shows signs of bursts. Every protocol has its own fingerprint, and we should be able to build a "database" of them. With this database, we can then determine whether a service is used maliciously or something is misconfigured. To start the analysis, Figure 6-1 shows a Time table generated from a sample set of traffic flows.

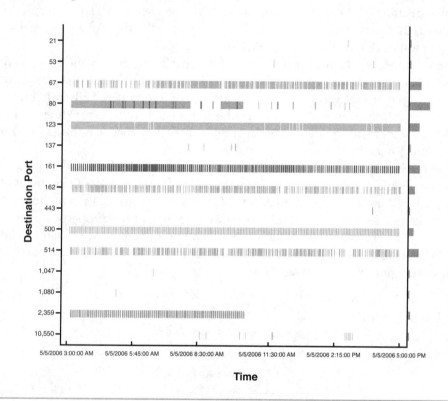

Figure 6-1   This Time table visualizes traffic flows. It shows how services are utilized over time.

Figure 6-1 shows time on the x-axis. Each service is represented with its own horizontal line. On the right side of the graph, a histogram summarizes the amount of traffic that has been seen for that protocol during the time shown. Unfortunately, analyzing the graph reveals that it is not possible to extract a fingerprint for each protocol. What if we also encode the packet size in the Time table as the thickness of each of the ticks? This idea is similar to the one pursued in Chapter 5, where the distribution of packet sizes was shown in a box plot. The Time table takes the distribution over time into account, whereas the box plots did not. It turns out that this is yet another dead-end. The patterns generated are not characteristic for a service. I was hoping to generate a unique fingerprint to identify individual protocols.

Ideally, it would also be possible to find tunneling activity. Identifying SSH tunneled over HTTP would be a great use for such fingerprints. Unfortunately, it turns out that multiple different traffic patterns are superimposed on each other. For example, most machines are using HTTP in its intended way, to browse Web pages. This generates various patterns that are superimposed—stacked on top of each other. An SSH tunnel over HTTP gets lost in all the other, regular Web browsing sessions.

Is there another way to analyze the time-based behavior of services and generate fingerprints? The basic challenge is to encode a lot of different time-series data points in a single graph. Is there any way of visualizing this type of information? Edward Tufte designed a visualization method for exactly this purpose. He calls it **sparklines**.[1] Check the sidebar for more information about sparklines, how they encode information, and how they are generated.

Figure 6-2 is a representation of traffic as sparklines. Each destination port is represented in its own graph. The x-axis shows time, and the y-axis encodes the number of packets seen at a specific point in time. Note that there are no units. Each of the sparklines has a completely different scale for the y-axis. Because of this property, we can compare traffic of individual ports with each other. The analysis of these graphs is interesting. Why do all the ports—echo, 20, 25, 53, 80, and 137—show similar patterns? They show a spike about midway through time.

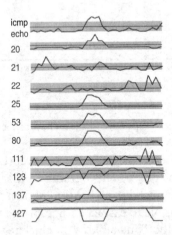

Figure 6-2   For each destination port found in the traffic flows, a sparkline encodes its behavior over time.

---

[1] www.edwardtufte.com/bboard/q-and-a-fetch-msg?msg_id=0001OR&topic_id=1

This graph is a great example of a visualization that answers some questions and poses other ones. For example, why does the echo traffic spike, too? All the ports are well-known services. Is someone scanning our machines? How can we find out? We need more information. Figure 6-3 therefore adds two more sets of sparklines to improve the picture.

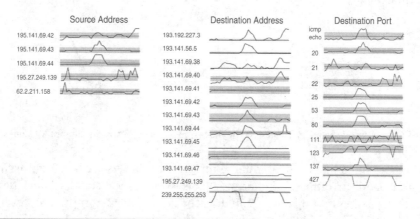

Figure 6-3 Three sets of sparklines encode traffic patterns over time. The left sparklines show the source addresses, the middle ones the destination addresses, and the rightmost sparklines encode the destination ports that we have already seen in Figure 6-2.

Figure 6-3 gives us more context for the traffic. We can see that the port patterns repeat in the destination addresses and in two of the source addresses, too. It seems that there were two source addresses generating all the traffic we were curious about a little earlier: 195.141.69.43 and 195.141.69.44. The destinations of this traffic seem to be few—all the ones that spike toward the middle.

To further analyze the traffic, we have to exclude some of the traffic. For example, all the port 427 traffic going to the multicast addresses 239.255.255.253 is something we can safely filter out. Both sparklines show exactly the same pattern and therefore seem to be related. We might want to go back and verify what the root cause for this traffic is. Most likely, we will find a machine that is misconfigured—after all, not many applications or services use multicast.

SPARKLINES

Edward Tufte invented sparklines for the purpose of encoding a huge amount of data in a small space. Absolute values are not of importance. Each individual sparkline can have a different scale. The only important thing is the development over time. Figure 6-4 shows a simple sparkline.

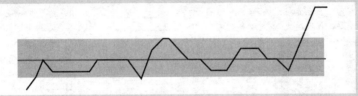

Figure 6-4   A simple sparkline, including the mean and variance of the distribution of values.

The horizontal line in the middle of the graph indicates the mean of the values. The gray band surrounding the mean depicts the statistical standard deviation. Everything falling into this band could be considered normal traffic, and everything outside of it could be flagged as an outlier. Statistically speaking, this would mean that, assuming a normal distribution of the data, 68 percent of the values will fall inside of this confidence band.

A first use of sparklines is to see development over time. A second use is to find outliers. And a third use is to compare multiple sparklines. The interesting thing, again, is that each sparkline's y-axis gets normalized. Therefore, we are not comparing absolute values, but relative values over time. This can yield interesting outcomes, as we have seen.

To generate sparklines, various plugins and libraries are available.[2] I found a free Excel plugin that I used for my graphs at http://excelidees.blogspot.com/2006/12/udf-et-sparklines.html. The implementation is not perfect, but it gets the job done. The problem I found is that the plugin generates an image for a set of data. Each update to the data generates a new image that is placed on top of the old one, instead of replacing it.

---

[2] http://en.wikipedia.org/wiki/Sparkline

Each step in the filtering process will yield a characteristic pattern that we can use to define a fingerprint for a specific application or service. As with the multicast traffic to port 427, we might find similar traffic fingerprints for other services.

A second way of analyzing sparklines is by looking for anomalies. By using the confidence bands in the sparklines (the gray bands), we can identify data points that fall outside of the statistical norm for a specific value. All the spikes identified earlier lie outside of the gray band, and thus indicate statistical anomalies. Other data points also fall outside of the norm. For example, the two sources 195.27.249.139 and 62.2.211.158 both show a spike in the beginning. The second machine, especially, goes back to fairly smooth behavior after that. The first one spikes again later. It would be interesting to know why the spike occurred. No directly correlated pattern in the destination addresses or destination ports reveals any further information about these spikes. The next step is to go back to the original logs and figure out what is causing the spike.

When analyzing the behavior of destination ports, we need to take into account that some protocols are going to show more chaotic or random behavior than others. For example, a Web server serves Web pages on a fairly constant basis. There are going to be variations, however, with respect to the time of the day, the day of the week, or holidays spread over a year. Apart from that, the distribution of traffic should be fairly smooth, unlike SSH, which is used on demand to manage servers. It is much more likely that you would see spikes and "anomalies" in port 22 behavior. Keep this in mind when you analyze sparklines.

SERVICE ANOMALIES

Looking into service characteristics, as we did in the preceding section, is one way of analyzing traffic flows. Another way of analyzing traffic flows is to look for anomalies in the way services are used. One way to spot anomalous traffic is to look for services that are hardly ever used. If we identify machines that access a service that is not normally accessed, we can spot machines that are behaving unusual and possibly are malicious. Network-based anomaly detection (NBAD) systems provide an automated way of analyzing network traffic for some of these signs. However, an expert who knows the environment can add insight that these systems cannot provide. By giving the experts visual tools, they can quickly get a feeling for the services and their behavior and compare them to the desired state. Ideally, the findings of an NBAD can be visualized, too, providing even more context to an expert's analysis.

We can use a treemap to identify services that are infrequently used. The bigger the boxes in a treemap, the easier they can be identified. This is exactly the inverse of what we are trying to do. We are interested in small tiles, the ones used by only a few machines. To solve this, we need to invert the size of the boxes. Boxes are bigger if fewer machines accessed the corresponding port. Figure 6-5 shows what such a graph looks like.

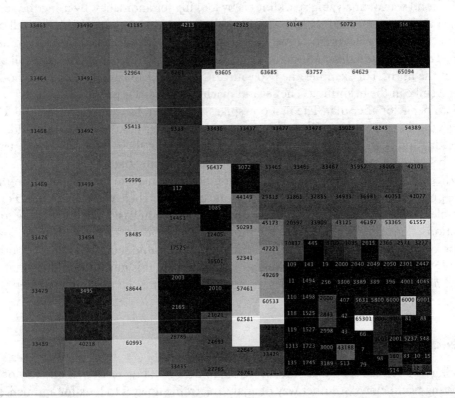

Figure 6-5   A treemap that is used to identify services used by only a few machines. The size of the boxes encodes the inverse number of machines accessing the service. The bigger a box, the fewer machines accessed the service. Color encodes the port number. The darker the tiles, the lower the port number.

In Figure 6-5, we can see that some of the largest boxes represent very high port numbers. This could be an artifact of a source/destination confusion. Due to the fact that large tiles are drawn on the top left of the graph, we should be looking for large, dark boxes. These boxes indicate low port numbers that were accessed. The larger the boxes, the fewer the number of machines that accessed them. We find large boxes toward the top of the treemap. Port 514 is one of the boxes located at the top and is probably the biggest one showing up. This box represents syslog traffic. The protocol by itself is nothing unusual. It seems that there were only a few machines that sent syslog messages; the box is really large. This is probably a good thing, considering that this was most likely unencrypted traffic. One of the next boxes that sticks out is the one for port 117. This port is a bit more worrisome. What is port 117 used for? No well-known service runs on this port. We have to go back to the original traffic to find exactly what traffic pattern generated this box. We can continue our analysis by looking at some more of these boxes.

Bright boxes in the bottom right of the treemap are another pattern we should be looking for. Those are services that are high port numbers, and they were accessed by a lot of different source machines. In fact, we can find some of these instances. For example, port 6000 and 65301 are two of them. There are others, but these two stick out. It is hard to say what port 65301 is, but it definitely would be worth trying to go back to the original log files and see what exactly the traffic is that is represented by these boxes. Port 6000 most likely represents X11 remote desktop connections.

GENERATING AN INVERSE-SIZE TREEMAP

The first step in generating a treemap like the ones in Figure 6-5 or Figure 6-6 is to extract the pertinent information from the log files:

```
argus -r traffic.pcap -w - | ragator -r - -nn -s dport | sort |
uniq -c > dport.uniq
```

This command instructs Argus to print the destination ports. The `uniq` command then produces a list of frequencies for each of the ports. To produce the inverse size for the boxes, we need to divide 1 by the frequency of an individual destination port:

```
cat dport.uniq | awk '{ratio=1/$1*1000000;
printf "%s    %s\n",$0,int(ratio)}'
```

For every entry in the file `dport.uniq`, `awk` divides 1 by the frequency. The treemap visualization program only takes integer numbers as sizes. The factor 1,000,000 is therefore used to round the ratio to be an integer. This is also the reason why in the `printf` statement `int(ratio)` is used to print the ratio. This rounds the number and eliminates the fraction after the period. Note that the separators for the two strings in the print command are tabulators.

A header line is now the only thing that is missing. The output then looks like this:

```
COUNT    PORT     RATIO
INTEGER  INTEGER  INTEGER
7029     20       1423
5556     25       1800
```

You can now use the Treemap tool (See Chapter 9, "Data Visualization Tools") to load this data and visualize it in a treemap. On the *Legend* tab, define the *Label* to be the port, the *Size* to be the ratio, and the *Color* to be the port, too. You can then change the color binning to define a gradient from white to black. This is, if you do not want the default green to be representative of the highest port numbers. Still in the color assignments, by playing with the scaling method form linear to square root to logarithmic, you can make sure that the port to color assignment is expressive enough. Depending on the distribution of your port numbers, a different distribution of the colors can help better identify interesting spots in the data. As a last step, I decided to not use any borders around the tiles, which can be defined in the main tab of the configuration. The effect of this configuration is that the tiles can take up slightly more space. Remember, increase the data to ink ratio—one of our design principles for good graphs.

Large, bright boxes on the top left of the treemap in Figure 6-5 are services running on high port numbers. They are used by only a few machines. These services deserve some attention. It might turn out that we are dealing with a source/destination confusion, but we might find that there is indeed a malicious service running on one of those ports. To continue the analysis, I generated a second graph where I filtered all the traffic to ports above 10000. The result of zooming this way is shown in Figure 6-6.

Filtering out traffic to ports above 10000 helps increase the legibility of the treemap in Figure 6-6. We have fewer boxes, which helps to identify ports represented by small boxes. In a perfect world, where everything is configured correctly and no attacks are targeting our machines, this treemap will show only a relatively small number of boxes. Unfortunately, this is not the case in Figure 6-6. The graph quickly draws attention to the lower-right corner, where ports 8080, 6667, 8000, and some others are popping out. This area shows that a significant number of services are accessing these ports. 8080 is most likely an HTTP proxy. Port 6667 is more alarming. Internet Relay Chat (IRC) is generally on this port. Although there might be a legitimate reason that this protocol is running, this is not a good sign. A lot of botnets are using IRC for command and control reasons. Therefore, it is definitely advisable to take a closer look at this traffic.

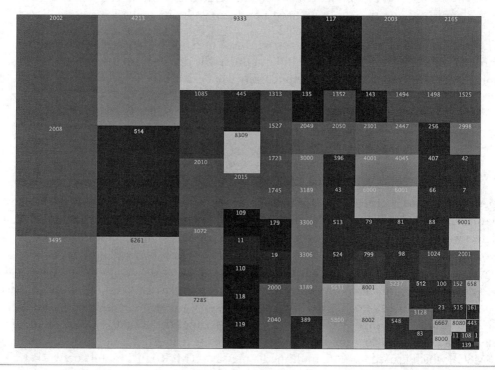

Figure 6-6 Treemap showing traffic to services on ports below 10000. The size of the boxes encodes the number of machines accessing the service. The larger the boxes, the fewer machines accessed the service. Color is used to encode the port numbers. Dark boxes encode low port numbers.

Ideally, we are able to justify every box that we see in the treemap and map it against the security policy to make sure the ports and services running over them are allowed or exceptions have been documented.

Some questions remain when looking at Figure 6-6:

- What do all the large boxes at the top left of the graph represent? What is going on with the ports in the 2000 range, for example?
- Why was syslog (port 514) used by only a small number of machines? Is this by design or should more machines report syslog?
- Why are there so many boxes that represent strange port numbers? Is this some sort of a misconfiguration or do we have a problem with our analysis method?

The treemap unfortunately does not answer these questions. They need verification through inspecting the traffic logs. Find out the traffic details from the packet captures. Sometimes only those details can help identify what exactly the traffic is about. We could also use some other visualization to help answer these questions.

This analysis showed only one possible way to find anomalies in traffic flows. There are many more ways that we could have chosen.

WORM DETECTION

Detecting worms is probably one of the simplest security/log analysis use-cases. Worms have a tendency to generate an enormous amount of traffic that is hard to miss. You can detect worms even without any network monitoring tools in place. One of the best worm detectors are employees. They will likely detect a slow network and start complaining. My point is that it is really not hard to detect worms.

I am discussing this use-case only for the sake of completeness. A book about security data visualization is not complete without a graph of a worm outbreak (see Figure 6-7). To make this section slightly more interesting, I use a nontraditional data source to discuss the analysis. The logs I am working with are from a Short Message Service Center (SMSC), which is used to route multimedia messages (MMS) in a mobile network. Call detail records (CDR) for these systems indicate who initiated a message and who received it. In addition, the CDRs also contain the message size and a few other pieces of information that are not relevant to our discussion. (See the sidebar "MMS Analysis" for more information on the log records.)

If you visualize the communications between the cell phones that were brokered by an SMSC, you will get a graph that looks like the one in Figure 6-7.

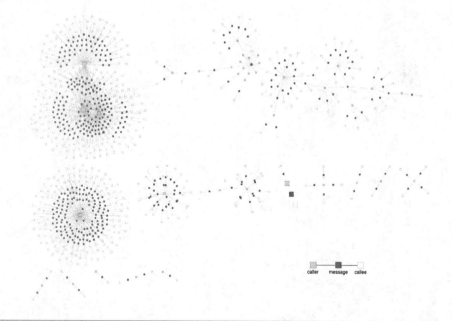

Figure 6-7 A worm outbreak visualized as a link graph. The entire cloud on the top right shows hand-helds that are infected by the worm. Notice the long chain. (This figure appears in the full-color insert located in the middle of the book.)

As you can see in Figure 6-7, it is really not hard to spot that a worm was spreading in this mobile network. If it does not look obvious, compare the graph with one generated when the mobile network was clean and free of worms (see Figure 6-8). In Figure 6-8, there are no chains of messages. The two circles in the middle of the graph seem odd. Who are the two originators who sent out messages to a fair number of recipients? It could be a proud dad who is sending a picture of his newborn to all his friends. Based on an examination of the records, these circles generally turn out to be service numbers. These are services that offer MMS messages in exchange for a payment, things such as ring tones, background images, and so on. Services are easily identifiable by their numbers. They are generally shorter than regular phone numbers; often they are three to five digits long.

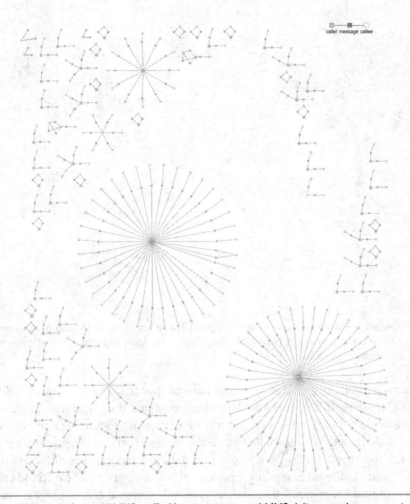

caller message callee

Figure 6-8   A picture of normal MMS traffic. You can see normal MMS delivery and some service numbers or spammers that sent MMS messages to a larger number of recipients.

MMS ANALYSIS

The log files I am analyzing to find worms in a mobile network are from a product called OpenWave[3] MAG. Two sample records look like this (the records are anonymized!):

```
20051117225657 GMT      20051117225657 GMT
4179543xxxx     4176448xxxx     0       63517
20051117225657 GMT      19700101000000 GMT
image/jpeg      CHEC1_MMSC1     MM4Rrecord      0
1       MM.1            22801351822xxxx
22802071035xxxx 2       1132 26821763098xxxx
19700101000000 GMT      message-id=67766686     0
mms.mnc002.mcc228.gprs  21      20      image/jpeg TT


20051117225651 GMT      20051117225651 GMT
4179286xxxx     4179256xxxx     0       11871
19700101000000 GMT      20051122015651 GMT
image/jpeg      CHEC1_MMSC1     MMSOrecord
2       MM.1            22801411834xxxx
22801211413xxxx 2       1132 26821906655xxxx
20051117225651 GMT      message-id=67766826     1
3       3       image/jpeg      TT
```

Immediately following the timestamps, you find the mobile device that sent the MMS. The next phone number is the one that received the message. Following this information, there are all kinds of individual pieces of information, such as the message size, the content type, the IMSI of the phones (i.e., the precise identifier for the handheld), and so on. To visualize the communications between different mobile devices, I just extracted the phone numbers (i.e., the MSISDN, as the mobile people call it) and put them into a link graph.

---

[3] www.openwave.com

This approach of visualizing MMS endpoints will not scale to millions of MMS messages. The graph would take a log time to render, and it would turn out to be completely cluttered. What can we do to solve this problem? Let's look at Figure 6-7 again. Is there anything we can see that might help us define a heuristic or a more deterministic way of processing the logs before we visualize them to detect the worms? The one sign that identifies a worm uniquely is long chains of messages. We could try to build an algorithm that computes the spanning tree for a graph and finds long chains. This turns out to be computationally fairly expensive. Another characteristic is the scanning behavior. An infected handheld sends messages to multiple recipients. This means that we can eliminate nodes that have fanouts below some sensible threshold. We could go on and on and find interesting ways of preprocessing the data.

A little later in this chapter when discussing botnets, I show how more sophisticated worm detection can be done by applying advanced heuristics. Most of the heuristics I am using for the botnet detection can also be used to implement more effective worm detection.

Using a visual representation of data to then identify heuristics for more efficient analysis is a common technique that visualization initiates. First the data is visualized. Then through human analysis, heuristics can be defined that simplify the analysis or speed it up. Without the initial visualization step, however, the heuristics would be very hard to find.

DENIAL OF SERVICE

Attacks that impact the availability of any of our computers, applications, or services, are considered DoS attacks. Unplugging a computer's network connection can be regarded as a DoS if the machine was offering services over the net. This particular case is an example of a physical attack. There are numerous logical, network-based DoS attacks. These attacks can target various different aspects of a computer or service. Other examples of DoS attacks include generating an amount of traffic that clogs the network and prevents real traffic from being sent or running a process that monopolizes the CPU. More generically, a process that uses up any type of resource, such as the available file descriptors on a machine, the hard disk space, memory, and so on, is an example of a DoS attacks. A DoS attack could also come in the form of a process or network traffic that puts the targeted machine into a state where it cannot process requests anymore. The WinNuke attack,[4] for example, uses a single packet that is sent to a Windows 95 machine to exploit a vulnerability in the network stack. Exploiting the vulnerability results in the target machine displaying a blue screen of death.

---

[4] http://users.nac.net/splat/winnuke

For this discussion, I am interested in network-based DoS attacks that are consuming network bandwidth. The environment I will focus on is an Internet service provider (ISP). This could also be a large corporation that operates a significant-size network where fluctuations in traffic patterns and large amounts of network traffic are nothing out of the ordinary. In such an environment, every traffic spike evokes the question whether the traffic represents a DoS attack or whether it is just a spike in regular activity. This is the question we are going to explore right now.

To investigate DoS attacks, we need to analyze the network traffic. Figure 6-9 shows a traffic graph captured on an ISP network that was under regular load. NFSen[5] was used to generate these network traffic graphs. NFSen is a graphical Web front end for the nfdump[6] tools, which are a collection of tools to process network flow data on the command line.

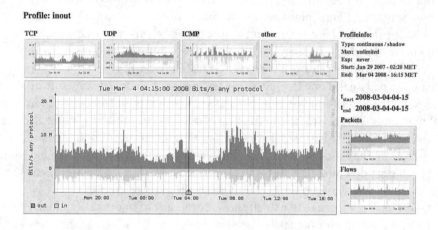

Figure 6-9   This traffic graph shows a normal traffic pattern on an ISP network.

The graphs in Figure 6-9 show various aspects of the network traffic over the past 24 hours. In the top row, you can see four graphs that show the traffic broken up by transport protocols. The fourth graph (other) summarizes all kinds of transport protocols, such as IP to IP tunnels, GRE tunnels, or IPsec traffic. The x-axis shows time, and the y-axis displays the number of bits transferred. Positive numbers of bits are outbound traffic and negative numbers (the lighter part of the graph below the x-axis) represent inbound traffic. The large graph in the middle of Figure 6-9 shows the number of bits

---

[5] http://nfsen.sourceforge.net/

[6] http://nfdump.sourceforge.net/

transferred, accumulated over all the transport protocols. The two graphs on the right-most side show the number of packets transferred over time and the number of flows over time, respectively. You can think of a flow as a session or also as a connection. One flow summarizes the traffic sent between the same machine and port pair.

What you can see in Figure 6-9 is a fairly constant number of flows over time (see lower-right chart). The number of inbound versus outbound flows is almost exactly the same. The two halves of the graph are symmetrical. The number of inbound versus out-bound packets is the same, too (although the number of packets fluctuates slightly over time). If we look at the traffic distribution of bits sent and received per protocol, we see varying patterns. There is more TCP traffic flowing out of this network than coming in. For UDP, the distribution is spiky and does not seem to have any real pattern or shape. ICMP looks very bursty. The bursts are evenly distributed over time. This seems interest-ing. A root cause is not obvious to me. The other transport protocols show activity only during business hours. This might be due to virtual private network (VPN) tunnels that use the IPSec protocol. These VPN tunnels are created when employees connect to the corporate network, which is generally during business hours. The number of bits trans-ferred for all the protocols shows a very regular traffic pattern.

With a baseline like the one in Figure 6-9, we are ready to detect someone executing a DoS attack, either against machines in our network or out of our network, attacking external machines. We have to be careful, however. Not every spike in traffic also means that there is a DoS attack. Suppose, for example, a big sports event or a big news story gets the attention of a lot of people. They will start browsing Web pages related to the event or even start downloading and watching video coverage. These events cause an increase in traffic that would quite certainly show up in these graphs.

Let's take a look at Figure 6-10, which shows some sort of anomalous pattern between 9:50 and 13:30. One sign immediately visible in the graph is the asymmetry between inbound and outbound traffic, flows, and packets. By looking at the breakdown by proto-col, we find that the asymmetric traffic is UDP and to a certain degree ICMP. The ICMP traffic shows symmetry, but with a different scale. There is more outbound traffic than there is inbound traffic. Is the asymmetric UDP traffic a DoS attack or is it legitimate traf-fic? Let's look at some of the other graphs to see what we can find out from them:

- There are a large number of flows. This means that multiple machines and ports are involved.
- The number of packets is very high. This by itself could be a video stream or any protocol that generates a large amount of traffic and therefore packets.
- The number of bits transferred is high, too, which is just an indicator of a lot of traffic.
- The majority of traffic is leaving the network.

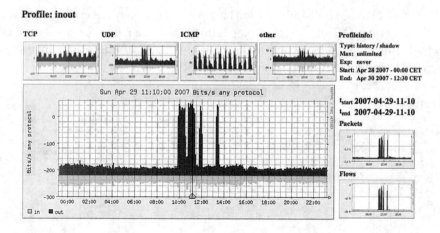

Figure 6-10 This traffic graph summarizes data suggestive of a DoS attack that started at around 9:50 in the morning and lasted until about 13:30.

It would be interesting to see a distribution of source and destination machines that are responsible for the traffic to see who exactly generated this traffic and whether multiple machines were involved. Without knowing more about this traffic, we cannot tell for sure whether this is indeed a DoS attack. The signs suggest that there is a machine on the internal network that launched a DoS attack to the outside world.

Note that another type of DoS attack (for example, a SYN flood)[7] would result in a different set of graphs. We would likely see a normal number of flows, a lot of TCP packets, and not very much traffic on the TCP protocol. We would only see a small amount of traffic because only SYN packets are sent and they can be kept very small. An example graph of a SYN attack is shown in Figure 6-11. The characteristics of a SYN attack are a normal distribution of flows, a normal amount of TCP traffic, but a large number of packets entering the network.

BOTNETS

In the world of IRC, bots have been used for many benevolent reasons. Trivia bots, for example, are used in certain chat rooms to entertain the audience. Soon after, people realized that bots were not just a means to develop games but also automate maintenance activities on IRC channels. The capabilities started to evolve, and the "bad" guys

---

[7] www.cert.org/advisories/CA-1996-21.html

figured out how to abuse bots for malicious purposes. Now they are even used in distributed denial of service (DDoS) attacks, to operate file sharing networks (such as ones used to trade music and videos), and to distribute spam. All of this is done by using the IRC protocol to instrument the bots.

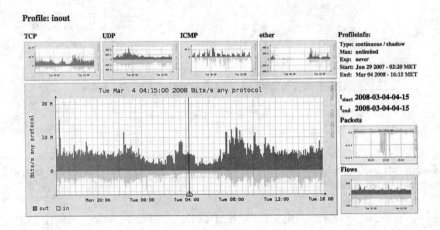

Figure 6-11   This traffic graph shows how a SYN attack manifests in a traffic graph.

The term *botnet* refers to large numbers of hacked systems that are under the control of a single user. The owner can control the zombies, the "owned" machines, with a set of commands. They can be instructed to, for example, launch an attack against a set of machines. Today you can even rent botnet time, very similar to the concept of grid computing. Spammers love this way of distributing email because it hides the true origin behind an innocent zombie machine.

An email from Dave Dittrich on the Honeysnap mailing list[8] inspired me to think about how to visually identify infected machines, machines that are part of a botnet. Dave, in his email, outlined the situation that he had flow records that he wanted to analyze:

> The malware in question is a peer-to-peer bot, which updates itself over the encrypted channel. I can see flow in the daily summary output that match (within a few thousand bytes) the size of the binary, and can tell when a peer sends my bot

---

[8]   Post from October 18, 2006, 16:24 subject: [Honeysnap] traffic analysis feature. Archives of this post are not available.

a new copy, at which point mine starts sending out copies to its peers. I want to detect the M+/-N byte inbound blob, followed by the multiple M+/-N outbound blobs and try to learn when/how the botnet updates itself.

One of the central pieces of information in an analysis would obviously have to be the packet sizes. How do you visualize a numeric quantity along with its distribution? Box plots come to mind. But then how do you link the box plots back to the traffic flows? I have an implementation of a parallel coordinate tool that can display numeric dimensions as box plots. The tool I am going to use for the following analysis is Advizor.[9] Unfortunately, this is a commercial tool. For this type of analysis, it nevertheless seemed to be the appropriate solution. I haven't found an open source tool yet that can do the same. The most annoying shortcoming of the tool—other than the fact that it is not available for free—is the fact that IP addresses are not supported as a data type. You will see in the graphs that the IP addresses are shown as numbers. This can be annoying, but for the botnet analysis it is not too important.[10]

The first step to start the parallel coordinate visualization is to identify the fields we need to extract from the traffic flows. We should probably look at the packet sizes (the received field in the graph). Then we should take a look at source and destination addresses. Do we need anything else? Port numbers? Probably not. These three properties should be sufficient.

Figure 6-12 shows a first graph I generated from the data. On the left side, the parallel coordinate display shows the communicating, entities along with the size of packets they transmitted. The leftmost column shows the source address, the middle column encodes the destination address, and the rightmost column represents the packet size. Note that for each packet, there is a line in the graph. If two machines exchanged multiple packets of different sizes, they all show as individual lines. The right side, a bar chart shows the distribution of packet sizes again. We will see in a minute why this can be useful.

We can see in the bar chart of Figure 6-12 that there were some really large packet sizes present in the data. Are they part of a botnet? By selecting the outliers (the largest packets in the graph), we can see what machines were involved in this type of traffic. This

---

[9] www.advizorsolutions.com

[10] I have a feature request pending with Advizor to fix this problem.

selection is shown in Figure 6-13. If this were traffic generated by the type of botnet we are interested in, we would see one machine on the left (the controller) that connected to a lot of machines in the middle (the bots) to update them. This is clearly not the case in Figure 6-13. Only one machine was responsible for generating traffic with very large packet sizes. We can therefore safely eliminate this traffic from the analysis. This feature is a strength of Advizor—it lets you eliminate selected data on-the-fly. Continue this process iteratively: Select the large packet sizes, check which machines are involved, and if they do not show an interesting or suspicious looking pattern, eliminate the data from the view.

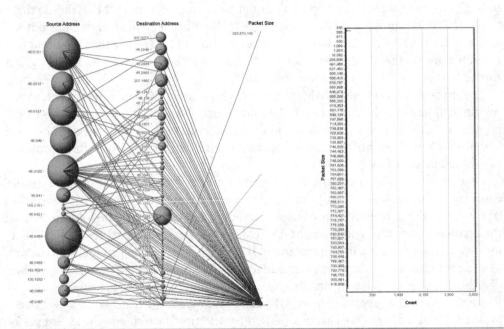

Figure 6-12   The first graph in the botnet analysis displays a parallel coordinate display of the communicating entities along with the bytes transferred by each of them. On the right side, the graph shows a bar chart of the distribution of packet sizes. Color is used to emphasize the packet sizes. (This figure appears in the full-color insert located in the middle of the book.)

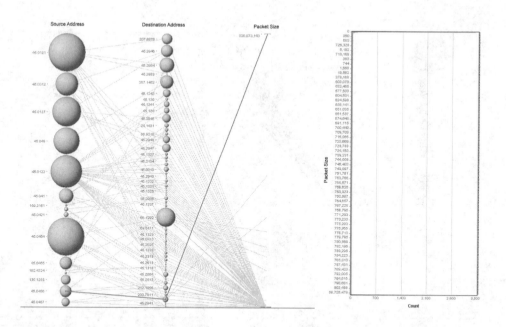

Figure 6-13   By selecting the large packet sizes (the red line), we can verify what the communicating entities are that are responsible for this traffic. If this were botnet traffic, we would see a pattern where one machine sent data to multiple other machines, which is not the case at this stage of the analysis. (This figure appears in the full-color insert located in the middle of the book.)

Eliminating outliers does not have to be restricted to selecting packet sizes that look uncharacteristic, as shown in Figure 6-13 and another example that is shown in Figure 6-14. In Figure 6-15, instead of selecting large packet sizes, there was one machine on the left that generated a lot of traffic (the biggest bubble). Is this possibly the control server that sends updates? By selecting it, we can see that this machine sent data to five other machines, and all the packets were 76 bytes in size. This is unlikely to be a botnet controller. If it were a botnet controller, it would connect to many more machines, and the traffic would probably be slightly larger. Let's eliminate it.

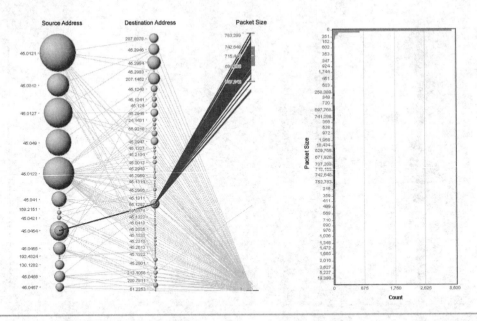

Figure 6-14 Iteratively eliminating packet sizes that do not show the characteristics identified in Dave's heuristic, we can narrow the scope of analysis more and more.

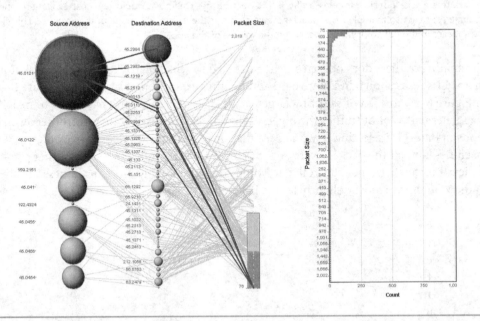

Figure 6-15 By selecting suspicious looking machines and investigating their traffic pattern, we can also eliminate data from the view or possibly find botnet controller candidates.

Continued elimination of outliers will result in one of two outcomes. Either we arrive at an empty dataset, which would indicate that we did not have any bots in our network or that we worked with the wrong heuristic, or we find that we do have bots in our network. The second outcome is what we can see in Figure 6-16. Can you see it?

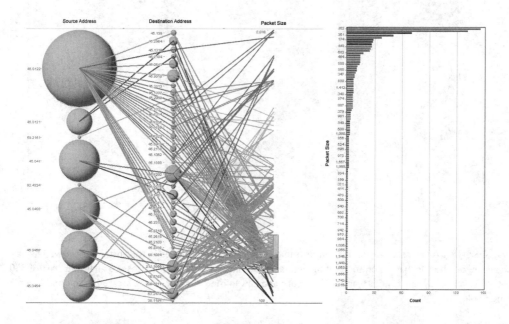

Figure 6-16 Not very visible, but in this graph enough data was eliminated to make it possible to detect a possible botnet controller. Color encodes the packet sizes. (This figure appears in the full-color insert located in the middle of the book.)

Although you might not see the botnet traffic in Figure 6-16, let me highlight some of the traffic. I chose to select packet sizes in the area of 400 bytes. There seemed to be an accumulation of packets of that size. Figure 6-17 shows the result of this selection.

Figure 6-17 shows fairly well that there was one machine on the left that connected to a series of other machines and the packet sizes were all in the range of 350 bytes. This looks like a winner.

Do we really have a winner? Did we find a botnet controller? We should now do a few things to verify this. The simplest thing is to capture the exact traffic and analyze its content. Does the traffic show signs of botnet commands? Another way to verify is to go to one of the machines and inspect it for signs of bots or malicious code.

This example should have shown you that interactive analysis of data can be a powerful tool to zoom in and concentrate on the interesting data. Imagine having to do this analysis with a textual log file.

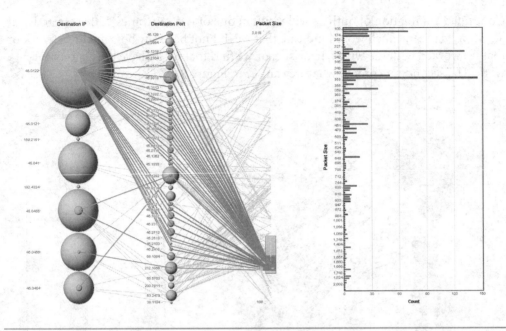

Figure 6-17   After iterative elimination of traffic in the graph, we can see in this instance that we have a machine on the left that is communicating with a lot of machines. The traffic sizes are all in the area of 350 bytes. This is likely our botnet traffic. (This figure appears in the full-color insert located in the middle of the book.)

POLICY-BASED TRAFFIC-FLOW ANALYSIS

Besides all the use-cases for traffic flows that we have discussed so far, they are also good candidates for monitoring usage policies. It might be company policy that peer-to-peer file sharing may not be used or Internet browsing has to go through the corporate proxy. Two approaches can be used to detect security violations through monitoring traffic flows:

- Analysis of traffic based on user roles
- Monitoring of the corporate security policy through network traffic analysis

The former case attributes all the traffic flows to users and visualizes this information. Figure 6-18 shows an example of a traffic graph that encodes, for each user (the source nodes), what role they belong to. Finance, HR, Engineering, and Sales all have different colors assigned to their respective nodes. The mapping is done based on the owner of the

Applied Security Visualization

Color Gallery

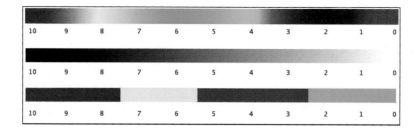

Figure 3-1

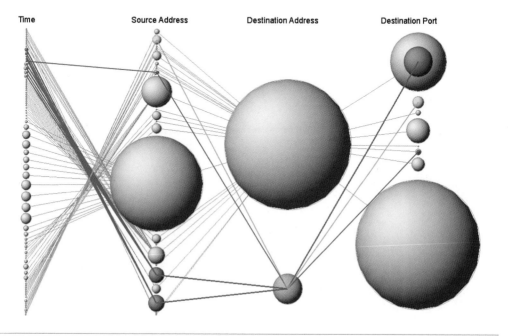

Figure 3-17

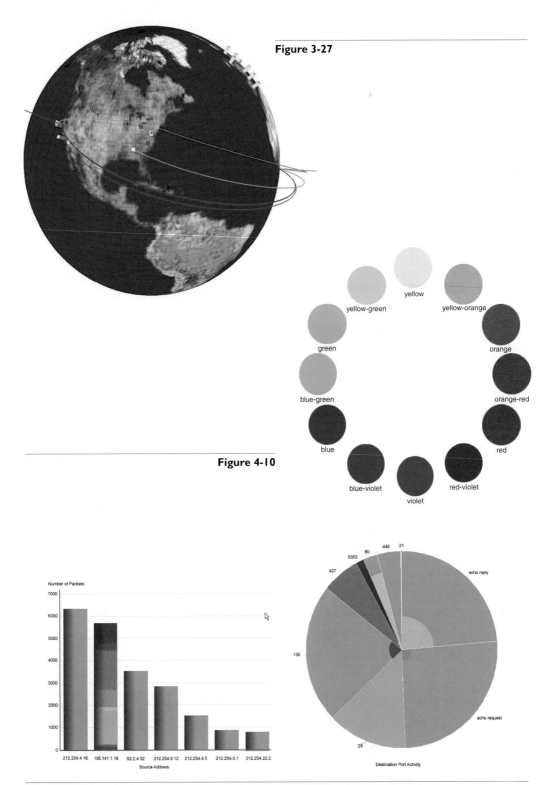

Figure 3-27

yellow

yellow-green   yellow-orange

green   orange

blue-green   orange-red

blue   red

Figure 4-10

blue-violet   red-violet

violet

Number of Packets

7000

6000

5000

4000

3000

2000

1000

0

212.254.4.16 195.141.1.16 62.2.4.52 212.254.8.12 212.254.4.5 212.254.0.1 212.254.22.2

Source Address

445 21

80

5353

427

echo reply

135

echo request

25

Destination Port Activity

Figure 3-39

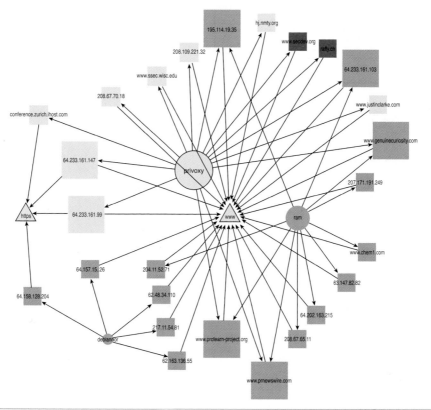

Figure 4-11

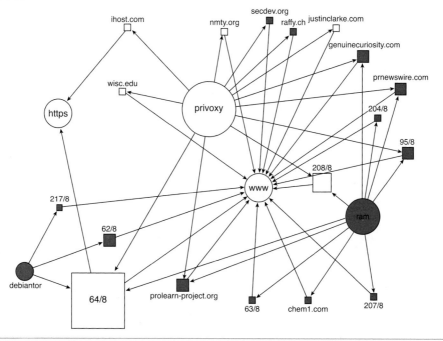

Figure 4-12

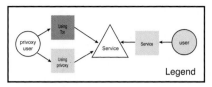

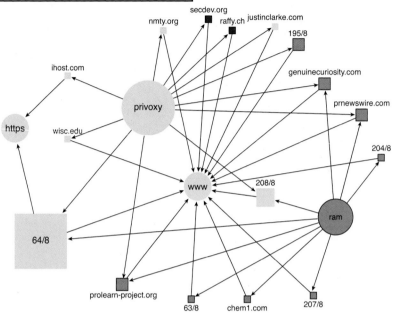

Figure 4-15

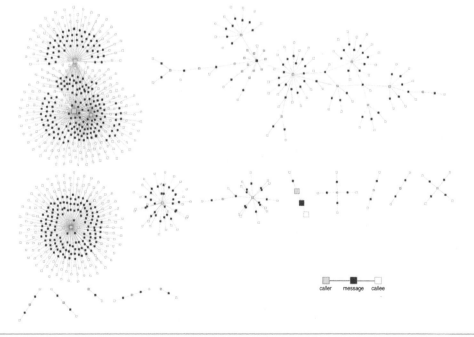

Figure 6-7

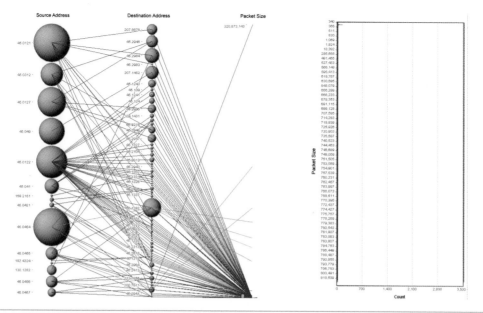

Figure 6-12

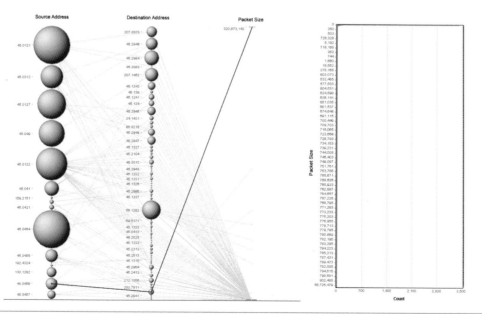

Figure 6-13

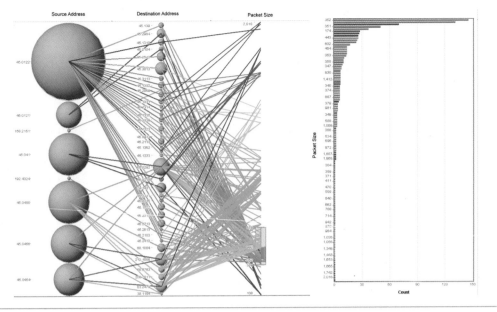

Figure 6-16

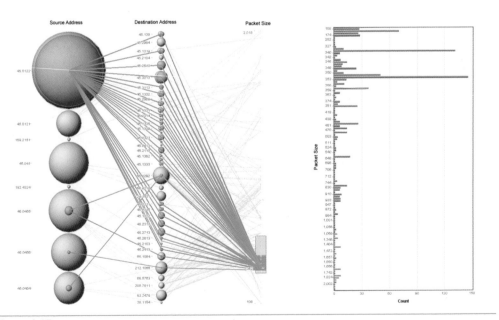

Figure 6-17

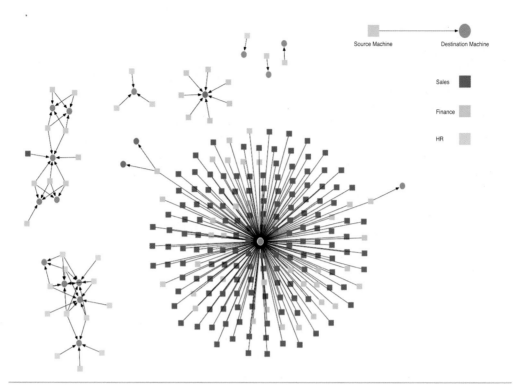

Figure 6-18

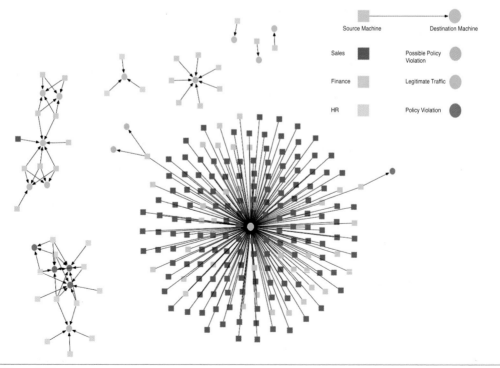

Figure 6-19

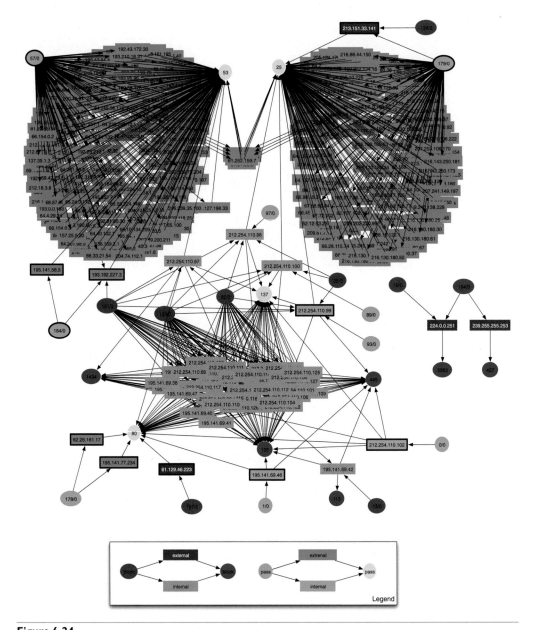

Figure 6-24

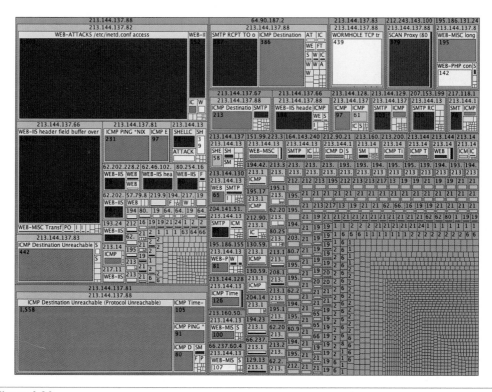

Figure 6-26

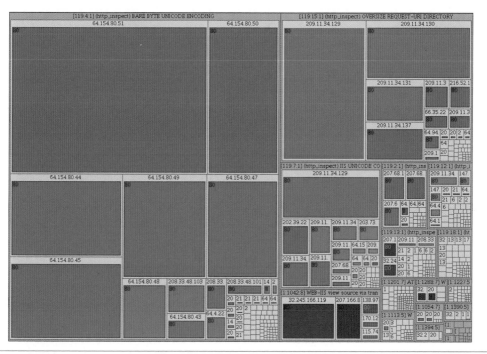

Figure 6-27

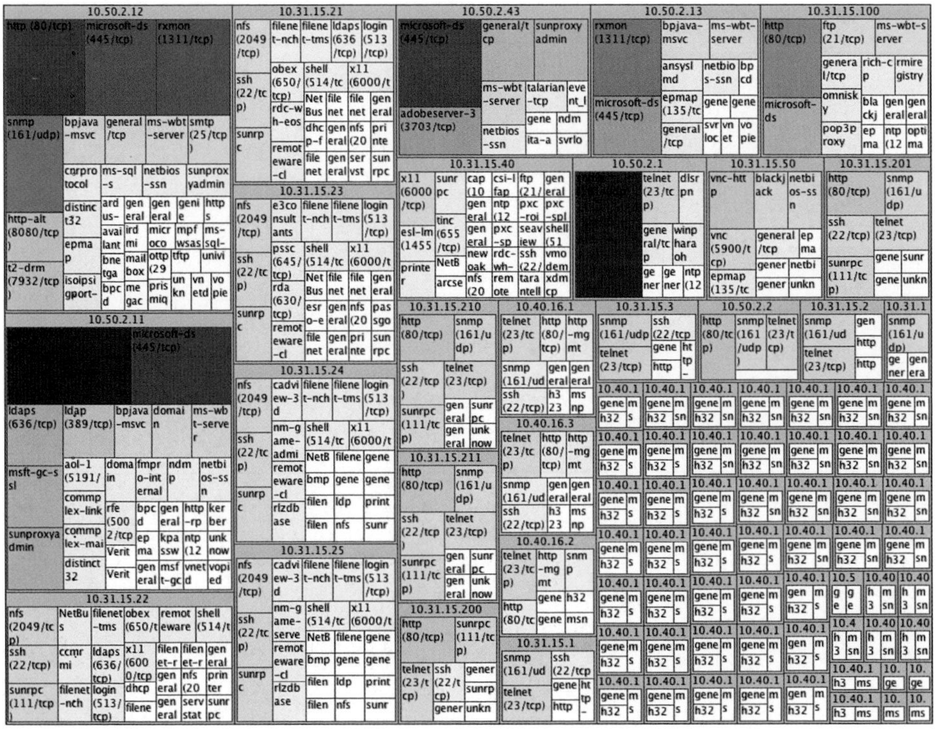

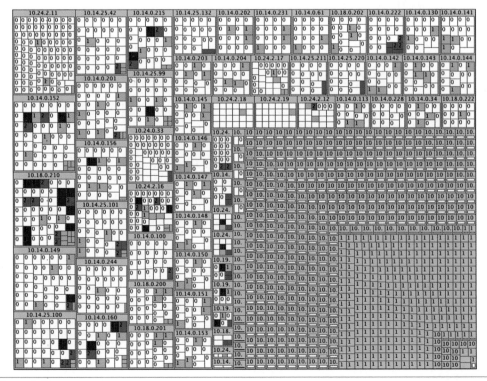

Figure 6-38

Figure 6-41

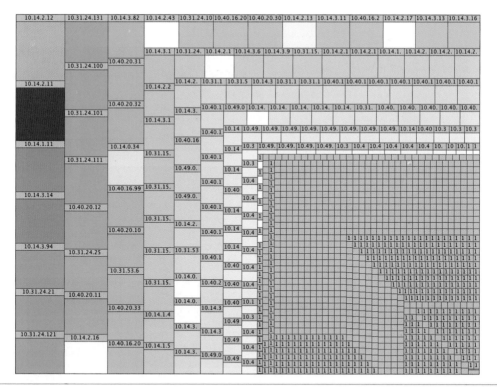

Figure 6-43

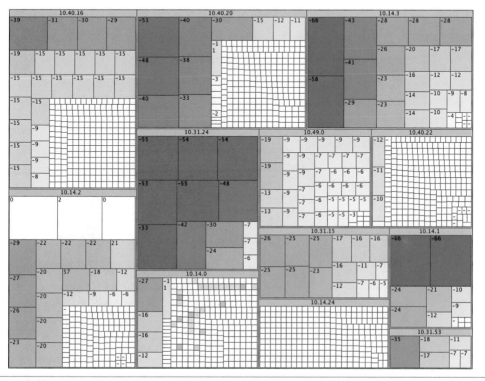

Figure 6-44

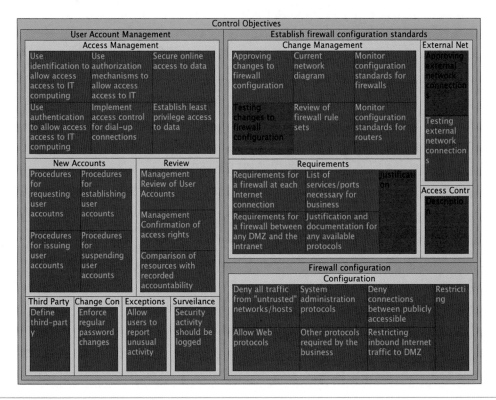

Figure 7-6

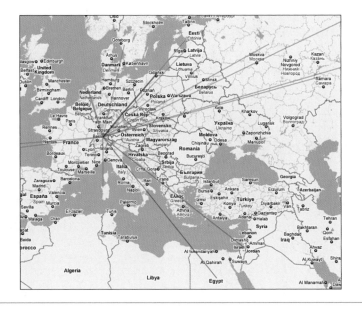

Figure 8-6

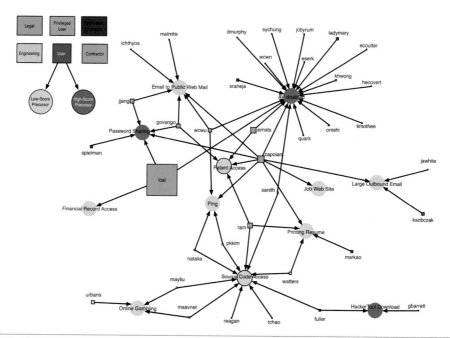

Figure 8-16

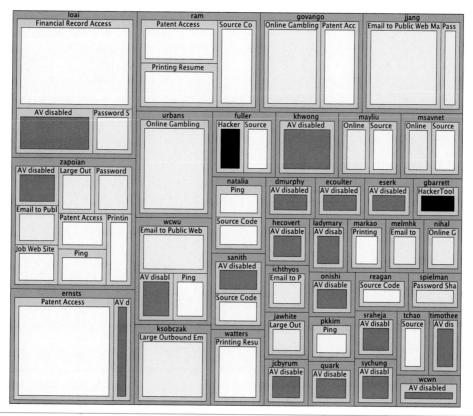

Figure 8-17

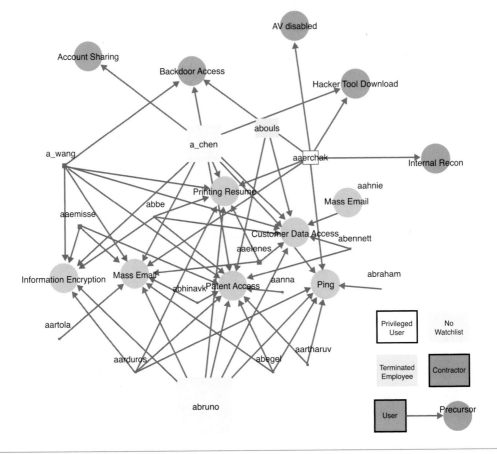

Figure 8-19

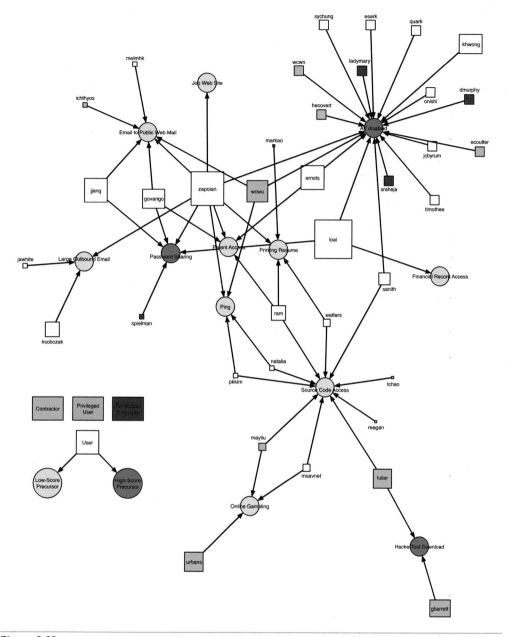

Figure 8-23

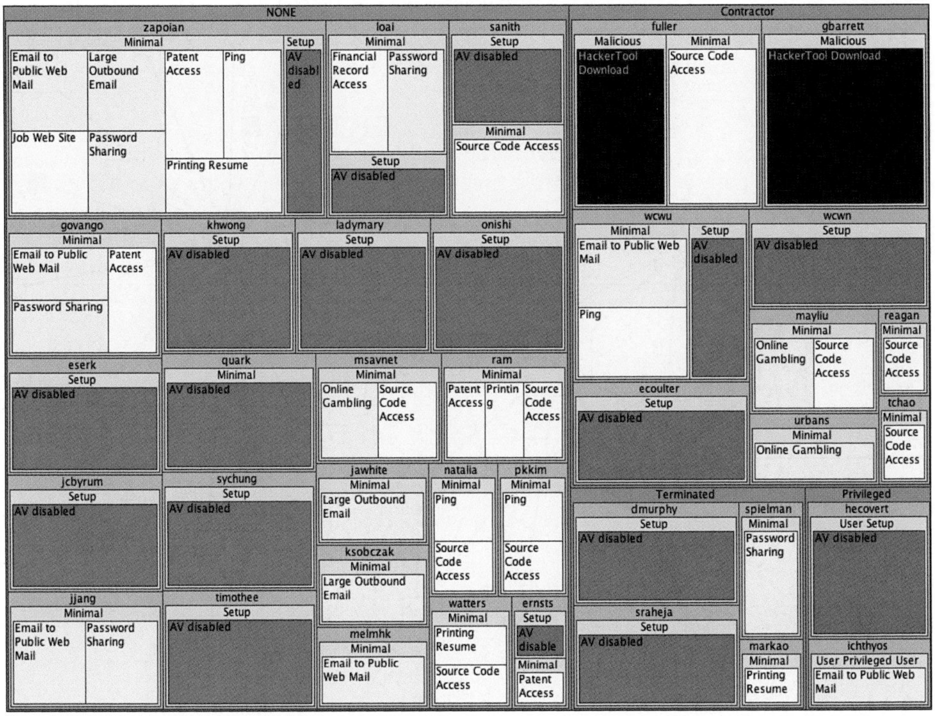
NONE
zapoian
Minimal
Email to Public Web Mail
Large Outbound Email
Patent Access
Ping
Job Web Site
Password Sharing
Printing Resume
Setup
AV disabl ed
loai
Minimal
Financial Record Access
Password Sharing
Setup
AV disabled
sanith
Setup
AV disabled
Minimal
Source Code Access
govango
Minimal
Email to Public Web Mail
Patent Access
Password Sharing
khwong
Setup
AV disabled
ladymary
Setup
AV disabled
onishi
Setup
AV disabled
eserk
Setup
AV disabled
quark
Minimal
AV disabled
msavnet
Minimal
Online Gambling
Source Code Access
ram
Minimal
Patent Access
Printin g
Source Code Access
jcbyrum
Setup
AV disabled
sychung
Setup
AV disabled
jawhite
Minimal
Large Outbound Email
ksobczak
Minimal
Large Outbound Email
natalia
Minimal
Ping
Source Code Access
pkkim
Minimal
Ping
Source Code Access
jjang
Minimal
Email to Public Web Mail
Password Sharing
timothee
Setup
AV disabled
melmhk
Minimal
Email to Public Web Mail
watters
Minimal
Printing Resume
Source Code Access
ernsts
Setup
AV disable
Minimal
Patent Access
Contractor
fuller
Malicious
HackerTool Download
Minimal
Source Code Access
gbarrett
Malicious
HackerTool Download
wcwu
Minimal
Email to Public Web Mail
Ping
Setup
AV disabled
wcwn
Setup
AV disabled
mayliu
Minimal
Online Gambling
Source Code Access
reagan
Minimal
Source Code Access
ecoulter
Setup
AV disabled
urbans
Minimal
Online Gambling
tchao
Minimal
Source Code Access
Terminated
dmurphy
Setup
AV disabled
sraheja
Setup
AV disabled
spielman
Minimal
Password Sharing
markao
Minimal
Printing Resume
Privileged
hecovert
User Setup
AV disabled
ichthyos
User Privileged User
Email to Public Web Mail

Figure 8-24

machines, or in some cases the owner of the network. For example, Sales owns the 192.168.0.0/16 subnet. Therefore, all those machines are displayed in dark blue.

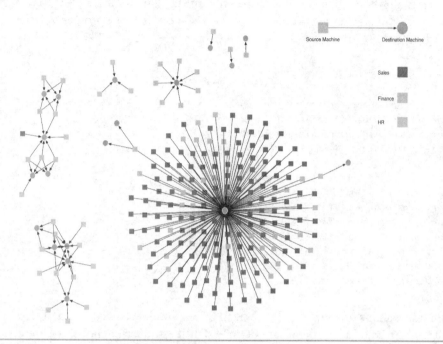

Figure 6-18 User role monitoring through traffic flows. The link graph visualizes the network traffic and attributes each flow to a user. User nodes are colored by their role. (This figure appears in the full-color insert located in the middle of the book.)

Figure 6-18 shows clear clusters of role behavior. Most of the clusters contain only users of a single role. This is what you would expect. Finance users are using their own systems. HR users have their systems, and no other role should access them. However, it seems that Sales and Finance share at least one machine (the big cluster in the middle). The graph also shows one possibly interesting access from a Sales user. On the left of the graph, a Sales user is accessing a machine normally accessed only by Finance people. This might be a problem.

GENERATING POLICY MONITORING GRAPHS

A traffic graph like the one in Figure 6-19 can be generated from any network traffic log. Extract the source and destination IPs, as well as the destination port from the traffic logs. This example assumes that the security policy allows certain network traffic and forbids the use of other traffic. For example, TFTP running on port 69 is a protocol that should not be seen on the network, because it transports data in clear text. After you defined a policy based on network protocols, write a configuration for AfterGlow that looks like this one:

```
shape.source=box
label=0
# sources are colored based on the subnet
color.source="blue" if ($fields[0] =~ /^45\.2/)
color.source="lightblue" if ($fields[0] =~ /^45\.0/
color.source="blue2" if ($fields[0] =~ /^45/)
color.source="green"
# targets are colored based on the port numbers
color.target="yellow" if ($fields[2] eq "80")
color.target="green" if ($fields[2] eq "443")
color.target="green" if ($fields[2] eq "22")
color.target="yellow" if ($fields[2] eq "123")
color.target="yellow" if ($fields[2] eq "110")
color.target="red" if ($fields[2] eq "69")
color.target="green"
```

First, the shape of source nodes is set to boxes, and labels are turned off for the nodes. Then, color assignments are defined. For the sources, I choose a different color for each subnet. In my network, each subnet is owned by a different role: Finance, HR, and so on. The target nodes are colored based on the destination port that was used by the traffic. Use your own color mapping scheme for the destination ports. You can, for example, map nonsecure ports to darker colors than secure ports as I have done here. You can also encode your corporate policy in the color scheme. Color nodes in red that are violations based on the security policy. This configuration will help you quickly identify which user roles are not adhering to the corporate security policy. It might turn out that some roles violate the policy all the time. Try to determine the root cause for this. It might be that some roles need certain network protocols to do their job, which in turn would suggest a need for a policy change and a security assessment of the said protocol.

Similar to the previous graph, we can generate a graph that helps us monitor the corporate security policy (see Figure 6-19). As before, a link graph is used to show the communication endpoints on the network. However, instead of using color to encode only the user's roles, color is used to also encode the security policy. Three different colors are used. Pink encodes policy violations. Brown nodes show possible policy violations. And green nodes encode legitimate traffic. The policy is based on the network protocols. For example, per the security policy, peer-to-peer traffic is prohibited due to copyright infringements and piracy issues. Telnet and TFTP are not allowed because they are unencrypted protocols, carrying potentially sensitive information in the clear.

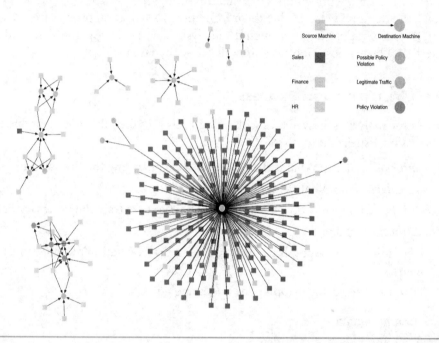

Figure 6-19 This traffic policy graph shows how the corporate security policy can be encoded in a graph. Red nodes indicate policy violations. (This figure appears in the full-color insert located in the middle of the book.)

The big cluster in Figure 6-19 shows Finance and Sales users accessing a common machine. The traffic is flagged as legitimate. However, a couple of Finance users accessed other machines, which has been flagged as possible policy violations. The graph makes this traffic easy to spot. The other cluster that asks for attention is on the left side. A number of HR users caused a policy violation while accessing some machines. This looks like possibly a legacy system that is used for HR purposes. This is one of those cases where an assessment of this protocol is in order, and possibly an update of the infrastructure is going to be necessary. A similar case is shown with the cluster on top, where Finance users are causing a possible policy violation. The fact that so many users are using only this one machine and all the traffic is flagged as a policy violation indicates that an infrastructure problem might exist.

FIREWALL LOG ANALYSIS

Most of us have dealt with firewall logs. Firewalls are very chatty. In principle, analyzing firewall logs is similar to analyzing traffic logs. The only additional information we get from firewall logs is whether a specific connection was passed by the firewall or denied. This gives us a few more possibilities to visualize the logs.

In my first attempt, I will be using the information visualization process from Chapter 4, "From Data to Graphs," to go through the analysis of a firewall log. In the second half of the section, I take a closer look at a firewall ruleset by visualizing it.

FIREWALL VISUALIZATION PROCESS

The process of analyzing firewall logs with link graphs uses the following steps, based on the information visualization process:

1. *Determine the problem:* What is the objective when analyzing the firewall log?
2. *Assess available data:* What fields does the firewall log contain?
3. *Process information:* How do we parse the log entries to extract the necessary fields?
4. *Visual transformation:*
   4.1   Determine the link graph configuration and the association of nodes to data fields.
   4.2   Determine the color mapping for nodes and edges.
5. *View transformation:*
   5.1.   Filter out unnecessary nodes.
   5.2.   Define aggregation for nodes.

Let's walk through each of the steps of a specific example.

1. Determine the Problem
We are interested in all outbound traffic that was blocked at the firewall. This means that we have to filter for log entries that indicate blocked connections. Through this analysis, we will identify either firewall ruleset misconfigurations or machines on the internal network that are misconfigured.

2. Assess Available Data
The firewall I am going to look at, OpenBSD pf, generates log entries of the following form:

```
Oct 13 20:00:05.760437 rule 179/0(match): pass in on xl1:
195.141.69.44.54700 > 64.156.215.5.25: S 462887145:462887145(0) win
32768 <mss 1460,nop,wscale 0,nop,nop,timestamp 3931103936 0> (DF)
```

It seems that all the information necessary is available. The log entries indicate whether a connection was blocked or passed and what the communicating endpoints were.

3. Process Information

We can use the pf parser from AfterGlow (http://afterglow.sf.net) to parse the log entries and extract the important fields:

```
tcpdump -n -e -ttt -i pflog0 | pf2csv.pl "sip dip dport action"
```

The next step is to then filter only for blocked traffic:

```
cat pflog.csv | grep "block$"
```

4. Visual Transformation

For the output to be useful, we would like to see the source address, the destination port, and the destination address. We want to see the internal machines, what service they contact, and on what machines they access those services. Therefore, the source node is going to be the source address, the event node is the destination port, and the target node is the destination address (see Figure 6-20).

Source IP   Destination Port   Destination IP

Figure 6-20 Configuration of the link graph for visualizing firewall logs.

Initially, we are just going to color internal machines as yellow nodes to be able to quickly identify which machines are the internal ones. In our example, it will inherently be all the source nodes because we are showing only outbound traffic. External machines are colored in blue. In addition to the identification of internal versus external machines, we are going to color the port numbers that are below 1024 different from the rest. Ports below 1024 are green and the rest is orange.

5. View Transformation

Without a sample graph, we do not know whether there will be a need to filter some additional nodes. We might come back to this. The same is true for aggregation.

It is time to generate a graph with the above configuration. The AfterGlow property file looks like the following, based on the previously discussed properties:

```
color="yellow" if (field() =~ /^111\.222\..*/);
color.event="green" if ($fields[1]<1024)
color.event="orange"
color="blue"
```

We can see in Figure 6-21 that there is a huge cluster of IP addresses around the node of port 80. To simplify the graph, we should try to aggregate the target nodes based on the IP addresses. Therefore, I am going to add the following line to the property file:

```
cluster.target=regex_replace("(\\d\+)\\.\\d+")."/8"
  if ($fields[1] eq "80")
```

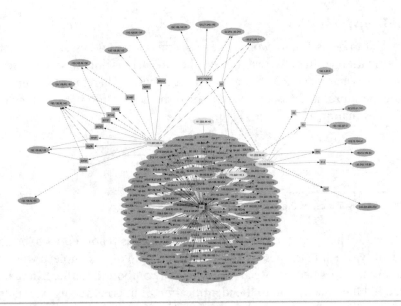

Figure 6-21   Link graph of blocked firewall outbound traffic.

This configuration line will aggregate all the IP address nodes around port 80 based on their A- class. Figure 6-22 shows the rest of this configuration.

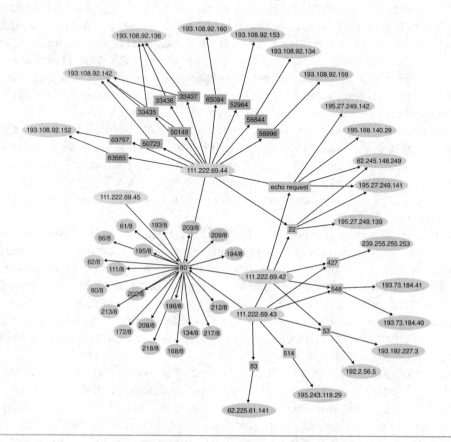

Figure 6-22   Link graph of blocked firewall outbound traffic with aggregated nodes around port 80.

Figure 6-22 visualizes all the outbound traffic that was blocked by the firewall. The orange rectangular nodes on the top of the graph are high ports that were blocked. Most likely, this traffic represents artifacts of packets that were either retransmitted or the session state on the firewall timed out. Before we completely dismiss all this traffic and attribute it to firewall state caches, we should make sure that they are not well-known ports that spyware is using. Joakim von Braun maintains a list of Trojan ports that can be found at www.simovits.com/trojans/trojans.html. In Figure 6-22, it does not seem like any of those ports are present.

All the other blocked traffic seems to be some sort of server misconfiguration. Let's look at some examples. Look at port 22 (SSH) and the echo request. A user on 111.222.69.44 might have deliberately initiated this traffic. He might have tried to access machines on the Internet via SSH and been blocked. Not knowing that he was actually blocked by the firewall, but realizing that he could not connect to the machines, he initiates some echo requests to see whether the machines are running at all. That traffic was blocked again. It is up to the security policy as to whether the firewall is actually misconfigured and the user should be able to connect to these two services or this actually is a policy violation.

The traffic involving port 514 (syslog) is interesting. It seems that a machine is trying to send syslog over the Internet to some foreign destination. It is not a good idea to send syslog over the Internet, especially when using UDP. Syslog is transmitted in plain text and could be abused by a third party to gain interesting insights. The traffic flagged in the graph is clearly a misconfiguration of the server and should be fixed. Fortunately, the syslog traffic was blocked.

Another node of interest is port 53. The fact that this traffic was blocked could indicate either a misconfiguration of the originating server or a misconfiguration of the firewall ruleset. There is a problem with the DNS setup. We would have to know how exactly DNS is configured to determine whether the servers are misconfigured or the firewall should pass the traffic. In general, it is advisable to have one machine as the dedicated DNS server in the network and have only that machine connect to the outside world and interact with the Internet's DNS infrastructure. Every internal machine exposed to public DNS traffic broadens the attack surface.

The blocks associated with port 80 can have one of two causes. The first possibility is that the three internal machines were trying to open Web sessions and were blocked. If these are servers, this sounds unlikely. It is more likely that incoming HTTP sessions timed out and the responses caused the blocks. We should verify whether there are indeed three internal machines that are serving as Web servers. If this is the case, some Web sessions timed out at the firewall and part of the traffic was blocked. A firewall keeps track of sessions that it has seen. It remembers the sessions and makes sure that the response and all the associated packets will be allowed through. To prevent the session cache from growing too large, firewalls implement a timeout. If a session is not completed, the firewall deletes the state after a certain timeout period has elapsed.

FIREWALL RULESET ANALYSIS

As the firewall administrator, it is important to know whether the firewall ruleset contains any misconfigurations. There are two ways to verify a firewall ruleset. One is to download the ruleset from the firewall and run some analysis on it. However, this type of analysis is not easy, and visualizing firewall rulesets is not very straightforward. It is fairly complicated because of different granularity levels that individual rules can have. For example, some rules block traffic to an entire subnet, whereas others are specific about an individual machine and port. It is hard to put this information into a visual display.

The other approach, which I will choose here, is to graph the traffic passing through the firewall. I use this information to identify the ruleset, in the hope that misconfigurations or problems can be detected. The obvious disadvantage with this approach is that we need historical data to visualize. This means that if there was a misconfiguration, it was abused already. This is, in a lot of cases, not a problem as the firewall has been running for a while and we want to know how well the setup performs.

The first step in the firewall ruleset analysis is to parse the firewall logs to extract the source address, the action, and the rule number:

```
$ tcpdump -n -e -ttt -i pflog0 | pf2csv.pl "sip action rulenumber"
68.121.121.53,block,197/0
62.245.245.139,pass,133/0
212.254.110.98,pass,166/0
```

Visualizing this information with a simple property file like the following one results in Figure 6-23:

```
color.source="olivedrab"
color.event="red" if ($fields[1] eq "block")
color.event="green"
color.target="blue"
```

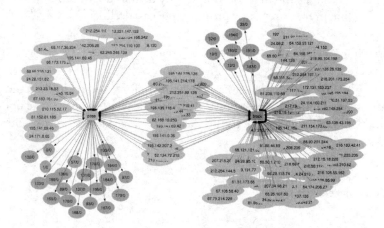

Figure 6-23   Simple firewall ruleset visualization using the source address, the action, and the rule number.

We can see two interesting things in Figure 6-23. The first thing that sticks out is some sources that have been both blocked and passed. That seems interesting, and I want to investigate this some more later. Note that every rule (blue nodes) is associated with either blocks or passes and that there are many more rules to pass traffic than there are to block traffic. It is interesting, in general, that there are explicit rules that pass traffic. This means that there are exceptions defined for some of the generic block rules. For example, there might be a generic block for traffic on port 22, but a couple of machines might be allowed to use SSH for remote administration.

To further analyze the ruleset, we need to see the destination addresses and the destination ports in the graph. The following command can be used to extract the pertinent information:

```
$ tcpdump -n -e -ttt -i pflog0 |
pf2csv.pl "action rulenumber dip dport" | perl -pe 's/,/\|/'

pass|57/0,80.80.7.210,53
block|19/0,224.0.0.251,5353
block|191/0,212.254.110.96,137
```

The graph I want to generate is one where I can see the rule number, followed by the destination address and then linked to the destination port. The nodes should then be colored based on whether the traffic was blocked or passed. However, AfterGlow can deal with only three columns. Therefore, I converted the first two columns into one by replacing the first comma with a pipe symbol. To not show the action as an explicit node, we have to change the first column to only be the rule number, without the action. The following line in the AfterGlow property file can do this:

```
label=$foo=field(); $foo=~s/.*\|//; return $foo;
```

This changes the label and removes everything before, and including, the pipe symbol. The rest of the configuration for AfterGlow then deals with coloring the nodes. The nodes should encode whether the traffic was blocked or passed. For the source node, this is simple:

```
color.source="red" if ($fields[0] =~ /^block/)
color.source="green"
```

For the event node, I also want to encode whether a machine is on the internal network, in addition to showing whether the traffic was blocked or passed. To do this, the following lines can be used:

```
color.event="palegreen" if (($fields[1] =~ /^212\.254\.110/) &&
  ($fields[0] =~ /^pass/))
color.event="palegreen" if (($fields[1] =~ /^195\.141\.69/) &&
  ($fields[0] =~ /^pass/))
color.event="green" if ($fields[0] =~ /^pass/)
color.event="red" if ($fields[1] =~ /^212\.254\.110/)
color.event="red" if ($fields[1] =~ /^195\.141\.69/)
color.event="deeppink"
```

This is a bit more complicated. I have two subnets that the firewall protects. If either of them is seen as the destination and the traffic was passed, the nodes are colored light green. If not, but the traffic was passed, the nodes are going to be green. If the traffic was blocked to an internal machine, the nodes are colored in red. The rest, external machines that were blocked, are colored dark red (deeppink). For the target nodes, the following configuration is used to apply light blue for passed traffic and blue for blocked traffic:

```
color.target="lightblue" if ($fields[0] =~ /^pass/)
color.target="blue"
```

Figure 6-24 shows the result of applying this configuration. It looks fairly complicated. The two clusters of dark green destination addresses at the top are the most dominant part of the graph. One little cluster stands completely separate on the rightmost side. The cluster shows rules 19/0 and 194/0. They block multicast traffic, judging by the destination addresses. The third cluster of rules is on the bottom of the graph. This looks really messy. The cluster shows a lot of traffic targeting internal machines (pink nodes) that was blocked. These are mostly external connections that got blocked while trying to access internal machines.

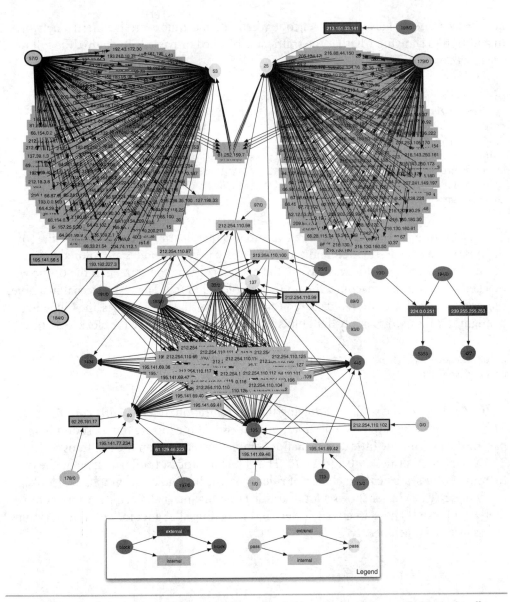

Figure 6-24   Firewall ruleset visualization based on recorded logs. Dark colors encode blocked traffic, and light colors encode passed traffic. (This figure appears in the full-color insert located in the middle of the book.)

Back to the two large, green clusters. These are some observations:

- The cluster on the left is associated with DNS traffic (port 53). What seems interesting is that two rules are responsible for letting the DNS traffic pass: 57/0 and 184/0. It seems that for 195.141.56.5 (on the left side in the graph), there was an exception defined in the ruleset. It is the only machine associated with DNS that is not linked to rule 57/0. It might be that 195.141.56.5 and 193.192.227.3 are external DNS servers and they are the only ones allowed to do a zone transfer over TCP port 53. It is odd that 193.192.227.3 is associated with the rule 57/0, 184/0, and also 191/0. Why did two different passes and a deny match?

  It turns out that rule 57/0 is allowing the internal DNS servers to externally resolve DNS names. This is the reason for the fan around that rule. 195.141.56.5 and 193.192.227.3 are external DNS servers that are used by the firewall itself for DNS lookups. It might make sense to reconfigure the firewall to do its lookups via the internal DNS servers. 193.192.227.3 shows up with the extra rule because it is the secondary DNS server for the domains hosted on this network. It therefore has to be able to execute zone transfers. This explains the special treatment of this machine.

- The cluster on the top right is associated with email traffic (port 25). Mail traffic was allowed outbound (dark green nodes) to a bunch of machines. However, one machine (on the top of the graph) was blocked by rule number 198/0. But its traffic was also passed by rule 179/0. What is this machine? The firewall ruleset does not show any exceptions for this machine. The only thing I was able to find was that the machine, based on a lookup of who owns this IP address, belongs to an Israeli company. There are no specific business relationships set up with Israel. It would be useful to take a look the email server logs to see what exactly this machine did.

If we shift our attention to the bottom part of the graph, we make the following observations:

- Two external Web servers (62.26.161.17 and 195.141.77.234) were accessed by internal machines. Why exactly two? These could be servers for software updates or maybe websites infected with malware. The next step is now to determine what those servers are.

- One internal machine tried to access an external Web server (61.129.46.223) but was not allowed. This is a good sign. The firewall ruleset seems to be strict, not just with regard to the traffic that is allowed inbound, but also regarding what is allowed outbound.

- There were a number of attempts to access internal servers on port 80. These are all the pink nodes in the middle of the graph that are connected to port 80.
- Apart from port 80, a number of other ports were probed and blocked: 1434, 113, 135, and 445. Port 1434 is used by Microsoft SQL Server, and port 113 is associated with the identd protocol, which is not used much anymore. All the other ports are associated with Microsoft Windows file sharing. These are likely worms trying to find new victims to infect.
- We seem to have two Web servers (212.254.110.102 and 195.141.69.46). They were successfully accessed on port 80.
- There was yet another machine (212.254.110.99) that got accessed on the Microsoft Windows ports 135, 137, and 445. The part that gives cause for concern is that this machine seems to also run a mail server (port 25). Looking a bit closer, we see a number of rules that actually blocked some of the traffic. We would need to look at the logs a bit closer to see what exact traffic was passed and what traffic was blocked.
- One concerning node is port 137. The traffic to this port was allowed by the firewall. This port is used by Windows file sharing, and this traffic should never be allowed over the Internet. We need to fix this hole and investigate whether any attacks have been successful over this hole.

This analysis of the firewall ruleset should not substitute for any other in-depth analysis of the rules themselves. However, as you saw, we were able to learn a lot about our rule-set, and in addition, we found a fairly significant bad hole in the ruleset through port 137 that is not blocked.

INTRUSION DETECTION SYSTEM SIGNATURE TUNING

Intrusion detection and prevention systems (IDSs and IPSs) are part of almost any defense in-depth architecture. They can provide a lot of insight into the corporate network and help us understand the posture and exposure of our networks. On the flip side, IDSs have a bad reputation because of the number of alerts these systems generate—and worse yet, they generate a lot of false positives. Over time, IDS technology has somewhat improved, and the problem of false positives has received a lot of attention. Modern IDSs apply different methods to try to get rid of the large number of false positives: verification against asset models, correlation with vulnerability data, and feeding the data into security information management (SIM) tools for cross-correlation with other log files and other additional information. However, even by applying all these approaches, the problem of false positives has not been completely solved. In fact, often you do not have the money, the resources, and the time to set up complicated security information management systems to help reduce the number of false positives. We still have to manually deal with the problem of false positives. The following lists shows a process that uses treemaps to analyze IDS alarms and reduces the number of false positives.

The generic IDS signature-tuning process looks like this:

1. Generate a treemap representation of your IDS alert log with one of the following hierarchies:
   - Source-based analysis: source address > destination address > signature name
   - Destination-based analysis: destination address > source address > signature name
   - Signature-based analysis: signature name > destination address > destination port

   The size of the boxes is configured to represent the frequency of the triples chosen (i.e., the hierarchy).

2. Based on the size of the individual boxes in the treemap, identify the most frequent triple. For example, in the source-based analysis, find the signatures that triggered the most between a specific source/destination pair. This comes down to choosing the largest box in the treemap.

3. Determine whether the traffic triggering the signature is a policy violation according to your security policy. Not every IDS signature looks for real attack instances. For example, signatures flagging ICMP traffic are considered a policy violation only in certain cases, depending on your specific environment and policies.

4. Check the network packets that triggered the signature to see whether the traffic matches the intention of the signature. For example, a signature looking for some type of Web attack should not be triggered by an email.

5. As an additional verification step, verify whether the target machines are actually vulnerable to the attack that was reported. An Apache Web server is unlikely to be vulnerable to a Microsoft Internet Information Server attack.

   At this point, there are two possible outcomes: You found a true positive, a real attack, or a false positive. If you found a false positive, you should go through these additional steps:

6. Eliminate these alerts from the graph to ease the next iteration of analysis steps.

7. Tune the IDS signature set. This is a tricky step and there are a few different ways to tune a signature:
   - The signature definition is wrong, and you can write a more specific one that still catches the attacks the signature was written for. Correct it. Make sure you share your findings with the community or your IDS vendor. They will appreciate it!

- The signature definition is correct and written at the right level of specificity. It is not possible to make the signature more precise. Tune the signature such that it won't trigger for the pairs of machines you identified.
- There are more, similar signatures that should be tuned the same way. Do it!
- Other alerts in the treemap originate in the same problem. Tune those signatures right away and clean up the treemap by filtering the alerts out.

8. Restart at Step 1 and go through the process until you end up with a manageable set of true positives that you can hand over to the incident response process.

SNORT ALERT DATABASE

Snort offers various ways of recording alerts. The simplest way is to use syslog. The logs are easy to collect and parse. However, the syslog records from Snort are not very expressive. They lack quite a few pieces of information. The alert log, which is a text-based log file, is a better solution if more details about an alert need to be collected. The problem with the alert log is that it is multiline. It is therefore not as easy to handle as the single-line syslog entries. The third and simplest method of collecting Snort alerts is in a database. You get all the information you need, and the data is easy to access and then parse. To configure Snort to log events in a MySQL database, edit your snort.conf file to contain this line:

```
output database: log, mysql, user=snort
password=password dbname=snort host=10.1.1.30
```

You have to set up the MySQL database and create the schema for the Snort alerts. You find the SQL statements to do so in the Snort distribution. After everything has been set up and you are logging data into the MySQL database, you can use the following command to extract alert information from the database:

```
mysql -s -u snort -ppassword snort -e 'SELECT
ip_src,ip_dst,tcp_dport
INTO OUTFILE 'out.csv' FIELDS TERMINATED BY ','
OPTIONALLY ENCLOSED BY '"' LINES TERMINATED BY '\n'
FROM iphdr,tcphdr WHERE
iphdr.sid=tcphdr.sid AND iphdr.cid=tcphdr.cid'
```

The output is written as a CSV file, out.csv. You can use this output directly for visualization.

IDS Signature Tuning Example

Let's walk through an actual example of tuning IDS signatures that applies this process. The very first step is to collect data for the analysis. This first iteration is going to be a source-based analysis, meaning that we will generate a treemap that uses a hierarchy of source address > destination address > signature name. The following command can be used to extract the information for the source-based analysis from the Snort MySQL database:

```
mysql -B -e "SELECT count(*),INET_NTOA(ip_src),INET_NTOA(ip_dst),
sig_name FROM event
LEFT JOIN signature ON signature=sig_id
LEFT JOIN iphdr ON (event.cid=iphdr.cid AND event.sid=iphdr.sid)
GROUP BY ip_src,ip_dst,sig_name" -u <user> -p<pass> snort
```

The query looks fairly complicated because Snort stores all the information about the alerts in multiple tables that need to be joined together. The previous command will generate tab-separated output that includes a header line. This makes it fairly easy to format the data as a TM3 file. The only thing you need to add is a second header line containing the data types for each of the columns:

```
Count    SIP      DIP      Name
INTEGER  STRING   STRING   STRING
1        12.149.87.130   213.144.137.88   ATTACK RESPONSES 403 Forbidden
2        12.154.254.96   213.144.137.88   SMTP RCPT TO overflow
```

Visualizing this information results in the treemap shown in Figure 6-25. The size of the boxes in Figure 6-25 is based on the count. Color has no significance at this point. We are interested in the frequency of the alerts and not any other property. Looking at Figure 6-25, we can identify hardly any signatures. Most of the boxes are illegible. However, two signatures stick out and need investigation. First, let's take a look at the WEB-MISC Transfer-Encoding: chunked alert that was triggered between 213.144.137.88 and 213.144.137.82. Both of these IP addresses are on the internal network. Most likely, this traffic is not an attack but a false positive. We should investigate this some more and then filter these instances from our data. In addition, if we are sure this is a false positive, we should define an exception in the IDS configuration to not trigger this signature anymore between these two machines. The next alert is WORMHOLE TCP traffic incoming. Let's step through the individual steps we discussed in the signature-tuning process to see whether this is a false positive. Table 6-1 shows the process steps and the individual decisions made.

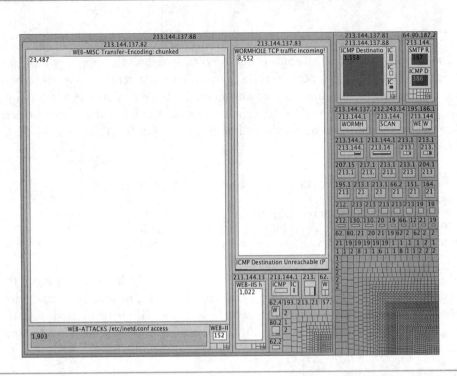

Figure 6-25   An initial attempt to visualize IDS alerts in a treemap. The configuration hierarchy is source address > destination address > signature name.

Table 6-1   Analysis of the WORMHOLE TCP Signature Based on the IDS Signature-Tuning Process

Step	Decision
3. Does the alert indicate a policy violation?	The WORMHOLE TCP signature is a custom signature that was written to specifically identify policy violations in the network. So yes, this indicates a policy violation.
4. Inspect the traffic which triggered the signature to verify the correctness of the alert.	We do not need to investigate the traffic that triggered this signature. The signature was written very generically, to look at traffic on certain ports. The traffic triggering the signature is clearly a policy violation.
5. Is the target indeed vulnerable to the attack?	The traffic that was identified is not necessarily an attack. The signature was only looking for traffic between specific port numbers. The traffic was not analyzed to identify an exploit of a certain vulnerability. Therefore, this step can be omitted.

The discussion in Table 6-1 shows that the WORMHOLE TCP signature is not a false positive. The traffic clearly signals a policy violation. To continue the signature-tuning process, I am going to filter all instances of the two signatures discussed.

We need to make sure that in parallel to the filtering we also initiate a response process. Ideally, there is a way to automate the response to this type of traffic. It might be possible to initiate an active response for every instance of these signatures. We need to be careful with this; but if our confidence in the signature is high enough, we should consider this approach.

After the elimination of the previous two alert instances, we should generate a new treemap and reiterate the signature-tuning process with one slight change. We will add color to encode the priority of an individual alert. Snort assigns a priority to every alert. We can retrieve the priority by expanding our SQL query from before:

```
mysql -B -e "SELECT count(*),INET_NTOA(ip_src),INET_NTOA(ip_dst),
sig_name,sig_priority
FROM event
LEFT JOIN signature ON signature=sig_id
LEFT JOIN iphdr ON (event.cid=iphdr.cid AND event.sid=iphdr.sid)
GROUP BY ip_src,ip_dst,sig_name" -u <user> -p<pass> snort
```

The output we need to format as a TM3 file again by using awk. Figure 6-26 shows the result of eliminating the two signatures we discussed above and using priority to color the boxes in the treemap.

Figure 6-26 can now be used to continue the signature-tuning process. Color can be used to keep an eye on the priority of the individual alerts. Dark red boxes encode high-priority alerts and should therefore get priority.

Instead of keeping the configuration hierarchy of the treemap as source address > destination address > signature name, you can reconfigure the hierarchy at any point in time to reflect any of the other configurations mentioned in the beginning of this section. You will be able to see different aspects of the signatures, which might help determine whether a signature is indeed a false positive.

Let's try another configuration to investigate the IDS alerts. The signature-based configuration can be useful to get a focus on the individual signatures. We therefore set the treemap hierarchy to signature name > destination address > destination port. The size of the boxes is the number of times this triple was seen. In other words, how many times did this signature trigger for a specific destination machine and service (i.e., port). We are going to change the color, too. Instead of showing the priority of the alerts, we are going to represent the number of distinct source addresses that have been seen. This helps identify attacks that originate from a broad set of sources versus ones that were specifically executed by a small number of sources. To get the necessary data out of the Snort database, use the following query:

```
mysql -B -e "SELECT count(*),sig_name,INET_NTOA(ip_dst),
tcp_dport,count(DISTINCT(sourceip))
FROM event
LEFT JOIN signature ON signature=sig_id
LEFT JOIN iphdr ON (event.cid=iphdr.cid AND event.sid=iphdr.sid)
LEFT JOIN tcphdr ON (event.cid=tcphdr.cid AND event.sid=tcphdr.sid)
GROUP BY sig_name,ip_dst,tcp_port" -u <user> -p<pass> snort
```

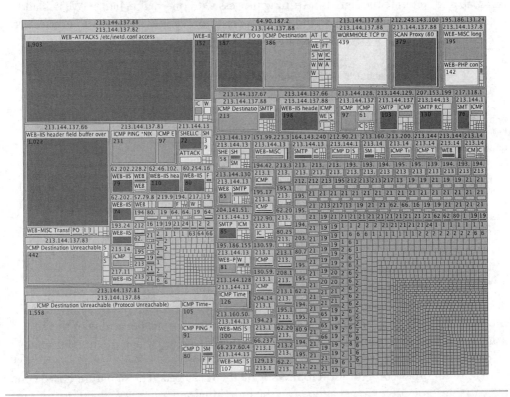

Figure 6-26 Treemap used for IDS signature tuning after eliminating some of the signatures and encoding the signature priority as the color of the boxes. (This figure appears in the full-color insert located in the middle of the book.)

Figure 6-27 shows a sample treemap that uses this information. Color is used to map the number of distinct sources that we extracted with the preceding above.

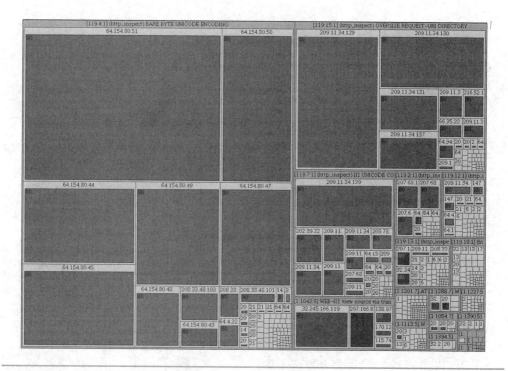

Figure 6-27 Treemap encoding IDS alerts. Size encodes the frequency of the alert triggering. Color encodes the number of distinct sources that triggered the signature. (This figure appears in the full-color insert located in the middle of the book.)

The green boxes in Figure 6-27 show signatures that were triggered by only a small number of sources. The red boxes indicate that a lot of distinct sources have triggered the signature. We can see in Figure 6-27 that all the alerts were triggered by traffic to port 80. Half of the alerts were generated because of the BARE BYTE UNICODE ENCODING signature. The other interesting finding in Figure 6-27 is that only a few signatures were triggered by multiple sources.

This example illustrates that a different treemap configuration provides yet another view on the data and reveals new properties and findings that can be used to filter the alerts and change the signature configuration of the IDS.

FIREWALL CROSS-CORRELATION MYTH

One of the myths in the field of analyzing IDS alerts is that the correlation of IDS alerts with firewall logs helps reduce false positives. Assume that an IDS generates an alert for an attack. Let's further assume that the firewall actually blocked the attack. The logical conclusion for this is that the IDS alert is a false positive. The attack could not be successful.

Let's take a closer look at this problem. Most attacks are using services that require TCP connections. For a TCP attack to execute code, it needs an established TCP session. The attack payload can only be sent after a TCP session is set up. In other words, a complete TCP handshake is necessary. For example, the Microsoft DNS RPC Management Vulnerability (CVE-2007-1748) attack requires that an attacker is able to open a TCP connection to the Windows RPC port. Assume the firewall indeed blocked this attack. This would mean that the firewall blocked the TCP handshake already. The attack payload cannot be sent by the attacker. In turn, there is no way that this attack could be seen on the wire.

There are only a few cases where this type of correlation is useful, and that is for UDP attacks. UDP is a stateless protocol, and there is no session setup. Most of the time, UDP attacks are single packet attacks. To weed out false positives, it is therefore useful to know whether the firewall blocked the attack.

A way to visualize these instances is by using treemaps as before. The color is assigned based on whether the firewall blocked or passed the connection. If blocked traffic was encoded in red, you can quickly find all the false positives in the treemap.

WIRELESS SNIFFING

Over the past few years, I have been attending DefCon, the largest hacker conference. During one of the days at the conference, I found myself sitting in the open area. This is where hackers show their latest hacking gear. It's among these guys that I had lunch—my laptop sitting next to me. It is hard to strike up a conversation with any of these people, so I opened my laptop and start playing around. Having nothing better to do, I realized that there was wireless Internet access. I happened to have Kismet[11] installed on my laptop, and just for fun I start recording some traffic. At first, I was not sure whether Kismet recorded some kind of a log. Fortunately, it did. Another 30 minutes later, I whipped

---

[11] www.kismetwireless.net

together some lines of shell code to parse the Kismet output, and I graphed the results with AfterGlow.

I discovered all kinds of interesting things with those graphs. The first one (see Figure 6-28), shows active machines on the network. For each of the machines, the link graph shows what SSID and channel the machine used to communicate. Color helps differentiate the machines with regard to how many different channels they used.

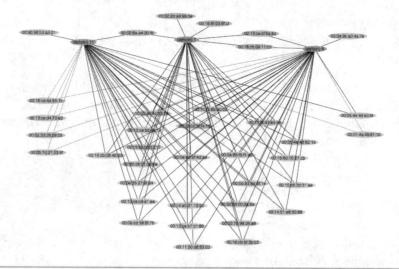

Figure 6-28 A link graph displaying the destination MAC addresses and the SSID, as well as the channel that the machines accessed. Blue nodes represent the SSID and channel. Machines are colored in green if they connected on a single channel, orange if they used two channels, and purple if they used all three channels on the wireless network.

ANALYZING KISMET LOGS

Kismet is a wireless sniffer. It puts your wireless access card into promiscuous mode and analyzes all wireless activity it can see. To start sniffing wireless network traffic, download and install Kismet. After you have configured it correctly, go ahead and start Kismet:

```
./kismet
```

This will bring up the Kismet interface and your machine is now recording wireless network traffic. You should then start seeing a set of log files in your Kismet directory. By default, there are four logs that Kismet writes:

- CSV: This file contains a list of all the machines that Kismet found communicating. It records the machine's IP along with all the parameters associated with that network, such as SSID or the channel.
- dump: The dump file is a PCAP file that contains the raw 802.11 frames captured on the wire.
- network: The network file contains a summary of all the networks that were found to offer wireless service.
- xml: The XML file contains the same information as the CSV file but in XML format.

The file that is of interest to us is the dump file. It records all the wireless traffic. To visualize the traffic, I am going to extract the source MAC address (i.e., the access point), the destination MAC address (i.e., the client), the channel, and the SSID from the capture file:

```
tcpdump -ennr Kismet-Sep-08-2007.dump |
grep "Probe Respone" | grep -v Retry |
perl -pe 's/.*DA:([^ ]*) SA:([^ ]*).*\((.*?)\).*CH: (\d*)/\1,\2,\3,\4/'
```

This command filters the Kismet captures to look at only probe responses. These are frames sent back from a wireless access point when it is probed for information. The probe responses contain the MAC address of the access point, the MAC address of the client that requested the information, and the SSID and the channel that was used for the communication. The output looks like this:

```
00:02:2d:84:c6:1e,00:0c:e6:00:04:66,meru-qq2,6
00:40:05:c5:cf:a1,00:0c:e6:00:04:66,meru-qq2,6
00:04:23:56:94:a8,00:0c:e6:00:04:66,meru-qq2,6
```

For the first graph, I am interested in the access points that are present. I am therefore using only the SSID, the channel, and the source MAC address for the graph. The result of visualizing this information is shown in Figure 6-29.

There are six access points in the network that Figure 6-29 represents. Each SSID has two access points (the pink nodes).

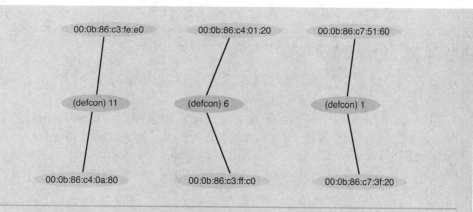

Figure 6-29   This figure shows the access points and the channel and SSID they are using.

After knowing how the infrastructure setup looks, I am interested in the clients. What access points are the clients connecting to? To generate a link graph for this information, I am going to extract the destination MAC, the SSID, and the channel information. The output I then format to look like this:

```
SMAC,SSID Channel
00:02:2d:84:c6:1e,meru-qq2 6
00:40:05:c5:cf:a1,meru-qq2 6
00:04:23:56:94:a8,meru-qq2 6
```

Before we can graph this, let's define an AfterGlow property file that colors the nodes based on how many access points a single client connects to. To do this, we need to look at the fanout of the source nodes. Here is a property file that does this:

```
variable=@col=qw{red green blue}
color.source=$temp=$sourceFanOut{$sourceName};
  $size=keys %$temp; return $col[$size-1];
```

The property file has only two properties. The first one defines a set of colors in an array (@col). The second line assigns a color to the source node based on the fanout of the node. The AfterGlow internal variable $sourceFanOut{$sourceName} contains a hash of all the neighbors of the current node ($sourceName). By using the $size variable, which counts the number of keys in this hash, we get a number that we can then use as an index into the $col array. We can now graph the log from before with the new property file:

```
cat wireless.log | afterglow.pl -c wireless.properties -t -f 1
```

You need to pass the -f parameter. It is used to filter nodes based on their fanout. The parameter is not really used, but you need to specify it in order to instruct AfterGlow to execute the code that evaluates the internal $sourceFanOut variable. The link graph generated with this configuration we have already seen in Figure 6-28.

Wireless traffic captures from a sniffer like Kismet can be used for visualization of other use-cases, too:

- Detect **new access points** by using a graph similar to the one in Figure 6-29. The graph shows source MAC addresses found in probe-response frames.
- Detect **rogue access points.** The difference between a neighbor access point (i.e., a new access point that is authorized to be on this network) and a rogue access point is that the neighbor access point is connected to the corporate LAN. A rogue access point is connected to a foreign LAN. You can determine whether an access point is connected to the corporate LAN by querying for the access point's MAC address on the LAN switches. If the MAC address does not show up in any of the MAC address tables, it is a rogue access point that is connected to some third-party network.

EMAIL DATA ANALYSIS

Email logs are a common security data source. A lot of people think of social network analysis in this context. However, many more use-cases can be addressed with email logs. This is especially true if not just the transaction or communication logs are considered, but also the log files from the email server itself. Those logs can prove very useful for a number of security use-cases.

In the following subsections, we take a look at email server logs to detect some common attacks and isolate the attackers. We then look at traffic characteristics to identify open email relays. Following that, we do some social network or clique analysis.

EMAIL SERVER ANALYSIS

To get a feeling for your email servers, it is a good idea to do some simple statistical analysis of the email transactions. The simplest form of analysis is to look at top senders, top recipients, and so on. Use simple bar charts for these visualizations. This analysis will give you some insights into who is sending email through your server. You might find some outliers that you would not have expected. By generating these graphs on a regular basis, you will be able to identify changes in email patterns. You'll see cases like senders that suddenly stop sending emails to recipients on your server. Why did they stop? Is there possibly a configuration problem with your mail servers? You might discover new entries in the top sender list. Why is that? Try to identify the root cause for these cases.

Instead of looking at top senders, recipients, or sender/recipient pairs, you can also look at the total amount and number of emails transferred (in terms of bytes, as well as in terms of emails themselves). You can use graphs similar to the ones used in the DoS analysis earlier. Does the average size of emails change? Why would that be? Are your employees receiving malware?

Email Attacks

By looking through the email server logs, you can identify a variety of anomalous or malicious activities. Adversaries use known attack patterns to probe and attack mail servers. If you look through the standard Snort ruleset, for example, you will find some of these patterns.

SMTP supports two commands to investigate email accounts hosted on a mail server. The first one is VRFY, which can be used to verify whether a given email address exists on the server. The second command is EXPN. This command can be used to expand an email address of a list of users to the individual users. Both of these commands can be used to for reconnaissance. You should not be seeing any of these commands under normal circumstances.

A simple way to analyze your Sendmail logs for this behavior is to run the following command and then visualize the outcome as a link graph:

```
egrep "EXPN|VRFY" maillog
```

This command retrieves all the EXPN and VRFY log entries. The following are some sample log entries:

```
Jun  2 03:02:31 ferengi sendmail[21129]: e5222V121129:
IDENT:root@[216.35.49.170]: VRFY 0000087648@seven.ch
```

```
Sep  2 08:02:40 ferengi sendmail[25097]: NOQUEUE:
CacheFlowServer@[208.169.102.230] did not issue MAIL/EXPN/VRFY/ETRN
during connection to Daemon0
```

The second type of log entry indicates that someone connected to the mail server without issuing any real command. We should treat these entries separately and analyze who caused a lot of these entries. This can easily be done in a bar chart. The other log entry shows someone trying to verify whether a specific email address exists on the server. We should take those entries and graph them. Here is how you extract the probing email address and the email address that got probed:

```
egrep "EXPN|VRFY" maillog | grep -v "did not issue" |
perl -pe "s/.*?(?: ([^ ]+\@[^ ]+) )+.*?/\1,\3/g" |
sed -e 's/IDENT://g'
```

Applying this command to my logs showed this other type of log entry:

```
Jun 17 14:52:11 ferengi sendmail[1327]: e5HDpe101327:
IDENT:insect@newton.zsmeie.torun.pl [158.75.61.4]: VRFY attack?
```

This is interesting. The mail server discovered by itself that someone was probing it. Back to the output from the preceding command. If we visualize the data with AfterGlow, we get a result like the one in Figure 6-30.

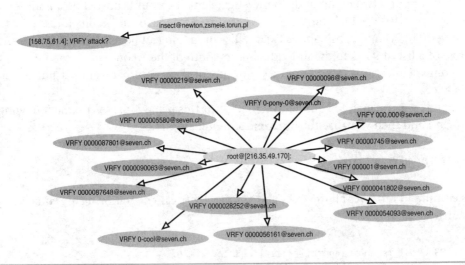

Figure 6-30   This link graph shows instances of VRFY commands executed against our mail server. Two offenders probed for multiple different email addresses.

As you can see in Figure 6-30, there are two offenders. One of them tried to check a set of different email addresses. It is not quite clear to me what the addresses are that were probed. They do not seem to make much sense. I would understand if the attacker was trying usernames to see whether they exist on the system. These users look like fairly random numbers. Nevertheless, we should make sure that this IP has not connected to our mail server and executed other commands or sent other emails.

We should go ahead and apply some other rules to the logs to find other potential problems. Single instances of violations are not necessarily interesting, but servers that tried multiple different attacks should be investigated more closely. Existing log analysis tools, such as logcheck,[12] are a great place to find more heuristics.

Open Relay

Every email server is responsible for specific domains or subdomains. Emails sent to an email address of those subdomains are accepted by the mail server and either forwarded to another mail server or stored locally. A mail server is said to be authoritative for a domain if it accepts emails for this domain. An **open relay** is an email server that accepts emails not just for the domains it is authoritative for, but also for any other domain. This setup can be abused by third parties to relay emails and therefore should be prevented. Here is a way to find whether your mail server was misconfigured and abused as an open relay.

In the following example, I am assuming that I am the administrator of the email server for the domain seven.ch. I am using Sendmail logs to detect whether someone was abusing my mail server to relay emails. To determine whether I am running an open relay, I have to see whether there was any email sent through the server, which originated from an email address that is not @seven.ch and was not sent to one of those addresses.

First we need to parse the email logs. I am using the Sendmail parser provided by AfterGlow. The command to parse the email records and extract the sender and the recipient is as follows:

```
cat maillog | sendmail2csv.pl "from to"
```

The output, which is formatted as CSV, can then be piped into AfterGlow to visualize it:

```
cat maillog | sendmail2csv.pl "from to" | ./afterglow.pl -t -c relay.properties
```

---

[12] http://logcheck.org/

The property file that I am using for AfterGlow looks like this:

```
color.source="red" if (($fields[0] !~ /seven.ch/) &&
  ($fields[1]!~/seven.ch/))
color.source="invisible"
color.target="orchid1" if (($fields[0]!~/seven.ch/) &&
  ($fields[1]!~/seven.ch/))
color.target="invisible"
```

I am trying to see whether there are any emails in the logs that were sent between email addresses that are not part of the seven.ch domain. I am using the invisible color to eliminate nodes that contain the domain name either as the sender or the recipient. This eliminates all the emails that were legitimately sent through my mail servers. Figure 6-31 shows the result of applying this configuration.

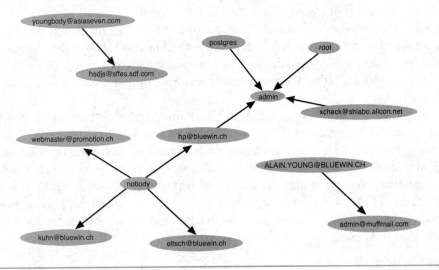

Figure 6-31 An email link graph that shows an email server that was abused as an open relay.

The graph in Figure 6-31 is not empty, which indicates that the mail server was abused as an open relay. We can see exactly which addresses were involved in the offense. However, we need to be careful. Some of the activities are false positives. The nodes that do not show an email address with a domain name (postgres, root, admin, and nobody, for example) are false positives. These are users on the mail server. They either received emails or were sending emails directly from the server. That is why they do not contain a domain name in the addresses. After discarding all this activity by filtering for only addresses that contain an @ sign, there are still two other emails that show a violation. It is probably time to verify the mail server configuration and make sure it does not allow relaying to prevent a future spam attack. If we indeed run an open relay, a spammer could abuse the server and send thousands of emails.

Large Email Delays

We can graph other aspects of the mail server logs, too. One of the fields in a mail server log is the delay. This field indicates how long an email was queued on the mail server after it was received from the sender and before it was forwarded to the recipient. There are multiple reasons why an email might be queued on a mail server for a longer period of time. For example, if the recipient email server is not available, the sender server is going to queue the mail locally, and it will retry periodically until it can either deliver the email or it has to give up. To visualize the email delays, we can use box plots. They are well suited to show distributions of numeric values. The information we need from the logs is the sender address and the delay:

```
cat maillog | sendmail_parser.pl "from delay" |
perl -pe 's/://g, s/,0+/,/g' > mail.csv
```

You might notice the substitution in the preceding command. This is used to convert the time (e.g., 00:12:22) into a decimal number so that it can be compared easily. By eliminating the colons, the time represents an integer that can be compared to a number. We also have to remove the leading zeros. Otherwise, the boxplot Perl code used later interprets the number as an octal number, which would mean that we had to compare octal numbers in the color assignments. To generate the box plot, we are using the boxplot.pl script from the AfterGlow[13] distribution:

```
cat mail.csv | boxplot.pl -f delays.png -l
```

The command instructs boxplot.pl to write the output to delays.png. Furthermore, the -l parameters generates a logarithmical scale for the x-axis. Figure 6-32 shows the result of visualizing my email logs.

If this generates too many records, we can use the -s switch for the box plot script that lets us define a minimum size for the delay. Any record with a smaller size than the one provided is disregarded. The emails were queued for various periods of time, up to multiple hours. Some of the senders caused multiple emails to be queued for a long time. We

---

[13] http://afterglow.sf.net

should go back and take a closer look at the senders that caused multiple emails to be queued for a long time. This might be people who send emails to lists of old and invalid recipients. Those email addresses might not exist anymore or something else might be wrong with those recipients. It could also be that these are spam emails that did not get delivered because the recipients do not exist anymore.

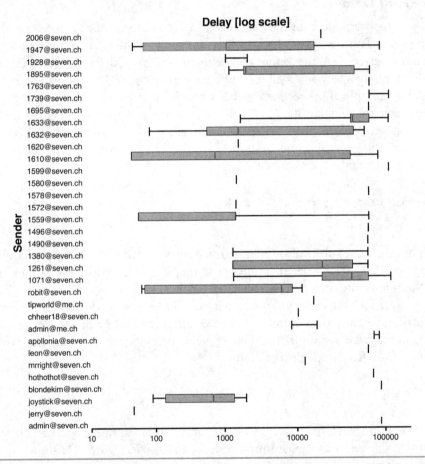

Figure 6-32   This box plot shows a number of email senders that caused the mail server to queue the email for a long time. The x-axis shows a log scale to better show the distribution of sizes.

Large Emails

Yet another analysis of email logs can be used to find people who are sending large emails. We can use the same concepts as before. The parsing command looks as follows to extract the sender, the recipient, and the size of the email:

```
cat maillog | sendmail2csv.pl "from to size" |
./afterglow.pl -c largeemails.properties
```

The AfterGlow configuration looks like this:

```
color.source="indianred" if ($fields[2] > 100000);
color.source="invisible"
color.event="lightcoral" if ($fields[2] > 100000);
color.event="invisible"
color.target="navy" if ($fields[2] > 1000000);
color.target="dodgerblue2" if ($fields[2] > 200000);
color.target="lightskyblue1" if ($fields[2] > 100000);
color.target="invisible"
```

This configuration colors different sized messages in different colors such that the larger the emails, the darker the nodes. Small emails are omitted so as to not clutter the graph too much. Figure 6-33 shows how a sample link graph looks with this configuration.

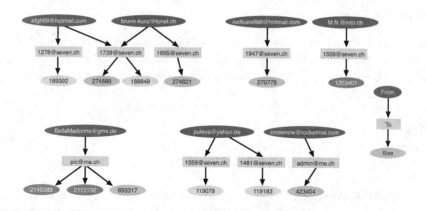

Figure 6-33 A link graph showing emails that are large in size. The sender, recipients, and the size of the large emails are visualized.

The link graph in Figure 6-33 shows various emails that were fairly large. Some of the emails are megabytes in size. Especially in the insider detection process (See Chapter 8, "Insider Threat"), we can use this information to determine people who are leaking information. Large emails are not pure text, but contain some attachments. If these emails are sent to noncompany addresses, this could help identify an information leak.

SOCIAL NETWORK ANALYSIS

Instead of analyzing the email server logs for specific properties, we can use them for social network analysis.[14] This can reveal communication patterns between different groups of people. There are two objectives for working with social network graphs:

- *Finding cliques of users:* Who are the popular users and with whom are they communicating? Do they just receive a lot of email or do they also send a lot? What is the role of the person sending and receiving the most email? Are emails mostly sent internally between employees or are they also sent to external recipients?

  Besides large cliques, are there people who do not communicate much? Do they only receive email or do they only send it? If they only receive it, maybe these are dead mailboxes? Should they be deleted? If they only send email, who are these users? Why do they not receive any email? Is someone abusing the mail server to just send emails?

- *Finding bridges:* People who connect or bridge two cliques deserve closer attention. These are likely "powerful" people who have multiple networks they are communicating with.

To do this analysis, I took an email log from a Sendmail server. The log contains about 8,500 entries, which translates into about 4,250 emails; each email generates 2 log entries. I used AfterGlow to generate a link graph of the email communications with the following command:

```
cat maillog | sendmail_parser.pl "from to" | sort |
uniq -c | awk -v OFS=, '{print $2,$1}' |
afterglow -t -c mail.properties | neato -Tgif -o mail.gif
```

This command first extracts the sender and recipient addresses from the email logs. The awk output simply rearranges the columns in my data and formats everything in CSV again so that it can be graphed with AfterGlow. Figure 6-34 shows the resulting communication graph.

The configuration file that I used to generate the email communication graph looks like this:

```
color="pink"
shape.source=triangle
label=0
```

---

[14] www.insna.org/

```
# Using the third column to size the nodes
size.source=$fields[2]
size.target=$fields[2]
maxNodeSize=1.5
sum.source=1
sum.target=1
```

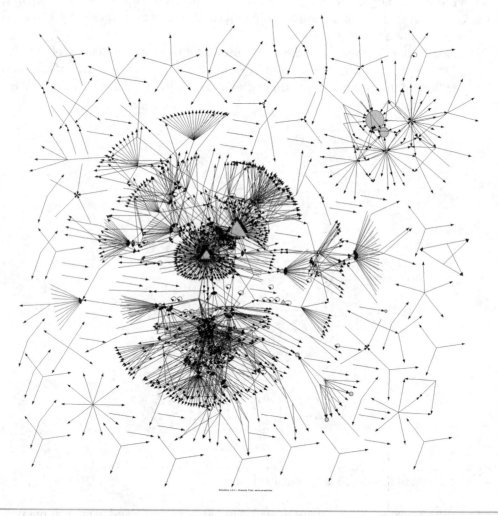

Figure 6-34   Email communication graph showing cliques of users.

The configuration instructs AfterGlow to use the number of emails sent between a sender/recipient pair as the size of the source and target nodes. The size is accumulative (`sum.source=1` and `sum.target=1`). The communication graph in Figure 6-34 is fairly messy, although it only consists of 2,200 nodes. I had to turn labels off (`label=0`) to not clutter the entire graph with labels.

Even though the graph is a bit messy, we can see some clear cliques and some small groups of people that are not communicating much. It is hard to further analyze this graph without interactivity.

To get a better understanding of the communication patterns, I tried to graph only a subset of the emails. You can see the result in Figure 6-35. I limited the number of emails to only 2,000, and instead of using `neato` to graph the result, I used `circo`, which generates a different layout.

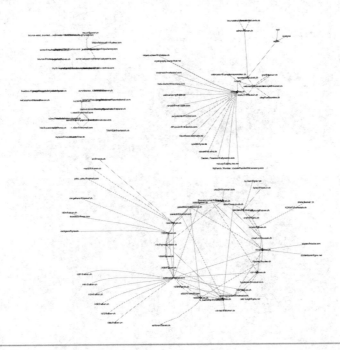

Figure 6-35   A smaller email sample visualized with circo.

The output in Figure 6-35 is hard to read. The labels are small and overlap at many places. However, the graph can be used to understand the big picture: It shows two large cliques and a set of individual communications on the top left. The cliques could be further analyzed based on the objective introduced a bit earlier—who are the popular users and so on. I am going to focus on the nodes on the top left, to work on the second objective. I therefore generated Figure 6-36, which only shows the emails that do not belong to the large clique. To filter the cliques, I used a graphics program[15] that allowed me to open DOT files. I then selected all the nodes in the cliques and eliminated them. It is nontrivial to automate this process. As you can see, this is where interactive visualization is of great help.

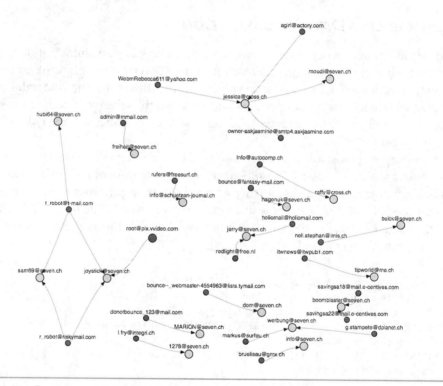

Figure 6-36   Email communications without the large cliques. Red nodes are external domains, and blue nodes are emails hosted on this mail server.

You can see multiple email addresses that only received emails. It looks like a lot of the email addresses hosted on this server only receive emails (blue nodes). Only one of them (jessica@cross.com) seems to be an active email that not just receives but also sends emails. The ones on the left side could be dead email accounts that still receive emails from mailing lists. There are more instances of the same all over the graph. You should

---

[15]   www.omnigroup.com/applications/omnigraffle/

put these email addresses on a watch list and see whether they show up as senders over the next weeks. If not, they are possibly dead ones and can likely be removed.

In conclusion, the analysis of social networks has been researched for a long time, and the visualization of such is a fairly hard job, as you can see with the link graphs in this section. Even a relatively small number of emails can render a graph fairly illegible.

VULNERABILITY DATA VISUALIZATION

When we talked about security data sources, we had a look at static information, such as processes running on a system or a machine's open ports. Another type of static information associated with a host is its vulnerabilities. If we know the vulnerabilities associated with machines on our network and we know the severity of each of the vulnerabilities, as well as the business value of the machines, we can assess the risk posture of our network.

For the purpose of visualizing vulnerability data, I am not going to start a discussion of risk. Take a look at Chapter 7, "Compliance," for a more in-depth discussion of risk. To visualize vulnerability information, we have to look at output from a vulnerability scanner. I used Nessus[16] to scan some machines on my network. The output from the scan I then saved as an NBE file, which is Nessus's default file format. These are some sample log entries of an NBE file:

```
timestamps|||scan_start|Mon May  5 21:03:41 2008|
timestamps||192.168.0.10|host_start|Mon May  5 21:03:42 2008|
results|192.168.0|192.168.0.12|ssh (22/tcp)
results|192.168.0|192.168.0.12|ssh (22/tcp)|10330|Security Note|An ssh
server is running on this port\n
results|192.168.0|192.168.0.12|http (80/tcp)|11213|Security Note|
\nSynopsis :\n\nDebugging
...
CVSS Base Score : 2 \n(AV:R/AC:L/Au:NR/C:P/A:N/I:N/B:N)\n\n
...
```

You can see that there are different types of output rows. The **timestamps** rows contain information about the timing of the scan: when was it started, how long it took, and so on. The **results** entries are more interesting. You can see that they call out the network that was scanned, the machine that was found, the port that was found open, and then

---

[16] www.nessus.org

the vulnerability found on that port. Along with the vulnerability, there can be a number of additional fields, as you can see in the last record. I erased some of the output to print it. The original entry contained much more information about the vulnerability, such as a verbose description of the vulnerability or a remediation recommendation. All of that information is not necessary for our purposes. What we are interested in is the CVSS score. The Common Vulnerability Scoring Scheme (CVSS)[17] is a standardization effort that assigns a set of scores to each vulnerability. The overall base score is broken down into individual components (the cryptic string in the preceding output). We are interested in the overall base score only, not all the additional data.

Scanning a network of 4,000 hosts creates a file that contains around 20,000 entries that record open ports and vulnerabilities. This is a lot of data. Treemaps are a visualization method that is well suited to this amount of data.

To visualize the NBE output, we need to write a parser that converts the pipe-delimited data into a TM3 file and filters out the unnecessary information. Here are a couple of lines of shell script that can help:

```
grep "^results" output.nbe | perl -naF'\|' -e 'chomp(@F);
$F[6]=~s/.*CVSS Base Score\s*:\s*([\d\.]+).*/\1/;
if ($F[6]!~/^[\d\.]+$/) {$F[6]="";} $F[7]=""; $,="    "; print @F; print "\n"'
```

This script is a quick-and-dirty way to parse the output. You can see that first I get rid of all the entries that are not **results** rows. The Perl code reads the input and splits it on the pipes. The input lines are then available in the @F array. The code further eliminates all the unnecessary information in the seventh field ($F[6]). The output is a tab-delimited row. Store this result as a TM3 file and add the necessary headers. This prepares the data for the treemap visualization. Here are some sample lines from the TM3 file:

Dummy	Network	DestIP	Service	NessusID	Severity	Risk
STRING	STRING	STRING	STRING	STRING	STRING	FLOAT
Results	10.50.2	10.50.2.16	general/tcp 11933	Security	Note	0
Results	10.50.2	10.50.2.17	general/tcp 11933	Security	Note	0
Results	10.50.2	10.50.2.11	domain (53/tcp)			

Note that the last record is valid, although it does not contain any information past the Service column. For our visualization, this is going to be missing data, but that is not a problem. Armed with this data, we can now visualize the vulnerability posture of our

---

[17] www.first.org/cvss

network. Let's take a look at two different ways of visualizing vulnerability data. I start with an analysis of the current risk posture based on the vulnerability scan data. In a second part, I show how you can use multiple snapshots to represent deltas in the security posture.

RISK-POSTURE VISUALIZATION

The first set of visualizations help us analyze the current risk posture of a network and its hosts.

I am going to load the Treemap tool (see Chapter 9) with the data generated earlier. The configuration hierarchy I choose as Service > DestIP. This shows each service and the machines that offer this service (i.e., that have that port open). In addition, the size and color of the boxes are set to represent the number of vulnerabilities on each machine. Figure 6-37 shows how this visualization looks.

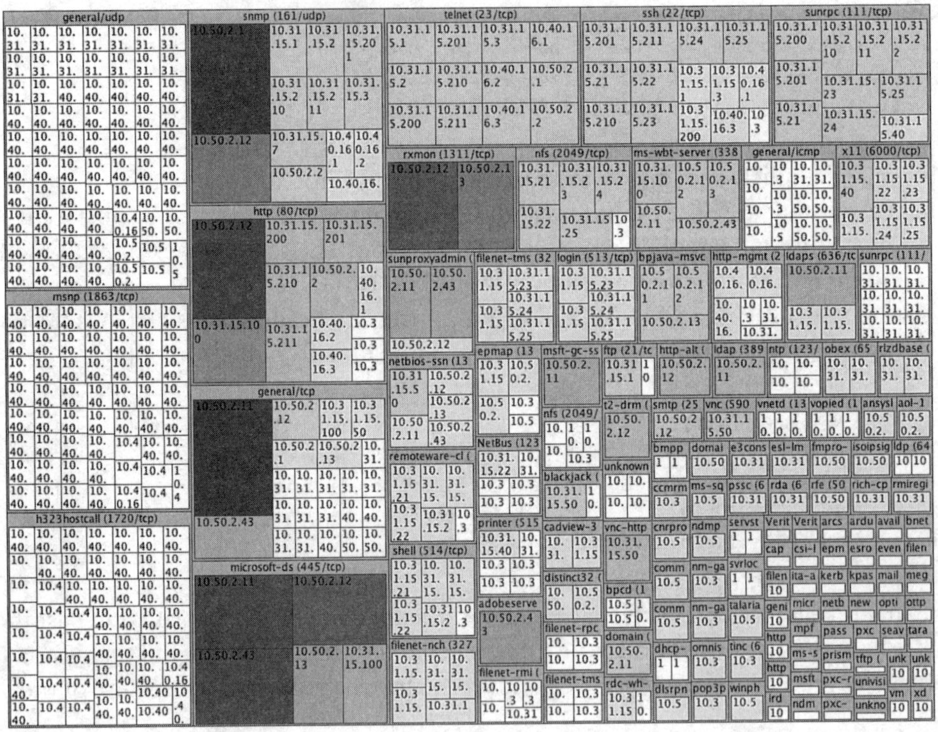

Figure 6-37   A vulnerability-posture analysis using a treemap. Color and size of the boxes both encode the number of vulnerabilities found on a host.

Figure 6-37 shows that there are a number of machines that have vulnerabilities associated with SNMP, HTTP, Microsoft DS, rxmon, and general TCP ports. This helps us understand which ports or services cause the most exposure to our network. We could then go ahead and instruct the firewall to block some of those ports to reduce the exposure of those vulnerabilities.

A second visualization that we should generate at this point is one the uses a hierarchy of DestIP > Service. This treemap helps with identifying machines that expose the most vulnerabilities (see Figure 6-38).

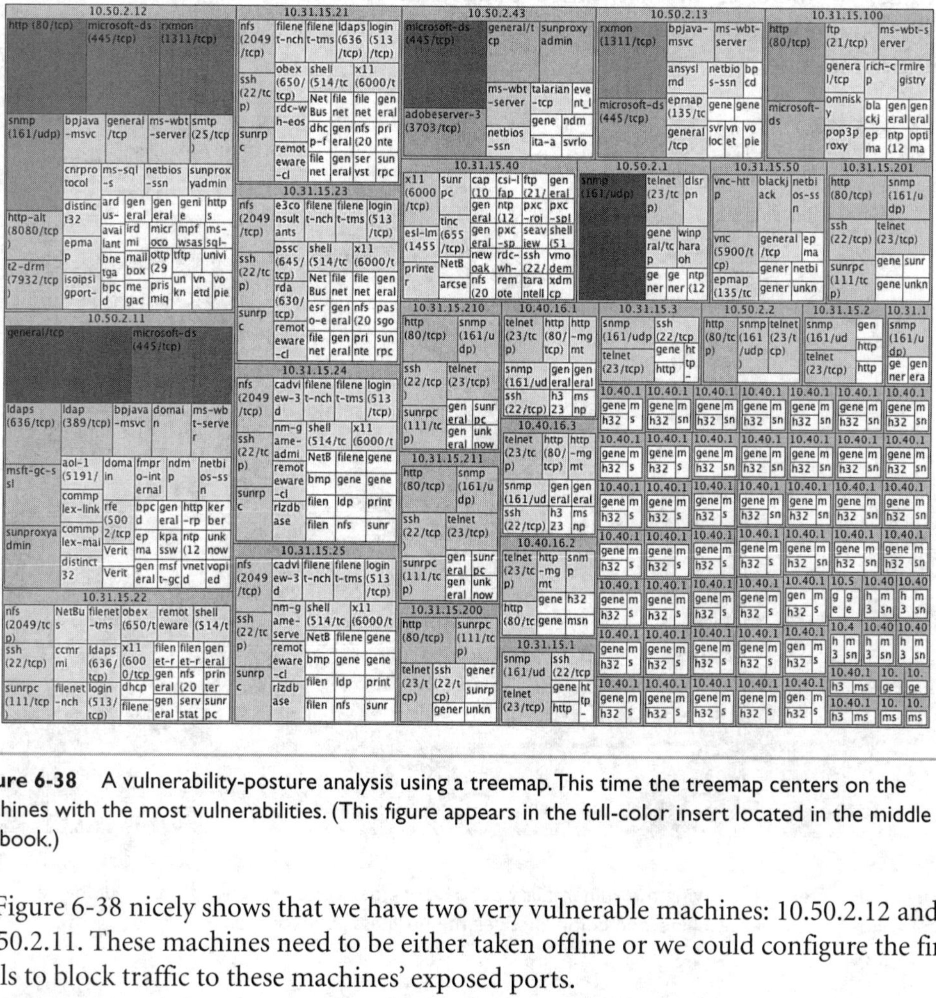

Figure 6-38 A vulnerability-posture analysis using a treemap. This time the treemap centers on the machines with the most vulnerabilities. (This figure appears in the full-color insert located in the middle of the book.)

Figure 6-38 nicely shows that we have two very vulnerable machines: 10.50.2.12 and 10.50.2.11. These machines need to be either taken offline or we could configure the firewalls to block traffic to these machines' exposed ports.

One question that comes up when looking at a graph like the one in Figure 6-38 is how critical those machines are. Are these test machines or are they critical production machines. If they are just test machines, we can probably take them offline. If they are critical production machines, we have to find another way of protecting them. I therefore include the business value of the machines in the visualization by adding an extra data column to the original data. The new column shows the business value for each machine. I hope there is an asset inventory that has a mapping of machines to their business value. This mapping is a manual process that needs input from the business process owners (see Chapter 7).

Figure 6-39 visualizes the data with added information about the business value per machine. The hierarchy of the treemap is such that it shows Service > DestIP. The size of the boxes represents the number of vulnerabilities and the color encodes the business value per machine.

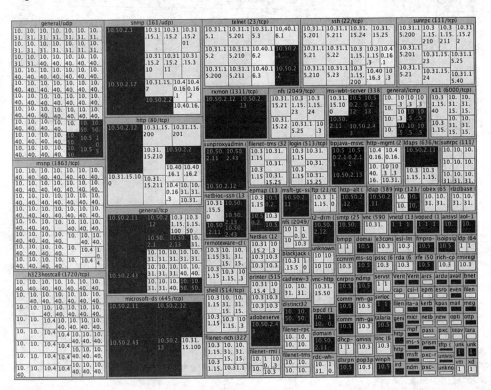

Figure 6-39   Treemap showing the vulnerability posture of a network. Size encodes the number of vulnerabilities found per machine, and color encodes the business value of such.

Figure 6-39 looks similar to Figure 6-37 except that now color encodes the business value of machines. Unfortunately, there are a number of large, dark boxes. This means that there are a large number of exposed vulnerabilities on business critical machines.

Although it is interesting to know how many vulnerabilities are exposed by each machine, it is more useful to know what risk is associated with the vulnerabilities. The data we are working with contains a risk field.[18] To incorporate the risk into the vulnerability visualization, I am going to keep the treemap hierarchy as Service > DestIP. In addition, the business value of the machine is encoded in the size of the boxes, and risk is shown as color. Figure 6-40 shows the results in the treemap.

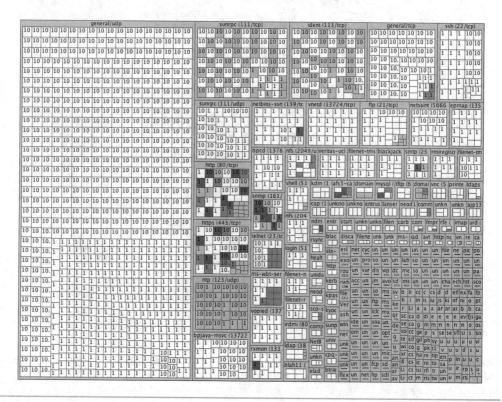

Figure 6-40 Treemap encoding the asset value as the size and the risk of the vulnerabilities as the color of the boxes. The hierarchy used in the treemap is Service > DestIP.

---

[18] Note that the risk in the data is not necessarily the business risk, but merely the CVSS definition of risk associated with a vulnerability. The overall risk would have to take into account the business value of the assets and the information hosted on them.

Figure 6-40 shows an interesting picture. We can see that most of the risk is associated with HTTP and HTTPS. Some of the problems surround SNMP, and a few smaller problems are scattered in other protocols. This treemap clearly shows that we should focus our mitigation efforts on the Web vulnerabilities.

To get yet another view on the data, let's reconfigure the hierarchy to get a destination-centric view again (see Figure 6-41).

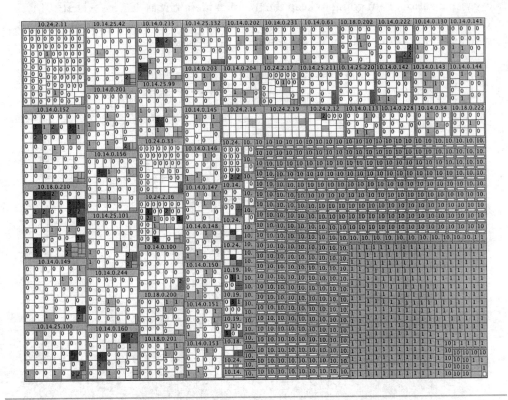

Figure 6-41   Destination-centric view of the vulnerability posture, encoding both the asset value (size) and the risk (color) of each vulnerability in the treemap. The hierarchy used in the treemap is DestIP > Service. (This figure appears in the full-color insert located in the middle of the book.)

Figure 6-41 shows an interesting finding. It is not the two machines identified earlier that are exposing the highest risk to our network. It is a single machine: 10.18.0.210. This machine exposes a number of very high-risk vulnerabilities (dark red boxes) and is of high value (large boxes).

While we are working with this treemap, we can try to filter the data down to the most critical machines and the vulnerabilities that expose the highest risk. Figure 6-42 shows only vulnerabilities that have a risk higher than 0 and assets that have a business value greater than 6.

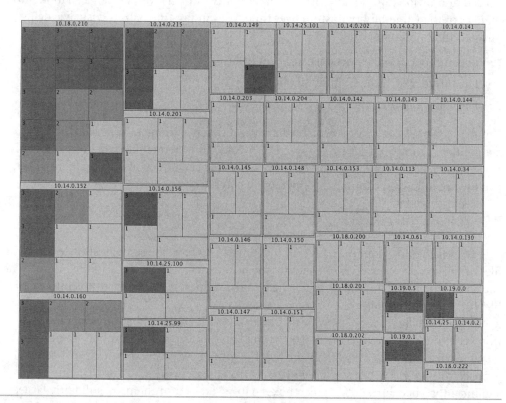

Figure 6-42 Treemap showing only the highest risk vulnerabilities on the most critical business machines. Color and the box labels encode the risk of the vulnerabilities.

Figure 6-42 is a view that can help prioritize remediation efforts. If we generate this exact treemap on a regular basis, we can potentially show some progress and reduce the number of machines that expose high-risk vulnerabilities over time.

We could generate many more visualizations based on vulnerability scan data, especially if we include some other pieces of information from the vulnerability scanner, such as the confidence about a reported vulnerability.

RedSeal (www.redseal.net) is a commercial product that takes vulnerability visualization to the next level by combining vulnerability data with network topology and access control lists. The product also uses treemaps to let the user explore different settings. The interactive nature of the product helps you quickly identify and report on the most vulnerable hosts in the network.

VULNERABILITY-POSTURE CHANGES

Instead of only looking at static risk or vulnerability information, we can also look into changes of the vulnerability posture over time. We can use treemaps to visualize deltas in various vulnerability metrics:

- The number of open ports per network or host
- The number of vulnerabilities per host
- The change in total risk per network or host

Figure 6-43 shows a sample treemap where the difference in the number of a host's vulnerabilities is compared for two consecutive weeks. To generate the data needed for this graph, you need to record the vulnerability scores for each week in a separate file. Then you use the following command to merge the two files:

```
merge_logs.pl week1.csv week2.csv | awk -F, -v OFS=, '{print $0,$3-$2}'
```

A weakness of this command is that it assumes you have the same hosts listed in both files. If the second week does not show some hosts, they will not show in the output. The awk command calculates the delta for the two risk values. If you convert this into a TM3 file, you can then visualize the data with Treemap.

Big boxes in Figure 6-43 show hosts that exposed a large number of vulnerabilities this week, and red boxes encode hosts that had an increase in the number of vulnerabilities since the last week. The darker the red, the more new vulnerabilities have been exposed this week. We can see in Figure 6-43 that the network's posture has improved significantly. There are a lot of green boxes. However, a lot of them are still fairly large, showing that they still expose a lot of vulnerabilities. It is even more concerning to find two large red boxes on the top left of the treemap. These machines have a high number of vulnerabilities this week, and they also show a large number of new vulnerabilities compared to the week before.

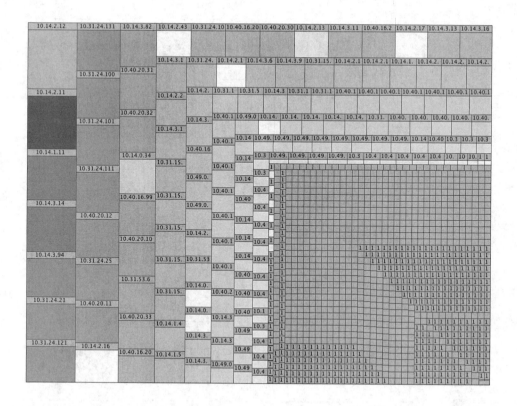

Figure 6-43 Treemap encoding the difference in the number of vulnerabilities per host measured for two consecutive weeks. Color encodes the delta between this and last week. Size encodes this week's score. (This figure appears in the full-color insert located in the middle of the book.)

Viewing the progress on a per-host basis can be important to address individual issues. If a higher-level posture assessment is necessary, we can reconfigure the treemap hierarchy to show the network or the subnet, rather than the individual hosts. Figure 6-44 shows such a network-centric view. The label of the boxes represents the delta in vulnerability counts. This gives a quick overview of which networks have improved over the past week and which ones still have a lot of vulnerabilities. The networks occupying large areas in the treemap need to be taken care of.

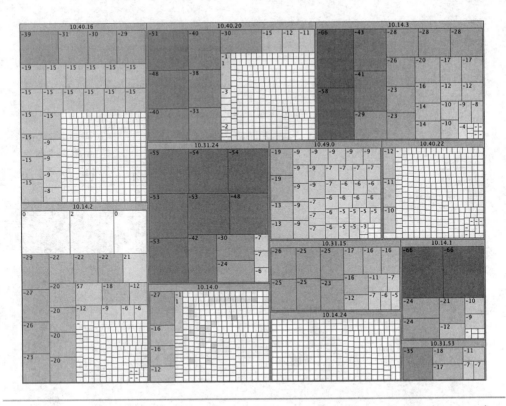

Figure 6-44   Treemap encoding the difference in the number of vulnerabilities per network measured at two consecutive weeks. Color encodes the delta between this and last week. Size encodes this week's score. (This figure appears in the full-color insert located in the middle of the book.)

This section about vulnerability data visualization has shown that it is possible to not only visualize a large amount of data on a small space, but it also showed that static information, rather than log entries, can be well suited to visual representation.

SUMMARY

This is the first of three chapters that are focused on specific visualization use-cases. Perimeter threat is a topic that greatly benefits from visualization. I picked a few subareas in the perimeter threat area to show how visualization can help to analyze problems and gain insight into a network's status.

The chapter started by discussing a number of use-cases based on traffic flows. We talked about how to find anomalies in communication patterns, detect worms in mobile networks, assess DoS attacks, find bots in the network, and finally, visualize network traffic to help identify security policy violations.

Firewall data is similar to traffic flows. In addition to the information about communicating hosts, the data indicates whether traffic was passed or blocked. Based on the information visualization process, we stepped through the analysis of data from a firewall log to find significant offenders. A section about firewall data analysis showed how a firewall ruleset could be analyzed.

False positives are an old topic in the world of intrusion detection systems. The section on tuning IDS signatures showed a new way of dealing with this old problem. We used treemaps to reduce the number of false positives in an efficient way.

Wireless network captures were our next topic. Rogue access points and wireless client communication patterns were the focus for this section. Link graphs helped us understand which access points are serving information to which clients.

We then left the realm of security devices and took a look at an example of an application log. We used email logs to analyze various properties of emails. We then used the email server logs to identify a mail server that was abused as an open relay. The second half of the section about email log analysis was concerned with visualizing email communications and showed how difficult it is to visualize social networks.

The chapter ended with a set of treemaps that we used to visualize the vulnerability posture of a network. By taking vulnerability scans from Nessus, we were able to not just visualize the risk exposure of a network but also communicate the changes in the network posture over time.

Compliance

For the past few years, the word *compliance* has been showing up all over the security landscape. Product brochures are filled with buzzwords and promises to help companies comply with the regulation of the day. Although I agree that there is a lot of hype around the topic, the compliance wave has caused some interesting and good progress in the computer security arena. Companies are being forced to invest money in security and compliance. Significant monetary motivations are involved. Noncompliance can result in fines and, in some cases, even time behind bars for company executives.

During the first quarter of 2007, a set of terms—*governance, risk,* and *compliance* (GRC)—started showing up. In a lot of cases, it even replaced the traditional compliance message of security companies. At first, I was confused. What is the new hype all about? All of the three pillars of GRC were well known to all of us. Years ago, before GRC even came along, I was working on governance initiatives. We walked up and down ISO 17799 (more about that later) to define governance interfaces and requirements. We made sure that companies provided the organizational structures and processes to ensure that IT supported and enabled the organization's strategies and objectives. Risk has been talked about for years, too. Although nobody has the magic formula that could be applied to actually measure IT security risk, there are numerous risk management approaches that are applied across the security industry. And finally, for at least the past couple of years, compliance has been on everybody's charter, too. Sarbanes-Oxley and HIPAA are part of our daily business and drive a lot of our decisions. That is why I was confused about the new GRC initiative. The only new thing is the clear focus on the business level. The governance aspect is concerned with aligning the business with regulatory laws. Risk is used to not just look at the downside, meaning how to minimize the risk, but more and more also for the upside. How does the risk have to be managed for new business initiatives? And finally, compliance is utilized to align and drive operational efficiency in a proactive way, rather than the traditional tactical approach of fixing deficiencies.

It is really nothing new. It is mostly a repackaging of older initiatives to try and marry them together, generating a more cohesive framework that can be used to manage information security or information technology in general.

Today, it is not an option for a company whether to comply with regulations. Regulations are written into law or are demanded by industry bodies. For example, the Bank for International Settlements put forward the Basel II framework, which banks around the world have to comply with it. What all these developments bring with them is an increased demand for data, audit records, and processes. Whereas 15 years ago you managed your compliance efforts with spreadsheets, you now need complex systems that help track, document, monitor, and audit all aspects of your compliance landscape. The trend continues in the direction of not just managing all your compliance processes with the implementation of work flows, but the trend clearly goes into the direction of measurement. *Business process management* and *business intelligence* are two key terms that you will find a lot in this context. This is exactly where visualization will also find a more and more prominent home. There are thousands of audit points, business metrics, risk factors, and so on that have to be analyzed in concert.

This chapter shows how visualization can be applied to compliance and risk management. I start out by describing the landscape of regulations, control frameworks, policies, and so on. After establishing the basics, I discuss business process management to focus the compliance work on the business. This is the basis for working on compliance monitoring, which needs to be a business-driven process. Risk management and the topic of how to visualize risk rounds out the more theoretical part of this chapter. At the end of the chapter, a discussion of two broader compliance use-cases shows how compliance visualization is more than visualizing risk or controls but can be used for auditing separation of duties and database applications.

POLICIES, OBJECTIVES, AND CONTROLS

The focus of this chapter is on the compliance and risk aspect of GRC, while still keeping governance concepts in mind. What exactly is *compliance?* It has to do with setting standards and then consequently implementing and adhering to them. Figure 7-1 shows a diagram of how compliance works. The diagram uses a number of concepts and terms that need some further definitions. They especially need definition because they are used slightly differently in many places. Sometimes they are even used in contradictory ways.

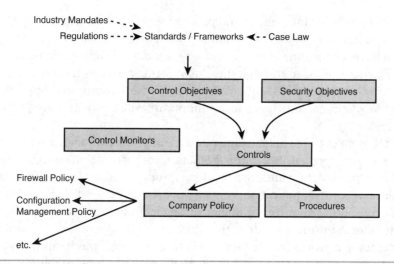

Figure 7-1 Compliance framework showing the relationship between control objectives, policies, procedures, controls, and control objective monitors.

Regulations are the driving factor in this process. They can be imposed by different entities. They can stem from the federal government or a specific industry. Because regulations are fairly nonspecific, there needs to be an entity that defines more precisely what has to be implemented and what the standards of measurement are. The regulation's requirement to apply due care is not enough. One additional input that influences standards and frameworks is case law. This is especially true for regulations enforced on a federal level, such as Sarbanes-Oxley.

The standards and frameworks define *control objectives*. These are the guidelines that need to be followed. An example is the requirement to review new user account requests. It does not define how this has to be done. To comply with these *control objectives*, a company develops a set of *controls*. Controls outline a way that the control objective is going to be addressed. They go into detail on how the implementation has to be done. For example, new user account requests have to be reviewed and approved before the account is generated to ensure that only authorized users have access to critical systems. The other input for controls is company *security objectives*. These are things that the company wants to implement and are not covered explicitly in a standard or framework.

To implement the controls, *policies* and *procedures* are put in place to implement, update, and monitor the controls. An example of a policy is an acceptable use policy, which covers the rules for appropriate use of computing facilities. A remote access policy covers the connection to the company's network from remote machines, be that from home or from laptops used on the road, and so on. Procedures are exact ways of implementing the control.

In parallel to defining the policies and procedures, *control monitors* should be put in place. These monitors can be used to monitor the controls in real time, or, in other cases, can be used to check the state of effectiveness of the controls on a periodic basis. Internal control deficiencies detected through these monitoring activities should be reported upstream and corrective actions should be taken to ensure continuous improvement of the system. As you might anticipate, the monitors are where visualization plays an important role.

Let us look at an example to help illustrate and make the compliance framework pieces somewhat more comprehensible. Our hypothetical company defines a security objective that states that the risk of unauthorized and inappropriate access to the organization's relevant financial reporting applications or data has to be minimized. This means restricting access to IT computing resources by implementing identification, authentication, and authorization mechanisms. To address this objective, multiple controls are defined. One of them is that if passwords are used for authentication (other mechanisms could be implemented instead of passwords), the organization should have established rules for password management and syntax. The technical implementation is not defined by the control, but an auditor can use the control to verify whether the objective is met. The bottom layer, the policy, is the setup of the operating system or application feature to enforce this control. It might, for example, define that an 8-character password has to be used, the password change interval is 30 days, and old passwords cannot be recycled for a year. The policy further details that on UNIX systems the implementation is done through the pluggable authentication module (PAM). The procedure in this case outlines who the people are that enforce these settings and how exactly they go about implementing them.

Now that we have an understanding of the basic concepts of compliance, we can look at the world of regulations and standards.

REGULATIONS AND INDUSTRY MANDATES

Conducting business as a company is a fairly well-regulated process. This is especially true for companies that are traded on the stock market. They need to comply with all kinds of regulations. In the United States, the Security and Exchange Commission (SEC) oversees publicly traded companies. But it is not only the government that regulates companies. Industry groups also impose regulations and requirements that companies have to follow if they want to do business with them. One such example is the Payment Card Industry (PCI) data security standard or the financial industry's Basel II. Noncompliance with these regulations can have various levels of consequences. In some cases, fines are imposed. In others (for example, where statutes are violated), executive management could be sentenced to jail.

Table 7-1 lists some of the most important regulations and gives a quick overview of the regulatory landscape. Companies have to comply with many more regulations than the ones mentioned in the table. The ones shown here are relevant for a broad set of companies. The table starts with regulations that are important for companies that are conducting business in the United States. Regulations that are important for companies doing business outside of the United States are listed at the end of the table. Table 7-2 lists industry regulations that mandate security requirements for companies that are doing business in specific areas.

Table 7-1   The Most Important Regulations

Abbreviation	Regulation	Sector	Short Description
HIPAA	Health Insurance Portability and Accountability Act	Health care	HIPAA is legislation that governs the security and confidentiality of identifiable, protected health information associated with the provisioning of health benefits and payment of health-care services. Requirements include, improved efficiency in health-care delivery by standardizing electronic data inter-change, and protection of confidentiality and security and privacy of health data through setting and enforc-ing standards.
			Internet: www.hhs.gov/ocr/hipaa/
SOX	Sarbanes-Oxley Act	Publicly traded companies	The SEC imposes the SOX act on all publicly traded companies in the United States. Section 404 of SOX addresses internal control over financial reporting, with the goal of improved corporate accountability. It encompasses every aspect of an organization that has access to financial information. SOX mandates the use of a recognized internal control framework to ensure compliance and security. It makes specific references to the recommendations of the Committee of Sponsoring Organizations (COSO) framework.
			SOX is not a standard and therefore does not define actual controls. A significant part of passing a SOX audit has to do with negotiations between the auditor and the company.
			The Public Company Accounting Oversight Board (PCAOB) has the oversight over SOX auditors. It releases an audit standard that contains guidelines for performing an audit of internal controls and provides important directions on the scope and approach of auditors.
			Internet: www.sox-online.com/sec.html

continues

Table 7-1 The Most Important Regulations (Continued)

Abbreviation	Regulation	Sector	Short Description
GLBA	Gramm-Leach-Bliley Act	Financial institutions	GLBA is a federal statute aimed at limiting the unauthorized use or disclosure of personal information by financial institutions. Requirements include the following: • Notify customers of their privacy policies. • Provide an "opt-out" mechanism for data sharing programs. • Protect against threats to personal information. Internet: www.ftc.gov/privacy/privacyinitiatives/glbact.html
FISMA	Federal Information Security Management Act	Government	FISMA is a United States federal law. The act was meant to bolster computer and network security within the federal government and affiliated parties by mandating yearly audits. The act is composed of many substandards and regulations, among them FIPS-199, NIST 800-53, and so on. Internet: http://csrc.nist.gov/sec-cert/index.html
J-SOX	Financial Instruments Exchange Law	Publicly traded companies	J-SOX is the informal name for a new legislative framework of internal controls over financial reporting (ICFR) that falls within the scope of the Japanese Financial Instruments and Exchange Law. The framework is modeled after the U.S. Sarbanes-Oxley Act. J-SOX requires the management all listed companies in Japan to provide an assessment of its internal control over its financial reporting. The regulation also requires that the registrant obtain an auditor's opinion on management's assessment. Just like the U.S. counterpart, it recommends modeling internal controls after the Committee of Sponsoring Organizations (COSO) framework. Internet: www.fsa.go.jp/en/policy/fiel

Abbreviation	Regulation	Sector	Short Description
EU DPD	European Union Directive on Data Protection	All companies	The EU DPD protects the right and freedom of people and in particular their privacy with respect to the processing of personal data.
			The directive tries to guarantee that personal data collected is
			• Used lawfully
			• Used for only the reasons explicitly stated
			• Adequate and relevant and not excessive with regards to the purpose
			• Is accurate and kept up-to-date
			• Kept no longer than necessary
			The directive outlines further rights that people whose data was collected have. They are, for example, given the right of access of the collected data, and the right to demand corrections in case of false records.
			Internet: www.cdt.org/privacy/eudirective/ EU_Directive_.html
PIPEDA	Canadian Personal Information Protection and Electronic Documents Act	Private sector companies	PIPEDA is a set of rules to govern the collection, use, and disclosure of personal information. It is meant to protect individual's privacy with regard to data collected about them. The act applies both to data collected
			• For a company's commercial use
			• About employees of the organization
			It is considered the Canadian version of the EU DPD.
			Internet: http://laws.justice.gc.ca/en/P-8.6/index.html

Table 7-2 The Most Important Industry Mandates

Abbreviation	Mandate	Sector	Short Description
PCI	Payment Card Industry	Retail	The PCI Security Standards Council's mission is to enhance payment account data security by fostering broad adoption of the PCI Security Standards, which enforce guidelines concerned with the protection of cardholder data. The organization was founded by American Express, Discover Financial Services, JCB, MasterCard Worldwide, and Visa International.
			Internet: www.pcisecuritystandards.org

continues

Table 7-2 The Most Important Industry Mandates (Continued)

Abbreviation	Mandate	Sector	Short Description
Basel II	Basel II	Financial institutions	Basel II is a risk management framework developed to respond to perceived poor risk management and fraud practices within the financial markets. Internet: http://www.bis.org/publ/bcbsca.htm

Already the definition of the regulations and industry mandates shows that they vary significantly in scope and detail. Some of them stay on a high level and merely require the application of due care with regard to IT security. A theme visible in most of the regulations is to not try to define a comprehensive IT security approach and framework that has to be followed. The regulations try to leverage already existing IT control frameworks to address their security objectives. The next section covers these frameworks.

IT CONTROL FRAMEWORKS

One of the challenges when defining policies and controls for an organization is the definition of a comprehensive set of control objectives. Fortunately, guidelines help us in the process of developing a set of objectives and corresponding controls. These so-called *control frameworks* are collections of control objectives. They do not delve into details of how to define the corresponding control, but they stay on the objectives level. For example, the control framework might require that every machine access be logged. The framework will not go into any further detail, and it will not describe exactly how to do this on all operating system platforms.

Multiple control frameworks exist and can be used as guidance for defining control objectives. Table 7-3 shows six control frameworks and outlines their focus area.

Table 7-3 IT Control Frameworks and a Short Explanation of Their Focus

Framework		Explanation
COSO	Committee of Sponsoring Organizations of the Treadway Commission	COSO is a voluntary private sector organization dedicated to improving quality of financial reporting through business ethics, effective internal controls, and corporate governance. The *Internal Control – Integrated Framework* publication outlines processes to achieve governance objectives. Internet: www.coso.org

Framework		Explanation
COBIT	Control Objectives for Information and related Technologies	COBIT is an overall control framework for IT. It does not define any detailed tasks and instructions about what to do, but instead outlines high-level control objectives to address IT governance requirements.
		Internet: www.isaca.org/cobit/
ISO 27000 Series	Information technology - Security techniques - Code of practice for information security management	ISO 17799 (which will be ISO 27002 soon) is a list of IT security control objectives.
		ISO 27001:2005 is a specification for an Information Security Management System (ISMS): It outlines the things you must do to set up an ISMS. The ISMS is the framework you need to have in place to define, implement, and monitor the controls needed to protect the information in your company.
		Internet: www.iso27001security.com/html/iso27000.html
ITIL	IT Infrastructure Library	ITIL is a set of best practice approaches intended to facilitate the delivery of information technology services. It outlines an extensive set of procedures that are intended to support businesses in achieving both high financial quality and value in IT operations. The framework addresses best practices from configuration management to service level management and security management.
		Internet: www.itil.co.uk/
BSI Standards 100	IT Grundschutzhandbuch	The BSI standards contain German federal recommendations on information security. Multiple substandards are in use:
		BSI-100-1: Information Security Management Systems (ISMS) • defines the federal standards for an ISMS. It is completely compatible with ISO 27001.
		• BSI-100-2: IT-Grundschutz Methodology describes (step by step) how IT security management can be set up and operated in practice.
		• BSI-100-3: Risk Analysis based on IT-Grundschutz outlines standard security measures required in the organizational, personnel, infrastructure and technical areas.
		Internet: www.bsi.bund.de/gshb
NIST 800-53	Recommended Security Controls for U.S. Federal Information Systems	NIST 800-53 defines security controls for federally owned/operated computing systems.
		Internet: http://csrc.nist.gov/publications/nistpubs/800-53/SP800-53.pdf

Regulations do not map one to one to control frameworks. In fact, regulations often leave it up to the company as to which framework to use or whether to use a framework at all. However, not using an established and known framework has a lot of disadvantages. For example

- Development of a framework takes time. Why duplicate effort by trying to create something that experts have been working on for years?
- Proof of a comprehensive approach (all the areas necessary are covered) is hard.
- Auditors will take longer to understand your framework and make sure you implemented all the necessary controls.
- New hires need to be trained on your framework. Their knowledge of existing frameworks only helps them peripherally.

Sometimes smaller companies take one of these frameworks and adapt it to their environment and their needs. It would be overkill for them to implement each and every control objective mentioned in the framework.

The control objectives of the different frameworks often overlap. The same objective can be used to address multiple frameworks. Therefore, by implementing a specific control based on the control objectives, you can satisfy two or more frameworks at the same time. It is not uncommon for companies to implement more than one framework. This is especially true because ISO is more focused on security, whereas ITIL is focused on IT service management. Some of the frameworks are complementary. For example, ITIL and ISO 17799 cover mostly complementary control objectives. Many GRC vendors and IT departments have created their own mappings from one framework to another. You can find an example mapping in NIST 800-53. It contains a mapping from the NIST sections to ISO 17799 and a couple of other frameworks in the appendix to the standard.

LOGGING REQUIREMENTS

This section summarizes the logging requirements for a number of regulations and IT frameworks. The list helps you navigate the jungle of logging requirements. Even if your company does not have to comply with any of these, you might want to consider following one of these recommendations. Most of the requirements and objectives outlined in standards and control frameworks benefit from some aspect of log management. The benefits may stem from efforts to monitor controls, enforce them, or show compliance through the recording and collection of audit records. Such records can be used to prove the presence of and adherence to control processes and objectives. Most IT control frameworks and standards have direct requirements for log management. Table 7-4 lists regulations, IT control frameworks, and standards that have specific logging requirements.

Table 7-4 IT Control Frameworks and Standards and Their Logging Requirements

Requirement Source		Description and Individual Sections Explicitly Demanding Logging	Extent of Logging Requirements
DCID	Director of Central Intelligence Directives	DCIDs are IT security requirements for infrastructure within the U.S. Department of Defense. Only a handful of these requirements have been made public. DCID 6/3 Appendixes. Appendix C, "Sample System Security Plan," includes an outline of audit requirements in section 7.4. Appendix D, "Required System Security Features and Assurances," summarizes the amount of auditing required as a function of the sensitivity/criticality of the data under consideration. Internet: www.fas.org/irp/offdocs/6-3_20Appendices.htm	• Monitoring user access. • Audit log review. • Hardware maintenance log requirements. • Audit log entries. • Audit log retention (5 years). • Real-time monitoring.

FFIEC	Federal Financial Institutions Examinations Council	The FFIEC is a body that governs financial institutions. It also makes recommendations to supervise financial institutions.
		
		Booklet: Information Security
		
		Section: Security Monitoring
		
		Internet: www.ffiec.gov/ffiecinfobase/booklets/information_security/05_sec_monitoring.htm
			• Covers logging on various levels. For example, sensitive applications should have their own logging of significant events.
			• Network intrusion detection systems combine the detection and logging of potential attacks with predefined response actions.
			• Network and host activity recording:
			  • Log transmission
			  • Log normalization
			  • Log storage
			  • Log protection

continues

Table 7-4   IT Control Frameworks and Standards and Their Logging Requirements (Continued)

Requirement Source		Description and Individual Sections Explicitly Demanding Logging	Extent of Logging Requirements
ISO 17799	International Organization for Standards and the International Electrotechnical Commission	ISO 17799 is a set of controls comprising best practices in information security. 10.10 Monitoring: • 10.10.1 Audit logging • 10.10.2 Monitoring system use • 10.10.3 Protection of log information • 10.10.4 Administrator and operator logs • 10.10.5 Fault logging • 10.10.6 Clock synchronization Internet: www.iso27001security.com/html/iso27000.html	• Monitoring systems. • Recording information on security events. • Identifying information system problems. • Verifying effectiveness of controls. • Verifying conformity to access policy model.
DISA	Recommended Standard Application Security Requirements	Recommended standard application security requirements for DoD systems, provided by the Defense Information Systems Agency. 4.12 Accountability:[1] • 4.10.1 Audit/event logging mechanism • 4.10.2 Configurable audit parameters • 4.10.3 Events to be audited Internet: http://iase.disa.mil/stigs/stig/applicationsecurityrequirements.pdf	• The application must log all security-relevant events. • Continuous, automated online auditing. • Audit events to be recorded.

NIST 800-92	Guide to Computer Security Log Management	NIST publishes sets of security recommendations that are in some cases made mandatory for the government to implement. Industry also adopts a lot of the NIST guidelines. NIST 800-92 is an entire publication concerned with all facets of log management.
		
		Internet: http://csrc.nist.gov/publications/nistpubs/800-92/SP800-92.pdf
			• Log management.
			• Log management infrastructure.
			• Log management planning.
			• Log management operational processes:
			  • Prioritizing log entries
			  • Storing logs
			  • Generating logs
			  • Responding to events

---

[1] The section is indeed 4.12; the subrequirements are 4.10.x.

Requirement Source	Description and Individual Sections Explicitly Demanding Logging	Extent of Logging Requirements

NIST 800-53	Recommended Security Controls for Federal Information Systems	NIST 800-53 is mandated by FISMA and defines security controls for federal information systems. The specific sections covering log management are
		
		• AC-13 Supervision and Review - Access Control
		• AU Audit and Accountability:
		  • AU-1 Audit and Accountability Policy and Procedures
		  • AU-2 Auditable Events
		  • AU-3 Content of Audit Records
		  • AU-4 Audit Storage Capacity
		  • AU-5 Audit Processing
		  • AU-6 Audit Monitoring, Analysis, and Reporting
		  • AU-7 Audit Reduction and Report Generation
		  • AU-8 Time Stamps
		  • AU-9 Protection of Audit Information
		  • AU-10 Non-Repudiation
		  • AU-11 Audit Retention
		• CM-4 Monitoring Configuration Changes
		• MA-4 Remote Maintenance
		• MP-2 Media Access
		
		Internet: http://csrc.nist.gov/publications/nistpubs/800-53/SP800-53.pdf	

PCI DSS	Payment Card Industry Data Security Standard	The PCI DSS is concerned with protecting cardholder data. One of the requirements explicitly talks about log management: Requirement 10: Track and monitor all access to network resources and cardholder data covers logging mechanisms and review. Internet: www.pcisecuritystandards.org/pdfs/pci_dss_v1-1.pdf	• Monitor access to cardholder data. • Monitor access to audit trails. • Clock synchronization. • Secure audit trails. • Log review. • Log retention.
FDA GXP	Food and Drug Administration Good Practices	The FDA has developed a series of Good Practices (GXP) regulations to better ensure the safety and efficacy of products manufactured by a large variety of life industries. The most central aspects of GxP are • Traceability (the ability to reconstruct the development history of a drug or medical device) • Accountability (the ability to resolve who has contributed what to the development and when) Internet: www.fda.gov	• Logging of all activity. • Secured logging information. • Litigation-quality auditing. • Log retention. • Nonrepudiation.

Table 7-4 is not a comprehensive list of regulations and standards that explicitly require a log management implementation. It should show, however, that more and more regulations are moving in the direction of demanding audit trails and log management. It is interesting to note the development in the direction of more specific requirements for log management. More standards demand log management. It is not just a mere guideline of "Thou shall log." Also keep in mind that apart from standards and frameworks explicitly demanding logging, a lot of the other requirements benefit greatly from log management, as mentioned earlier.

Visualization of log data is not a requirement and likely will never be. However, the application of visualization techniques greatly helps manage the number of logs generated in the environment. Also remember that auditors are hardly ever log analysis specialists; therefore, by using a graphical representation of log files, instead of textual logs, you can greatly improve communication with your auditors. You can find a great example of this can at the end of this chapter when I cover separation of duties (SoD). I show how much more efficient it is to present the data visually rather than manually when analyzing SoD data to identify conflicts.

AUDIT

Implementing an IT control framework is the first step toward complying with the regulations imposed on the company. The next step to actually show compliance is an *audit*. An audit verifies that the control objectives are correctly implemented and processes to monitor them are in place. To attest compliance with a specific regulation, external auditors verify the control implementations and their mapping to the regulations. Companies of a certain size have not just an external auditor that does the final attestation of compliance, but they also have an internal audit group, which makes sure the external audit is successful. An internal audit group generally reports to someone who is responsible for compliance in the company. More and more, this is the chief compliance officer. The roles of internal audit are the following:

- Understanding the policies that apply to the company. There are federal statutes and industry regulations.
- Mapping the regulations to recognized frameworks or standards to address the regulation and translating the standards into relevant control objectives.
- Defining controls that support the objectives to guarantee reliability of processes and effectiveness and efficiency of operations.
- Monitoring the implementation of controls and policy compliance.

- Auditing the controls using a risk-based sampling and testing approach.
- Report problems identified and negotiate action plans with management to address the deficiencies.
- Executing external audits; being the liaison between the company and external auditors.

If there is no internal audit group, the tasks still have to be executed. Most of the responsibilities will generally end up in the IT security group. The problem with this approach is clearly that there is no separation of duties, which might negatively influence the implementation of and adherence to controls.

To better understand how visualization can help in the audit process, we should not only understand what an audit is about but also how an audit is conducted.

PCI LOG REVIEW AUDIT

The Payment Card Industry (PCI) Data Security Standard (DSS) demands that audit logs be reviewed daily. Auditors want to see proof that such reviews indeed happened. Some log management tools have an audit capability that records all user activity. These records can then be used to show to the auditors that the logs were reviewed.

A sample audit record from Splunk[2], for example, looks like this:

```
Audit:[timestamp=Mon Mar 31 16:34:19 2008,
user=ram, action=search, info=granted
page 0-9 50000  [ search failed login ]][n/a]
```

This record shows that the user `ram` executed a search for the term `failed login`. Each activity is recorded in this way.

Instead of asking the auditors to go through these logs, a chart could be drawn that shows on a daily basis whether the system was used. The report could be further refined to show specific types of searches that indicate that the daily log review process was indeed implemented. In Figure 7-2, you see a sample chart that shows that there was no activity on March 30, showing immediately that the daily log review process was not implemented completely.

---

[2] Splunk is an IT data search engine often used as a log management tool. Also see www.splunk.com.

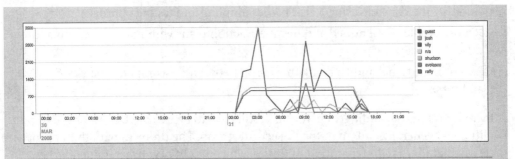

Figure 7-2   Audit records of a log management system showing that the daily log review process was not executed every day. This report was executed by using the following search: `index=_audit | timechart count(_raw)` by user.

Instead of using Splunk, you could use `script`, a UNIX tool to record all the commands executed in a shell session while the log review process is executed. However, the reporting over these results is slightly more involved.

Let's consider a company that needs to comply with the PCI DSS (see Table 7-2). The gist of PCI is to make sure that cardholder data is secured. The company therefore has to make sure that all the transmissions, and the storage and processing of credit card (or more generally, cardholder) data is secure. For an external auditor to gain an under-standing of the environment and the places where cardholder data resides and is processed and transmitted, he starts with an architectural overview. This overview involves the **network architecture,** which shows which machines are on the network and how they are interconnected. The second step after the architectural overview is a look at the **transaction flows.** The auditor will be asking questions about how data moves through the network. How does cardholder data, or credit card data, enter the network? Where is it processed, transmitted, and stored; and where does it leave the network and in what manner? The third component is the people element. The questions for this component are concerned with roles and responsibilities. What is the **organizational structure?** Who is responsible for the individual machines, and who has access to the machines and systems that store or process cardholder data? Who is responsible for the network? Who manages the security safeguards such as firewalls, SSL concentrators, and so on? This is important for the next step, where the individuals owning components of the infrastructure are interviewed. This includes anything from firewall and system administrators to database administrators and process and business owners who use this data. During these interviews, the processes for changes, installations, additions, and so on are of interest. Are there processes in place? Who signs off on them? Who controls the changes? Are there audit records? And so on.

The next step is to use all the knowledge accumulated in the interviews and architectural discussions and start conducting some checks. Are the processes that were mentioned in the interviews really in place? Are the standards implemented correctly? To manage the number of checks that can be executed in a limited amount of time, only a sample is generally looked at. There is no time to check every single process and control. The sample size is generally determined by the frequency of a control. A control that has to be executed on a daily basis is looked at much more in depth and with a larger sample size than a control executed quarterly.

Control verification and testing can happen in two ways: continuous monitoring and ad hoc testing. Some controls are important enough that it is necessary to monitor them continuously with a monitoring system, such as a security information and event management (SIEM) solution. These systems take feeds of audit trails and monitor them for control violations in near real time. This continuous monitoring is especially necessary if monitoring is used as a **compensating control.** Assume that one of the control objectives is to disallow network traffic coming from the Internet to go directly to the financial servers. The general approach is to install a firewall that implements this policy. However, there might be reasons why that is not possible. In those cases, instead of putting in a preventive control, a compensating control could be implemented that detects direct connections from the Internet to our financial servers. In this case, continuous monitoring is absolutely crucial. Note that in this example a preventive control is more desirable and less maintenance intensive. Once in place, we can more or less forget about the control. The firewall will block the traffic without any intervention.

In our example, even though a firewall is in place as a preventive mechanism, the firewall could fail or the firewall ruleset could reflect incorrect policies. To mitigate this risk, ad hoc testing or control verification is implemented. On a periodic basis, the ruleset is audited, and changes are mapped to tickets in the change management system. Every change to the ruleset needs to be approved and documented. This process is often a manual one. Ideally, all the changes are recorded automatically in a monitoring solution, but not everybody has such systems in place.

If the control test on the samples turns out to be well implemented or effective, there is no need to further probe those controls. However, if it turns out that some of the controls were deficiently implemented, a control deficiency is filed and has to be addressed by the process owners. As soon as the deficiency is addressed, another (most likely bigger) sample is taken and audited. This continues until all the controls meet a defined and acceptable standard. The audit of controls not only makes sure that the controls themselves are implemented, but it also makes sure that the control monitors are implemented correctly and that they are actively monitored.

This example for PCI translates almost one to one to other regulations. The only difference is that for most other regulations, it is not the regulation itself that dictates the individual control objectives, but it is the chosen IT control framework that is consulted for guidance on the set of control objectives to implement. However, the overall process stays the same.

AUDIT DATA VISUALIZATION

You have probably been wondering since the beginning of this chapter how visualization applies and relates to all of this. Audits always deal with a significant amount of data. Therefore, visualization is useful in all the auditing steps. And if visualization was used during regular operations, it could be useful during the audit, too. The following are some areas where an IT security audit benefits from visualization:

- Communicating the state of compliance (i.e., the status of a set of controls) in a dashboard for both upper management and operations.
- Increasing the sample size for audits due to making data processing more efficient.
- More efficient communication between the auditors and the rest of the organization that has to collect and present/report the data.
- More efficient and quicker assessment of control objectives. An example is shown later in the chapter for separation of duties.
- Takes less time to read and understand a graphical representation of a control state as opposed to reading textual reports.
- Improved and easier communication with upper management and between individual teams.

One of the drawbacks of visualization is that often visualization aggregates information. Auditors, on the other hand, are not interested in aggregate information. They need the raw information, which is mostly gained by sampling the actual evidence that is generated. Again, the drawback is also an opportunity. Visualization can be applied to the raw data and make it more accessible to the auditors and data owners. Instead of manually processing the data, an auditor can interact with a visualization of the data to assess it.

Another area where visualization plays a significant role in compliance audits is for **gap reports.** A sample gap report is shown in Figure 7-3. The treemap shows all the sections of ISO 17799, grouped by their ISO chapters. If a control for one of the sections failed, the treemap highlights the corresponding node.

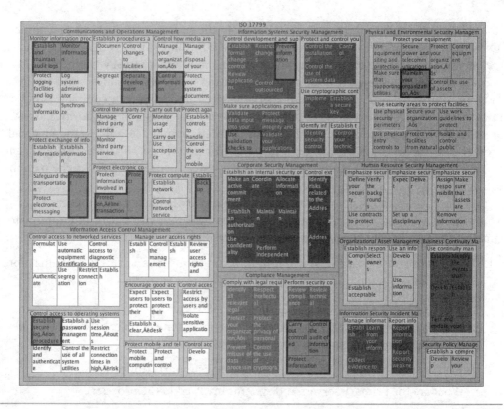

Figure 7-3 A treemap used as a gap report for an organization that is using ISO 17799 as an internal control framework.

Figure 7-3 indicates, for each of the 12 sections of ISO, which controls are currently out of compliance. If a control verification fails, the box is marked with a black border. The gap report can be used either as a report that is updated on a periodic basis or it can be used as a dashboard that is automatically updated.

This leads us to the next compliance topic: business process monitoring. The discussion will help us move decisions into the business layer to prioritize remediation efforts.

BUSINESS PROCESS MONITORING

The only real way to prioritize remediation efforts to eliminate identified material weaknesses in our environment is to identify business processes driving these controls. A material weakness, when reported by an auditor, suggests that a significant misstatement (for example, the financial results) could occur. In the end, it is the business that guides our efforts, and it boils down to money. Therefore, a business-process-driven approach is the only one that can help prioritize and assess the individual control violations.

The following list shows how to go about mapping controls to business processes. This approach needs to be repeated for every business process in your company. You might want to start with your most important one and then expand out slowly. Do not boil the ocean. If you are dealing with Sarbanes-Oxley compliance, address the financial processes. If you are in retail, map out the quote-to-cash process and have a close look at where cardholder data and credit card records are stored. Use the PCI DSS to help establish individual control objectives.

Pick the business process you want to monitor and apply the following seven steps. This process will help you to configure dashboards and other visual control monitors to supervise and document compliance efforts:

1. Draw out the business process with input from the business side of the organization.
   - What are the individual steps involved in the process?
   - What is the importance of this business process?
   - Calculate loss for the case where the process fails (for example, how much money is lost per hour if the process is nonfunctional).

2. Identify, together with IT, the infrastructure that supports this process.
   - What are the primary servers and systems involved in the process?
   - Where are the servers located?
   - What is the networking infrastructure that the data travels on?
   - What are the applications involved in the process?

3. Map data/information to assets.
   - Where does data reside?
   - How does data flow through the assets?
   - What type of data is flowing?

4. Map transactions to users.
   - Who are the users and which accounts are used for the transactions?
   - How does the application server connect to the database? What user is it using?

5. Get access to data feeds that can help monitor process properties.

- Operating system logs for logins and configuration changes.
- Database logs for logins and auditing.
- Application logs for transactional activity.
- Networking infrastructure monitoring data (e.g., traffic flows, network devices logs, and device configurations) to audit configuration changes.

6. Define dashboards for monitoring.

- Who needs a dashboard?
- What's the data?
- How can the data from across the stack be mapped into the dashboards?

7. Monitoring process.

- Who is accessing what data for what reason at what time?
- Who else is accessing the assets involved in this process and for what reason at what time?
- Does the process complete all the time? Are there errors?

Going through this process is not easy. A lot of data points need to be collected. An interesting discovery will be that while collecting all the information, security problems will already be surfacing. For example, it could turn out that the database that hosts the cardholder also hosts marketing data. From a PCI standpoint, this is fairly significant. It means that the system hosting cardholder data is accessible by some marketing people. This is most likely a violation of separating cardholder information from all other data.

To illustrate how the fairly theoretical process can be used, I use a simplified quote-to-cash process illustrated in Figure 7-4. Imagine a website that offers software for purchase. The user buys the software according to the following steps:

1. Search the website for desired product.

2. Click the Purchase link.

3. Enter customer information.

4. Enter credit card information.

5. Receive license key and URL to download the software.

6. Download the software.

On the back end, this process maps to the one shown in Figure 7-4. Drawing this diagram is part of the first step in the process above. We also have to identify what the overall value and importance of this process is to the company. Assuming this is a very small shop and the online Internet presence is the only way customers can purchase goods, this process is the most important one the company operates. It is a fairly simple task to even assign a dollar value to this process. The company will know what the average daily sales volume is and can assign that number directly to this process. The second step in the process requires us to map the process to the underlying IT infrastructure. You can see this in Figure 7-4, too. The company identified four main systems. The first is an application server used as the front end. It serves the Web page and handles all the customer interaction. Next, IT uses a customer relationship management (CRM) system to store all the customer-related information. The third system has to do with the interaction with the financial application takes care of registering all the sales. And finally, the licensing server is used to track and issue license keys for the product. Figure 7-4 not only shows the servers involved in the transactions but also the supporting network infrastructure. This is important as soon as we assess the overall exposure of the infrastructure. For example, if one of the routers goes down, the process is not working anymore, and the company loses money.

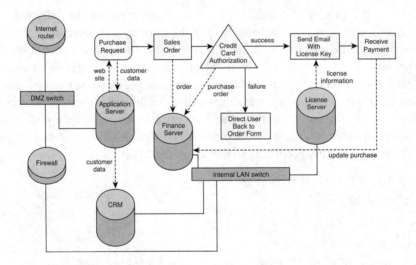

Figure 7-4 Quote-to-cash process example. The process is mapped to the IT infrastructure and to the data and users involved in the process.

The next layer of information that we need is the user names associated with the individual accesses. Table 7-5 shows the relevant users associated with the sample process.

Table 7-5   Data Flow between Servers Showing Respective User Names Used

Server	User	Data Passed
Application server to CRM	app_crm	Customer data
Application server to Financial server	app_fin	Store order
Application server to License server	app_lic	Request for new license key

Beware: This is an idealized view and shows only the way data is *supposed* to flow and which users related to this specific process are accessing the machines and applications. It does not show all the users unrelated to the one quote-to-cash process who have access to the same data. Gathering all the extra information about other processes utilizing the same infrastructure, other users capable of accessing the customer data, and so on is a great exercise and needs to be part of an infrastructure security assessment. However, for our purposes, that is out of scope.

This concludes the upfront mapping process. The next step, Step 5, in our process is to get access to the data feeds. Hopefully, there is a way to get a feed from all the components involved in the process. Only that way can we monitor the process end to end. Various infrastructure challenges are associated with this step. How do you collect all the data? How do you access the data after it has been collected? I am going to assume that there is a system in place that deals with all of this. One such system is Splunk. It helps collect all IT data in your environment and makes it easily accessible. For more detailed information, see www.splunk.com. When the data feeds are in place, we can finally move on to the fun part of our journey. We are going to define the dashboards and other visualizations that help monitor the quote-to-cash process. These visualizations will help us monitor our state of compliance (i.e., they are our control monitors).

What we just talked about can be found in the literature under *business process management* (BPM). BPM is even broader in scope than what I presented here. I was taking a slight detour into BPM to show that compliance monitoring is not something that should be motivated by control frameworks and controls, but by the business and its processes.

By mapping the control objectives and IT infrastructure to a business process, we can map our efforts to financial numbers. We are able to calculate what it costs if a control is out of compliance. We just assess the impact this control violation has on the business process.

COMPLIANCE MONITORING

In the beginning of this chapter, when I introduced the compliance framework (see Figure 7-1), I mentioned the function of **control monitors.** These monitors are individual tests that can be used to certify that a control is in place and operating effectively. Taking multiple control monitors together, we can then try to define a dashboard that shows a live compliance status.

To define a compliance dashboard, the first step is to define who the target audience is. Who will look at this dashboard and how frequently? Is it a daily task? Maybe the dashboard is used in real time? These questions have an impact on the type of data collected, its detail, and the granularity of data the dashboard is going to display. Various people could benefit from a compliance dashboard. Pretty much everybody from the operations folks at the front line to the chief security officer could use a dashboard to show data related to the current compliance state. Whereas the CSO is probably not interested in up-to-the-second details and all the technical nuances, the operations people definitely need that type of information. Table 7-6 summarizes possible consumers for a compliance dashboard. It also lists what type of information the dashboard should display and how frequently.

Table 7-6 Compliance Dashboard Consumers and the Data That Needs to Be Presented in Such a Dashboard

Consumer	Information Display Examples	Update Frequency
Operations	• Patching status	Real time/daily
System Administration	• Antivirus status	
	• Compliance with configuration guidelines	
	• System health (processor utilization, and so on)	
	• Business process flow	
Networking	• Network equipment inventory (including software versions and patch levels)	Real time
	• Network equipment health (e.g., CPU and memory utilization)	
	• Network reachability (e.g., routing state)	
	• Network traffic metrics (e.g,. bandwidth, latency)	
Security	• Security device alerts	Real time
	• Intrusion and attack attempts	
	• Communication trends (who is accessing what data)	
	• Vulnerabilities and exposure of systems	

Consumer	Information Display Examples	Update Frequency
Operations manager	• Mean time to repair • Number of open tickets • Statistics on resolving open tickets	Real time/hourly
IT manager	• Location-based view of control objective violations • Trend of open/resolved tickets over time • Currently active projects per region	Daily
CIO/CISO	• Trend of risk over time • Compliance trend over time • Information security status • Critical business process status	Daily/weekly
Audit	• Control monitors across the application and IT stack • Where does critical data live? • Who has access to critical data?	Daily/weekly
Business users	• Business process view • Transaction round-trip times • Transaction integrity • Business process infrastructure status	Real time
CFO/CEO	• State of business process compliance • Compliance breaches • Measures and metrics around compliance issues	Real time/daily

All the dashboards for the individual roles in Table 7-6 are interesting to look at. We previously discussed the CISO dashboard in Chapter 5, "Visual Security Analysis" (see the reprint in Figure 7-5).

If we cross-check that dashboard with the requirements shown here, we are pretty much right where we need to be. We can reuse that dashboard without modification. Therefore, I do not discuss it further here. I will also not discuss most of the other dashboards. Remember, we were talking about compliance monitoring. Although most of the consumers listed in the table would benefit from some sort of compliance view, it is not their main focus. The operations people, for example, benefit from the information in this chapter through prioritization of their work items. Instead of looking at trouble tickets in a vacuum, they now have a way to map those to a business process and assign a priority, based on the importance of the business process they support.[3] A compliance dashboard would not add much benefit to an operator's daily tasks—except for perhaps the security people, who should be reacting to some compliance violations immediately. However, the security operations people do not need to know what exact regulation a control is part of and how this relates to the overall compliance state. If a security control failure occurs, they need to assess how important it is and then take reactive action and make sure it does not happen again.

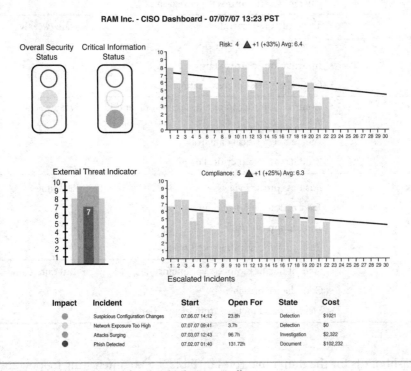

Figure 7-5   Compliance dashboard for the chief security officer.

The operations manager, who is one of the remaining consumers, might be interested in some compliance-related indicators. However, he is going to be more concerned with the performance of his teams. What is the mean time to repair (MTTR), average time cases stay open, and so on. Although this definitely plays into the compliance efforts, it is

---

[3]   We have not quite arrived at the stage where you would make these decisions; but later in the chapter, you will see exactly how control objectives are prioritized.

not core to them, and he does not need a compliance monitor for assessing his team's performance. What he needs is similar to what the operations people need: a prioritized view of tasks and tickets.

The next group is IT managers. What would their compliance dashboard look like? The objective is to see which areas of the IT organization need attention. If the company is big enough and we are redesigning the dashboard to cater to IT managers, we might have to partition the controls per geographic region. This requires that the data be collected on a per-region basis. In addition, a higher-level dashboard should be built to summarize the states of all the regions for a top-level manager who has the responsibility over worldwide compliance. That way, he can tell immediately which parts of the world are in compliance and which ones are not.

On a regional basis, the data can be sliced in various ways. One approach is to use the control framework sections to show how the control objectives are met in each of the sections. This is what I used in Figure 7-3. Another possibility is to slice the data based on technical controls. For example, all firewall control objective monitors would be grouped together, all access management, all remote access, and so on. This is a role-based approach, where individual control owners can quickly check whether their controls are compliant. Figure 7-6 shows a sample dashboard that partitions the data based on functional roles.

The figure shows four areas where compliance violations occurred. All four areas are located under the topic of "Establish firewall configuration standards." This helps you to quickly identify that all the compliance problems are in the area of firewall management. All the other areas are doing fine. This information can now be used to, for example, allocate resources to get the firewall controls back on track.

This leaves us with two more groups of people we have not dealt with yet: auditors and businesspeople. Businesspeople are increasingly interested in compliance. Although they are traditionally interested in areas such as bringing in money, increasing profit margins, decreasing operational costs associated with their business process, and so on they are starting to include compliance in their planning process. However, it shouldn't be their main focus to manage those aspects of the business. This is where the auditors' responsibility lies; they need to assess whether procedures are followed.

Does the audit team need a dashboard? They would very likely benefit from one. What does an auditor's compliance dashboard look like? What are some of the indicators? How frequently should the dashboard be updated?

Let's take a look at the update frequency first. Do auditors need a real-time view on the compliance state? Generally, the answer is no, although in some cases it could be useful for the internal auditor to have this view. The granularity auditors generally need to verify control objectives is maybe a day. In general, this is even too granular, and a weekly update would suffice. In addition, auditors are interested in looking at the entire application and IT stack, not just the application layer itself. They need to assess transaction level or application level controls, but also pay attention to the database, operating system, and network layers. Even information about physical controls is important.

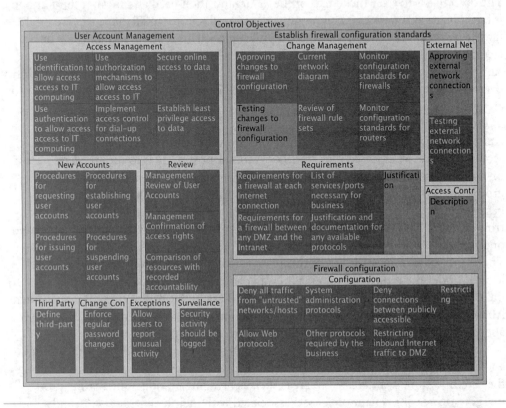

Figure 7-6   Control objective monitoring dashboard arranged by technical controls. Compliance violations are highlighted. (This figure appears in the full-color insert located in the middle of the book.)

Who else needs a compliance dashboard? Who did we forget? What about the chief risk officer and possibly the compliance team or whoever has the mandate to handle compliance? In bigger companies, this is increasingly an independent department that deals with risk and compliance. In some cases, it falls under the financial umbrella, where the controllers are responsible for compliance activities. And don't forget that the CEO (or even more likely, the CFO) is, in some cases, interested in the compliance dashboard, too. In the end, he is responsible for meeting statutory compliance. He cannot transfer that responsibility. All of those people need a view on the compliance state. The following are some objectives for this group of people:

- Real-time (or highly frequent) view on the state of compliance in the context of individual business processes
- Instant notification of compliance breaches with business process context
- A common point of reference for compliance-related issues
- Assessment of compliance breaches in a business and risk context
- A common set of measures and metrics for compliance issues

To address these objectives, we need to elevate our discussion and include some way of presenting and assessing the control violations in a business context. What does that really mean? The business side of a company is concerned with generating income and (we hope) profits. In the course of the business, certain decisions need to be made that generally involve some type of risk. Should the additional money be spent to produce a new product? Many risk models and approaches can be used to assess the business risk. We need to be doing the same when we manage our IT security efforts. We have to assess control objective violations in a risk context. Which controls should we fix immediately? What's the risk of not fixing them?

RISK MANAGEMENT

So far, we have looked at how to prioritize the mitigation of control failures through association with the business processes they influence. Elevating this concept one more layer positions us in the realm of risk management. The idea is to describe and monitor the controls in the context of the risk posed to the company.

The topic of risk management is a huge field. In the context of computer security, risk management causes a lot of discussion and controversy. Simple questions such as "How do you manage risk?" and "How do you measure risk?" are heavily discussed.[4] My intention here is not to claim that I have the correct answers to all the questions. The goal of this section is to present some ideas and concepts for enriching your risk management approach with visualization. To dig into risk management, you can check out two good guides on risk management published by the National Institute of Standards and Technology (NIST). The Risk Management Guide for Information Technology Systems

---

[4] For example, at www.securitymetrics.org

and the Guide on Managing Risk from Information Systems are available on the NIST website.[5] The former is a guide that provides the foundation for the development of a risk management program. It contains both the definitions and the practical guidance for assessing and mitigating risks identified within IT systems. The latter guide provides guidelines for managing risk from an organizational perspective. The Federal Information Security Management Act (FISMA) defines an effective security program to include the following:[6]

- Periodic assessment of risk
- Effectiveness of information security policy
- Detecting, reporting, and responding to security incidents

These three points are great motivators and guidance for using visualization in risk management.

To frame our discussion, here is a definition of **risk management** that I found on a Canadian government website:[7]

> Risk management is a systematic approach to setting the best course of action under uncertainty by identifying, assessing, understanding, acting on, and communicating risk issues.

I am not quoting the definition of risk management that NIST establishes. I don't like it. It is too complicated and talks about risk assessment and so on. The definition I provided here is much cleaner and simpler to understand. However, the definition immediately poses the question of what *risk* is. Without being scientific about defining the term, we can view **risk** as a way of looking at the probability that an event happens, also called the **exposure,** and the **impact** or consequence this event has on the business. Consequently, we need to understand the events that make up the total risk and are of importance to the compliance effort. Simply put, risk is the product of exposure and impact.

---

[5] You can find the NIST risk management guide at http://csrc.nist.gov/publications/nistpubs/800-30/sp800-30.pdf. There is also the *Guide on Managing Risk from Information Systems,* which is available at http://csrc.nist.gov/publications/drafts/800-39/SP-800-39-ipd.pdf. NIST-800-39 is in draft state at the time of this writing.

[6] There are five more items that FISMA calls out, but the ones mentioned here are the ones applying directly to visualization.

[7] *A Management Framework for the Government of Canada,* www.tbs-sct.gc.ca/pubs_pol/dcgpubs/RiskManagement/rmf-cgr01-1_e.asp.

CONTROL OBJECTIVE PRIORITIZATION

We have already talked about the events that are the key components to define risk in the beginning of this chapter. The control monitors are perfect candidates to represent the events in the *risk* definition. If we put the monitors in the context of the business process, we end up with a nice framework that we can use to address risk management.

For every control objective, we have to figure out the impact of the control failing and multiply it by the exposure of the control (i.e., the probability of the control failing). How do we measure the exposure and impact for an individual control objective? We could look at the information protected by it. Let's look at an example. Assume that the control objective is to disallow direct root access to database servers. Assume further that we are monitoring this control objective for our main database server that stores financial data. The *impact* of this control failing or not being in place is fairly minimal. Someone still needs the root password to access the server. The one big problem with allowing direct root access is accountability. You cannot associate actions taken with a person. Who was using the account? You do not know. This is something that the auditors will definitely dislike! The *exposure* of this control is very low, too. The effect on the target host is really none for the control not being in place or failing. A potential adversary still has to know the password and go through the authentication mechanisms or circumvent the authentication mechanism with a more sophisticated attack to access the machine.

I am not giving formal definitions for impact and exposure. There is no well-known and accepted risk management framework that makes it easy to define these parameters. One good source for a possible definition is the Common Vulnerability Scoring Schema (CVSS), which defines an actual score to measure exposure and impact (www.first.org/cvss). For our purposes, it is enough to use colloquial definitions.

As we have just seen, to make an impact assessment, we need a way to classify assets in our environment. The impact is close to none if the control objective in our example the failing of a test server. If we classify our assets based on the data they host and the business processes they are taking part in, we can then determine the impact of a control failure.

To classify assets, you can use multiple approaches. A very extensive and thorough discussion on asset classification can be found in the Federal Information Processing Standards 199 standard. As the name implies, the FIPS standards covers all kinds of standards for the U.S. federal government. FIPS 199 addresses the *Security Categorization of Federal Information and Information Systems.* In great length, it describes how all the information systems should be classified with respect to the three aspects of security: confidentiality, integrity, and availability (CIA). Although you might not want to follow these more complex guidelines, make sure you consider the CIA properties when you classify your systems.

The net effect of mapping the control objectives to risk (i.e., exposure and impact) is that the prioritization is elevated a level to include risk and not just the context of the business processes involved. The previous visualization techniques are therefore not changing, but the inputs to the assessments do.

RISK VISUALIZATION

Approaching the task of managing risk, we can definitely reuse some of the visualizations we developed under the compliance monitoring section. However, some specific properties of risk management are worth monitoring in more detail. The central question to carry us through the discussion is how to improve visibility into the risk landscape. The goals to address with risk management and, specifically, visualization are the following:

- Conveying the overall state of risk to both internal and external parties
- Tracking changes (i.e., progress and trends)
- Facilitating prioritization of security requirements and allocation of resources based on impact on the business
- Providing insight into security weaknesses and deficiencies
- Supporting decision making based on organizational priorities

To manage risk across the organization, we need to extend our compliance dashboard to include a risk-based approach. Figure 7-7 shows an example of a treemap that shows business units by their state and the risk associated with their failure. In the treemap, exposure is encoded as color. The darker a box, the higher the exposure. Encoded in the size of the boxes is the impact associated with the corresponding control. The larger the box, the greater the impact. Note that the impact is not a function of the control. The impact of one and the same control is different for every host the control protects. This is why the size of a control varies, depending on where a control violation was detected.

The reason for using the size of the boxes for the impact and not the exposure is fairly obvious. The exposure is control specific and therefore would result in all same-sized boxes for the same control. That would not be helpful. The impact, however, communicates another piece of information: the information under control. The objective of this visualization is to identify controls and departments exposed to high risk and which should be investigated immediately.

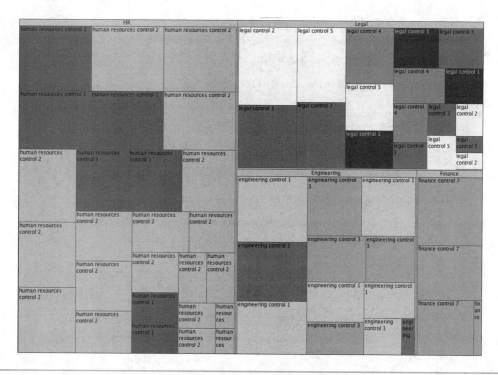

Figure 7-7 Treemap representing controls that failed verification. Color indicates the exposure associated with the control and the size represents the impact.

GENERATING FAILED CONTROLS TREEMAPS

The following explains how to generate a treemap showing controls that failed verification. This process was used to generate Figure 7-7. As a starting point, you need to collect data about risk for all the departments that you want to track. Then format the data to look like this:

Count	Dep	Control	Exp	Impact	Risk	Fail
INTEGER	STRING	STRING	INTEGER	INTEGER	INTEGER	INTEGER
2	Eng	engctrl	3	10	30	1
5	Finance	finctrl	7	5	1	5

This is the TM3 format that Treemap[8] is using to visualize the data. Load the data into Treemap and configure the following:

- The hierarchy to be just the Department (Dep)
- The label to be the Control
- The size to be the Impact
- The color to be the Exposure
- The color binning to use a color palette that distinguishes well between colors

The configuration of the last four items is shown in Figure 7-8.

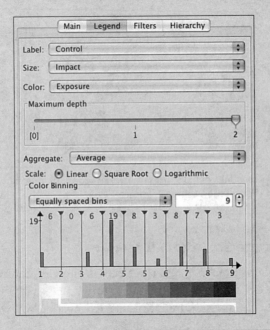

Figure 7-8   Treemap configuration used for Figure 7-7.

What we are looking for in Figure 7-7, once again, are large and dark areas. Those are the controls that expose high risk. Note again that the treemap shows only failed controls. Also notice that the same control shows up multiple times (because the same control can fail on multiple machines, applications, or users). A look at the treemap quickly reveals

---

8   www.cs.umd.edu/hcil/treemap

that the HR department needs attention. Control number one is failing at three places and exposes significant risk. Furthermore, the HR department shows a lot of controls that failed. Engineering also needs to be looked at as a second priority. Control number 2 is a fairly high-risk control and needs to be fixed, especially in conjunction with all the other engineering controls that failed.

Another way of looking at the same data on control failures or violations is shown in Figure 7-9. The scatter plot representation helps us understand the distribution of impact and exposure. The dots at the top right of the graph are the ones of interest. The graph does not identify the exact control that failed, unlike the preceding figure. However, by encoding the business unit as the shape of the dots and the asset classification as the color, we can quickly identify which business unit and which types of assets are exposed to high risk. In the figure, we see a significant number of dark dots on the right side of the graph. This environment definitely needs some attention. The fact that the dots are dark shows that the assets affected are of high criticality, yet another reason to have a closer look at this environment. By looking at the shapes, we can determine that the business process associated with the triangles is probably the one to investigate first.

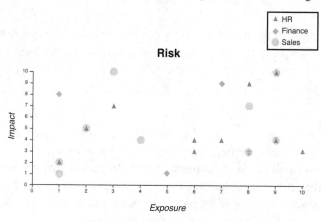

Figure 7-9 Risk map showing impact and exposure for all the controls. Shape encodes the business unit that was affected, and color encodes the asset classification.

To improve the rendering of the graph, we should apply a method called **jitter.** Multiple data points with different colors and shapes are located in the same place. This makes it impossible to identify all the individual points and their corresponding values. With the use of jitter, the dots are moved slightly to make them not overlap. Figure 7-10 shows an example of how jitter can help increase legibility. The figure uses the same data as used in Figure 7-9. You can see that at various places, for example, at the exposure level of 2 and the impact level of 5, there is a group of different data points. Jitter moved them around slightly to not crowd the same place and to thus make all the data values visible.

This method works especially well for this type of graph in which there are discrete data values on each of the axes and they are fairly far apart; in other words, moving the data points slightly does not decrease the capability to identify the exact values represented.

ADDING JITTER TO DATA VALUES

You can apply jitter to a scatter plot by adding a random number to the original data values. In Perl, you could use the following code to iterate over the data array and add some jitter:

```
# iterate through all array elements
for (my $i=0; $i<=$#data; $i++) {
  # $max is the maximum value in @data
  $data[$i] += int((rand($max/$#data)- $max/$#data/2;
}
```

This code snippet changes each value of the array (@data) by adding a random amount to it. The last term in the assignment inside of the for loop adjusts the value to also go negative and not just increase the original values.

The best way of using the risk map in Figure 7-10 is by using it as a view into the risk landscape present in your organization. Introducing the additional dimension of time can help you monitor all kinds of properties and helps justify investment. Before elaborating more on that concept, look at Figure 7-11, which shows yet another way of visualizing the risk landscape. This time we plot the risk over time. Multiple data series are plotted on the same graph, one data series per department.

The first thing that you will notice in Figure 7-11 is that the legal department had a huge surge in risk mid month. They were able to bring the risk back down over the course of the month, but not to the level originally seen at the beginning of the month.

A graph of this type, in which the risk is plotted over time, has a few really interesting applications:

- By analyzing the graph, you should be able to explain every change. Why was there a surge or a drop in risk? Did you implement a new control? Was a new asset introduced in the environment?

- Use the graph to justify investments. If you just implemented a security program, you can immediately verify whether it was successful in reducing the risk.

- Running a security awareness program does not necessarily have to happen across all departments. Focus on the departments with the highest risk.

- Check the development of risk after a security awareness program has been implemented. If it was successful, the risk should be decreasing. This can be used to show a direct return on investment (ROI).

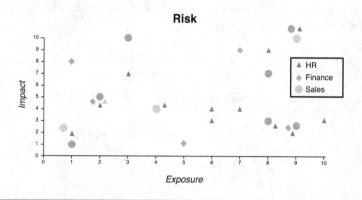

Figure 7-10   Risk map showing how jitter renders the risk map more legible.

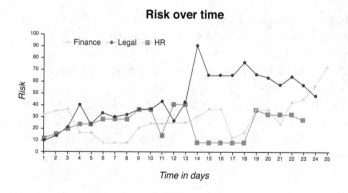

Figure 7-11   Line chart showing a risk profile over time for three business units.

Analyzing rates of change and identifying trends is a necessity when making decisions about resource allocations and investment decisions. Is the risk constantly going up? You might want to consider changing something in your security program. Figure 7-12 shows a graph to analyze the rate of change and trends with respect to risk.

GENERATING A RISK TREND CHART

The risk profile shown in Figure 7-12 was generated in Microsoft Excel. List all your risk values in a column and add another column for the moving average. Table 7-7 shows what a sample table in Excel would look like. The last column shows what formula to use to compute the moving average.

Table 7-7   Basic Setup for a Risk Trend Chart (The moving average chosen is over three values.)

	A	B	
1	Risk value	Moving average	Formula
2	5	5	=A2/1
3	4	4.5	=SUM(A2:A3)/2
4	5	4.66	=SUM(A2:A4)/3
5	3	4	=SUM(A3:A5)/3
6	4	4	=SUM(A4:A6)/3

The moving average used in Table 7-7 is over three values. You can see this in the formula by looking at the divisor in the last three rows. The last three values are summed up and then divided by three. The first two rows are anomalies. They are the lead in. You do not have a three-value moving average available yet. Only one or two values are available to do a computation.

Graph these values in a line chart. By double-clicking the individual graph elements in the Excel chart, you can then work on optimizing the data to ink ratio. Get rid of the grid lines, the background color, and so on. All that visual clutter is unnecessary.

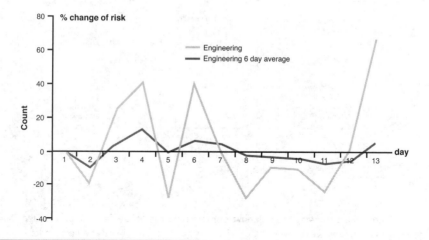

Figure 7-12   Line chart showing a risk profile over time. The chart shows a daily summary and a weekly average to emphasize relative progress.

The graph in Figure 7-12 shows two different data series for the same data. In Chapter 5, when I discussed time-series data analysis, I introduced this method of analyzing trends in data. What you can see is the risk over time in the engineering department. On a daily basis, the risk changes quite a lot from day to day. A word of caution: The underlying data is not very granular. The values are from 1 to 10, so a change from a risk of 5 to 7 is a 40 percent increase. That explains some of the radical spikes you see. The second data series is the moving average of risk over a period of 6 days. The interesting data points are now where the two lines intersect. Those are points where the daily risk increase significantly changes compared to the 6-day average. At those points, you can see whether the daily risk increase is trending above or below the weekly average.

An important change can be seen at day 5. The daily risk falls below the moving average. This indicates good progress and should be an indicator for a good trend. However, the day after, there is another crossover of the two averages, invalidating the positive development of the preceding day. Day 8 changes the situation for a longer time period. Things start to look better. The daily average stays below the 6-day average. Unfortunately, this is the case only until day 12, when the risk shoots through the roof again (indeed, so much that the moving average also moves above 0 again).

A way to look at the risk tendencies at a specific time is the sector chart, shown in Figure 7-13. This chart is used to visualize the last day of risk development and how each of the four departments compare in terms of risk development.

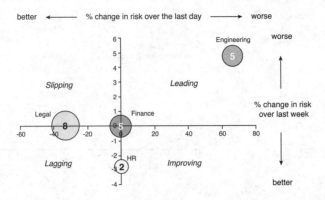

Figure 7-13 Sector chart showing the risk development over the past week. The percentage changes indicate how much more risk was present. "Good" values are located toward the bottom left.

GENERATING SECTOR CHARTS

Sector charts are essentially scatter plots. The one in Figure 7-13 was generated in Microsoft Excel. The chart type is a bubble chart. The location of the points is determined by the percentages of change over the past day and over the past week, respectively. The size is determined by the current risk value. We therefore need three data values to plot a single point.

Let's take a look at how to arrive at plotting the data point for the Engineering department. Table 7-8 shows some sample data that uses the percentage change over the past day and the percentage change over the past two days, instead of over the past week. If the entire week were shown, there would be a lot of empty rows. The principle stays the same.

The calculations for the C column are such that you take the average of the past two days as a reference and then compare the average of the past two days plus today to that value.

With this data, we can now go ahead and generate a bubble chart in Excel. When going through the wizard, choose any field as the data source. When the graph is generated, right-click the newly generated bubble and choose Source Data. You now see a dialog box that lets you add new data series to the plot. We only need one series for our example table. Provide a name in the right side of the dialog box. For the X Values, choose the last entry of the data (B6 in our case). For the Y Values, choose the entry in cell C6. The size is the risk value itself, so cell A6.

That is it. You successfully created a sector chart with one data series. Repeat this for additional data series of other departments that you want to add to the chart.

Table 7-8 Data Used to Generate a Sector Chart (The Formula columns show how to compute the Percentage Change columns.)

	A	B		C	
1	Risk Value	% Change Last Day	Formula	% Change Last Two Days	Formula
2	5	—		—	
3	4	−20	=100/A2*(A3-A2)	—	
4	5	25	=100/A2*(A4-A3)	3.73	=100/AVERAGE(A2:A3)* (AVERAGE(A2:A4) -AVERAGE(A2:A3))
5	7	40	=100/A2*(A5-A4)	18.51	=100/AVERAGE(A3:A4)* (AVERAGE(A3:A5)- AVERAGE(A3:A4))
6	5	−28.57	=100/A2*(A6-A5)	−5.55	=100/AVERAGE(A4:A5)* (AVERAGE(A4:A6)- AVERAGE(A4:A5))

Dots located on the top-right quadrant are ones that performed really poorly over the past week, as well as over the past day. The engineering department seems to be in pretty bad shape. They have had a 5 percent increase in risk over the past 6 days, and an increase of more than 60 percent over the past day. The other three departments have either been stagnant (finance) or have even seen a decrease over the past week (HR) or the past day only (legal). The size of the bubbles indicates the current risk value. You can see that the legal department has a current risk of 8, but there was a decrease from the last day. The HR department looks pretty good. They experienced an absolute value of 2 and a decrease of overall risk over the past week. Whatever measures were taken over the past week were successful.

The charts in Figure 7-12 and Figure 7-13 are fairly volatile and will change fairly significantly for each day. The nice thing, however, is the display of a current and detailed state. It might be useful to, instead of using the change of risk over the last day and the last week, monitor the risk changes over the past week and the past month or maybe even the entire year.

Monitoring the risk over time and providing a comprehensive view into the risk landscape is crucial for any risk management initiative. When defining the control objectives (and in turn, their monitors), we need to keep the focus on an end-to-end security model. It is absolutely crucial that we not only monitor the network layer but the entire network stack. Too often, only the application layer is monitored. For example, the financial application can be instructed to enforce roles. Expensive consulting engagements make sure that separation of duties is correctly implemented and enforced. Sometimes the logs are even audited to find access control violations. But all of this happens on the application layer. What happens if someone circumvents the application and goes directly into the database to change records? The application is completely blind to this type of activity. It will never know. This is the reason for monitoring and protecting the entire stack. Unfortunately, no commercial products help address this problem. There are definitely initial approaches that, for example, the security information and event management market is taking, but this entire field is still in its infancy.

This ends our discussion on risk and compliance visualization. The following sections delve into some specific visualization examples in the compliance world. They illustrate how specific visualizations can help improve effectiveness of implementing and maintaining monitoring mandates.

SEPARATION OF DUTIES

A security concept that auditors are familiar with is called *separation of duties,* or SoD for short. This concept is especially important in the world of enterprise and finance software, where employees enter invoices, make payments, and generally manage the finances of a company. The SoD concept helps make sure that the likelihood of abuse in such a system is as minimal as possible. It is used to set up the user privileges such that no one person should be able to execute a critical or financially significant task. For example, creating an invoice and also authorizing the payment of it would circumvent the paradigm of SoD. At least two people should be involved in such a transaction. This makes it more expensive for an attacker to circumvent the system. A recent case where the principles of SoD were not exercised happened at the Société Générale Group in France.[9] An insider caused damage of multiple billions of dollars by placing trades of significant amounts that he should not have been able to place without someone else signing off on them.

---

[9]   www.sp.socgen.com/sdp/sdp.nsf/V3ID/D22EA4F2E1FB3487C12573DD005BC223/$file/08005gb.pdf

The overall idea behind SoD is to have more than one person required to execute a critical task. The concept is not only applied in enterprise resource planning (ERP) systems, but it should also be enforced in the IT department. No one person should be able to create an administrator account on any system without a second person authorizing it. Administrator accounts are especially critical because they enable a user to control almost every aspect of a system, and the potential for abuse is fairly high. Other areas where SoD should be considered and implemented include the following:

- Requiring online management authorization for critical data entry transactions
- Instituting code reviews for the software development and maintenance process
- Using configuration management processes and technology to control software
- Requiring review and approval of system modifications

An SoD audit deals with a lot of data. A shortage of staff members trained in ERP and security makes it especially hard to conduct an efficient and cost-effective SoD audit. In addition, no good standardized security solutions are available to help conduct these audits.[10]

AN EXAMPLE OF APPLYING VISUALIZATION TO AN SoD AUDIT

The following example shows how visualization can be applied to an SoD audit. We will have a look at an ERP system: SAP in this example. In SAP, there is a concept of **transaction codes,** or t-codes for short. Every transaction code identifies a unique action in the system. Examples are *V-04,* which stands for Create Invoice Recipient (Sales), and *SU01,* used for User Maintenance, which are activities such as authorization changes to a user. Another important concept for an SoD audit is **user roles.** Every user is assigned one or more roles in the system. Every role in turn has a set of t-codes associated. These are the actions that this role has privileges to execute. The role Maintain Security, for example, could be set up to cover the t-codes associated with user management, such as SU01. The trick is now to find t-codes that are conflicting, meaning that no user should have both of these t-codes assigned. If he was associated with both t-codes, this would indicate a violation of the SoD principle and that he has the capability to commit fraud in the system.

In contrast to most other analyses we have been doing so far, an SoD audit does not operate on log files or real-time data. An SoD audit is done on static tables; in our example, it is done on the t-code assignment of roles. The monitoring of real-time activity to

---

[10] "ERP Security and Segregation of Duties Audit," by David Hendrawirawan et al., *Information System Control Journal,* Volume 2, 2007.

see violations of the SoD principle falls under the topic of **access control,** which is similar to what we are going to do here, but auditors draw a clear line between the two.

To conduct our analysis, we first need a list of all the roles and their t-code assignments. In addition, we should try to either obtain or create a list of conflicting t-codes. An example is t-code *FD01*, which stands for Create Customer (Accounting) and t-code *VA01*, which is Create Sales Order. No user should have both of these t-codes assigned. If anyone who can enter a sales order were allowed to create new accounts, he could create accounts that get paid and ship goods. Sometimes the creation of a new account requires the target company to go through a credit check. If a sales clerk could just create a new account, this process could potentially be circumvented. Figure 7-14 shows how these two pieces look when they are visualized.[11] The four- or five-letter codes represent t-codes, and the light-gray nodes stand for user roles. There are multiple, independent clusters. This is what you would expect; t-codes are generally not shared among different roles. However, as you can see in Figure 7-14, a few roles share the same t-codes. These t-codes and roles should be looked at, and it should be verified that the assignments are wanted and legitimate. The Sales Agrmts/Contracts and Maintain Security roles provide an example of two roles sharing the same t-code. They share the t-code *1KEA*, which stands for Post Selected Data CO > EC-PCA. I am not an SAP expert, and I really don't know exactly what that means. What is important is that these two roles should probably not share the same code, and this conflict needs to be investigated.

Note that there is a second instance that we should be looking at. The SoD graph shows those instances fairly clearly with the dark-gray t-code nodes. These are nodes that are used by some role and there is a known conflicting t-code. You need to verify whether any of the conflicting t-codes were used by the same user role. To have a closer look at those instances, I generated Figure 7-15, which shows only the sales roles and only the t-codes for which a conflicting t-code is known. All the additional conflicting codes and roles are filtered out.

The graph shows two roles, Sales Order Entry and Sales Order Release, each of which has conflicting t-codes associated with it. The Sales Order Entry role, for example, has privileges to execute t-codes *F.34* (Credit Management - Mass Change) and *V.23* (Release Orders for Billing), and those are in conflict.

---

[11] Note that the role to t-code mapping was not taken from a real system because of confidentiality issues. The mappings used will probably not make sense in most cases. However, for our purposes, this is not important; the concept stays the same.

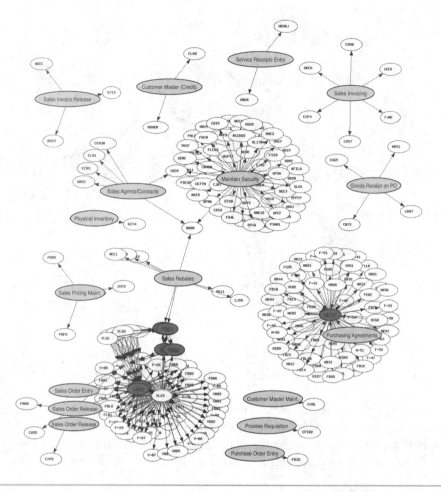

Figure 7-14 Link graph that shows the t-codes for each user role. Cases of SoD violations are shown as dark nodes.

What about the Sales Rebates role? There is no direct conflict between FD01 and FD05, but indirectly they conflict. The question that we need to ask ourselves now is whether t-code conflicts are transitive, meaning that if there is a conflict between A and B and one between B and C, is there an implicit conflict between A and C? The answer is that it depends. For certain conflicts, it makes sense to enforce the transitive property. For others, it does not. In practice, this means that we should make sure that the list of t-code conflicts we are working with explicitly calls out the conflicts and does not assume we resolve them. When in doubt, verify all the instances manually. This is not as bad as it sounds because we already limited the amount of data to look at!

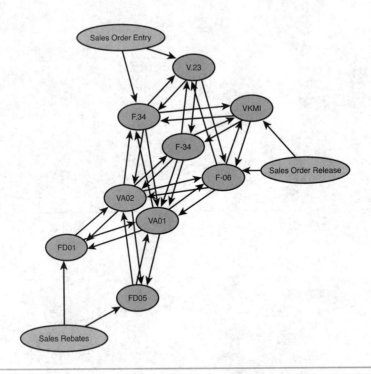

Figure 7-15 User roles and their associated T-codes for only the sales roles.

The interesting thing to note here is that through visualizing the t-code conflicts, we arrived at the question of whether t-codes are transitive. Had we not seen how the conflict layout looks, we might never have discovered that there could be such a concept hidden in the data, and we might have missed some significant violations.

GENERATING SoD GRAPHS

I show in a few simple steps how the graphs used for the SoD analysis can be generated. The only tools used were AfterGlow (with the help of GraphViz,) and some command-line magic using awk and grep.

To start, a list of all the conflicting t-codes, as well as a list of the "role to t-code" mappings is needed. You can get this information out of your ERP system, and either your auditors can give you a list of conflicting t-codes or you can try to get it from the Internet.[12]

---

[12] I found a list of SAP t-code conflicts at www.sapsecurityonline.com/sox_sod/fullconflicts.xls.

For the following, I assume that the t-code conflicts are stored in a CSV file (conflicts.csv), listing the conflicting t-codes as two columns. The "role to t-code" mapping file (sap_role.csv) has two columns, as well:

```
Sales Order Entry,V.23
Sales Order Release,F-06
```

The first column represents the role, and the second one the corresponding t-code. With these two files, you execute the following command:

```
awk -F, '{print $2}' sap_role.csv | sort | uniq
| grep -f - conflicts.csv > sap1.csv
```

What this does is extract only the conflicting t-codes that are actually used by any of the roles in the sap_role.csv file. The sap1.csv file now contains all the t-codes from the roles file along with the corresponding conflicting t-code. What is missing in this file is the "role to t-code" mapping, which I am going to add to sap1.csv with the following command:

```
cat sap_role.csv >> sap1.csv
```

This is what we have to do to prepare our data file. The next step is to configure the colors for the link graph, to highlight conflicting t-codes. Create a file called sap.properties with the following content:

```
color.source="lightblue"
color.sourcetarget="orange3"
```

Now run AfterGlow with the following command:

```
cat sap1.csv | afterglow -t -e 1.3 -c sap.properties
| neato -Tgif -o sap.gif
```

The AfterGlow parameters instruct the tool to use a two-column input (-t), use a default edge length of 1.3 (-e), and use the file sap.properties as its property file (-c). Neato is one of GraphViz's layout tools that takes a DOT file as input and generates a link graph based on the spring model. After the command is run, the generated link graph is stored in the file sap.gif.

To separate the nonconflicting roles from the rest, as was done in Figure 7-15, you need to filter either your data file or apply some processing on the graph. There is no easy configuration that could be applied to AfterGlow to filter out those nodes. If you assume that the t-codes are not transitive (see discussion earlier), you can filter all the t-codes that are not directly used by a user role. This can be done with a property entry like this:

```
color.target="invisible" if ($fields[0] =~ /^[A-Za-z_\-0-9]{4,7}$/)
```

This makes the assumption that t-codes consist of alphanumeric characters and can include underscores or dashes. It further assumes that t-codes are between four and seven characters long. Anything else would identify a role name. This is a pretty poor configuration, but it does its job. The application of this configuration will significantly reduce the amount of data shown in the graph.

DATABASE MONITORING

Compliance efforts, especially the Sarbanes Oxley (SOX) act, often focus on protecting data. In the case of SOX, it is financial data, which is generally stored in some sort of a database. Monitoring databases is, therefore, an important objective. Tasks such as making sure that financial records were not altered and only authorized personnel have seen the financial results are crucial to companies under the umbrella of SOX. But it is not just SOX that we need to be concerned with here. Other regulations, such as PCI or HIPAA, are also concerned with database monitoring.

Each database has different ways of enabling auditing. Oracle, for example, has at least four ways of logging data.[13] **Fine-grained auditing** is the most powerful of all methods. It can log anything down to row-level audit information. It stores the logs in a specific audit database. **Oracle audit** logs are by default written into an internal, virtual database table. They can log database access, as well as changes to the database structure. The location of the log can be changed to be a file, rather than a database table. **System triggers** can be invoked through specific system events, and various **system logs** are written by the database system itself. Before you deploy any of the auditing methods on one of your databases, make sure you understand all the impacts this can have on your

---

[13] You can access a good article on Oracle logging at www.securityfocus.com/infocus/1689.

system. Performance impact, privacy implications, and resource exhaustion (such as filling up the SYSTEM tables with log records that, in turn, will crash your system) need to be considered!

Let's take a look at an Oracle setup. First, add this line in your init.ora file to enable the Oracle audit logs to be written into a file rather than a database table:

```
AUDIT_TRAIL=OS
AUDIT_FILE_DEST=/var/log/oracle/audit.log
```

Now you configure the commands and activities to log. You can establish a sample configuration a simple `audit create session` command. Make sure you are running the command as sysdba. This will enable auditing[14] for all session-related activity. Every login will now create a log entry like the following one:

```
Thu Jun 25 9:30:00 1976
ACTION: 'CONNECT'
DATABASE USER: '/'
OSPRIV: SYSDBA
CLIENT USER: ram
CLIENT TERMINAL: pts/2
STATUS: 0
```

If you are not just interested in connection information, but also database table access, use a command similar to the following:

```
audit SELECT, INSERT, DELETE, UPDATE on user.table by ACCESS;
```

A sample log entry resulting from this configuration looks like this:

```
Thu Jun 25 9:39:00 1976
ACTION: 'update salary set amount=10000 where name='Raffy''
DATABASE USER: ''
OSPRIV: SYSDBA
CLIENT USER: ram
CLIENT TERMINAL: pts/2
STATUS: 0
```

---

[14] For more options on the **audit** command, check the Oracle reference, http://tinyurl.com/28e3ly.

These log entries are fairly simple to read for a human. To parse them, it takes a bit of log parsing magic to combine the multiline entries into a single line programmatically. An interesting and important fact about the log entries is that the client user is recorded along with its activity. The client user is really the operating system user that was used to connect to Oracle. In the case of remote access, this user field will be empty. Oracle is not passed the user information. This is great news because it enables us to correlate these logs with the operating system logs. Also note that the entire SQL query was logged, which is yet again great news in terms of our being able to conduct all kinds of analyses.

Microsoft SQL Server has a similar log format that logs even more information than Oracle. Here is a sample log entry to compare with the Oracle entry:

```
0         11/11/2007 17:02:53    11/11/2007 17:02:53    0.009   0.009   5.000
172.16.36.57    172.16.20.70    3066  1433    0         0         192     389     1
1       0.000    -         -         -         -         EM006     PubAnonymous    PUB     17
5703    0        Warning::Changed database context to 'mycorp'. ,Changed language
setting to us_english.         -         0         Login:PubAnonymous@3066 mycorp   386
```

You can see all kinds of information, such as the client IP address, the server port, the OS of the user who connected, the database user, and so on.

What are we going to do with these logs? Our proclaimed goal is to monitor people accessing database tables. I therefore visualized the client-user and database user as a link graph. Figure 7-16 shows the result.

The dataset I used in Figure 7-16 is fairly small and therefore does not show too many exciting things. However, one of the interesting things is that the user bizsvc used two different database users (U2006 and U2004) to access the database. Most likely, this is a business application that uses different users to query different database tables. It would be more of a concern if two users were using the same database user account. Fortunately, this does not seem to be the case in this log file. One of the properties of the graph is that the source nodes are color coded with the user's role. The legend is shown at the top of the graph. Among other scenarios, the role of information can be used to verify that only authorized users are using privileged database accounts. In Figure 7-16, no DBA users are using a privileged database account. The opposite is shown in Figure 7-17, where a non-DBA user is connecting as sysdba. This is definitely a warning sign.

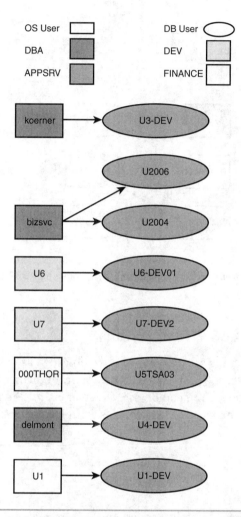

Figure 7-16 Link graph of a database audit log. Color encodes the role of the operating system user.

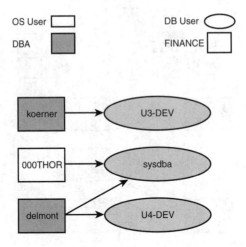

Figure 7-17   Link graph showing privileged database access from a non-DBA user account.

DATABASE AUDIT LOG VISUALIZATION

The first step in generating an audit log visualization such as the one shown in Figure 7-16 is to extract the pertinent information from the raw audit record. There are multiple ways to do so. You could write a regular expression that extracts the users from the log file or, what I prefer for this audit log, use awk to extract the fields:

```
grep select query.dat | awk -F'        ' '{printf"%s,%s\n",$22,$23}'
```

This command assumes that
- We are only interested in select statements.
- The 22nd field is the database user.
- The 23rd field is the operating system user.

Also, notice that the argument to the -F parameter is a tabulator, not a set of spaces. The parameter defines the field record separator in query.dat, which is a tab.

After we extract the data, we need to get it into AfterGlow to visualize. To assign colors based on the user's roles, build a properties file with content similar to the following:

```
shape.source="box"
color.source="gray91" if ($fields[0] eq "U6")
color.source="gray61" if ($fields[0] eq "finsvc")
color.source="gray61" if ($fields[0] eq "bizsvc")
```

This will instruct AfterGlow to use boxes as the source nodes and color the different users (U6, finsvc, and bizsvc) based on their roles. gray91 is used for developers, and gray61 is used for the financial service role. Then use the following command to generate the graph:

```
cat data.csv | afterglow.pl -c db.properties -t
| dot -Grankdir=LR -Tgif -o db.gif
```

This command instructs AfterGlow to use the properties from db.properties and use only two columns as input (-t). The output is then piped to the dot command, which we instruct to use a left-to-right ordering (-Grankdir=LR). This generates a vertical graph rather than a horizontal one. The output is then stored in the file db.gif.

It seems that there are no other scenarios worth investigating in the graph of Figure 7-16. Wouldn't it be interesting if we could see exactly which database tables these users accessed? The logs we looked at, both from Oracle and MS SQL, record the SQL query that was executed. It should therefore be possible to extract the databases tables from the query strings. It turns out that doing so is not trivial at all. It involves some regular expression magic to deal with all kinds of different and complicated queries. It would be much easier if the database explicitly logged all database tables involved in a specific query, but they do not. Maybe someone will come up with a good script to extract the database table information. For now, I hacked some regular expressions to extract the table information from a SQL query.[15] Figure 7-18 shows the result of visualizing a database log with OS username, database username, and database table.

You will realize that in Figure 7-18 not only does the database show tables as target nodes but also specific SQL queries (e.g., SERVERPROPERTY('ProductLevel')). Apart from accessing database tables, you can use SQL commands to execute operations other than just accessing database tables.

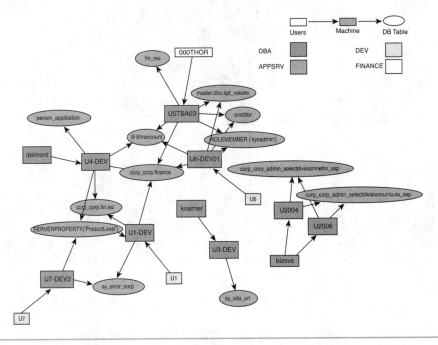

Figure 7-18 Link graph of a database audit log showing table access and database commands.

When doing this type of analysis, make sure you understand the extent of the underlying data that you are analyzing. SQL logs, for example, might contain queries that execute as a user other than the log record explicitly identifies. SQL has a command, execute as, that enables a user to execute a query under the credentials of another user.

---

[15] The command I used as a hack is really ugly. It could be much improved, and it should be. I am almost ashamed to put it here:

grep select query.dat| "awk -F'   ''{printf"%s,%s,%s\n",$23,$22,$31}' | perl -pe 's/([^,]*,[^,]*).*from (.*?) (where|by|order)?.+/\1,\2/' | perl -pe 's/is_.*/ADMIN_FUNCTION/' | perl -pe 's/.*declare.*?select.*//' | grep -v "^\s*$"

This could derail your analysis fairly significantly. Make sure there are no such or similar cases in your logs before you start visualizing them.

Let's go back to Figure 7-18. Notice first the three clusters of connected nodes. The one cluster on the right of the graph seems to be some kind of an automated application that queries regular database tables. The user bizsvc is most likely an application account used by the application tier to access the database. The second cluster is the smallest one, where the DBA user koerner seems to be accessing the sy_site_url table. The fact that this is a DBA (based on the color coding of the source node) should encourage us to take a close look at what this user is doing. The database table name seems to indicate that this is a table that contains URLs. There is probably nothing to worry about. You might realize that it can be really hard to determine whether a specific database access was critical. The table names can be cryptic. Case in point, read some of the other node values in the graph. It is really hard to understand what type of data is hidden in those tables. For this reason, include your database people in this type of analysis or let them do it altogether. They have the domain knowledge to do it.

Having looked at the two smaller clusters in Figure 7-18, we need to attack the bulk of the graph. We have two ways to approach this. We either start with the user nodes or we look at the database tables that were accessed to identify anomalous or suspicious activity. Let's do the latter. Reading through the tables, we see a few things that look interesting: corp_corp.fin.sal, corp_corp.finance, person_application, fin_res, and creditor. The latter two tables were accessed by a finance user, 000THOR. This seems right. One of those tables was also accessed by a developer, which seems reasonable, too. The other tables were accessed by both developers and DBAs. That is interesting. Why would a DBA (delmont) query from the financial tables? There is something wrong. It would be okay if the DBA executed table maintenance commands such as grant or alert, but definitely not SELECTs.

Another way to look at this data is by using parallel coordinates, as shown in Figure 7-19. The parallel coordinates chart was generated in Advizor (see Chapter 9 "Data Visualization Tools").[16] The first column shows the user's roles. The second and third columns show the OS username and the database username, respectively. You can see that there are mostly one-to-one relationships between the set of usernames, except for the bizsvc database user. The link between the database users and the database tables is a bit harder to analyze. We should be looking for scenarios where DBAs are accessing the same tables as finance or appsrv users. As mentioned earlier earlier, privileged users (DBAs) should not be reading data from pure data tables. They have no business looking

---

[16] Unfortunately, I have not found a parallel coordinate visualization tool that is freely available and practical.

at those entries. There are exceptions for overlaps: tables such as the @@trancount, for example. The figure has marked all the tables that are "data tables" using a black dot in the middle of the table bubble. The first three were identified by following the finance users to their tables. I identified these tables manually and left the two system tables or internal SQL tables out of the picture. Going back from these three tables, there should be no privileged user who accessed them. As we already know, the user delmont violated this policy.

Following this paradigm, we will miss another table that shouldn't be accessed by a DBA user: corp_corp_fin.sal. If we look at a dataset spanning a longer period, we might see financial users accessing this table, too. Note that I didn't mention the dev users at all. As soon as a database or a table is in production, they should not be accessing it. During development, this might be a scenario that is okay.

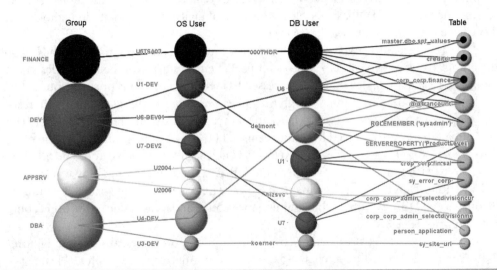

Figure 7-19   Parallel coordinate graph of a database audit log showing table access and database commands.

SUMMARY

This chapter started with a journey through the world of compliance. How does compliance fit into the world of governance, risk, and compliance (GRC)? I introduced the concepts of policies, controls, and monitors. To ensure context and show how these concepts fit into a bigger picture, I outlined some regulations that could be imposed on your company. The regulations themselves are not specific about how to implement and run an IT infrastructure. This is where IT best practices or IT frameworks, such as COBIT, enter the scene. These frameworks provide guidance on defining control objectives.

To narrow the scope and help with navigating the IT frameworks and regulations, the chapter took a look at some of the regulations to highlight where explicit logging requirements are specified. This can also be useful as guidance for your log management implementation if you do not have to comply with any specific regulation.

To approach the topic of "visualizing compliance," I first addressed the topic of an audit, which is the central point in a compliance effort. From there, the chapter worked its way into monitoring controls and the design of a compliance dashboard. This discussion led to the topic of risk management, to guide the prioritization of control-deficiency remediation.

The chapter closed with the discussion of two specific compliance efforts that greatly benefit from a visualization approach. How can visualization assist in the process of finding separation of duties violations? Monitoring database access and role abuse is the second use-case that can significantly benefit from a visual approach.

The controls implemented for compliance can be translated into their own projects. In the next chapter, about perimeter threat, a lot of these controls (both individual and sets of) are discussed. You can then use them for your compliance program. After all, as you have learned, compliance is not an isolated effort; it has myriad relationships with other IT projects.

Insider Threat

8

Managing security used to be an easy task. The expectation was that you installed a firewall to protect the corporate assets from attackers. Every now and then, you had to poke a hole into that firewall to enable some application to talk to the Internet or vice versa. If things were taken really seriously, you also had to install a network-based intrusion detection system (NIDS) to monitor the traffic entering the corporate network. It was a lot of fun—maybe I am just a masochist—to look at the NIDS logs to find how many times you were scanned in the past 24 hours. It got a bit frustrating every now and then when you did not really find any important events that would indicate someone actually attacking you. However, you did your job and everyone seemed to be happy.

Unfortunately, those times are over. If you are responsible for security at your company, now you not only have to make sure that there are no attacks from the outside, but you also must deal with the threat from within. It is no longer just the evil hacker on the other side of your firewall who you have to protect your users from. It could be your coworker, your teammate who is the one you have to turn in after the next investigation. The malicious **insider** is the new threat that we need to protect from, in addition to all the threats coming from the outside.

In this chapter, I take a close look at the insider threat problem. We take a look at what the insider threat really is. I answer questions such as, "Why should you have an interest in insider threat?" and "Why does visualization play an important role in dealing with malicious insiders and mitigating the insider threat?" To make the insider threat problem slightly more tangible, I walk through three sample insider attacks and show how they can be detected with visualization of audit trails and electronic log files. After you have a better understanding of the types of malicious insider activities, I present a generic framework that can be used to mitigate the insider threat problem by visually identifying possible malicious insiders in an early stage. The detection process that I present is by no means a complete insider threat solution, nor do I claim it will necessarily detect all of them. The approach, early-stage research, needs to be extended and refined to become more efficient and reliable. However, the process has been applied to real data and has yielded successful results! The interesting property of the detection process is that it is extensible by design. Changes in the threat landscape or new findings and knowledge can be incorporated easily.

INSIDER THREAT VISUALIZATION

Why should visualization be used to detect malicious insiders? To analyze insider threat, we have to consider huge amounts of data—much more than for other security analysis tasks. This problem differs from others where we can just monitor violations. Malicious insiders often have legitimate access to machines and data. These activities won't be logged by security-monitoring solutions. They are not exceptions or breaches. Log levels might have to be turned up to detect malicious insiders. In addition, we are not dealing with network layer problems. Firewall log files will be of limited use to identify malicious insiders. Fraud, especially, is almost exclusively visible in application logs. In some cases, however, we need the network level logs, too. Again, here is another factor that increases the amount of data at hand. So far, you could still make the argument that deterministic or statistical methods could be used to do the analysis. This is where the core strength of visualization comes in. Often, the questions, the things to look for, are not known in advance. They are uncovered during the analysis process. Visualization is a great tool for provoking those questions and helping find answers to them.

The dynamic nature of fraud makes it a particularly challenging detection problem for static algorithms. Fraudsters quickly adapt to fixed threshold-based detection systems. With a visual approach, we are looking for any unusual patterns, making it an effective strategy for identifying new classes of fraud.

Visualization is a key technique to help identify and analyze insiders.

WHAT IS A MALICIOUS INSIDER?

To understand insider threat, we should start by defining what a malicious insider is:

Current or former employee or contractors who intentionally exceeded or misused an authorized level of access to networks, systems, or data in a manner that targeted a specific individual or affected the security of the organization's data, systems or daily business operations.[1]

Malicious insiders are people with legitimate access to information. They are not trying to circumvent any access control mechanisms to gain access to interesting information. They already have access. This is a really important point. It means that traditional security devices do not have the capabilities to find these types of attacks. The NIDSs, as we know them, are monitoring network traffic for known patterns of malicious behavior. They are completely useless in scenarios where there is no attack and no violation of communication policies. The same is true for firewalls, host-based IDSs, antivirus, and so on. All these devices are good at detecting malicious traffic or behavior.

The market has realized that this is a shortcoming and created a new market segment for "insider threat tools." But these tools are no panacea. They might claim to have the capabilities to detect malicious insiders, but that's unfortunately an illusion. How are you going to find a malicious insider who is selling company secrets to the competition if all he does is take printouts of confidential financial statements he uses for his daily job with him when he leaves work? No tool or device will prevent him from doing so. Even if there were some kind of a device to detect documents when they are leaving the company premises, who says that the employee is not authorized to take the documents home to work on them? I think you get the point. It is illusive to believe that any device or tool can detect all insider crimes. However, what does exist are tools that can *help* detect malicious insiders. We will see in this chapter that these tools are not necessarily specific devices, but often log files of systems and application behavior that will help convict the guilty.

THREE TYPES OF INSIDER CRIMES

The insider threat space can be subdivided into three categories, as shown in Figure 8-1. The boundaries between the three categories are smooth. The categories overlap in many ways. For example, an information theft case can also be a sabotage and a fraud case at the same time.

---

[1] "Insider Threats in the SDLC: Lessons Learned From Actual Incidents of Fraud, Theft of Sensitive Information, and IT Sabotage," by Dawn M. Cappelli, Randall F. Trzeciak, and Andrew P. Moore (www.cert.org/archive/pdf/sepg500.pdf).

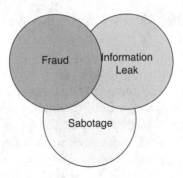

Figure 8-1   Insider threat can be subdivided into three categories: information theft, fraud, and sabotage.

The following are short descriptions for each of the insider threat categories:

- **Information theft** is concerned with the stealing of confidential or proprietary information. This includes things such as financial statements, intellectual property, design plans, source code, trade secrets, and so on.
- **Fraud** deals with the misuse of access privileges or the intentional excess of access levels to unjustly obtain property or services through deception or trickery. Examples range from selling confidential information (social security numbers, credit card numbers) to modification of critical data for pay (driver's license records, criminal record, welfare status) to stealing money (through financial applications, tampering with order processing system, and so on).
- **Sabotage** has to do with any kind of action to harm individuals, organizations, organizational data, systems, or business operations. Examples include the deletion of information, bringing down systems, website defacements, logical bombs, and so on.

Let's take a separate look at each of the three types of insider threat individually to understand better what is involved in each of these three types of insider threats.

INFORMATION THEFT

Information theft is incredibly hard to detect. Information is intangible. Copying information is quick and simple. We all carry huge data stores around with us: cell phones, USB sticks, iPods, and laptops. They can all be used to store and transport thousands of documents. It is almost impossible to detect someone sneaking out a confidential document loaded on a cell phone. It is not feasible to inspect all phones of people as they leave the office. And often, information is not removed on a physical device. It is put into an email message sent to a recipient outside of the company.

Protecting information to prevent it from being leaked turns out to be a challenging task. Insiders have legitimate access to confidential information. They need this information to do their daily jobs. Stealing confidential information does not involve an act of access violation or an attack. Customer records, for example, can be accessed by support personnel, the finance department, sales, professional services, and so on. Source code for computer applications needs to be available to all developers. They often have access to the entire product or, even worse, all the products that are hosted on the same source code control system.

An entire market space has formed around protecting information. There is still some confusion as to what to call this space. Some call it **extrusion detection,** alluding to the fact that there is not an intruder, but something is extruding. I personally think this is a horrible name, but that's my opinion. The space is also called **information-leak prevention** (ILP) or **data-leak prevention** (DLP). These names resemble much better and more descriptively what these information protection tools are doing.

Data-Leak Prevention Tools

What exactly are DLP tools doing? I usually point out two features. The first one is nothing really new. A DLP watches the network traffic, much like an IDS (except that the DLPs focus more on the application layer than IDSs do). It is configured with signatures that are looking for confidential or sensitive information leaving the network (for example, social security numbers or credit card numbers). NIDS could do this, too. The difference is that the DLPs are specifically built to do this type of analysis. A DLP would, for example, monitor network traffic for credit card numbers. If traffic is identified, the DLP can display the violating transaction. Transactions can be emails, IRC chats, Web connections, and so forth. DLP interfaces are optimized toward displaying this type of information. NIDS are not meant to display this type of information in the context of a transaction. They are good at flagging the violation, but not at showing the original transaction. NIDS are also not optimized toward application layer protocol analysis, such as email dissection.

Although the DLPs have the upper hand when it comes to information display, they could really learn from their NIDS colleagues. The products I have seen require configurations to be done in text files, don't support full regular expressions, do not have a good way to update the signatures, and so forth.

The second feature that DLPs offer is document watermarking or document tracking. This is where things are getting interesting. Your financial statements, for example, are documents that are not written for general consumption. With a DLP, you can register this document with a centralized document registration server. It then monitors the network traffic and finds instances of the document floating around. This is only the beginning. The DLP can also detect whether someone copied the Word document into an Excel spreadsheet. Or, if someone takes a paragraph of the original document and pastes it into an email, the DLP can still detect the document.

Logging In Data-Leak Prevention Tools

Most DLP products are horrible at logging! One of the products does not even have pre-defined logging built in. The user has to define, on a per-rule basis, what the log messages look like. Bad idea! Don't let the user muck with logging. If security device vendors cannot get logging right, how are users supposed to? On top of that, not defining a logging format makes integration and interoperability a nightmare. I am digressing, but I had to bring this up.

The second drawback of DLPs is one that might sound familiar to a lot of you: **false positives.** These products have exactly the same problems that NIDS have. It is extremely difficult to configure the DLPs precisely enough to detect all the cases of information leaks while not flagging benign instances. Assume you want to watch for social security numbers floating around on the network. You would configure a rule to monitor all the traffic for strings of the form \d{3}-\d{2}-\d{4}. This corresponds to three numbers followed by a dash, then two numbers, another dash, and then followed by four numbers. Depending on where this sensor is placed, there might be legitimate traffic containing social security numbers. You now have to go ahead and teach the DLP all the instances of traffic where it is okay to see social security numbers. Try to be exact. You need to configure every client that should have access to this data as an exception to the rule. If an entire subnet of machines is allowed to access the data with social security numbers, but a couple of machines should be prohibited, you need to define these exclusions! Be careful about **false negatives** while setting up your policies. In various cases, policy violations can be missed. For example, encrypted traffic or unsupported versions of documents make it impossible for the DLP to analyze the documents. It is really exactly the same problem as IDS signature tuning. The fact that DLP vendors have not tried to learn from the NIDSs is not helping.

Information-Leak Examples

Take a look at Table 8-1. It shows a few examples of information theft and information leaks. It is worth noting that none of the attacks require technically sophisticated means or knowledge. Anyone can commit information theft.

Table 8-1   Examples of How Information Can Be Leaked

Activity	Example
Printing documents	When information is on a sheet of paper, it is simple to remove it from the workplace and share it with other people.
Copying information to disks	Similar to printing documents, information can be removed from the workplace without anyone noticing. Has anyone ever checked your cell phone for data before you left a facility?
Sending information via email	A common scheme is to send documents via email. A lot of times, private Web mail accounts are used to receive the information on the other side.

INFORMATION LEAK: EXAMPLE

In February 2007, a fairly large information-leak case made the news.[2] Scientist Gary Min faces up to 10 years in prison for stealing more than 16,000 documents and more than 22,000 scientific abstracts from his employer, DuPont. The intellectual property he was about to leak to a DuPont competitor, Victrex, was assessed to be worth $400 million. This is an extraordinary event of information leakage. However, similar cases occur all the time when employees are leaving their jobs. Shortly before actually leaving the company, they start collecting documents, emails, source code, and so on. In a lot of cases, the employees feel that they are entitled to this information. However, for the company this could mean significant losses, as the preceding case shows.

What can be done to detect these cases? Is it even possible to prevent them? Information leaks always have to do with people accessing information. Most often, the people have legitimate access to this data, which makes it a bit harder to detect mischief. Log entries will not flag suspicious activity. In addition, hardly anyone is auditing all document access. This is the precondition for this type of analysis. Access to critical documents needs to be audited. When this in place, visualization can be used to analyze the access logs. Figure 8-2 shows an example of a document access log. If your applications do not write an access log that contains this type of information, you could use file auditing (see Chapter 2, "Data Sources") to audit document access.

---

[2]   www.informationweek.com/news/showArticle.jhtml?articleID=197006474

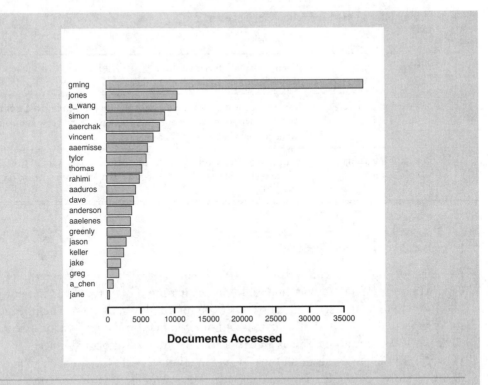

Figure 8-2   This bar chart shows how many different documents each user accessed.

If DuPont had been monitoring a document access graph like the one in Figure 8-2, they would have seen that Gary was accessing a lot of documents. The logical next step would have been to walk over to his desk to figure out why he was looking at all these documents. Granted, this is a focused way of monitoring activities. You would have to be specifically monitoring document access. This approach does not necessarily scale. The number of things to monitor is likely going to explode. Therefore, we need a more generic way of monitoring user activity. Figure 8-3 shows a slightly more generic way of monitoring user activity in a stacked bar chart. It is now possible to encode not just document access, but any type of activity in this chart. In this example, it is very visible that gmin showed the most activity. This is a fairly good indicator that you need to have a closer look at what he is up to.

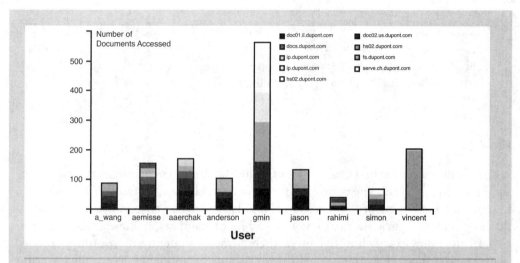

Figure 8-3 This stacked bar chart shows a way of monitoring data access on servers. Each user is represented as an individual bar, split by the different servers that were accessed. Each access constitutes a unit on the y-axis.

Yet another way of monitoring users would be to use a link graph, where each machine's amount of access (to, say, certain servers) for a user is encoded as an edge in a graph. The activity of just gmin is shown in Figure 8-4.

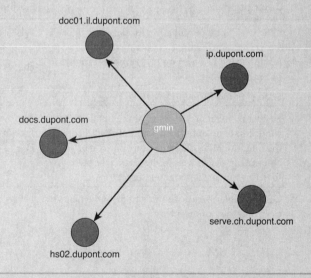

Figure 8-4 A link graph showing a single user's access of servers.

The size of the circles can be used to encode the amount of activity seen from that user. This graph can be extended in various ways. For example, the user nodes could be colored based on a separate property. Using the role of the user as the color shows how users behave relative to their role.

FRAUD

A class of insider threat that causes a lot of headaches in the corporate world and some significant loss is **fraud.** The reason for the activity and interest in fraud is, of course, that the potential monetary gain is compelling. This attracts well-organized and sophisticated groups that turn out to be involved in a lot of fraud cases. These groups are experienced and know exactly how to conceal their crimes. Frequently, these groups do not commit fraud themselves, but persuade people inside of companies to execute the crime in return for payment. There are many different types of fraud. Table 8-2 discusses some types that could likely be identified through electronic logs or electronic audit trails. Because of the difficulty of detecting these fraud cases in log files or audit trails, the table does not list tax fraud, real-estate fraud, insurance fraud, bribery, and so on.

Table 8-2   Different Fraud Categories and Examples

Fraud Category	Description	Examples
Occupational fraud	"The use of one's occupation for personal enrichment through the deliberate misuse or misapplication of the employing organization's resources or assets" Source: *Fraud Examiner's Manual*	False overtime Payroll and sick-time abuses
Financial statement fraud	Deliberate misrepresentation of the financial condition of an enterprise accomplished through the intentional misstatement or omission of amounts or disclosures in the financial statements to deceive financial statement users	Improper revenue recognition Overstatement of assets
Misappropriation of assets	Cash receipt schemes, fraudulent disbursements of cash, and theft of inventory	No receipt issued Sales during nonbusiness hours Any type of stealing of checks issued to the company

Fraud Category	Description	Examples
Financial institution fraud	Fraud related to banking institutions	Any false accounting entries
		Unauthorized withdrawals
		Unauthorized unrecorded cash payments
		Account sharing
Computer and Internet fraud	Tampering with computer programs, data files, operations, and so forth resulting in losses sustained by the organization whose computer system was manipulated	Phishing
		Auction and retail schemes

Each category in the table has its own detection mechanism. Most of the fraud cases can be identified by system irregularities—either through audits and checks in the applications or through monitoring of system-level parameters, such as changes of files, accessing of critical files, or accessing of database tables. Often it also helps to monitor access paths to uncover new paths or detect unauthorized access.

The Fraud Triangle

To determine how to detect fraud, it helps to understand what it takes for someone to commit this crime. For a person to commit fraud, a concept known as the **fraud triangle** has to be satisfied. Three factors must be present, as shown in Figure 8-5.

Figure 8-5   The fraud triangle, identifying the three preconditions for someone to commit fraud.

The first factor is **perceived opportunity.** The fraudster needs to have a way to override the antifraud controls or at least be confident enough that he has the capabilities to do so. An opportunity has to be present. A simple example is that the fraudster is left alone in a room where the object of desire is situated. If there is no electronic surveillance, an opportunity presents itself. The second factor is **pressure.** This can be either from inside of the organization or from the outside. Something has to drive the fraudster. Some of the pressure can also stem from financial needs that the fraudster has. The third factor is **rationalization.** It is interesting to know that rationalization has to be present already before the crime takes place. The fraudster does not view himself as a criminal. He therefore has to justify his misdeeds before he ever commits them.

How does this materialize in a person's behavior, and how is this going to help us with detecting fraud? We need to look for opportunity. After-hours activities, for example, are important to watch. We can additionally monitor for pressure situations. For example, you could monitor a salesperson who did not make his or her quota, someone who was put on a performance improvement plan (PIP), someone who has not received a raise, and so forth. All these indicators are important when we are monitoring for fraud cases.

Fraud-Detection Solutions

The market has identified fraud as a problem, and a number of companies provide solutions to help address it. Interestingly enough, no universal antifraud solution is available that covers all types of fraud. Each type of problem has its own solution. And even among these solutions, there does not seem to be a common theme. They do not rely on one specific way to detect fraud, such as reviewing audit logs. Some of the solutions help verify that provided information about an individual or a company is accurate. Others monitor the user of a service closely and make sure that the probability of impersonation is low. Yet others statistically analyze data to find irregularities or anomalies, such as irregularly high revenues per employee.

This means that we have to come up with different analysis methods on a case-by-case basis.

FRAUD DETECTION: EXAMPLE

A while ago, I received a phone call from my credit card company, and they told me that they had blocked my card because of concurrent transactions happening in different geographic locations in the United States. It was physically not possible for me to be in both those places at the same time. This is a fairly common heuristic that credit card companies use to detect fraudulent transactions. A similar situation is associated with user accounts. If the same user account logs in from two different subnets in a short period of time, there is probably something wrong.

Doing such an analysis can be done in various ways. The following is a sample application log entry that shows access to my Web portal:

```
217.139.17.162 - ram [21/Nov/2006:02:26:00 +0100]
"GET / HTTP/1.0" 403 2898 "-" "-"
```

For each of the IP addresses in the log file, we have to determine its geographic location, which we can do based on a method similar to the one introduced in Chapter 4, "From Data to Graphs." The difference is the library I am going to use here. We need to retrieve not the country name, but the actual longitude and latitude of the IP address location:

```
cat access_log | perl -naF/.-/ -M'Geo::IP::PurePerl'
- e '$geo=Geo::IP::PurePerl->new("GeoLiteCity.dat", GEOIP_STANDARD);
my (undef,undef,undef,undef,undef,$long,$lat)=
$geo->get_city_record($F[0]);
print "$F[0],$long,$lat\n";'
```

With the list of IP addresses, longitudes, and latitudes, we can then generate an XML file that can be read by the Google Maps API. The output format we need is the following:

```
<markers>
  <line color="#008800" width="2">
    <point lat="$lat" lng="$lng"/>
    <point lat="47.368527" lng="8.538503"/>
  </line>
  <line color="="#008800" width="2">
    <point lat="$lat2" lng="$lng2"/>
    <point lat="47.368527" lng="8.538503"/>
  </line>
  ...
</markers>
```

Each record in our log needs to generate an entry like this. I hard-coded the location of the second point. It is the location of my Web server that stays fixed. We can switch up the color of the individual polygon lines to match what we need them.

I leave it up to the reader to build a little script that translates the CSV output from the first command into an XML format like the preceding one. The next step is then to find whether a single IP address is using more than one user name. This is fairly simple:

```
less access_log | perl -pe 's/\.\d+ /\. /' |
awk '{print $1, $3}' | sort | uniq |
awk '{print $2}' | sort | uniq -c |
grep -v "\s*1 "
```

The Perl command summarizes the data by class-C network. The crazy sequence of sorts first looks at unique IP address: user pairs. Then the IP address is left off, and the command checks whether there was an instance where two IP addresses from different class-C networks used the same user. The grep command filters for only violations. If this sequence of commands shows any output, there was a concurrent access of the same user from different subnets. You can then use this information to color the edges in the graph from before. Sample output looks like the map in Figure 8-6. The red edges indicate access with the same user name but from different subnets. Be careful when flagging malicious activities with this approach. If you are analyzing data that ranges over a longer period of time, you might have users who traveled and now access the systems from a different location, resulting in an IP address from a different network.

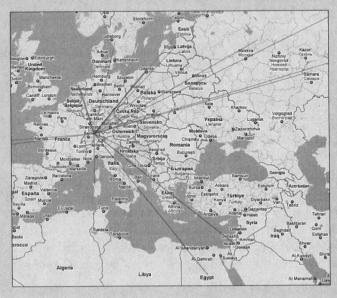

Figure 8-6   Map that shows access of a website that is located in Zurich, Switzerland. Red lines indicate concurrent access of the same user name but from different subnets, which could indicate stolen user IDs. (This figure appears in the full-color insert located in the middle of the book.)

To generate the map in Figure 8-6 through the Google Maps APIs, you need to use the JavaScript sample code from http://econym.googlepages.com/example_map7.htm. Save the source file on your machine and change the filename from `example4.xml` to the name you gave to the XML file generated earlier. Then open the HTML file on your machine and you should see the map you just defined.

SABOTAGE

Sabotage is not just a costly crime for the victim, but also one that is hard to fix. Operations might be impacted for extended periods of time and the effects will be felt for a long time. The following list is an attempt to classify different types of sabotage:

- **Information destruction,** such as deletion of files, databases, programs, backup tapes, or planting a logic bomb
- **Denial of service,** such as modifying passwords and user accounts, crashing systems, and cutting cables
- **Theft,** such as stealing computers, backups, and so forth
- **Harming organizations or individuals,** such as defacing websites, posting customer credit card data, modifying system logs to frame innocent people, and modifying a system or data to present embarrassing information

Interestingly enough, *fewer than half* (according to various studies) of sabotage cases involve sophisticated technical means. This would suggest that sabotage should be fairly easy to detect, at least in terms it being a relatively frequent occurrence.

Unfortunately there are no sabotage detection tools. The types of crimes are too different for one tool to address them all. The only category of sabotage that has created a software market early on is network-based denial-of-service (DoS) attacks. There is a fair collection of tools that help with detecting DoS attacks. They even mitigate them through different means, such as black hole routing or setting up firewall rules to block the offending traffic. There are challenges associated with these mitigation approaches. Using a firewall rule to block DoS traffic that clogs your Internet connection, for example, is useless. You have to filter before the traffic comes close to your corporate firewall. The only way to mitigate the problem is to collaborate with your ISP to block the attack closer to the attack origin.

Other types of DoS can be detected by monitoring tools. The simplest form of such a monitoring is ping. You ping machines to see whether they are available. A more sophisticated approach would be to establish connections to all the available services and make sure they are functional. There are tools, some in the open source space, that implement this functionality (see, for example, www.nagios.org). This helps guarantee that services are available and functioning correctly.

Other sabotage cases can be detected with file-integrity monitoring tools. These tools can be used to monitor critical files on machines. Each time a critical file gets modified, the tool can report the change. This is useful for detecting changes in system configuration files or cron jobs on critical machines. This can be an addition of new cron jobs or a change to an existing one. An open source solution for file integrity monitoring is the advanced intrusion detection environment (AIDE).[3]

The problem with these monitoring tools is that system administrators have access to the tool's configurations. It is fairly easy for them to alter the configuration to conceal their sabotage activities. A solution to this is to centrally collect configuration changes and make sure separation of duties is implemented with regard to alerting data. There should be no way for a system administrator to change a configuration change record. An additional problem in a lot of sabotage cases is the absence of electronic trails. Even where there are trails, no tools exist to mine the logs for sabotage instances.

SABOTAGE: EXAMPLE

One way for a system administrator to execute a sabotage attack is to plant a cron job that will execute a malicious command at some point in the future. The following is a simple script that can be used to check how many cron jobs are scheduled on a list of machines. The list of machines can be stored in a file called hosts.list:

```
for host in `cat hosts.list`; do
  count=`ssh root@$host 'find /etc \( -name crontab
    -o -name 'cron.\*' \) -exec grep -P "^\d" {}\; | wc -l' `
  echo `date +%D`,$host,$count >> cron.watch
done
```

The script goes through the list of hosts and uses SSH to execute a find command on each of them. The find command tries to find all cron jobs located in the /etc directory. For each of the files, it extracts the number of actual cron jobs

---

[3]   http://sourceforge.net/projects/aide

scheduled. The result is then written to a file called cron.watch. Running this script will generate a file that looks something like this:

```
04/17/08,vidar,4
04/17/08,thor,4
04/18/08,vidar,4
04/18/08,thor,6
```

I have two machines, vidar and thor. You can see that on April 18 two additional cron jobs were added to the machine. This might be okay, but it might not be. Figure 8-7 shows the deltas of the number of cron jobs found for each day. You can see that on January 8 two new jobs were added to all the machines under surveillance. Given this kind of finding, you would now go ahead and investigate this phenomenon.

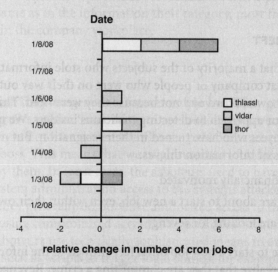

Figure 8-7   For each day, this chart shows the number of added or deleted cron jobs per machine.

The graph in Figure 8-7 was generated in Microsoft Excel. You need to build an additional column into your data series, which is the difference between the current number of cron jobs and the number from the previous day. Then use a stacked bar chart, where each series is one of the hosts.

A DETECTION FRAMEWORK FOR MALICIOUS INSIDERS

After looking at three different examples of how malicious insiders can be detected and studying the malicious insider personae, we now understand the insider threat space well enough to define a proactive approach to detecting malicious insiders.

The problem we already encountered a little earlier is that no devices identify a malicious insider when she or he enters the building or becomes active on the network. Similarly, no warning devices can warn us about malicious insider activities. The traces of malicious insiders are hidden all over throughout different applications and log files.

To help us identify malicious insiders, we need to know that they do not just decide one day that they will commit a crime and then execute it. There is a reconnaissance or preparation phase where the malicious insider slowly prepares his or her crime. We should go back to the insider personae discussed earlier. One key fact we learned from the different malicious insider types is that we have to not only monitor our current employees, but also need to have an eye on former employees. You might think that's an easy task. Former employees should not have access to any resources after they leave the company. I hope you are right. If your company is really good about its termination processes, all the user accounts will be disabled and all access will be revoked. However, reality shows that this is rarely the case. You are probably well off monitoring former employee accounts! Keep in mind that you need to take care not just of accounts directly associated with that person, but also shared accounts that the employee had access to.

It would be ideal if you not only monitored former employees but also employees who are on their way out, employees who show signs of resigning soon, and employees who show "suspicious" behavior. These groups of employees are especially prone to committing a crime.

In the following subsections, I first discuss a simple process to detect malicious insiders. The process discussion starts with the topic of **precursors.** Precursors are activities that we should be monitoring to detect malicious insiders before they become active. You will see that precursors are most useful for detecting saboteurs. Following the precursor discussion, we look at **watch lists,** and following that, we look at how to improve the detection process.

Visualization is going to play a role in almost each step of the detection process. Before we can start the discussion of the detection process, we need to look at the concept of precursors, which are the building blocks for the entire process.

PRECURSORS

To detect malicious insiders, we have to monitor user behavior and activities. The activities can be collected from applications, network traces, physical security devices such as badge readers or IP cameras, and so on. Some activities can be used to immediately flag someone as a malicious insider (for example, a regular employee who installs a key logger on a colleague's machine). This means that a subset of all the activities that users execute can be considered precursors:

> A **precursor** is an activity that, when observed, flags the associated user as a potential malicious insider. Each precursor can be assigned a score, which reflects the extent to which the precursor classifies someone as a malicious insider. Precursors are a way to differentiate "good" users from the ones that are up to no good and might potentially turn into the malicious insider.

Precursors are based on user activity. Qualifying an activity as a precursor can be done through one of three possible processes:

1. *Signature matching:* A predefined keyword, a specific action, and so on is defined, and activities are matched against the signatures.
2. *Policy monitoring:* The activity is compared against a set policy. A violation constitutes a precursor. Examples include people accessing certain data, using specific applications, surfing forbidden websites, and so forth.
3. *Anomaly detection:* First normal behavior is identified to create a profile or a baseline. Once established, the profile is used to assess behavior and determine whether it is "abnormal" or falls inside the boundaries of being "normal."

Table 8-3 lists a short sample of precursors. These precursors help flag users or machines that should be looked at a bit more closely. You can find a more comprehensive list of precursors at the end of this chapter.

Table 8-3 Sample Precursors and Their Detection Method

Precursor	Detection Method
Accessing job websites such as Monster.com	Signature matching
Salesperson accessing patent filings	Policy monitoring
Printing files with *resumé* in the filename	Signature matching
Sending emails to a large group of recipients outside of the company	Anomaly detection

Many precursors can be used to flag potential malicious insiders. The problem is that a lot of the tools that can identify some of this behavior have a high rate of false positives and therefore need to be complemented with some other way of confirming the precursor activity. Note that not all the precursors manifest themselves in electronic trails or log records. That is unfortunate.[5] A lot of precursors are hard to record. Things such as the family situation, personal problems of employees, and so forth do not leave an electronic trail that we could consume. I don't discuss any of these precursors, although experience shows that these are useful ones. A way to still capture these precursors is to use a simple application where the situation of each employee can be registered. One last point about monitoring people's activities: A number of countries have laws that prohibit the recording of user activity without a prior notice to the user or a legal case made. As an employee, I wish more countries had privacy laws covering these issues.

How do we compile a list of precursors? One way is to go through all your log files. Take each of them and identify activity that suggests suspicious behavior. Try to elicit input from as many people as possible. Application owners are, most of the time, the experts in understanding their log files. They generally have a fair understanding of what precursor you should be looking for to detect suspicious activity. You will have to get fairly creative. Think out of the box. It is not always the case that the log entry screams at you, asking for you to look at it. Things such as printing resumés can be on the list of precursors. This does not mean that someone printing a resumé is automatically a malicious insider. What you identify are precursors for users in general. In conjunction with other behavior, the fact that someone printed a resumé might help flag him or her as a malicious insider. It is likely that someone who prints a resumé is on his or her way out of the company. Along with printing the resumé, the person might be starting to collect proprietary information to bring along. Of course, this does not have to be the case. It might be that a manager was printing a resumé before interviewing someone. Or the person is leaving the company on good terms. However, some precursors are much more indicative of suspicious behavior. A salesperson should never access a company's patent filings. And an engineer should not access the financial records.

ASSIGNING SCORES TO PRECURSORS

Each precursor needs a score indicating the "badness" or level of suspiciousness of the activity. The higher the score, the more likely it is that the machine or user is malicious and needs to be looked into. A low score is associated with behavior that is common and could be seen any time. In most cases, a low score indicates normal behavior. Table 8-4 shows the same list of precursors from before, but now adds a score to each of the entries.

---

[5]   Fortunate from a privacy perspective! Unfortunate, if we put our log analysis hat on.

2. Visualize the Insider Candidate List

Visualizing the insider candidate list is the main step in the insider-detection process. The goal of this step is to produce a graph that helps identify a set of likely malicious insiders and weed out unlikely ones. Instead of using visualization to process and analyze the list of insider candidates generated in the preceding step, we could use a deterministic approach, especially since we have a score associated with all the attributes. Although this would be a valid solution, visualization offers some unique capabilities that we want to exploit:

- Visualization is nondeterministic. A script does exactly what it is programmed to do. Visualization provides the viewer the possibility of making his or her own interpretations and lets him or her find and discover new patterns.

- Machine-based detection methods are largely static, whereas the human visual system is dynamic and can easily adapt to the ever-changing techniques used by malicious insiders.

- Visualization brings up questions you have not thought about, instead of just answering existing questions.

Let's step back for a second to think about what exactly we want to accomplish. This is a list of three goals we are seeking to accomplish:

- Get a feeling for groups of users. Which users exhibit approximately the same behavior? Do any users not fall into any groups? Are there outliers in otherwise consistent clusters? Why?

- Adding information about a user's role helps determine whether a precursor is indeed a warning sign. For example, printing a resumé is part of an HR person's regular job and not generally a sign of a malicious insider activity.

- Find users with high scores (i.e., users who triggered a significant number of precursors).

Identifying Groups of Users with Similar Behavior

The first goal we can accomplish by visualizing the users and their precursor behavior. Figure 8-9 shows an example. The graph draws users with similar agendas in proximity. This is an effect of using link graphs, which try to find an optimal placement of the nodes. This helps grouping users of similar roles together.

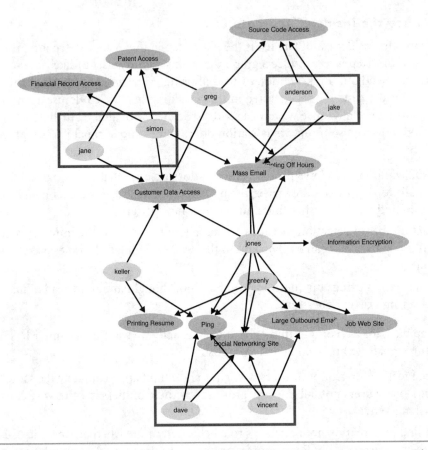

Figure 8-9   This graph shows how users can be grouped into roles by analyzing their precursor behavior. Users of the same role exhibit similar precursor behavior.

I used rectangles in Figure 8-9 to annotate users who exhibit similar behavior. It does not necessarily mean that these users have a similar job role, but their observed activities suggests so. Note that the grouping was done loosely. The users do not exhibit exactly the same behavior. Nevertheless, it seems that the users' roles are related. For example, both Jane and Simon are accessing patent information, as well as customer data. Hopefully, both of these users are working in legal and have a real need to do so. Greg, on the other hand, seems to be accessing patent data and customer data. In addition, he is printing off-hours and is trying to access source code. This is not a good combination of activities. If the attempted accessing of source code were not in the mix, this user could also belong to the same group as Simon and Jane, but not with the attempted accessing of source code. The graph helps quickly identify such instances.

Also note that not all the user nodes in Figure 8-9 are annotated with a rectangle. Jones and Greenly most likely do not belong to the same role, even though they are drawn very closely to each other. Jones is exhibiting much more activity than Greenly, and Greenly distinguishes himself by the additional customer data access. These are sub-tleties that need to be taken into account when grouping the users together. However, the visual representation greatly helps finding users that might be related.

This type of clustering or grouping helps us accomplish the first goal; we have a way to identify groups of users.

Augmenting the Analysis with User Roles

If, in addition to the precursor logs, we have an actual list of roles for each user, we can augment our graph with that information. This will ease our analysis of user groups and provide an additional data point. Instead of guessing what role various users belong to by comparing them, their roles are explicitly encoded in the graph. Figure 8-10 shows the same graph as before, but this time the roles of the users are encoded as the color of the user's nodes.

Coloring the nodes based on the role of the users simplifies our precursor analysis immensely. We can see that two of the groups that we found earlier, the ones covering the users on the top of the graph, indeed coincide with real user roles (engineering and legal). However, we also see that Greg is an engineer, yet he exhibits behavior that is unique to legal workers. This was not obvious in the previous graph.

The bottom of the graph shows a different picture. We identified the two users, Vincent and Dave, to be of the same group (see Figure 8-9). This is, however, not the case, as Figure 8-10 shows. The single finding in Figure 8-10 that gives the most cause for concern is related to the marketing people. They are all over the map in terms of trigger-ing a number of precursors. Looking at which exact precursors they trigger, however, mitigates this concern; they all seem fairly benign. None of them really poses a signifi-cant threat.

So far, we are only identifying groups of users, without making any statement about how bad those activities really were. The next step is going to address this objective by starting to use the precursor scores.

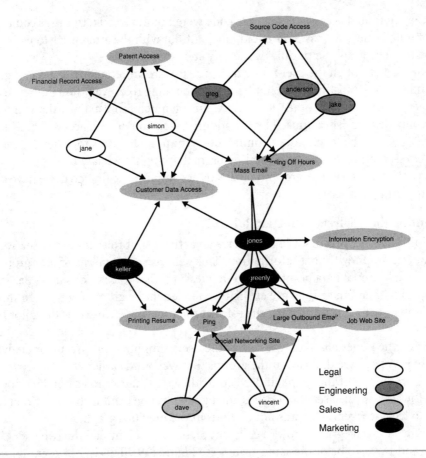

Figure 8-10 Users and their precursor activity. User nodes are colored by using the user's role. This way the identification of outliers becomes much easier.

Identifying Users with High Scores

It is now time to make use of the precursor scores to identify users who triggered many of the precursors. We can add an additional property to the graph to encode the precursor scores. Figure 8-11 uses a new set of data than the previous graphs have used. In the new graph, the size of the user nodes (the rectangles) encodes the cumulative score of a user. Note that the size of the circles is kept the same for all nodes and does not encode any information.

In Figure 8-11, malicious precursors are colored black. These are all the ones with a score of 5 or higher. Precursors that could just as well be benign behavior are gray.

Malicious precursors should never be seen. However, the problem of false positives prevents us from taking immediate action if a user triggers them. A user who triggers multiple malicious precursors increases the certainty of something being wrong.

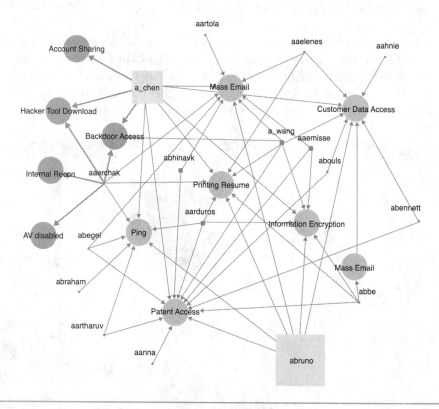

Figure 8-11 Users and their precursor activity. Malicious precursors are colored in black, and precursors that could as well indicate benign activities are represented in gray. The size of the rectangles encodes the score a user accumulated.

In Figure 8-11, we notice two users right away: abruno and a_chen. They seem to be triggering a lot of precursors. It looks like abruno is the worst person in the mix and deserves some closer attention. Is that right? Take a look at the precursors abruno triggered. They are all benign ones (gray circles). Not a single one of them is a malicious one (black circles). On the other hand, a_chen triggered some of the malicious precursors, and so did aaerchak, who shows up as a small node compared to the others—the reason for this being that the user only triggered its precursors once, whereas other users have triggered some of the precursors many times. This is why aaerchak accumulated a relatively small score. Having a closer look at the individual precursors, it seems that aaerchak should be investigated closer.

This finding is fairly interesting. It seems that someone who triggers a few malicious precursors can almost fly below the radar. Maybe a link graph is not the best way to visualize this type of data?

What happens if we take the same information and try another type of visualization? In Figure 8-12, you can see how the same information looks in a treemap. The users are on the top of the hierarchy, followed by the precursor they triggered. Color encodes the score of the precursor. The darker the squares, the higher the precursor score. The size of the boxes encodes the number of times a certain precursor was observed.

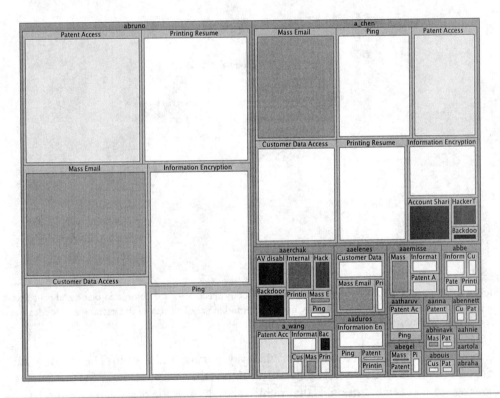

Figure 8-12   Precursor activity encoded in a treemap. The hierarchy is User > Precursor. The color represents the score that a certain activity represents, and the size of the boxes is the amount of times a certain behavior showed up.

We are interested in big dark boxes. With this treemap, we can quickly identify the same group of potentially malicious users who we already found with the link graph. Abruno shows a lot of low-score behavior, whereas aaerchak is noteworthy for triggering significant and potentially malicious precursors. Compared with the link graph (Figure 8-11), the treemap makes it easier to spot the users who triggered high-score precursors.

This concludes Step 2, the visualization of the insider candidate list. We will later see how some of the shortcomings of our visualization methods can be addressed through an improved detection process. The next step in the insider-detection process is going to help us manage larger insider candidate lists.

3. Apply the Threshold Filter

The graphs that visualize insider candidate lists can grow large quickly. We have to find some filtering techniques to narrow down the list of users to focus on.

Filtering the candidate graph can be done in various ways. The most obvious is to focus on the size of the user nodes. We can define a threshold to remove small nodes. Small nodes represent users who did not accumulate a high score. To determine a good threshold, various approaches can be applied. One is to choose a trial-and-error method, whereby we slowly increase the threshold to filter out more and more nodes until the graph represents a small and workable set of users. *Small* in this case is relative. It can be any size that you are comfortable working with. A simple way to see what happens if such a threshold filter is applied is to look at a bar chart that shows the score plotted for each user. Figure 8-13 shows a bar chart for the example we looked at before.

Based on the distribution of users and their scores, you can now make a decision where to set the threshold. Be cautious, though. The bar chart in Figure 8-13 shows a long tail. This would suggest we set the threshold somewhere above 50. This would then leave us with only the two users with the highest scores. However, as we have seen in the previous graphs, the next user down (aaerchak) is worth having in the picture, too!

Another way of setting a threshold is to sort the values and always pick the top *n* users, where *n* can be any number. This is can be dangerous, too. If the "*n* plus 1" user is one who behaves in an anomalous fashion or even maliciously, you just missed him. However, it seems that the scoring process should be able to take care of that and not the filtering process. We will investigate what we can do to improve the scoring process to circumvent these problems.

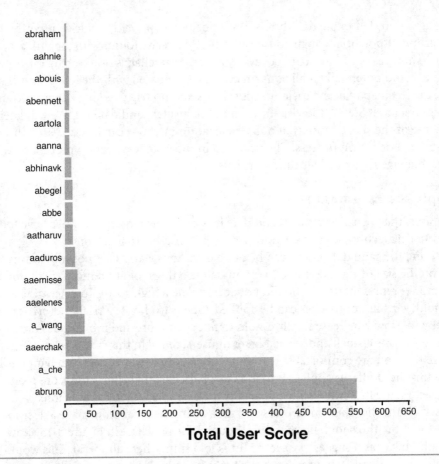

Figure 8-13   Bar chart showing the accumulated score per user.

As soon as we determine how to filter our list of insider candidates, we can use the new list to generate a graph for only the remaining users. To continue on the example from before, if we filter the graph, we end up with Figure 8-14. The threshold was set to include only the top three users, which was the outcome of the previous discussions.

This step almost concludes the insider-detection process. The only step we have left is tuning the precursor list, which is discussed in the next section.

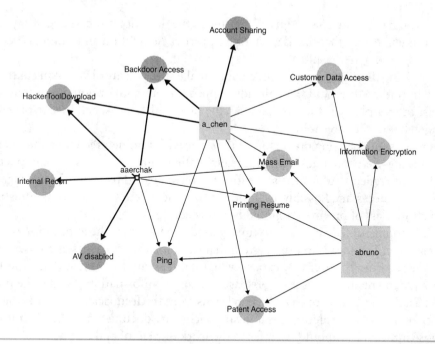

Figure 8-14 A link graph of malicious insider activity, filtered to show only users who accumulated a high score.

4. Tune the Precursor List

The last step in the insider-detection process involves tuning the precursors and their scores. The goal of this tuning process is to arrive at a score for each precursor that helps to clearly identify a malicious insider, but at the same time it should not flag benign actors.

In the previous steps, we recognized that four different situations can apply to a precursor:

1. A precursor turns out to flag benign activity all the time. *Remove it.*

2. A precursor is missing. Some activity is not caught. *Define a new precursor.*

3. A user triggers a precursor although the activity is absolutely benign for this user. *Define an exception for this user.*

4. A score for a precursor is either too high or too low. *Adjust the score.*

After you have made these adjustments, rerun the detection process and verify the result. You will realize that this is an iterative process. Adaptation and tuning is necessary to get better and better results.

When going through tuning of precursors, make sure you are also looking at the graph without the threshold filter already applied. The reason for doing so is that you will miss the people flying below the radar, the ones with a low score. Precursors could be hidden below the threshold.

The process of changing precursor scores starts with finding precursors that seem to either escalate users too quickly or with realizing that some activity is more important than the score reflects. Adjust the score for the precursor and pay attention to why the change seems necessary. Possibly, it is not just this one precursor that needs adjustment, but an entire class of precursors should be adjusted.

A more sophisticated approach to tuning precursor scores is the application of an **expert system.** The idea is to use a system that can tune the scores based on user feedback. It learns from the user (the expert) who interacts with the system. The expert makes a judgment about a user's score based on all the information present: the precursor, the user's role, and so on. The system learns from the feedback and adjusts the scores of the precursors. Many algorithms and approaches are documented in the literature. For more information about this, refer to the work of Maloof and Stephens.[8]

SUMMARY OF INSIDER-DETECTION PROCESS

We looked at a lot of things in this section. It is time to stop and summarize what we have covered. Figure 8-15 graphically summarizes the insider-detection process. We started out with defining a precursor list. As mentioned earlier, a fairly large list of precursors can be found at the end of this chapter. After defining the precursors, we discussed how to assign a score to them. Once this was done, we put the precursors in action. We have seen that devices flag behavior based on the precursors or the precursors can be used to analyze behavior via log files. The application of the precursors resulted in a list of insider candidates that we then visualized. Using the candidate graph and some meta information about the users, we conducted a role-based analysis of the user activities. To reduce the size of the graph and eliminate the "not so bad" users from the analysis, we discussed how to apply thresholds. The last step before closing the process circle was the analysis of the output, which directly led to a discussion about tuning the precursor list and scores.

---

[8]   "ELICIT: A System for Detecting Insiders Who Violate Need-to-Know," by Marcus Maloof and Gregory Stephens, RAID 2007.

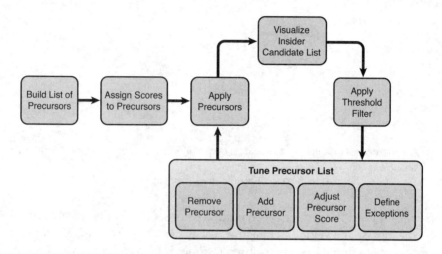

Figure 8-15   Flow diagram of the insider-detection process.

Tuning the precursors will be a work in progress, and precursors will have to be added and removed constantly over time. New precursors will be necessary for many reasons: new detection technologies, new threats, new users, new types of users, and so on. When a single round of the insider-detection process has been completed, the process starts over again.

Before we take a look at how this process could be improved and address some of its shortcomings, let's take a look at an example insider case.

INSIDER-DETECTION PROCESS AT WORK

This section considers the insider-detection process again, but this time with a more practical, hands-on approach. Each step of the process outlines how the data has to be prepared and how the graphs can be generated.

To start the insider-detection process, we define a set of precursors. You can find a sample set of precursors at the end of this chapter. The list is a good starting point for our sample use-case. The precursors in the list are already scored based on the methodology introduced earlier. We therefore do not have to go through the scoring process.

The detection process starts with applying the precursors to the log files at hand. The following is an example of how to do this. Assume we want to find users who printed resumés. On a Windows print server, you can use the printer logs to check which files have been printed. A sample log entry looks like this:

```
Event Type: Information
Event Source: Print
Event Category: None
Event ID: 10
Date: 8/5/2002
Time: 8:32:39 AM
User: Domainname\User1
Computer: Server
Description:
Document 208, Microsoft Word - resume.doc owned by ram was printed on HP DeskJet 550C
Printer/User1/Session 12 via port
\\sa-01\Sales\TS012. Size in bytes: 128212; pages printed: 3
```

You can collect these log entries from Windows print servers in the application log. To access the logs on the Windows machine, use the `wmic` command (see Chapter 2). The simplest way to find users who printed resumes is to `grep` for the word *resumé* in multiple languages:

```
wmic ntevent where "LogFile='Application' and EventCode='10'" GET format:csv |
grep -i "(resume|lebenslauf|cv)"
```

Extract the user from the event (for example, by using the `awk` command) and store records that look as follows in a `precursor.list` file. It contains the user, the precursor name, the role of the user, and the precursor score:

```
user,precursor,role,precursor score
ram,printing resume,engineering,1
```

The roles can be retrieved from either a directory service, such as Active Directory, or from a static mapping between users and their groups, depending on what data you have available. You get the precursor scores from the precursor list, which you can find at the end of the chapter.

Repeat the preceding step for each of the precursors you are monitoring. Do not forget to automate his process, for example, via a `cron` job. This will enable you to monitor the precursors on a regular basis.

When this step is completed and we have a `precursor.list` file, we are ready to generate a first graph. I am using AfterGlow (see Chapter 9, "Data Visualization Tools") to create the candidate link graph. To decorate the nodes correctly, create a property file like the following one and save it as `ithreat.properties`:

```
 1 # Variables
 2 variable=@violation=("Backdoor Access", "HackerTool Download", "AV
   disabled", "Account Sharing", "Internal Recon", "Password Sharing",
   "Classification Breach", "Unauthorized Web Site", "Locked Account",
   "Hacker Site");
 3 # shape
 4 shape.source=box
 5 # size
 6 maxnodesize=1.5
 7 sum.target=0                # do not accumulate target node size
 8 sum.source=1               # source node sizes are cumulative
 9 size.source=$fields[3]     # the fourth column indicates the size
10 size=0.5
11 # color
12 color.target="royalblue3" if (grep(/^\Q$fields[1]\E$/,@violation));
13 color.target="skyblue1"
14 color.source="#b2e2e2" if ($fields[2] eq "Contractor")
15 color.source="#66c2a4" if ($fields[2] eq "Privileged User")
16 color.source="#b30000" if ($fields[2] eq "Terminated")
17 color.source="#6dc200" if ($fields[2] eq "Legal")
18 1 color.source="#edf8fb"
```

The configuration file first defines a variable (violation) that contains the names of the precursors that denote a significant violation. This variable is then used to determine the color of the target nodes in line 15. If the second column ($fields[1]), the precursor, shows up in the list of violations, the node is drawn darker than otherwise. On line 7, the shape of the source nodes (the users) is defined to be a box. Lines 9 to 13 define the size of the nodes. First the maximum node size is set to 1.5. Then we instruct AfterGlow to accumulate the size of the source nodes. For each time that the source node (i.e., the user) shows up in the log file, we add the score to determine the size of the node. In line 12, we define that the fourth column ($fields[3]), the precursor score, is used to define the source node's size. In the last few lines, we define the color of the nodes. Color is determined by the third column in the data, the user's roles. Each role has its own color. Add your own roles here, if you are using different ones.

After defining the properties file, run AfterGlow with the following command:

```
cat precursor.list | afterglow -t -c ithreat.properties |
neato -Tgif -o candidate.gif
```

The result of running this command on a sample data set is shown in Figure 8-16. You can see that there are some large green boxes. These are users in the legal department who triggered a number of precursors. It seems that we can more or less visually group the different user groups in this graph. Around the Source Code Access precursor, there are a number of engineers and contractors. The legal people have the Patent Access in common and so forth. It would now be useful if we could find outliers or users who behave atypically for their role. In this particular graph, it is hard to find such outliers. Not a single user seems to pop out or draw attention. Users are too entangled and are sharing a lot of the precursors among the roles. We had to serially scan the graph to find possible violations of separation of duties or users who acted atypically for their roles. Your graph might not suffer from this, and you might see clear clusters of users and outliers thereof.

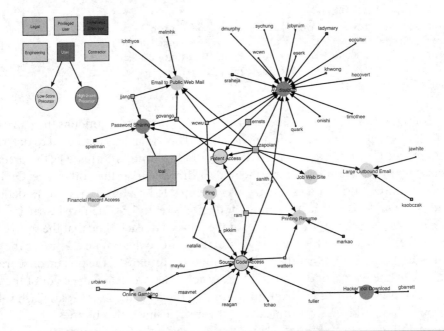

Figure 8-16   Link graph showing users and the precursors they triggered. Color is used to encode the role of the users on the source nodes and the severity of the precursors on the target nodes. The total score a user accumulated determines the size of the user nodes. (This figure appears in the full-color insert located in the middle of the book.)

One of the interesting things in Figure 8-16 is the number of people who disabled their antivirus software (AV disabled). This does not have to be malicious. In fact, it is probably a sign that the AV software gets in the way of a number of employees' regular work and they disabled it. However, from a security standpoint, this is a warning sign, and someone needs to follow up on it. Another interesting finding is that there seem to be a handful of users who are on the Terminated Employees list, and they show up around various precursors. These are a couple of initial findings that call for action. To gather some more information about the actors, we can use the treemap visualization shown in Figure 8-17. To generate a treemap with the Treemap 4.1 tool, we have to generate a TM3 file (see Chapter 9) first. The first step is to manually enter the header lines:

```
COUNT      User    Precursor   Role      Score
INTEGER    STRING  STRING      STRING    INTEGER
```

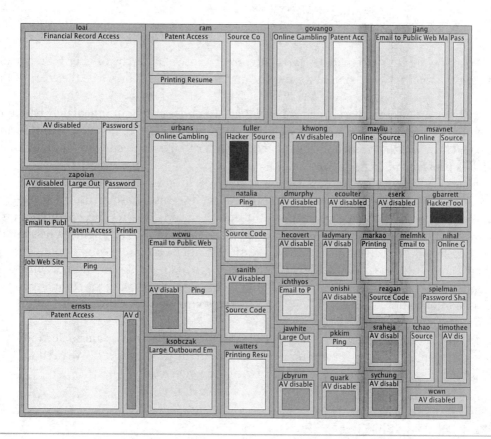

Figure 8-17 This treemap visualizes the candidate list. It uses a configuration hierarchy of User > Precursor. The size of the boxes is determined by the number of precursors run up, and the color encodes the precursor score. (This figure appears in the full-color insert located in the middle of the book.)

Make sure tabs separate the tokens. Then use the following command to translate the CSV file, precursor.list, into the TM3 format:

```
cat precursor.list | sed -e 's/,/        /g' | sort | uniq -c |
perl -pe 's/^\s*//, s/ /        /' >> precursor.tm3
```

Note the two tabs in the command. The output then looks like this:

```
COUNT    User      Precursor     Role         Score
INTEGER  STRING    STRING        STRING       INTEGER
1        dmurphy   AV disabled   Terminated   4
1        ecoulter  AV disabled   Contractor   4
```

Load the file with Treemap 4.1 and configure it to use a hierarchy of User > Precursor. Assign the total score to be used for the size and the precursor score to be the color of the boxes.

Figure 8-17 has the interesting property that two nodes pop out immediately based on their dark color. These users trigger only a small number of precursors that do not seem too bad. The fact that someone downloaded a hacker tool is interesting to know, but by itself is probably not a huge concern.

Instead of looking just for dark boxes, we can look for users who triggered a lot of precursors. They show up at the top left of the map. It seems that some users triggered interesting precursors and combinations thereof. User ram is interesting. He did not just access patents and source code but also printed resumés. If this is an engineer, he should not be accessing patents. If he is a lawyer, he should not be accessing source code. The combination of these three precursors could be a sign of an employee who is leaving the company. He is printing his resumé and at the same time is browsing for company confidential information to take with him: patents and source code. A closer investigation should be initiated.

In line with the discussion at the end of the introduction to the insider-detection process, we realize that there are some deficiencies to the process as it is. We need to improve a few things, which we address in the following section.

IMPROVED INSIDER-DETECTION PROCESS

We have identified a few weaknesses in the insider-detection process as it stands. Namely, if a user triggers the same precursor multiple times, he gets escalated very quickly, even if the precursor was quite benign. The process also does not incorporate any external information, such as a list of terminated employees. Lastly, we would like to treat users differently based on their role. For example, an administrator should be allowed to run a vulnerability scanner, whereas a salesperson has no business of doing so. To address these issues, we are going to explore the concept of watch lists. Following the discussion of watch lists, we examine how we can add the watch lists to our insider-detection process. This leads us to trying to prevent users' scores from shooting through the roof because of a single precursor that is triggered multiple times. The solution to this problem is grouping precursors into buckets.

Watch Lists

The insider-detection process used a fairly simple way of scoring activities and flagging potential malicious insiders. A malicious insider was identified by adding scores based on the precursors an actor triggered until a certain threshold was exceeded. We have seen that there are some problems associated with the scoring scheme. Following is a list of features we should include in the detection process to make it more powerful and address some of the problems identified earlier:

- External and dynamic intelligence should feed into the detection process (for example, watch lists defined by HR). These lists can be used to flag groups of employees and monitor them more closely than others (for example, terminated employees or employees on a performance improvement plan).
- Certain user roles should be monitored all the time (for example, administrators or privileged user accounts). These users have a lot of power over the system, and it is comparatively easy for them to circumvent detection systems. We also need to know who these users are to define exceptions for a lot of the precursors; they trigger a lot of them throughout their workday (e.g., scanning the internal network, using password crackers).

Watch lists, which are nothing other than lists of actors (users or machines), can be used to address these objectives. They incorporate external data into the insider-detection process and can be used to give special treatment to subsets of users. The detection process can be extended to utilize watch lists in a couple of ways:

- Precursors can be restricted to monitor users on specific watch lists only.
- Precursor scores can be adjusted based on membership in specific watch lists.

Table 8-6 is an overview of a sample set of watch lists. These lists are fairly generic ones and should be extended with ones specific for your environment.

Table 8-6   Watch Lists and the Activities/Precursors That Are Relevant and That Should Be Monitored for the Users on These Lists

Watch List	Monitored Activity / Precursors
Terminated employees	All activity executed by accounts that are associated with people who left the company are a warning sign. In reality, there will be automated scripts or similar activity that is going to show up. However, all of this activity needs to be eliminated.
Privileged users / administrators	Users with administrator accounts or privileged user accounts for any system should be monitored closely, especially changes to systems, such as adding new users, giving more access rights to users, changing critical settings on systems, and so forth. All of these can be used to prepare for attacks or install backdoor access. This type of activity should have a change request ticket associated with it to justify the action. In addition, even regular activity should be monitored for administrator or root accounts. Generic activity should not be executed with privileged accounts!
New hires	Don't trust new hires from the first day of employment. They need to prove themselves and earn trust. Monitor their activities and be more stringent about what they are allowed to do. Practically, this means that the precursor score for these users is going to be slightly higher than for employees who have been with the company for a while. The first couple of weeks of employment can also be used to build up a usage profile or "normal" behavior pattern for a user.
Contractors	Contractors are generally given access to the corporate resources, such as the network. Under certain circumstances they are even given privileged access to systems and applications. It is therefore crucial to monitor these users extra carefully. Verify the hours of operation and make sure the accounts are terminated when their work concludes.
Finance users	"Finance users" is just one example of a set of watch lists that can be instantiated to monitor access to specific resources. There is a finite set of users who should be accessing financial system or other specific resources. The better these groups can be defined and monitored, the smaller the chance for abuse.

The detection process needs to be extended to utilize the watch lists. We can use them to define exceptions for precursors and restrict certain precursors to actors on specific lists only. The second way of using them is to use the watch lists to adjust the precursor scores. Table 8-7 shows a way to adjust the scores for precursors depending on what watch list a user belongs to.

Table 8-7 Adjustment Table Showing, for a Set of Precursors, How Their Score Is Adjusted Based on the Actor Belonging to a Watch List

Watch List	Precursor	Score Adjustment	Final Score
Terminated employee	Any activity	+6	<10
Privileged users	Access information outside of need to know	+2	5
	Use of anonymizing proxy	+1	4
	Deleting audit logs	+1	5
	Creation of backdoor account	+n	10
	Disabling of anti virus or security software	+1	5
	Changes to critical files	+2	5
	User account sharing	+1	8
	Direct data table access	+2	8
New hires	Any Precursor	+2	N
Contractors	Not complying with configuration guidelines	+2	5
	Web traffic bypassing proxy	+3	7
Owner of critical data	Unauthorized encryption of information	+2	5
	Failure to create backup	+1	5
	Unauthorized information transfer	+4	7
	User account sharing	+1	8
	Anomalous email activity	+2	4
	Storage device attachment	+3	7
	Traffic to suspicious countries	+3	7
IT security staff	Not complying with configuration guidelines	+2	5
	Physical anomalies	+1	10
Everyone except IT security staff	Download of password crackers	+2	5
	Downloading of hacker tools	+1	8
	Promiscuous network interface	+1	5

Table 8-7 uses the list of precursors that is printed at the end of this chapter. Not all of them are incorporated in the table because a lot of precursor scores are not impacted even though the actor belongs to a watch list. To understand the adjustment table, let's look at the first row. If activity is detected from a terminated employee, the score of that precursor is increased by 6 points. However, the score should be kept below 10. This adjustment has the effect of increasing very low scores. Very low scores are not assigned an automatic 10. Only precursors with an original score between 4 and 9 will be bumped up to a 10.

Figure 8-18 visually summarizes how scores are adjusted for an actor based on belonging to one of the watch lists. Per the watch list, the treemap shows which precursors are getting adjusted. The darker the color of a box, the bigger the adjustment of the precursor score.

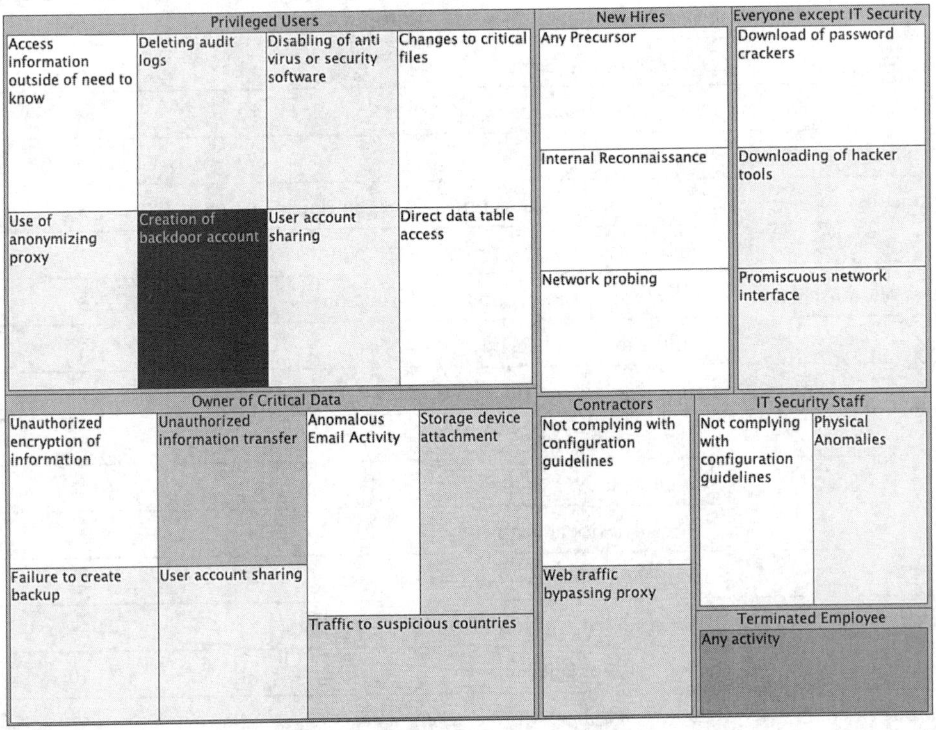

Figure 8-18 Treemap showing how the watch lists increases the scores for specific precursors. Color encodes the amount of the change; the darker the color, the bigger the adjustment.

Watch lists need to be kept up-to-date. Ideally, populating them is part of a regular IT process. For example, the new hire list should be populated as soon as IT creates the user accounts for a new employee. The terminated employee list should get an update from HR as soon as an employee leaves the company.

ADDING WATCH LISTS TO THE INSIDER-DETECTION PROCESS

The insider-detection process introduced in this chapter has some deficiencies, including the following:

- If a user triggers the same precursor multiple times, he gets escalated very quickly, even if the precursor was quite benign. Printing many documents off-hours, for example, quickly flags an employee as a malicious insider.
- Depending on which watch lists an actor belongs to, we would like to use a different set of precursors. Changes to files, for example, should be monitored mainly for privileged users and not for the entire staff.
- Depending on the watch list, different scores should be used for the same precursor. A new hire conducting an internal reconnaissance should be rated higher than if an administrator did the same.

To address some of these deficiencies, we can use the watch lists introduced in the preceding section. The first step is to adjust the precursor scores according to Table 8-7. In addition, we can use the watch lists to color the user nodes. The result of incorporating these new data inputs into the insider-detection process is shown in Figure 8-19. If we look at the graph in Figure 8-19, we can see a few things:

- Color is used to highlight users who are on a watch list.
- The size of the user nodes has changed according to Table 8-7.

The net effect for Figure 8-19 is that a new user suddenly draws attention to himself: abouis. This user is on the terminated employee list and therefore his score was bumped up significantly. You might notice that aaerchak's node has grown, too. This means that this user deserves more attention than if he were a regular one. This is a privileged user, and he should therefore be monitored closely due to his extended access and capabilities.

Coloring the users according to the watch list they belong to has yet another benefit. It is suddenly possible to visually group user nodes and compare activities with the watch list attribution in mind. One thing to watch for, for example, is privileged users triggering precursors clearly outside of their domain, such as a privileged user accessing patents.

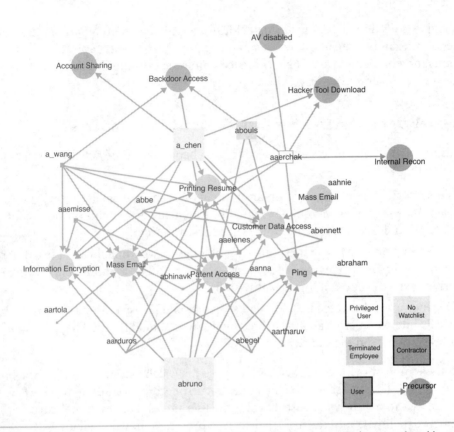

Figure 8-19   The insider candidate list shown as a link graph. The precursor nodes are colored based on how "bad" a precursor is deemed. The actor nodes are colored according to the watch list that the actor belongs to. (This figure appears in the full-color insert located in the middle of the book.)

GROUPING PRECURSORS INTO BUCKETS

The approach of using watch lists to adjust users' scores and also color nodes in the candidate graph is promising. However, we still have not addressed one of the most pressing needs we identified throughout the insider-detection process. We need a way to improve scoring. The first problem we should address is that a user who executes the same activity over and over again will keep triggering the same precursor and therefore drive his or her score higher and higher.

To address this problem, we are going to group the precursors into five buckets. Each bucket can only accumulate a maximum score of 20. This way, the maximum score that a user can ever reach is 100. This will prevent a single precursor, or even a set of precursors, from compounding and driving the score for a user through the roof. The five buckets are the following, based on the original score of the precursors:

- Precursors representing minimal or no impact—original precursor scores of 1 and 2
- Precursors showing signs of a setup for a malicious act—original precursor scores of 3 and 4
- Precursors indicating malicious behavior, activity that is clearly not normal but under certain circumstances or for certain user roles the activity is benign (e.g., scanning internal machines is a precursor that is bad, but a system administrator scans internal machines every now and then)—original precursor scores of 5 and 6
- Malicious behavior (behavior that should *never* be seen)—original precursor scores of 7 and 8
- An insider crime—original precursor scores of 9 and 10

This way of grouping the precursors into five buckets has a nice side effect. We can define a tiered system to classify users. A user with a score between 81 and 100 is regarded as malicious with a very high likelihood of committing a crime. Given the new scoring schema, the user needs to trigger at least one precursor in group 5, which is a real malicious insider act. In the range of 61 to 80, we can be fairly certain that a user is malicious. He needs to trigger a lot of precursors and not just in the benign tier, but in some of the others, too. Figure 8-20 shows a classification of users, based on the score they accumulated. From 0 to 20, there is not much to worry about. From 21 to 60, users are on a bad track, and there seems to be something going on. From 61 to 80, an actor has executed some malicious activities and seems to be worth checking out. Actors with a score above 80 deserve some attention. There is something going on.

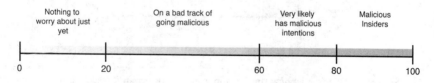

Figure 8-20 A tiered system to classify users based on their accumulated score.

Note that a user could trigger a precursor with a score of 9 or 10 once, which by our definition of the scores constitutes an insider crime. However, because of the rating, the overall score of the user will not trigger an alarm. Only if this user also triggers some other precursors would he be noted. Depending on the precursors, this has to be adjusted, and these precursors have to be given a higher individual score to escalate the user more quickly. For some precursors, on the other hand, this fact can be used as a way to reduce false positives and make sure that a user was indeed malicious.

CANDIDATE GRAPH BASED ON PRECURSOR BUCKETS

The candidate link graph is not going to change much with this new way of capping the size of nodes. The only difference is that the size of the nodes is not going to increase infinitely. In cases where a maximum node size is specified, the smaller nodes will show up slightly larger due to the new scale that is applied. A way of reporting the scores per user is to use a stacked bar chart that encodes per user the scores for each of the buckets. Figure 8-21 shows an example of such a bar chart. This chart is best used for a small number of users. As soon as the list gets bigger, users need to be filtered.

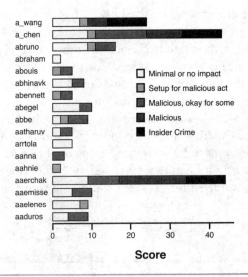

Figure 8-21   Stacked bar chart, encoding the score per precursor group for each user.

A more scalable solution is to use a treemap representation. An example is shown in Figure 8-22. The configuration hierarchy of the treemap is Watch List > User > Precursor Bucket > Precursor. What we should focus on are large, dark boxes to identify malicious insiders or users that are misbehaving. The darker the box, the higher the score of the precursor represented by the box. The size of the box represents the total score accumulated for that precursor. In other words, if the precursor has a score of 5 and a user triggered it 6 times, the box would have to be drawn with a size of 30. However, because we allow only a maximum score of 20, the box is capped at the size of 20! Dark patches in the treemap represent users who triggered a lot of significant precursors.

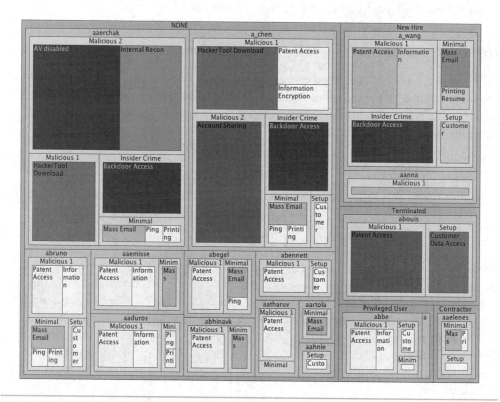

Figure 8-22   Treemap showing the accumulated score per user. The configuration hierarchy for the treemap is Watch List > User > Bucket > Precursor. The size of the boxes is based on the score a user accumulated. The color is based on the score of the individual precursor. The darker the boxes, the higher the score.

In Figure 8-22, we can quickly identify that aaerchak is one of the users we need to investigate closer. We can also see from the treemap that this user is not on a watch list. The other user that deserves attention is a_chen. He also triggered a lot of high-score precursors.

Another way to look at the treemap, instead of identifying big red patches, is to start with the watch lists. We can see some activity from users on the Terminated Employee list. The activity of those users is represented with dark patches. This is yet another set of users that deserve our attention.

This treemap should be used as a working graph. Have it generated either in real time or at least on a regular basis to review activity in your environment. By going through the insider-detection process, and specifically the tuning step, you will see that this is going to become a great tool for understanding your environment.

IMPROVED INSIDER-DETECTION PROCESS SUMMARY

With the previously discussed extensions to the insider-detection process, we can address the shortcomings of the initial version of the process. We started using two new concepts: watch lists and grouping of precursors into buckets. The watch lists added the capability to:

- Incorporate external input from, for example, HR. An example is a watch list for terminated employees.
- Limit the scope of precursors to just certain actors that are on specific watch lists.
- Adjust precursor scores based on what watch list an actor belongs to.
- Color actor nodes in the candidate graph.

In addition, we introduced buckets of precursors. Each precursor lives in one of five buckets. The maximum score a user can accumulate in a bucket is then limited. This has the effect that individual precursors can escalate an actor only to a specific limit, unlike before when a single precursor could run an actor ad infinitum.

The basic insider-detection process from before did not change. The only change is in how scores are accumulated and how the candidate graph is drawn. Let's continue on with our example from earlier and see how the extensions to the process change the visualizations.

EXTENDED INSIDER-DETECTION PROCESS AT WORK

Earlier in this chapter, we started to look at an insider case by applying the insider-detection process. At that point, we did not know about any of the more advanced techniques that we just discussed. Let's revisit that insider example and augment it with the new techniques.

Previously, in the regular insider-detection process, we had the following data elements to generate our graphs:

- *User:* The user triggering the precursors
- *User role:* The role of the user to analyze user behavior relative to their roles

- *Precursor:* The precursor triggered by the user
- *Precursor score:* The score of the precursor

The extended insider-detection process adds the following pieces of information to the analysis:

- *Watch list:* The watch list a user belongs to
- *Precursor bucket:* The bucket that the precursor falls into
- *Total user score:* The accumulative score of the user across all buckets

To generate the candidate graphs, we need to prepare our data. The central problem is the calculation of a user's total score. The calculation has to respect two properties:

- There is a maximum score that can be accumulated in each precursor bucket.
- Watch lists influence the score of precursors. They can either limit the applicability of precursors, or change the score depending on what watch list a user belongs to.

The product of our data preparation needs to be a file that contains the user, the precursor the user triggered, and the total score a user accumulated:

```
govango,Password Sharing,8
govango,Email to Public Web Mail,8
govango,Email to Public Web Mail,8
govango,Patent Access,8
natalia,Ping,1
```

Note that we need to include the total score a user accumulated in this file and not the individual score of a precursor. The reason for this is that we need to guarantee that a user does not accumulate more than a certain maximum score per precursor bucket. When visualizing the candidate list, AfterGlow would blindly add all the scores for the individual users, even beyond the maximum that is allowed per precursor bucket. This is precisely what we did before. This is why we have to deal with the calculation of the total score per user outside of AfterGlow.

How do we calculate the total score for a user? Unfortunately, no single command line could do this. It is slightly more involved than that. Let's see what a possible approach would look like.

The first step is to adjust the precursor score based on the watch lists, and then in a second step we cap the scores based on the precursor buckets. To adjust the scores per watch list, I use a set of awk scripts that look similar to this one:

```
awk -F, -v OFS=' '
  '/govango|peter|john/ {$4=$4+2}  # first watch list, adjust by 2
  /annen|baumann|stillhard/ {$4=$4+4} # second watch list, adjust by 4
  {print}' activity.csv > new_activity.csv
```

Each line of users represents a watch list, for which the precursor scores are adjusted. In this example, we're adding two points for the first watch list and adding four points for the second.

In addition to using the information about the users and their watch lists to adjust the scores, we store it in a file (`watchlist.csv`). The file has to list the user along with the watch list the user belongs to:

```
dmurphy,Terminated
ecoulter,Contractor
fuller,Contractor
```

After all the adjustments have been done and the watch list file has been defined, we then have to calculate the total score for a user. You need to write a little script or manually go through the data to guarantee that a user does not accumulate more than a certain maximum score per precursor bucket. I wrote a little tool to do this. You can find the tool (`capper.pl`) on this book's CD. Here is how you run it:

```
./capper.pl user_activity.csv precursor.csv > user_activity_new.csv
```

The script takes two inputs: a file with all the user activity (user, precursor) and a file with precursors and their scores. The precursor file also lists the bucket for each precursor and not just the precursor score. The `capper.pl` script does nothing other than add the score for each user and make sure that, per bucket, the user does not exceed its maximum. The output then looks as shown earlier.

Insider Candidate Link Graph

After all the data has been prepared, we are ready to define the properties for the insider candidate graph. We need to build another property file for AfterGlow to format the link graph correctly:

```
1 # Variables
2 variable=@violation=("Backdoor Access", "HackerTool Download", "AV
  disabled", "Account Sharing", "Internal Recon", "Password Sharing",
```

```
     "Classification Breach", "Unauthorized Web Site", "Locked Account",
     "Hacker Site")
  3  variable=open(FILE,"<watchlist.csv"); while(<FILE>)
     {chomp; split(/,/); $wlist{$_[0]}=$_[1]}
  4  # shape
  5  shape.source=box
  6  # size
  7  maxnodesize=1.5
  8  sum.target=0                    # do not accumulate target node size
  9  sum.source=0                    # source node sizes are cumulative
 10  size.source=$fields[2]          # the third column indicates the size
 11  size=0.5
 12  # color
 13  color.target="royalblue3" if (grep(/^\Q$fields[1]\E$/,@violation))
 14  color.target="skyblue1"
 15  color.source="#b2e2e2" if ($wlist{$fields[0]} eq "Contractor")
 16  color.source="#66c2a4" if ($wlist{$fields[2]} eq "Privileged User")
 17  color.source="#b30000" if ($wlist{$fields[2]} eq "Terminated")
 18  color.source="#6dc200" if ($wlist{$fields[2]} eq "Legal")
 19  color.source="#edf8fb"
```

The property file is similar to the one we used previously. The only big difference is the way we are using the watch list. In lines 6 and 7, we are reading the watch list from watchlist.csv into an internal variable. It is then used in lines 19 through 22 to check whether the user is on a specific list. Also note that we are not accumulating the score for the source nodes (line 13). We already did the calculations in our preprocessing.

Figure 8-23 shows the result of visualizing this information.

The graph in Figure 8-23 does not look much different from the one we generated with the simple insider-detection process. Notice that the user nodes are colored based on the watch list they belong to and not based on their roles (as previously). Also note that the size of all the nodes has changed. The user ioal is not the single biggest node anymore. Other users are now drawing attention to themselves, as well. Analyze the graph more closely by using the colors to see whether any of the users on a watch list are behaving strangely. Look for large, colored nodes.

This is a great starting point for tuning the precursors. In some cases, you might find that you need to define exceptions for specific groups of users. For example, you might realize that privileged users are triggering specific precursors (such as using ping) all the time. For these cases, consider defining an exception to not show those instances anymore.

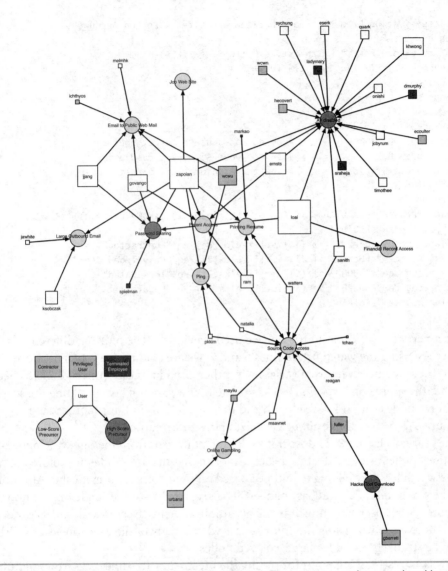

Figure 8-23   The insider candidate list shown as a link graph. The precursor nodes are colored based on how "bad" a precursor is deemed. The actor nodes are colored according to the watch list that the actor belongs to. (This figure appears in the full-color insert located in the middle of the book.)

Insider Candidate Treemap

After going through the link graph, we can move on to the treemap visualization. The input for the treemap differs slightly. We cannot use multiple files to generate the treemap. Let's start out by defining a CSV file that contains all the necessary information and then convert it to a TM3 file that can be read by the treemap visualization tool. As input, we need a file that looks like this:

```
User,Precursor,Precursor_Score,Total_Score,Watchlist,Precursor_Bucket
jjang,Email to Public Web Mail,2,2,NONE,Minimal
jjang,Password Sharing,2,2,NONE,Minimal
khwong,AV disabled,4,4,NONE,Setup
ksobczak,Large Outbound Email,2,2,Contractor,Minimal
```

The calculation of the total score in this case is a bit trickier. Treemaps can display visual properties of leaf nodes only. What does that mean? In our example, we are using a hierarchy of Watch List > User > Bucket > Precursor. This means that the precursors are the leaf nodes, and therefore we can use properties of the precursors to be graphed as the box properties. However, we would like to make sure that the total size of the user boxes is set to a specific value, the total score a user accumulated. To do so, we have to go through some tricky calculations that adjust the total score in the input and assign it to the precursor's size. Here is the formula to do so for each precursor:

$$\text{New precursor score} = (\text{Total user score} / \text{Sum of precursor scores for this user}) * \text{Precursor score}$$

This will distribute all the precursor scores evenly, not paying attention to a maximum score per bucket. The sum of precursor scores for each user is now going to add up to the total score of the user. You can run the `capper.pl` script with the –a option, to do this calculation for you:

```
./capper.pl –a –u user_activity.csv -p precursor.csv –w watchlist.csv >
user_activity_new.csv
```

The following columns are needed in the preceding files:

- `user_activity.csv`   `user, precursor`
- `precursor.csv`   `precursor, bucket, precursor_score`
- `watchlist.csv`   `user, watchlist`

Example output from the preceding command then looks like this:

```
ladymary,AV disabled,4,4,Setup,Terminated
spielman,Password Sharing,7,7,Malicious,Terminated
onishi,AV disabled,4,4,Setup,
```

When this all is done, we can convert the CSV file into a TM3 file (see the earlier discussion of converting a CSV file to TM3 in the section "Insider-Detection Process at Work") and then generate the treemap shown in Figure 8-24.

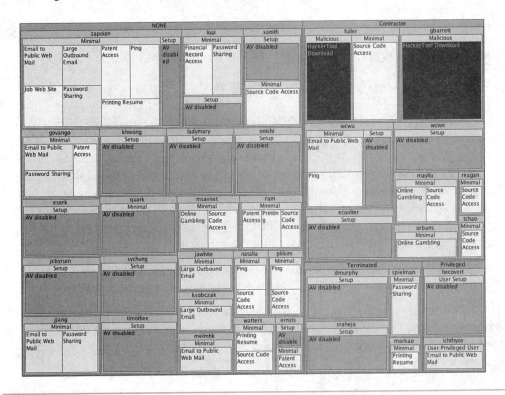

Figure 8-24   Treemap showing the accumulated score per user. The configuration hierarchy for the treemap is Watch List > User > Bucket > Precursor. The size of the nodes is based on the score a user accumulated. The color is based on the score of the individual precursor. The darker the boxes, the higher the score. (This figure appears in the full-color insert located in the middle of the book.)

We can see that Figure 8-24 now sizes the user boxes according to their total score. The precursor boxes are then proportionally distributed over that box. We can see some high-score precursors on the top right, indicated by the dark red boxes. We can also see that those precursors were triggered either alone or with one other precursor. Depending on the role of the users, this is not very significant. The fact that contractors triggered these precursors might be a bit alarming, unless these are security consultants. On the top left, we see that the user who accumulated the most points is zapoian. This user triggered quite a few precursors. However, all of them are in the low range of scores. It is probably still worth having a chat with this person.

The next step in the process is now to go ahead and tune the precursors. Based on the two graphs, we should go ahead and investigate more closely what all the activity signifies. Some of it will turn out to be absolutely benign, whereas other activities will probably be reason for concern.

CHALLENGES

One challenge remains with the insider-detection process. We worked with the assumption that all activity can be traced back to a user. However, a lot of precursors involve monitoring log files that do not contain information about the user executing the specific action. In the worst case, the log file does not contain any information about the subject. In some cases, there will be some sort of a subject represented in the log, but not the actual human responsible for the activity. A lot of log files will show an IP address, for example. There are three approaches to this problem:

1. All the activity can be traced back to machines (i.e., IP addresses), and this is all we care about. There is nothing else we need.

2. Each machine that generates traffic can be mapped one to one to a user, and we are in the possession of the mapping. We can use the mapping to track down the user responsible for the actions.

3. We use an additional source of information that links the activity from machines to users. Logs that contain this type of information are DHCP logs, authentication logs, identity and access management (IAM) logs, and so forth.

Another challenge in this context is an identity management problem. A user typically uses multiple user names across different systems. I use the user ram on my UNIX systems, but I am rmarty in the Windows domain of my employer. And even worse, sometimes I log in to systems as root rather than using su or sudo to switch from my user account to the root user.[9] Who is responsible for commands executed by the root user? This is definitely tricky and falls in the area of identify and access management (IAM). To get as close as possible to tracing back activities to users, collect as much information as you can and link things back to the real actor or user responsible for the activity. Also look at other data sources that might prove useful. For example, collect login information. If you know that a user logged in from a specific machine using the user identity ram and then the same machine opened a connection using another user rmarty, you

---

[9] Although I restrict this on most of my machines, sometimes I do log in as root on my desktop or laptop to do some maintenance work.

can be fairly certain that these user IDs belong to the same person. There are caveats, but this might be a viable source from which to start constructing user account maps.

This concludes our discussion of the insider-detection process. You should now have a starting point to address your information protection and insider abuse problems and challenges. Let's discuss some proactive approaches that may enable you to counter the insider threat problem.

PROACTIVE MITIGATION

The insider-detection process we developed throughout this chapter is a great step toward dealing with the malicious insider problem. However, unless we define exceptionally good precursors, the process is very much a reactive one. What we really need is a way to proactively mitigate the problem of insider crime. *Insider threats can be stopped, but it takes a complex set of policies, procedures, and technical means to do so.*

To prevent the problem of malicious insiders, we need to implement a comprehensive and effective security program. That is really what it comes down to. As you know, that is not an easy task, and there will always be gaps or areas that are not addressed by policies or technical safeguards. This means that all the work we did to identify users before they turn into malicious insiders is still relevant.

What this also means is that in addition to the insider-detection process we should try to mitigate some of the problems by implementing a "good" security program. A lot of processes that can help with mitigating the malicious insider problem do not directly relate to IT and computer systems but are human resource processes. Things such as awareness training or background checks are examples. The following list of IT security practices can be used to further minimize the window of opportunity for malicious insiders. All the following practices can be monitored via log files.

- Application of least privilege
- Access path monitoring
- Separation of duties
- Privileged access
- Rigorously following processes for configuration management
  - Deactivate access for users following termination
  - Strict password and account management policies and practices
  - Actively defend malicious code

- Use of layered defense against remote attacks
- Implementation of secure backup and recovery

One way to use this list is to define precursors and use those for detecting malicious behavior or preparation for insider crimes. Another, more effective way of using the list is to implement processes to enforce these properties. Separation of duties, for example, could be monitored via log files, but the disadvantage is that only cases of active violations can be detected. On the other hand, if you were to analyze the configuration of your systems to make sure that there are no conflicting roles associated with users, you could completely mitigate the problem. Take a look at Chapter 7, "Compliance," for a discussion about what such a verification could look like.

An overall solution should implement both prevention and detection measures. It is fairly likely that some cases will be missed by preventive measures. Perhaps those will be detected with the insider-detection process, however, and can be mitigated before any real harm is caused.

SAMPLE PRECURSORS

Precursors are an integral part of the insider-detection process. This last section of the chapter provides a collection of precursors that you can use to monitor actors in your own corporate environment. The precursors are organized in a set of tables. They list the precursors themselves, mention what electronic record or log file can be used to find the precursor, identify how the precursor is detected in the log, classify the precursor in one of the three categories of detecting the precursor (signature matching, policy monitoring, or anomaly detection), assign a score to it, and in some cases even show a sample log entry to illustrate what the precursor looks like.

Table 8-8 discusses precursors that apply to all three categories of insider crime: categories: sabotage, fraud, and information leaks. The following tables then discuss precursors specific to one of the insider crime categories.

Whereas some precursors apply to more than one of the insider crime categories, others are specific to a single category. Sabotage- and information-leak-specific precursors are listed in Table 8-9 and Table 8-10, respectively. And finally, Table 8-11 shows precursors for fraud.

Table 8-8   A Sample Set of Precursors That Apply to All Three Types of Insider Crime: Sabotage, Fraud, and Information Leaks

Precursor	Description	Data Source	Detection Method	Score	Detection Category
Use of organization's systems in violation of acceptable use policy	Activities such as playing games, using company equipment to work on personal projects, and so on.	Operating system	Log analysis.	1	Policy

	Windows event log example:
	
	`EventlogType=Security`
	`DetectTime=2005-04-29 14:15:16`
	`EventSource=Security`
	`EventID=592`
	`EventType=Audit_success`
	`EventCategory=Detailed Tracking`
	`User=COMPANY\yfan`
	`ComputerName=NIGHTLESS`
	`Description=A new process has been created`
	`New Process ID=4856`
	`Image File Name=\Program Files\Windows NT\Accessories\pinball.exe`
	`Creator Process ID=3532`
	`User Name=yfan`
	`Domain=ARCSIGHT`
	`Logon ID=(0x0,0x1BDF9)`				

Printing activity	Each of the following scenarios could indicate employees who plan to leave: • Printing resumé • Printing off-hours • Excessive printing	Printer logs	Log analysis.	1	Signature Anomaly

Windows printer log example (someone pasting information into a Notepad document results in the following log entry):

`#Document 92, Untitled.txt - Notepad owned by ram was printed on HPIJ via port`
`HPLaserJet4050Series.  Size in bytes: 12342; pages printed: 5`

Precursor	Description	Data Source	Detection Method	Score	Detection Category
Job Web page access	Accessing job Web sites could be a sign that an employee is about to leave the company and is looking for new opportunities.	Proxy NetFlow Router Firewall	Log analysis with list of job websites.	1	Signature

OpenBSD pf firewall example:

`Feb 18 13:39:27.667326 rule 71/0(match): pass in on xl0: 195.27.249.139.63280 > `**`66.218.84.150.80:`**
`S 948010585:948010585(0) win 32768 <mss 1460,nop,wscale 0,nop,nop,timestamp 24077 0> (DF)`

Access of Web sites prohibited by acceptable use policy	Accessing websites violating of the acceptable use policy could indicate employees who are not committed to their work anymore.	Web proxy	Log analysis.	2	Policy

Privoxy log example:

`Apr 01 13:13:05 Privoxy(b55aaba0) Request: www.sex.ch/index.html`

Account creation outside of normal business hours	Depending on the work habits of the system administrators, this could indicate a problem.	Operating systems Applications	Log analysis.	2	Signature
Download and use of password cracker	Regular users do not need these types of tools.	Web proxy Operating system (file change monitor)	Log analysis.	3	Signature

Privoxy log example:

`Apr 04 19:45:29 Privoxy(b65ddba0) Request: www.google.com/search?q=`**`password+cracker`**

continues

Table 8-8   A Sample Set of Precursors That Apply to All Three Types of Insider Crime: Sabotage, Fraud, and Information Leaks *(continued)*

Precursor	Description	Data Source	Detection Method	Score	Detection Category
Access of information outside of need to know	Users should not be accessing data unnecessary for their job.	Operating system Web server Applications	Log analysis: Define what is normal for each user or role.	3	Policy
Not complying with hardening or configuration guidelines	Not deploying patches or making necessary configuration changes could indicate deliberately left vulnerabilities that later could be exploited.	Configuration and Patch management Software distribution Vulnerability scanner	Log analysis: Look for patch or configuration management violations.	3	Policy
Use of anonymous proxy	Anonymizers can be used to conceal the destinations of connections and also encrypt their content. This helps evade detections mechanisms such as IDSs or DLPs.	Proxy NetFlow Router Firewall	Log analysis with list of public proxies.	3	Signature

Privoxy log example:

`Apr 04 20:25:11 Privoxy(b7df9ba0) Request: www.anonymizer.com/cgi-bin/open.pl?url=http%3A%2F%2Fraffy.ch%2Fblog`

Precursor	Description	Data Source	Detection Method	Score	Detection Category
Internal reconnaissance	Browsing applications and shares on servers could be a sign of someone doing reconnaissance. At a later stage, this knowledge could be used to execute an attack.	Applications Operating system NIDS	Log analysis.	3	Policy Anomaly

Precursor	Description	Data Source	Detection Method	Score	Detection Category
Deleting audit logs	Audit logs should be archived and only in rare cases should they be deleted. Deletion could be an attempt to hide traces.	Operating system (file change monitoring)	Log analysis.	4	Signature
Web traffic bypassing proxy	If a proxy setup is in place, all the Web traffic should be leaving via the proxy to guarantee accountability.	NetFlow Router Firewall	Log analysis: Look for direct Web connections.	4	Signature
Unauthorized use of coworker's machine left logged in	Utilizing someone else's equipment attributes activity to the wrong person and can be used to draw attention to an innocent third person.	Physical access control	Log analysis: User is either physically not in the building or in another building while his computer is being accessed.	5	Policy
Physical anomalies	Impossible concurrent physical access Logical access without physical access Access of off-limit facilities	Physical access control Operating system Applications	Log analysis: Correlate physical logs with logical access logs.	9	Policy
Creation of backdoor account	Unauthorized modems Creation of user accounts without a change request	Vulnerability scanner Operating system Applications	Log analysis.	9	Signature

Table 8-9   A Sample Set of Sabotage Precursors

Precursor	Description	Data Source	Detection Method	Score	Detection Category
Network probing	Regular users do not have any justification for scanning or probing machines on the internal network. This is reserved for security staff or auditors.	IDS NBAD	Checking for abnormally high traffic volumes or specific indicators of scans.	3	Policy Signature
Unauthorized encryption of information	If data is encrypted and the encryption key is lost, the data cannot be restored anymore. This could be an act of sabotage	NIDS	In some cases, a NIDS uses statistical analysis methods to detect encrypted traffic on the wire. It is another problem to then map the activity back to a policy and verify whether encryption was allowed.	3	Signature?
Changes to critical files	System configuration changes, or new cron jobs, both executed without an associated change ticket, are potential signs for mischief.	Operating system	Log analysis.	3	Signature
Disabling of anti-virus or other security software	Turning off security software will allow the user to execute commands that would otherwise be reported or blocked. This could be used to prepare for an attack.	Operating system Security tool log	Monitoring the shutdown of these tools or disabling of the service on the operating system level.	4	Signature

Precursor	Description	Data Source	Detection Method	Score	Detection Category
Failure to create backups as required	The next thing after omitted backups is usually a failure somewhere. This could indicate a setup for an act of sabotage.	Backup	Log analysis.	4	Signature
Download and installation of hacker tools or malicious code	Unless someone is a virus researcher, this is definitely not normal behavior. Rootkits and password sniffers are not part of the normal repository of applications for a user.	Proxy IDS	Log analysis Possibly monitoring sites known for virus code distribution.	7	Signature

Table 8-10   A Sample Set of Information-Leak Precursors

Precursor	Description	Data Source	Detection Method	Score	Detection Category
Anomalous email activity	Emailing documents to public Web mail accounts. Emails going to the competition.	Email Data-leak prevention Intrusion detection system	Log analysis with specific lists of recipients to watch. Analyzing cliques to find communication anomalies.	2	Policy
Unauthorized information transfer	Any piece of critical information in the wrong hands could lead to direct or indirect financial loss.	Proxy Application Email Instant messenger	Log analysis.	3	Policy
Checking someone else's email	Users should read their own email only.	Email	Log analysis.	4	Signature

Microsoft Outlook example:

COMPANY/ram logged on as /o=COMPANY/ou=US/cn=Stefanie Boem Recipients/cn=ram on database "COMPANY\zurich(VMSG32)". For more information, click http://www.microsoft.com/contentredirect.asp

Promiscuous mode interfaces	This is one example of security parameters to monitor. Promiscuous interfaces are a sign that someone is sniffing traffic. Except for networking or security people, this is not something an employee should be allowed to do.	Operating system	Log analysis.	4	Signature

Precursor	Description	Data Source	Detection Method	Score	Detection Category
Storage device attachment	The attachment of storage devices, such as CD-ROMs or USB storage, especially on server machines, could be an attempt to steal or remove data.	Operating system	Log analysis.	4	Signature
Traffic to suspicious countries	Some companies are more sensitive to where connections are going. If the company operates in Switzerland only, connections inside of Europe might be normal, but outside of that, they might raise suspicion.	Router Firewall NetFlow Proxy	Log analysis with either a white list or a black list to monitor the traffic endpoints.	4	Policy
Sharing passwords or user accounts	Each person should have a unique user account to guarantee auditability and accountability.	Operating system Application	Detecting access of one and the same account from two either physically separate places or different logical networks.	7	Policy
Laptop theft	No automated systems will detect a stolen laptop. However, the owner of the system should report it as soon as the theft is detected. That way, any future use can be flagged, and other necessary precautions can be initiated.	Human	Every company should have a theft-reporting process. This is a manual process.	8	N/A

Table 8-11   A Sample Set of Fraud Precursors

Precursor	Description	Data Source	Detection Method	Score	Detection Category
Changes to critical files	Changes to critical files can be used to mask behavior, change intrinsic properties of systems, and serve as a pathway into fraudulent activity.	Operating system Applications	Log analysis.	3	Signature
Direct DB access	Generally, databases are accessed via applications, and data is not directly changed in the database itself. Direct changes in the database can be used to circumvent application layer security controls.	Database Application	Monitor specific tables to ensure access via the dedicated application only.	6	Policy
Role-based access monitoring	Each user role has specific activities they execute. Monitor for violations. For instance, database administrators accessing data tables in the database might be a bad sign.	Database Application Operating system	Monitor logs to ensure user actions stay in their roles.	6	Policy

The precursors listed here are only examples. Many more precursors can be used, especially if you define precursors significant for your own environment. Use these precursors as a starting point and let them inspire you to extend the list.

Figure 8-25 summarizes the lists of precursors from this section in a graph. The graph will help you get a feel for the types of precursors the tables introduced and in what areas we might have to spend some more time to define new ones. You can see four groups of data points. The cluster on the left identifies all the generic precursors, the ones that apply to all three categories of insider crime. The next cluster represents the fraud precursors, followed by information-leak precursors, and then on the right side you can find the precursors that flag saboteurs. The graph shows that most of the precursors have a score associated with them that is in the range of about 3 or 4. This indicates that it is not trivial to find precursors with a high score. Furthermore, there are hardly any precursors colored in black, which are ones that use anomaly detection to find precursor activity. It seems that generic precursors, ones that apply to all three insider threat categories, are the easiest ones to find.

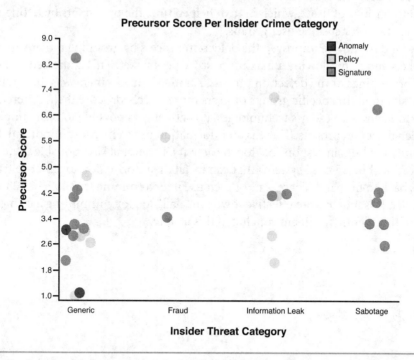

Figure 8-25   Summary of all precursors introduced in this section and their associated scores.

SUMMARY

Implementing a security program is not finished when the perimeter is secured. Although that is an important and necessary task to prevent external attackers from abusing our computing resources and stealing information, we also need to protect our systems and information from malicious insiders. The problem with detecting malicious insiders is that no security devices or programs can generate an alert when malicious insiders become active. It is more complicated than that. A lot of data has to be analyzed and monitored to detect malicious insider activities.

In this chapter, we explored an insider-detection process that can be implemented to find instances of insider crimes and people setting the stage for such activities. We have used visualization to analyze the vast amount of data and narrow it down to pertinent information. We have discussed precursors that can be used to trigger when malicious activity is detected. Using a scoring schema, we then rated the activities to focus on users who drew a lot of attention. Using visualization, we analyzed all the precursor activity. This insider candidate graph helped determine whether the activity was commonly observed for groups of users, which in turn helped tune the precursors by letting us define exceptions for specific user groups.

In a second round, we improved the detection process by grouping the precursors into buckets and only allowing a maximum score per bucket. This addressed one of the initial shortcomings of the detection process. Another improvement was the addition of watch lists to monitor specific groups of users more closely or score them differently.

Unfortunately, with today's technologies, it is not always possible to easily implement the insider-detection process. There is an information problem. Most important, few log files identify the human responsible for the activity. It is not always possible to do so for an application, but we need systems that can tie all the information together to trace activities back to humans. There is not much use in determining that 192.168.23.1 was the offender. It is much more effective if we can "nail" Joe for committing a crime. A discussion of this identity problem concluded this chapter.

Data Visualization Tools

9

Throughout this book, I have used various tools to generate graphical representations of log files and security data. In some instances, I have shown how to configure the tools to generate the visualization. What this chapter does is summarize a huge set of mostly freely available tools that you can use to generate your own graphs. At the end of this chapter, you will find a big table that summarizes all the tools and shows their capabilities side by side.

Pay attention while you are reading through the descriptions of all these tools. You will realize that there is no one tool that I deem "the best" for visualizing data. They all have things they do well, but they also have shortcomings and lack one feature or the other. Even when looking into the commercial space, there are some really good products, but there is not one that I think would address all of your security visualization needs. I guess we will have to wait for someone to build a tool and continue working with what we have. You might even have to write a little bit of code to achieve your goals.

Accompanying this book, you will find a live CD, DAVIX, that contains all the tools discussed throughout this chapter. You can use DAVIX, which stands for Data Analysis and Visualization UNIX, to try the tools without having to deal with any installation problems. All the tools are ready to go. If you need to quickly analyze a set of log files and you do not want to deal with installing various tools and configuring them, you can use the CD and load your data very quickly analyze the given log files. In addition, you will also find some log files on the CD that you can use to test the tools. You can find more information about DAVIX at http://davix.secviz.org.

The list of libraries and tools I present in this chapter is by no means complete. It is simply a collection of visualization aids that I have come across during my journey through the world of visualizing security data. Also note that I do not focus on reporting libraries and tools. The focus is on real visualization tools that do more than just generate a pie chart. The office products, for example, can be used to generate some charts. Clearly, that is not what I discuss here.

The chapter is structured such that I first discuss freely available visualization packages. This should give you a good start for visualizing your own data. I then discuss various open source programming libraries. This is definitely not something for everybody. Some of the libraries are fairly complex to be included in your own programs. Others are fairly simple. However, they offer a lot of flexibility, much more than any program would. I then discuss some of the tools that the commercial world has to offer. To start the chapter, I wrote a short section that talks about data inputs or data files. The visualization tools all use different types of data files. The first section explores their formats so that you can use them with the appropriate tools. I then cover the open source tools, the libraries, some online tools, and finally, the commercial tools.

DATA INPUTS

The tools introduced in this chapter cannot directly read data from your security devices. They will not understand, for example, a Snort log. Some exceptions can read PCAP files (see Chapter 2, "Data Sources"). Interestingly enough, only one tool that I found, R, connects to a database to read data. All the other tools require some form of file-based data format to read the data from.

The most common and important file formats for you to know are comma separated value (CSV), the TM3 format, GraphViz's DOT format, and the Graph Markup Language (GML). Let us have a brief look at them to understand how we can convert our own logs into these formats.

COMMA SEPARATED VALUES

A comma separated values, CSV, file stores fields or data dimensions separated by a comma. The following shows an example:

```
10.0.0.2,10.2.3.1,80
10.2.3.1,10.0.0.2,29122
10.2.3.1,10.0.0.2,53
```

You can see three columns or data dimensions. The first column represents the source address, the second column the destination address, and the last column the destination port. Note that you cannot derive this from the file alone. In some cases, the tools expect a header line that gives a name to each of the columns. Other tools don't respect such a line and assume that the first line is also part of the data.

What happens if you need to represent a value in a column that contains a comma itself? For example, consider the string 80,443,993. We want to keep this string as a single value and not break it up into individual columns. In that case, you need to quote the string, which will look like this: "80,443,993". That's all. Most programs can understand this format. Now you might wonder how to represent a quote. You need to double it: "He said:""don't worry""". But don't worry. This is rarely ever needed when you analyze security logs.

One more thing about CSV files: If you are really not good with awk, use Excel or OpenOffice to manipulate the files. They both fully support the CSV format with a limitation on the number of rows that either of these tools can handle. Excel, for example, has a limitation of 65,535 rows.

Some tools support a TSV, a tab separated values format. This is nothing other than a CSV file where, instead of commas, tabulators are used. This is not very common, but you might run into this.

TM3

The TM3 file format is a bit more complex, but also more expressive, than the very common CSV files. The main benefit of TM3 files is that a data type is assigned to each of the data columns. This is done by utilizing header lines. The first two lines in the file are dedicated headers. The first line defines the name of the column, which is purely cosmetic, and the second line defines the data type for the column. Generally, the accepted values are STRING, INTEGER, FLOAT, and DATE. Tabulators separate columns. Here is a simple example:

```
Name            Age       DOB
STRING          INTEGER   DATE
Raffael Marty   31        6/25/1976
```

You get the idea. Quotes can be used to surround fields, but are optional. The data types have the advantage that the tool reading the file knows what type of data to expect. This has an influence on sorting, operations that can be applied to the fields, and the way the field is displayed.

Sometimes, the TM3 format is used slightly differently, where an additional hierarchy is imposed. This is, for example, what the Treemap tool can be used with. However, it works just fine with the simple format. If you add an additional hierarchy, each row is appended a variable number of columns that define a hierarchy for the current record. Our example from earlier will then look like this:

```
Name            Age      DOB
STRING          INTEGER  DATE
Raffael Marty   31       6/25/1976   Switzerland   St. Gallen   Wil
```

This defines a hierarchical structure for where the person lives. As you might imagine, the Treemap hierarchy will then be represented by the additional columns.

DOT

The DOT attributed graph language is what its name suggests: a simple language that defines a link graph. Each node and each edge has an entry in this file that describes exactly how the nodes and edges have to be represented. Attributes such as color, size, shape, and so on can be specified. In addition, global options can be specified. These are applied to the entire graph. Things such as pagination, size of the drawing, and so forth are specified as global options. Note that depending on what layout algorithm you use in GraphViz, the parameters that can be used for nodes and edges, as well as the global graph options, are slightly different. The main ones stay the same, but options specific to the layout algorithms vary. Note that this property of DOT files breaks the paradigm of separating data from presentation. DOT files are not pure data input files, unlike GML files. For more information about DOT files, refer to the man page or find the documentation online at www.graphviz.org/doc/info/attrs.html.

The following is a simple DOT file that illustrates the structure and expressiveness of the file format:

```
digraph structs {
      graph [label="AfterGlow 1.5.8", fontsize=8];
      node [shape=ellipse, style=filled, fontsize=10, fillcolor=green];
      edge [len=1.6];
      "ram" -> "Printing Resume";
      "mar" -> "Information Encryption";
      "ram" [fillcolor=white, label="Raffael", shape=box];
      "mar" [fillcolor=blue, label="Marty", shape=box];
}
```

This example first defines the global properties for generating the graph. The graph keyword indicates global settings for the graph, the label in this case. These properties are followed by default values for node and edge properties. If a node or edge definition is not specifying anything different, these are the settings that are used. The example then defines the edges in the graph. There are only two edges. Following the edge definitions, special properties are defined for two of the nodes. The color, label, and shape for these two nodes are not the default ones, but the ones specified. Figure 9-1 shows how GraphViz renders the example DOT file.

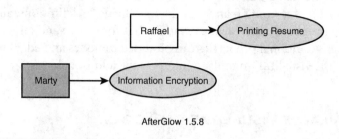

AfterGlow 1.5.8

Figure 9-1   Simple example of a DOT file rendered with GraphViz.

GML

One way of representing a link graph is by using a DOT file. A number of visualization tools do not support DOT files but are using a very similar format, the Graph Modeling Language (GML).[1] This format is similar to a DOT file. It consists of a hierarchical key-value list. The following is a simple example graph:

```
graph [
  comment "This is a sample graph"
  directed 1
  IsPlanar 1
  node [
    id 1
    label "Node 1"
  ]
  node [
    id 2
```

---

[1]   www.infosun.fim.uni-passau.de/Graphlet/GML/gml-tr.html

```
    label "Node 2"
  ]
  edge [
    source 1
    target 2
    label "Edge from node 1 to node 2"
  ]
]
```

A graph has some global parameters. Those are followed by a definition of all the nodes. The nodes are required to contain an id. Following the node definitions, all the edges are defined by using the source and target keys. The IDs for source and target are the IDs used in the nodes. Additional properties can be added to nodes and edges in key-value form. It is up to the visualization tools to interpret the additional keys.

FREELY AVAILABLE VISUALIZATION TOOLS

A cheap and easy way to start visualizing data is to use a freely available visualization tool. You do not have to invest any money up front or even start a big project of evaluating the right tool for your needs. You can get started immediately. You also do not have to develop your own programs, as is the case for visualization libraries. Note that some of the tools introduced are only free if they are not used for commercial purposes.

Unfortunately, I cannot recommend any one tool for all types of visualizations. All the tools have their strengths, weaknesses, and generic capabilities. All the tools I cover here are tools that take actual data and not coordinates to create the graphs. There are other tools that you have to feed coordinates to generate a graph. I have looked at two basic types of graphing and visualization tools: ones that generate static data graphs and stand-alone applications. Static data generation tools are ones that you can script and use on the command line to generate image files, such as GIF or SVG. They do not provide a viewer, nor do they provide any interactivity to manipulate or navigate the generated graph. This is in contrast to stand-alone applications, which have a user interface that offers varying degrees of capabilities to interact with and manipulate the graphical output.

In the following sections, I do not discuss the tools in their entirety all the time. In some cases, I might simply not know about additional features; in other cases, I might decide to leave some discussion out because of space and time restrictions.

STATIC DATA GRAPHS

This section introduces some visualization tools that generate static graphs as output. In contrast to interactive, stand-alone applications, these tools mostly come in the form of scripts or tools launched on the command line. The output is generally written to an image file. The disadvantage of these tools is that we cannot interact with the visual output to interactively explore the content. On the other hand, these tools can be scripted and be used in processes to automatically generate graphical output.

Often, the data we want to visualize is available in CSV format or may be stored in a database. However, some of the tools require more complicated data input formats (for example, a DOT file). To bridge the gap between a simple CSV file and a DOT file, you can use AfterGlow, the first tool introduced in this section. It is not a classical visualization tool, but it helps translate a CSV file into a DOT file, based on a set of configuration parameters. Following the discussion of AfterGlow, I introduce various visualization tools that you can use to generate static data graphs.

Table 9-1 compares the tools discussed in this section. The most important properties are shown in the columns so that you can easily find the ones that satisfy your needs and you can compare the tools.

Table 9-1   Static Data Graph Visualization Tools

Name	URL	Last Release Data	Platform	Interactivity	Input Data	Visualizations
AfterGlow	http://afterglow.sourceforge.net	9/2007	Perl	No	CSV	DOT
GraphViz	www.graphviz.org	11/2007	UNIX, Linux, Windows, OS X	No[2]	DOT	Link graphs
Large Graph Layout	http://sourceforge.net/projects/lgl	08/2005	Perl	No	Space separated	3D link graphs
Gnuplot	www.gnuplot.info	09/2007	Linux, UNIX, OS X, Windows	No	CSV	Bar charts, box plots, line charts, scatter plots, 3D scatter plots

continues

---

[2] lneato, which is part of the GraphViz distribution, is a stand-alone application. I am separately discussing lneato in the section on stand-alone applications.

Table 9-1 Static Data Graph Visualization Tools (Continued)

Name	URL	Last Release Data	Platform	Interactivity	Input Data	Visualizations
Ploticus	http://ploticus. sourceforge.net	06/2006	UNIX, Linux, Windows, OS X	No	CSV	Bar charts, pie charts, box plots, scatter plots, maps, link graphs, and so on
R	http://www. r-project.org	10/2007	UNIX, Linux, Windows, OS X	Limited	CSV, SQL, etc.	Bar charts, line charts, parallel coordinates, box plots, scatter plots, 3D scatter plots, treemaps, maps, and so on

AfterGlow

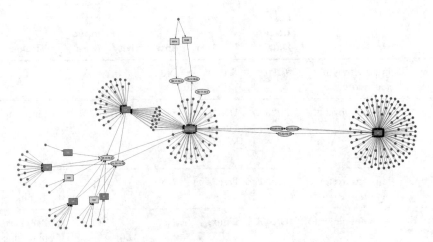

AfterGlow is a collection of scripts that facilitate the process of generating link graphs. The tool is written in Perl and needs to be invoked via the command line. As input, AfterGlow expects two- or three-column CSV files, and it outputs a DOT file, or it can generate input for the large graphing library (see below). As you can see by going through the list of visualization tools, a number of them use DOT files as input.

Generating those files manually is not easy. AfterGlow bridges this gap and enables users to use simple CSV files to generate their DOT graph descriptions.

Invoking AfterGlow to generate a DOT file from a CSV file is done with the following command:

```
cat file.csv | perl afterglow.pl > file.dot
```

AfterGlow supports a variety of features for transforming CSV input into a graph:

- Node filtering based on node name, frequency of occurrence, and fan out
- Coloring of nodes and edges
- Sizing and assigning a shape to nodes
- Aggregation of nodes

To define all of these properties, AfterGlow uses a property file that is passed as an argument on the command line. The property file consists of a set of assignments.

Let's assume we are processing a CSV file with three columns. The source address for an event is in the first column, the destination address is in the second, and the destination port in the third column. The following property files can then be used to assign color to the graph nodes:

```
color.source="yellow" if ($fields[0]=~/^192\.168\..*/);
color.source="red"
color.event="yellow" if ($fields[1]=~/^192\.168\..*/)
color.event="red"
color.target="blue" if ($fields[2]<1024)
color.target="lightblue"
```

The property file basically consists of three assignments: `color.source`, `color.event`, and `color.target`. These values map to the three nodes in Figure 9-2. A complete graph is made up of multiples of these individual nodes and edges.

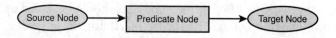

Figure 9-2   Three-node configuration used by AfterGlow to identify individual nodes.

A color assignment in the property file is a Perl expression returning a color name. The expressions are evaluated top to bottom. As soon as an expression matches, the color for this node is assigned. Another important fact is that color configurations can reference the values of the current log entry, which are made available in the @fields array. The first column of the data is therefore accessible with $fields[0].

Getting back to our example, you should now understand what the property file is doing. Whenever the first column of the data ($fields[0]) starts with 192.168., the node is colored yellow. If not, red is the default color that will be used. The same logic applies to the event nodes, this time referencing the second column ($fields[1]). For the target nodes, we want to color them blue if the target port is below 1024 and light blue if it is equal to or greater than 1024.

A slightly more complex and feature-rich configuration is one that I used to generate some of the graphs in Chapter 8, "Insider Threat":

```
# Preparing watch lists
variable=@violation=("HackerTool Download", "AV disabled");
# Highlight watch list behavior
color.target="red" if (grep(/$fields[1]/,@violation));
color.target="green"
# Score determines the node size
maxnodesize=1
size.source=$fields[2]
sum.target=0
sum.source=1
# Change shape of source nodes
shape.source=box
```

The first assignment of this configuration defines a new array, which identifies "violations." There are two possible values. The first color assignment then checks whether the second column ($fields[1]) has the value of one of these violations. If so, the color red is assigned to the node. Otherwise, the node is colored in green. The next block is used to define the size of the source nodes. The size is determined by the third column in the data file. The definition of the maxnodesize makes sure that the nodes do not grow indefinitely. In other words, the largest value found in column three will be assigned a size of 1. A value of 0 in the third column is used to mean a node size of zero. The two next assignments are used to define whether the node sizes should be added up if the same node shows up multiple times in the original log file. If not, the largest value found is chosen to determine the size. The final assignment is then used to draw source nodes as boxes rather than the default ovals.

If you use Perl expressions to evaluate the values for individual properties, an incredible set of possibilities open up. It is possible to read files, process external input, and so on. Your imagination is the limit.

If you are interested in generating an interactive link graph that enables a user to click the nodes to execute a specific action, you can use AfterGlow to generate an image, along with an image map. An image map is a piece of HTML code that defines for specific areas or locations in an image what the URL should be that is opened upon clicking that area of the image. To generate a Web page with an image map, define the url parameter in the property file to define the base URL to be followed:

```
url=http://localhost:8000/\N.html
```

The placeholder \N is used to specify what part of the URL should be replaced with the value of the node. The example assumes that there are pages available on the Web server for each node. The naming convention for the HTML pages is node name followed by .html.

After defining this property in the AfterGlow property file, you have to generate both the image and the image map with GraphViz:

```
cat file.csv | perl afterglow.pl -c sample.properties
| neato -Tgif -o image.gif -Tcmpax -o image.map
```

The file image.map will then contain an image map similar to the following:

```
<map id="structs" name="structs">
<area shape="poly" href="http://localhost:8000/\10.0.41.102.html"
title="10.0.41.102" alt="" coords="419,349 416,343 408,338 395,333
378,331 360,330 342,331 325,333 312,338 304,343 301,349 304,355 312,361
325,365 342,368 360,369 378,368 395,365 408,361 416,355"/>
<area shape="rect" href="http://localhost:8000/84.52.92.94.html"
title="84.52.92.94" alt="" coords="421,395,525,421"/>
...
</map>
```

You need to now construct an HTML file that displays the GIF image and applies the image map. An HTML file looks like this:

```
<HTML><BODY>
<!-- insert image map from before here -->
<IMG border=0 SRC="image.gif" usemap="#structs" ISMAP>
</BODY></HTML>
```

After you have placed this file along with the image on your Web server, you have an interactive graph that opens up individual pages whenever you click an image node. Obviously, you have to build all the individual pages for the nodes. If you are using some more sophisticated configurations and Web server technologies, you can use this approach to build some quite interesting applications.[3]

GraphViz

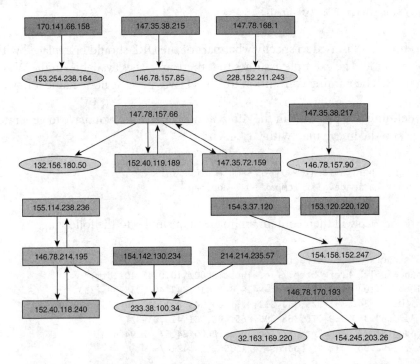

The tool that I have probably used the most during the process of writing this book is GraphViz. When it comes to generating link graphs, this is one of the better tools available. The GraphViz package consists of tools that translate a description of a graph into an image. The output format can be anything from GIF to SVG. However, GraphViz is a scripted tool, and the output is static. GraphViz ships with two tools that can be used as stand-alone applications. I discuss them as separate tools later in this chapter. The

---

[3]   I have built an integration between AfterGlow and Splunk this way. You can find instructions on how to get the two working together in my blog at http://blogs.splunk.com/raffy/2007/09/16/afterglow-and-splunk/.

GraphViz package implements a variety of layout algorithms for link graphs. Each algorithm is represented by a different tool that can generate the graph output:

- `dot` generates hierarchical layouts.
- `neato` is used to draw graphs by using a spring model for computing the layout.
- `twopi` draws graphs using a radial layout.
- `circo` draws graphs using a circular layout. It generally generates very big graphs that are not very useful.
- `fdp` uses a different spring model to layout the graphs.

All the tools read DOT attributed graph language files. The format is fairly simple and is documented at http://en.wikipedia.org/wiki/DOT. (For more information, see the beginning of this chapter.) Each tool has a variety of parameters it understands. Have a look at the man pages to explore them.

Here is a sample way of rendering a graph:

```
cat input.dot | neato -Tgif -o output.gif
```

This command instructs `neato` to render the input from the file `input.dot` and create a GIF image.

Included in the GraphViz distribution are all the previously listed tools and some graph editing tools. One tools that is useful is the `unflatten` command. If you have ever tried to generate a hierarchical graph with DOT, you might have encountered the problem that the graph turned out really wide and very thin, pretty much rendering the graph useless. The `unflatten` command corrects that problem and makes visualizing those hierarchies more space friendly. A sample way to run it is as follows:

```
cat input.dot | unflatten | dot -Tgif -o output.gif
```

Another interesting tool that is part of GraphViz is `gvpr`. It helps traversing and processing graphs. The tool operates on a DOT file, transforms it, and writes a DOT file back out. The transformations are written in a simple language whereby you can specify what should happen to edges and nodes. If you are interested in this type of graph processing, have a look at the man page of `gvpr`.

Large Graph Layout

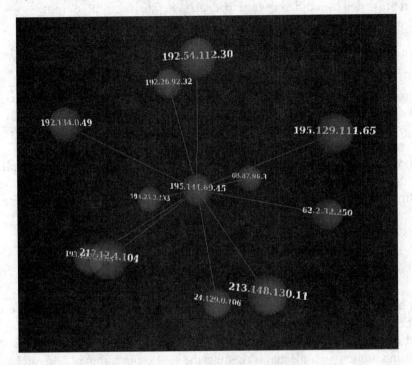

Visualizing data in a three-dimensional space is something that the Large Graph Layout (LGL) library was built for. It renders a 3D link graph based on the definition of nodes and their links. It is not a display of three data dimensions, but the 3D space is used to display the two data dimensions.

Installing the tool requires you to change the `bin/lgl.pl` file after you download and extract the package. On line 41, you need to change the `LGLDIR` to the path where you have LGL installed. After that, you are ready to generate a visual representation of your data. The input has to be formatted as a space-separated, two-column dataset. There is one restriction for the data. It has to be unidirectional, meaning that if you have an edge A > B, you cannot have an edge B > A. You need to filter those instances. After your data complies with these constraints, make sure your data file ends in `.ncol` and execute the following command:

```
perl -Iperls bin/lgl.pl data.ncol
```

This process might take some time, especially if you are trying to compute a graph with a large number of nodes and edges. When the process finishes, you will find a file in

/tmp/lgl_temp that has a number followed by _new_lgl.lgl, and a file called final.coords. You need these two files in your next command:

```
./perls/genVrml.pl /tmp/lgl_temp/1172375515_new_lgl.lgl /tmp/lgl_temp/final.coords
```

This command generates a VRML file that you can then view in a VRML browser. The VRML file generated by the preceding command is called final.coords.wrl.

The interesting aspect of LGL is that you can render graphs in 3D, and the layouts generated are actually really good. The drawbacks of the tools are the long runtime and looking at the graphs after they are generated. Navigating in 3D space is not easy, and I find it really hard to analyze a dataset this way. One interesting aspect of LGL is that the project offers an online service where you submit your edges and receive back the coordinates of your 3D graph. This is the first visualization tool that I know of that does this.

Gnuplot

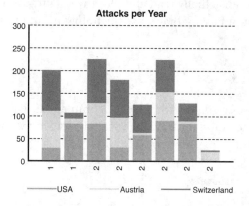

One of the most common tools for visualizing numeric data is gnuplot. It is strong in dealing with the use-cases that it was built for (plotting mathematical functions). The types of graphs supported are therefore a bit limited, although the last few releases added some more charting capabilities. Mainly scatter plots and some variants on them are supported. The other limitation of gnuplot is that the data input has to be formatted as numeric values. Gnuplot does not deal with strings or IP addresses. It does deal with dates, however. This limitation means that you have to convert your IP addresses and other string fields into some type of ordinal or continuous values before you can use it. This can make interpreting the graphs confusing, except when you are just interested in certain trends and you do not need to go back to the original data values.

Plotting data with gnuplot is done either interactively or in batch mode. To get into interactive mode, just start gnuplot. You will be presented with a prompt where you enter your commands. To run gnuplot in batch mode, just provide your script file on the command line as an argument. Here is a simple set of commands to plot a CSV sample file:

```
set datafile separator ","
set xdata time
set timefmt "%d/%b/%Y:%H:%M:%S"
set yrange [1:2]
set xlabel "Time"
set ylabel "Amount"
plot "data.csv" with points
```

The first line instructs gnuplot to expect a CSV file. Then we define that the first column is a date. The range for y-values is only from 1 to 2, so scale the graph. Further, set the labels of the axes, and then actually read and plot the data from data.csv. That's it. If you need to save the output as an image, use the following additional commands:

```
set output "plot.png"
set terminal png
```

If you now regenerate your graph with the plot command, it will be saved as a PNG image. To generate a line graph rather than a scatter plot, you would change the plot command to the following:

```
plot "data.csv" with linespoints
```

To learn more about how to use gnuplot, there is a great tutorial on the IBM DeveloperWorks site at www-128.ibm.com/developerworks/linux/library/l-gnuplot/. The tutorial also shows how to use gnuplot to draw box and error plots.

Ploticus

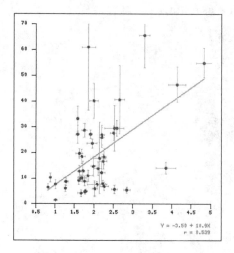

Another scripted visualization tool is Ploticus. It allows for both a configuration file that describes all the parameters of a graph or the configuration of a graph via the command line. The definitions of the graph parameters can be very specific. It therefore turned out to be fairly frustrating to get exactly right. On the other hand, this gives the tool great flexibility to configure pretty much every aspect of a graph. Here is an example of using ploticus on the command line:

```
ploticus -prefab chron  data=data.ploticus x=1 y=2 unittype=time
mode=line xrange="13:39:10 13:39:30" yrange="0 30" -png xinc="2 second"
xstubfmt=ss
```

This command invokes Ploticus and generates a PNG file based on the data.ploticus data file. data.ploticus is a TSV file and has the following content:

```
13:39:14        8
13:39:15        12
13:39:19        15
13:39:25        18
13:39:26        28
```

The same definition of the graph could have been entered in a configuration file rather than on the command line, as follows:

```
#proc getdata
file: data.ploticus
fieldnames: time amount

#proc areadef
    xscaletype: time hh:mm:ss
    xrange: 13:39:14 13:39:30
    yrange: 0 30

#proc xaxis
    stubs: inc 2 seconds
    minorticinc: 1 second
    stubformat: ss

#proc yaxis
  stubs: inc 10
  grid: color=orange

#proc scatterplot
xfield: time
yfield: amount
```

To generate a graph with this configuration, save this file as `example.ploticus` and invoke the tool as follows:

```
ploticus example.ploticus -png
```

This script generates a scatter plot rather than a bar chart and enables slightly more control over all the graph parameters. This illustrates the flexibility that this tool has.

The output of Ploticus is as manifold as the graph types it supports. All the usual graph types are supported, and output can be stored not just as image formats, such as PNG, but also as image maps to generate interactive websites.

R

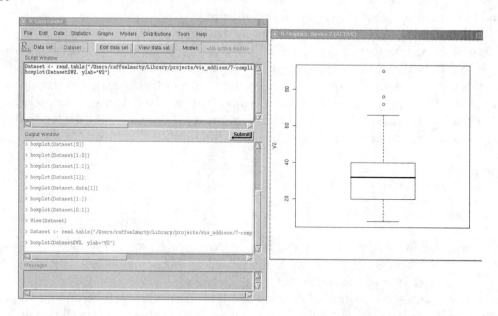

The R project is a statistical suite that supports quite flexible charting. The learning curve for this software package is steep. To get you started, type the command R --gui x11 on the command line. Numerous add-on packages are available that can be used to extend the functionality of R. One of the packages I could not have worked without is Rcmdr. You should download it from http://cran.r-project.org/src/contrib/Rcmdr_1.3-8.tar.gz and then install it with the following command:

```
R CMD INSTALL Rcmdr_1.3-8.tar.gz
```

After you have installed it, start R and execute library(Rcmdr). This should bring up a GUI that exposes the most important functions of R. To load a dataset, navigate to Data, Import Data (from text file or clipboard). Specify the necessary parameters and click OK. Now select a data file (for example, a CSV file) and load it. The data is then available in R for further manipulation and visualization. You can interact with R via the user interface or enter your commands directly in the top panel. After you enter a command, you need to click Submit to actually execute the command. For example, use the following command after you have loaded a dataset:

```
boxplot(Dataset$V1, ylab="Spread")
```

This command generates a box plot of the first column in your data. This assumes that you loaded a dataset that has a numeric first column.

One interesting aspect of R is that it can read data from databases. The main advantage of working with data in a database is that the data types are automatically assigned based on the type of the database column. You have to install a special database package for this purpose. Multiple ones are available depending on what database you want to connect to.[4] You can use the same method as described previously to install the packages, after you have downloaded the tar.gz file. If you are using RMySQL,[5] use the following sequence of commands to load a dataset from a MySQL table:

```
library(RMySQL)
mycon <- dbConnect(MySQL(), user='ram', dbname="secviz", host="my",
  password='secviz')
res <- dbGetQuery(con, "select * from table")
```

After you have loaded the data with the preceding commands, you can work with res as if it were any other data result. Note that this procedure differs slightly based on the type of database you are trying to connect to.

A more comprehensive discussion of R's features and its language is beyond the scope of this book. A great place for exploring the graphical capabilities of R is the R Graph Gallery located at http://addictedtor.free.fr/graphiques/allgraph.php. Other places that provide great tutorials include the following:

- www.cyclismo.org/tutorial/R/
- www.stat.auckland.ac.nz/~paul/RGraphics/rgraphics.html
- www.harding.edu/fmccown/R/
- http://freshmeat.net/articles/view/2237/

STAND-ALONE APPLICATIONS

Stand-alone visualization applications do not just visualize a certain dataset. They also display the output and let the user interact with it. Interaction is crucial for data exploration. The applications presented here offer different levels of interaction. Some offer only the most basic operations, such as zooming. Others offer full interactivity, with brushing, filtering, and even graph editing. Table 9-2 summarizes all the applications and some of their properties.

---

[4] If you are dealing with an ODBC connection, use the RODBC package (http://cran.r-project.org/web/packages/RODBC/index.html).

[5] http://cran.r-project.org/web/packages/RMySQL

Table 9-2 Stand-Alone Visualization Applications

Name	URL	Last Release Date	Platform	Interactivity	Input Data	Visualizations
GGobi	www.ggobi.org	09/2007	Linux, Windows, OS X	Yes	CSV, XML	Bar charts, parallel coordinates, scatter plots, scatter plot matrix, time series, link graphs (optional)
Mondrian	http://rosuda.org/Mondrian	05/2007	Java	Yes	CSV	Box plots, bar charts, scatter plots, parallel coordinates, and a couple more
Tulip	www.labri.fr/perso/auber/projects/tulip/	07/2007	UNIX, Linux, Windows, OS X	Yes	DOT, GML, and so on	Link graphs, treemaps
Cyptoscape	http://cytoscape.org	07/2007	UNIX, Linux, Windows, OS X	Yes	CSV, GML, and so on	Link graphs
GUESS	http://graphexploration.cond.edu	08/2007	Java	Yes	GDF, GML	Link graphs
Real Time 3D Graph Visualizer	www.secdev.org/projects/rtgraph3d	12/2007	Python	Limited	White-space delimited	3D link graphs
Walrus	www.caida.org/tools/visualization/walrus	03/2005	Python	Yes	LibSea graph format	Custom 3D link graphs
Dotty and lneato	www.graphviz.org	11/2007	UNIX, Linux, Windows, OS X	Yes	DOT	Link graphs

continues

Table 9-2   Stand-Alone Visualization Applications (Continued)

Name	URL	Last Release Date	Platform	Interactivity	Input Data	Visualizations
Treemap	www.cs.umd.edu/hcil/treemap	02/2004	Java	Yes	TM3	Treemaps
glTail	www.fudgie.org	10/2007	Ruby	No	Apache, IIS, Postfix, Squid, Postgres, MySQL, and so on	Custom animated network visualization packet
Parvis	www.mediavirus.org/parvis	03/2003	Java	Yes	STF	Parallel coordinates
Shoki	http://shoki.sourceforge.net	03/2004	Linux	Yes	PCAP	3D scatter plots
InetVis	www.cs.ru.ac.za/research/g02v2468/inetvis.html	11/2007	Linux, Windows	Yes	PCAP	3D scatter plots
TimeSearcher	www.cs.umd.edu/hcil/timesearcher	12/2002	Java	Yes	TQD	Custom time visualization
TNV	http://tnv.sourceforge.net	01/2007	Java	Yes	PCAP	Custom time-oriented view
NVisionIP	http://security.ncsa.uiuc.edu/distribution/NVisionIPDownLoad.html	11/2004	Java	Yes	Textual Argus input	Custom network packet visualization

Name	URL	Last Release Date	Platform	Interactivity	Input Data	Visualizations
Rumint	www.rumint.org	09/2007	Windows	Yes	PCAP	Custom network packet visualization
MRTG / RRD	http://oss.oetiker. ch/mrtg/ http://oss.oetiker. ch/rrdtool/	04/2007	UNIX, Linux, Windows, OS X	Limited	SNMP queries to routers	Custom network traffic histogram
EtherApe	http://etherape. sourceforge.net	09/2006	Linux, UNIX	No	PCAP	Custom network traffic visualization

The first few applications discussed here are general-purpose visualization tools that can output various kinds of visualizations, such as bar charts, line charts, parallel coordinates, and so forth. These applications are followed by a set of applications that can be used to generate link graphs. Applications to generate treemaps, parallel coordinates, and 3D scatter plots are next. The section ends with a look at applications that use custom visualizations to display packet captures.

GGobi

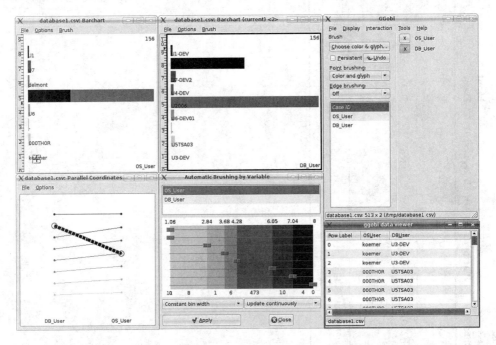

GGobi is probably one of the most powerful freely available visualization tools. It is a general-purpose visualization application that can display data in a variety of ways: bar charts, line charts, parallel coordinates, and so forth. Multiple views on the same data can be used simultaneously to show different aspects of the data. The views are fully linked to support brushing. This means that if you select one bar in a bar chart, it will update that selection across all the other charts and highlight the data just selected.

Under Automatic Brushing, you can define the color assignment for all the graphs. It even supports binning of colors, which makes it a great tool to explore the data through the color dimension. You can also add, move, and delete lines between points in the data, which makes it easy to update and tune a visualization for presentation purposes.

Unfortunately, there is no native OS X port available. It needs an X emulator. However, on my Ubuntu machine, I had GGobi installed in no time:

```
aptitude install ggobi
```

The only unfortunate drawback when using `aptitude` to install GGobi is that it does not support GraphViz. You have to compile the sources yourself and manually turn on support for GraphViz through `./configure`.

GGobi reads CSV and XML files. An integration of GGobi and R allows the user to transfer data between R and GGobi. After the data is loaded, it is easy to open different views on the same data to get an idea of the data. By filtering outliers and using the brushing feature, data can be investigated quickly. To not clutter the displays, GGobi does not show all the labels for the data elements. However, you can hover over the individual data points and have GGobi identify the underlying data.

Mondrian

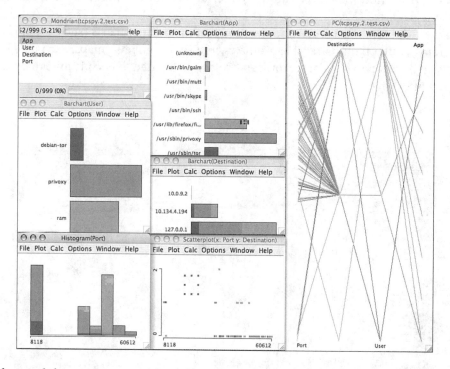

Another tool that supports a wide variety of graphs and enables you to simultaneously show multiple views is Mondrian. The views are all linked; selecting a value in one graph automatically propagates the selection to the other views. The data can be sorted, and individual values can be excluded. Mondrian allows you to color individual values. You have to first select a certain value and then use the META-1 to META-9 keys to assign a color. When you click away and make a new selection, the previous selection will have a color assignment. This can prove useful when analyzing data. You can distinguish individual values from each other much more quickly.

Some of the functionality of Mondrian needs R and Rserv installed. Most of the visualizations, however, work without that.

Mondrian reads TSV files. By adding /C or /D in front of the column name, you can instruct Mondrian to interpret a data column as either continuous (/C) or categorical (/D). Here is an example:

```
SourceIP      DestIP       /CBytes Transferred
10.0.0.2      10.2.1.2     100
10.0.0.3      10.2.1.3     213
```

In the example, Mondrian is instructed to interpret the third column as a continuous or a numeric field.

Unlike GGobi, Mondrian does not just support the normal charts (such as bar charts, histograms, scatter plots, parallel coordinates, and so on) but also maps. Each polygon in a map can be mapped to a data record, and color can be used to encode information for that part of the map.

Tulip

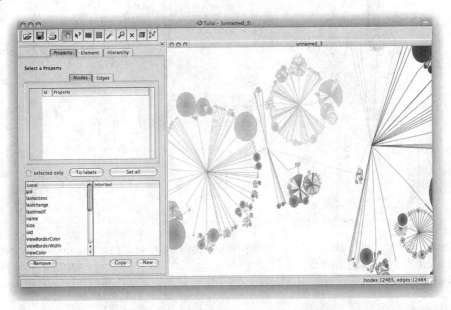

If you are not satisfied with the command-line interface that GraphViz is offering you to visualize DOT files, Tulip is the right tool for you. It offers a graphical interface that can be used to not just visualize DOT files, but also GML files and other graph formats. The graph output is a fairly interactive link graph. Rotation, zooming, moving nodes, and deleting nodes are some of the interaction features. Tulip offers a variety of layout algorithms; not just 2D, but also 3D ones. The tool offers all kinds of algorithms to find reachable subgraphs, color by various metrics (for example, the fan out of a node), and resize the nodes. To explore some of these features, I highly recommend going through one of the tutorials contained in the Help. They are great!

When you first import a data file, you will be a bit surprised not to see much on your screen. The first thing you must do is go to Algorithm > Layout and choose a layout algorithm to render your graph. After you do this, you are good to go. You might notice that a lot of the functionality is available only if you have data organized in a tree. For example, treemaps are that way.

If you are looking for a programming library, Tulip also offers a C++ library that you can use to code against. This tool is a must-try if you are working with link graphs!

Cytoscape

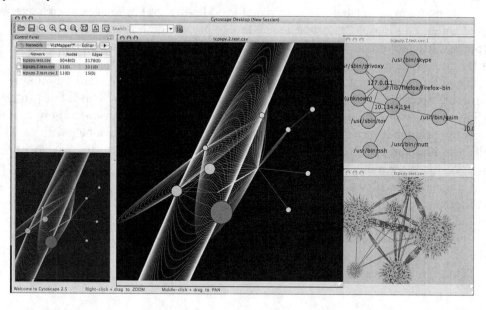

Cytoscape is another tool in the category of link graph visualizers. Importing data is fairly simple. This tool assists greatly in loading CSV files. The import capability lets you configure the parameters on-the-fly and gives you immediate feedback by showing the impact of your changes on the first 100 lines of your log file. This made it very easy to load one of my datasets.

After the data is loaded, Cytoscape offers many different layout algorithms to draw graphs. With a variety of layout algorithms available, chances are that one is well suited for the data that needs to be visualized. Cytoscape offers four control panels: the Network panel, the VizMapper, the Editor, and the Filter panel. The **Network** panel shows all the datasets loaded. The **VizMapper** exposes all the graph, node, and edge properties and lets you change them. Anything from color to size, labels, and even line styles can be adjusted here. The **Editor** enables you to add new nodes and edges just by dragging the symbol from the pane into the graph. By right-clicking nodes, you can change their properties. Anything from color to labels can be adjusted this way. The **Filters** panel enables you to eliminate nodes. It lets you define filters based on all kinds of graph properties. The interaction with the filter interface is a bit confusing, and I was not able to delete individual filter conditions after I added them. I had to delete the entire file and start over.

Exploration of graphs is flexible. You can zoom, pan, rotate, move nodes, and select subsets of nodes to work on. There is also a search facility in the toolbar that you can use to locate nodes by their labels. To rearrange the nodes in a graph, you can align a selected set of nodes. This makes Cytoscape a great tool to prepare graphs for presentations or reports. Often, automatic layouts of nodes do not produce an optimal placement; with little human interaction, this can be fixed.

In addition to the layout algorithms and the fairly nice graph interaction, a minimal clustering operation is offered through one of the layout algorithms. This is fairly interesting when you are trying to see clusters in your data. The simplest way to apply clustering is to select the Inverted Self Organizing Maps layout from the layout algorithms. This will draw nodes in proximity that belong together. More advanced clustering algorithms are available as separate plugins.

A unique feature that Cytoscape offers is the plugin architecture (and not just the architecture itself; the website offers about 40 plugins for download).[6] A lot of them are related to biology because the tool was initially developed by biologists. Plugins to find the shortest path or even an integration via XMLRPC are available from the download page.

---

[6]   http://cytoscape.org/plugins2.php

GUESS

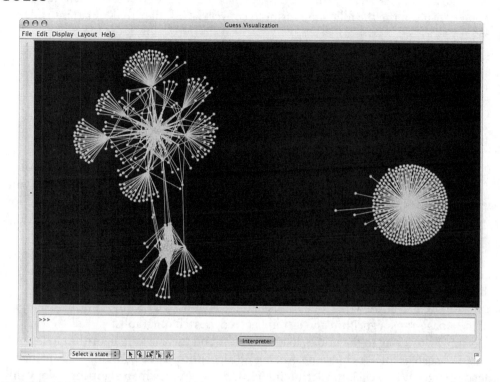

GUESS is fairly unique in its capabilities. This visualization tool renders link graphs by using one of a set of layout algorithms. In addition, the tool has a completely scripted programming language that enables you to interact with the graph.

To start the tool, I had to change the `guess.sh` script to point the `GUESS_LIB` variable to the current directory. Executing `guess.sh` after that successfully launched the application. Loading data was not too complicated either. The proprietary GDF format is fairly simple and can quickly be generated from a CSV file. A GDF file looks like this:

```
nodedef> name
10.1.1.2
10.10.39.10
edgedef> node1,node2
10.1.1.2,10.10.39.10
```

As you can see, the file starts with a definition of the nodes, followed by a definition of the edges. You can use the following script to convert a CSV file (`input.csv`) into GDF format:

```
echo "nodedef> name";
awk -F, '{print $1; print $2}' input.csv
| sort | uniq; echo "edgedef> node1,node2";
cat input.csv
```

After loading the data, choose a layout algorithm to change the layout of the graph. GUESS offers a variety of layout algorithms (although not as many as Cytoscape). After the data has been laid out, GUESS provides all the common interaction capabilities you need to navigate the graphs (panning, zooming, selecting nodes, and deleting a selection of nodes). You can change node attributes either globally or on a per-node basis through a right-click.

The benefit of a scripted interaction language is that all the graph elements are available in the scripting language. Therefore, it is fairly simple to implement graph algorithms on top of GUESS (for example, a clustering algorithm). You can find a set of scripts for GUESS at www-personal.umich.edu/~ladamic/GUESS/index.html. Examples include a page-rank algorithm and a simple greedy search on graphs.

To apply clustering to the graph, load your data and use a layout algorithm to lay out the nodes, such as the Fruchterman-Rheingold algorithm. Then go to the website mentioned previously and click the Script link for the Girvan-Newman algorithm. Copy this script into your clipboard and go back to GUESS. Then navigate to Edit > Paste to Console in the menu bar. Click within the console (the bottom pane) and press Return to execute the algorithm on the given data. The colors now highlight individual clusters.

Real Time 3D Graph Visualizer

The Real Time 3D Grapher (RTG) is a tool to visualize link graphs in 3D. It uses a physics model to lay out the nodes. The output is simple and by default does not even show the node labels but just the nodes themselves. From an interaction standpoint, you can click the nodes. Furthermore, nodes can be moved around to change the arrangement and layout.

I could not get the tool running on OS X. On Ubuntu, I had to download some additional files to make the tool work. Depending on your Linux distribution, you might have to install additional libraries. The first library I had to install was `pyinline`, which I found on SourceForge. In addition, you need to search for "povexport," and then download the file and save it as `pyexport.py` in the same directory as you have `rtgraph3d`.

That did the trick for me. After you have all of these files installed, run the tool with `./rtgraph3d.py`. An output window will open, but nothing will happen at this point. You need to then open `./rtg_cli.py`, which is an interactive client, to add edges to the graph. By entering

```
edge raffy san_francisco
```

two nodes will be generated: one for `raffy`, one for `san_francisco`. An interesting and fun application is to now script something against the CLI. Try, for example, the following:

```
sudo tcpdump -nnli ath0 | perl -pe
's/.*?(\d+\.\d+\.\d+\.\d+).*?(\d+\.\d+\.\d+\.\d+).*?$/edge \1 \2/; $|=1'
| ./rtg_cli.py
```

This will run tcpdump and extract the IP addresses. For every connection, a node is added to the graph in real time! By using the right mouse button, you can rotate your graph. Have a look at the output. It's fairly interesting to see your traffic live onscreen! Unfortunately, there is no way to eliminate certain nodes from the screen. If you have a lot of different IP addresses showing up in your tcpdump, they will quickly clutter your screen.

Walrus

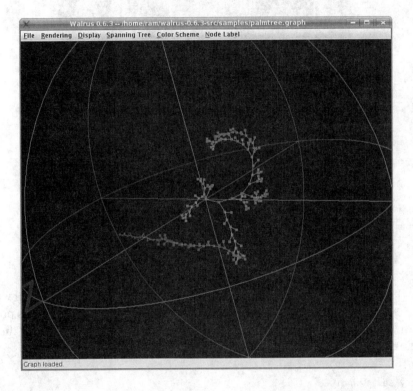

If you are looking to visualize a large amount of data as a link graph, take a look at Walrus. By utilizing a specialized 3D view based on a fisheye-like distortion, it supports the rendering of arbitrary numbers of nodes and edges. Interacting with the graph is easy and common for these types of 3D tools; it offers the common interactions such as rotation and zooming. In addition, you can interactively prune the graph to subgraphs to reduce occlusion. To encode more data in the graph, you can use colored nodes. The output of Walrus looks pleasing. Given that the tool can visualize a large set of nodes and edges, this is a great selling point. However, don't be fooled by the visual presentation. Unfortunately it is fairly hard to get data into the tool. You need to meet a lot of restrictions and conditions. First of all, only connected graphs with reachable nodes are supported. Second, you need to provide Walrus with a meaningful spanning tree for your graph. And third, the input format that Walrus accepts is based on the LibSea library from CAIDA.[7] The format is fairly complex but also powerful. As a minimum, you need to provide a list of all the links and nodes, as well as the spanning tree. Unfortunately, I have not found an easy way to generate all this based on my CSV files. Maybe someone has a good tool to do this.

Walrus runs without any problems on Leopard (OS X). On Ubuntu (Linux), it was a bit more challenging to get it running. I had to download the correct Java 3D libraries. It works now, but for some reason it seg-faults every now and then, locking up the entire machine.

If I had an easy way to convert my CSV files (or log files) to the input format that Walrus expects, I would definitely use the tool regularly. Even a minimal example that just draws a couple of nodes results in a fairly complex input file.

Dotty and Ineato

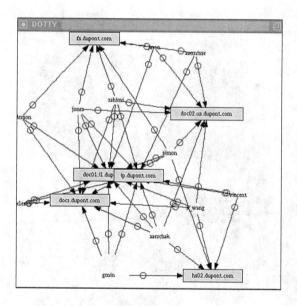

GraphViz ships with two applications that can be used to not only render DOT graph files, but also interactively explore them. Dotty and Ineato are both equal in functionality. The difference is just the layout algorithm used to render a DOT file. Whereas dotty

---

[7] Check www.caida.org/tools/visualization/libsea/ for more information about LibSea.

is based on dot to render a hierarchical layout, lneato uses neato to lay out the nodes. The interaction with graphs is fairly limited and basic. Commands can be accessed through right-clicks. You can, for example, zoom into a specific area of the graph and then open a bird's eye view to orientate yourself in the graph. You can also use a search capability to locate a specific node by its label.

Various keyboard shortcuts enable you to navigate the graphs. For example, Z and z can be used to zoom in and out, respectively. By using either a right-click on a specific node or by selecting a node and then using some of the keyboard shortcuts, you can, for example, delete nodes (d). By just clicking in the graph, you can add new nodes and add edges between them. This makes it easy to improve DOT layouts, add new nodes, and delete others. When you are satisfied with a set of nodes, you can then save the graph as a new DOT file. This eliminates the need to interact with the DOT files themselves.

Treemap

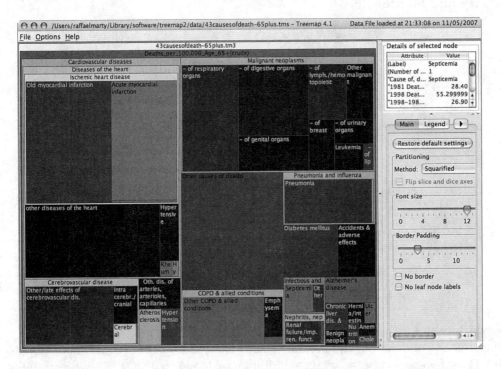

The research team led by Ben Shneiderman, the inventor of treemaps, implemented this version of a treemap visualization tool. The tool is completely interactive. It lets the user specify all the parameters for the treemap with easy-to-understand configuration panels. There are four main configuration panels. The first one (**Main**) lets you choose basic display options for the treemaps, such as font size and border paddings. The second panel (**Legend**) controls the labels of the boxes, what variable is used to control the size of the boxes, and what variable controls the color. The **Filters** panel can be used to filter the data by each of the data fields. The user can move sliders to interactively adjust the treemap view. The **Hierarchy** panel is used to define the fields and the order of fields that drive the hierarchy displayed as the treemap. Each of the data fields can be added and ordered to make up the hierarchy best suited for the data at hand. The treemap view updates in real time. The real-time feedback helps explore the different settings, such as different hierarchies.

By clicking individual boxes in the treemap, you can zoom in (double-click) and out (right-click). By hovering over individual boxes, you can display the underlying values in a little popup; and on the top of the rightmost panel, all the details of the selected box are shown.

An interesting feature is auto refresh. To enable auto refresh, navigate to Options > Reload Data File. If the data file changes, you can tell the tool to refresh the graph and display the new data. It keeps all the configurations from before, so you don't have to reapply them.

Treemap handles strings and integers differently in the input data. You can use strings and integer fields to define the treemap hierarchy and the box colors. To define the size of the boxes, you need to use an integer field. The data type of the input fields is defined in the TMS input file's header. To generate the input file, I generally translate my log files to CSV. Then, I add the header line manually to label the columns. As the first column, I add a Count column. The data types I define based on the data columns present in my data. To populate the Count column, I run the following command on my data:

```
cat file | sort | uniq -c | sed -e 's/,/       /g'
```

This command sorts my file, adds the Count column, and translates commas to tabulators. Do not forget to do this before you add the two header lines. A sample file looks like this:

```
Count    Department     Control    Exposure  Impact  Risk
INTEGER  STRING         STRING     INTEGER   INTEGER INTEGER
3        Engineering    engineering control  1       3
2        Engineering    engineering control  1       3
```

glTail

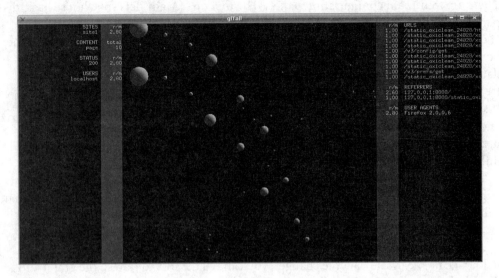

A fun tool that does not just render static images, but even animates them, is glTail. The installation on Ubuntu was fairly simple. Running the `gl_tail` code prompted me one by one to install a few libraries. After all of them were installed, I had to build a configuration file. When you run `./gl_tail -n`, glTail generates a sample skeleton for a configuration file that can be modified to reflect the correct parameters. The tool is written for a specific case where people are tailing remote log files. This is not the case for me. I want to look at local files. To do so, I just configured the host to be localhost, where I am running an SSH server anyway. This enabled me to get everything running. Currently, glTail ships with built-in parsers for a few sources such as Apache, IIS, PIX, Postfix, and Squid. I think the tool would benefit from a generic CSV input where you could use your own parsers to get to the data. I would rather provide my own parsing and input CSV data into glTail.

Once everything is set up, run the tool and watch a live data stream of your data on the screen. On the left and right side, all the data dimensions are drawn horizontally. Under each field name, a list of current values appears. The pane in the middle of the screen uses moving bubbles to represent active traffic. The bubbles are emitted from the legends on the sides, and they move toward the other side. Gravity pulls them down to the bottom of the screen.

The visualization is extremely cool. However, from a data representation standpoint, the utility of the visualization is questionable. You can't see much except data volume and frequency. You get only a qualitative feel for the actual values of the log entries. It is not possible to quantify them because the screen updates too fast. Also note that if you are not constantly monitoring the screen, you will miss potentially important activity.

With the tool in its current incarnation, you can use it to get a rough idea of the distribution of values in a log file. After you have a broad understanding of the data, you can then go in and either use another visualization method to look at details or look at the raw log files. It would be helpful to have a VCR-like control to navigate in time. That way, users could have a closer look at individual time slices.

Parvis

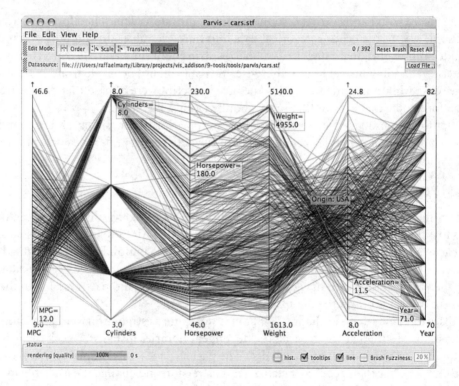

Parvis is a specialized visualization tool. It supports only the generation of parallel coordinates. Because it is so specialized, the rendering of the parallel coordinates is really well done.

To start the tool, use the parvis.bat file that is provided, even if you are on a UNIX system. Unfortunately, the input format and the general capabilities of the tools are not that great. The input format is a special format called the Simple Table Format (STF). It is not very different from a TM3 format. However, it is slightly more complicated.

The first line defines how many columns are present in the file. The following lines then define all the column names and data types, followed by the actual data. Here is an example:

```
3
Name        String
School      String
Quiz1       Real
John  St.Pauls     93
```

The problem with Parvis is that it supports only continuous data. Therefore, you need to find some way to turn your categorical data into numeric values. In addition, you must include both the original categorical values (as string columns) and the converted numeric values in your data file. Otherwise, the data will not be labeled, and it won't make sense while analyzing it. It would be nice if a script were offered that did the translation for people that are not that savvy about writing STF files.

After the data is loaded successfully, Parvis supports brushing, sizing, and rearranging of coordinates. It also enables you to highlight the data values under the cursor to further explore the data.

Shoki (Packet Hustler)

Part of the Shoki application is a visualization capability called hustler. Hustler can be used to either visualize live network traffic or recorded PCAP files. It lets you visualize the packets in a 3D scatter plot. Along with the 3D representation in one of the quadrants, the three other quadrants simultaneously show the isometric views of the data. They help a great deal with navigating the 3D representation and partly deal with the problem of occlusions in the 3D space.

I discovered that the installation of Shoki is not quite as straightforward as it should be. First, make sure that you have all the dependent libraries installed. Check the Read Me for exactly which libraries are needed. The package does not compile with a gcc compiler that is newer than gcc-3.3. Install an earlier version and change the Makefile to compile the package. In the Makefile, change the line

```
CC=cc
```

to

```
CC=gcc-3.3
```

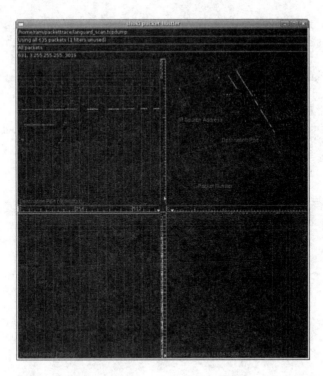

After you make this change, go ahead and configure and make the package:

```
./configure --with-fftw=/usr/lib --with-pcre=/usr/lib \
  --with-gtk=/usr/lib
make
useradd shoki
groupadd shoki
make install
make chroot
```

This will execute the installation. Now copy the sample filter such that the default configuration is working and hustler can be started:

```
cp /usr/local/shoki/conf/sample_filterlits.conf \
/usr/local/shoki/conf/ip_filterlist.conf
```

Running hustler is now a matter of providing the capture file on the command line:

```
/usr/local/shoki/bin/hustler -r pcacp_file
```

Different axis configurations will help identify different situations. A useful one is to define the axes as source address, destination address, and destination port. To change the axes assignment, right-click in one of the quadrants and choose Axis Variable, followed by the variable you want to display. Another configuration is to assign the packet number to one of the axis, along with the destination address and destination port on the other axes. This configuration helps identify port scans.

As I discussed earlier in this book, 3D representations suffer from occlusion. The innovative use of the three isometric views, however, provides a good way around this.

InetVis

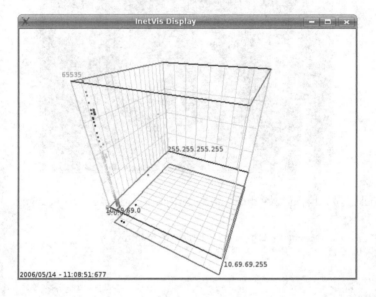

One more tool that is in the category of network traffic visualization is InetVis. The tool represents either live network traffic or recorded packet captures in a 3D scatter plot. InetVis has some limitations that are very unfortunate. For example, the axis assignments are fixed. You can visualize only source address, destination address, and destination port. What is interesting about the tool is the VCR-like controls to replay network captures (much like rumint). Very nicely done is the fading of older events. This helps keep the screen from getting too cluttered. The capability to color the points based on a few data properties can come in handy, too. The drawback is again the limited number of options. It seems that this tool should be integrated with rumint. I base this observation on some similar concepts that these tools apply.

TimeSearcher

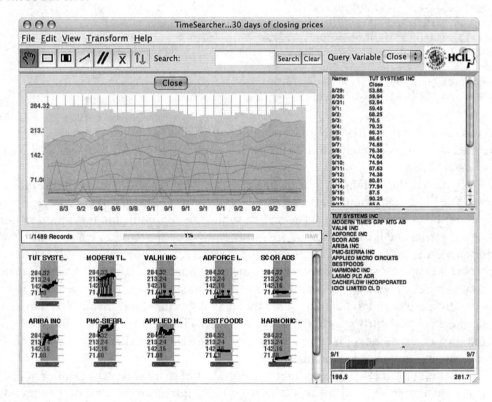

TimeSearcher is a time-series analysis tool. It is unfortunate that the tool uses some proprietary data format. The TQD file format requires a specific header that defines the title, static and dynamic variables and their data types, the number of data points for each record, the number of total records, and then the labels for each of the time units. Here is an sample file:

```
#title
DMZ access last month
# static attributes
machine,String
# Dynamic atts
Access
#  of time points=n
30
# of records k
2
```

```
# time point labels
8/29,8/30,8/31,9/1,9/2,9/3,9/4,9/5,9/6,9/7,9/8,9/9,9/10,9/11,9/12,9/13,9
/14,9/15,9/16,9/17,9/18,9/19,9/20,9/21,9/22,9/23,9/24,9/25,9/26,9/27
#stat1, dynamic @ t1, dynamic @t2, ....,dynamic @tn
192.168.0.10,58,58,59,59,58,59,58,57,58,59,58,58,57,57,56,57,57,56,59,59
,59,59,59,59,59,58,58,58,57,59
192.168.0.100,51,53,56,57,58,56,55,55,59,55,55,57,60,61,63,62,60,62,61,6
1,58,61,63,66,64,66,68,68,66,66
```

As you can see, this is fairly elaborate and does not reflect any of the file formats we are used to. This is definitely a hurdle for people who want to use the tool with their own data.

Once started, the tool shows four main areas. The lower left shows all the individual series. The lower right shows all the series as a textual list. The details of the selected series are shown on the top right. The top left shows the minimum and maximum values of all data series and is called the data envelope. This is also the window where you start your queries. Select the rectangle in the toolbar to start setting up your query. By selecting View > Graph Overview, you can enable the individual data series in the top-left view.

Many more interactions are available. One of the interesting queries is the angular query. This enables you to find data series that have a specific slope. If you need to find data where you had fairly significant spikes, this can be interesting. To find out more about the various modes of interaction and features of TimeSearcher, have a look at the accompanying, very detailed manual.

The output of TimeSearcher resembles the concept of sparklines. A large amount of data is visualized in a very small area. This makes it an interesting tool to compare trends over time for multiple variables. For example, use the destination ports as individual series. Looking at an individual port series, you can find suspicious behavior quickly. For example, if you are running a non-Windows environment and you see traffic on port 135 (NetBIOS), you should probably investigate further and find out what is generating this Windows-related traffic. By comparing multiple series with each other, you can find trends and commonalities between multiples services (i.e., destination ports).

TNV

Analyzing packet captures is something that most of us have had to do at some point. The challenge with an unknown dataset is always to get a quick feeling for what the data covers, which hosts are communicating on the network, which protocols were seen, and possibly find some sort of anomalous activity. TNV helps quickly visualize the captured traffic in a single display. The screen is partitioned into multiple parts. It uses the horizontal axis for time. The time slider on the bottom lets you control the time window

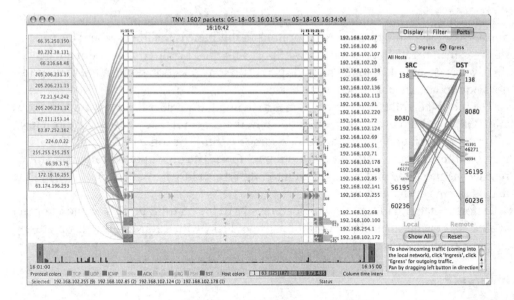

displayed. On the left side of the screen, TNV displays all the external machines. External machines are all the ones that do not reside in your home network.

The home network can be configured in the settings on the right side of the screen. One thing that I had to learn the hard way was that the setting of the home network variable is not just central to displaying data in TNV, but it also requires a reload of the dataset if the value is changed. A reload literally means reimporting the data, not just clicking the Reset button. This can be fairly annoying, especially if you are analyzing a dataset that you are not familiar with and you have to determine the home network first. Once the home network is set, TNV shows each of the internal machines on the vertical axis of the main grid display. Connections are then displayed as lines between the individual hosts. This enables you to quickly identify the communications between internal and external machines and among internal ones. Inside of the grid, little arrows indicate traffic from different protocols. They point in the direction that the traffic was flowing. Color is used to encode the protocol and, in the case of TCP, also the TCP flags.

To interact with the data and explore it, you can double-click within a cell to zoom in. A right-click brings up a context menu that enables you to either execute some predefined commands for that IP address, such as a DNS lookup, or choose the option to show packet details of the selected communications.

The rightmost side of the display contains a pane that has three different options. The first one is to configure the display properties, such as the home network. The second one is to filter and highlight individual connections based on certain criterion. You can, for example, choose to highlight all connections with a TTL larger than 128.

Unfortunately, the filter options are fairly limited, and not all the protocol fields are supported. The last of the three possible options in this pane is the Ports pane. This pane shows a small parallel coordinate view of port activities. I realized that, unfortunately, this display is not linked to the main display at all. Any selection done in the main grid does not update the parallel coordinate view.

The tool is fairly flexible when it comes to defining the colors for the protocols, hosts, and TCP flags, but beyond that, unfortunately, there are not many options. Quite a few controls are missing. I wanted to exclude some machines or some traffic from the display, but there doesn't seem to be an option to do so. The only option I found was to reorder the machines and group them into interesting clusters. With a lot of hosts in the data, this can get challenging.

Unfortunately, I had trouble with loading a 7MB file on my laptop. It wouldn't open it at all. I kept trying smaller files until I finally got lucky with a 1.5MB file that was, to my surprise, opened really quickly.

NVisionIP

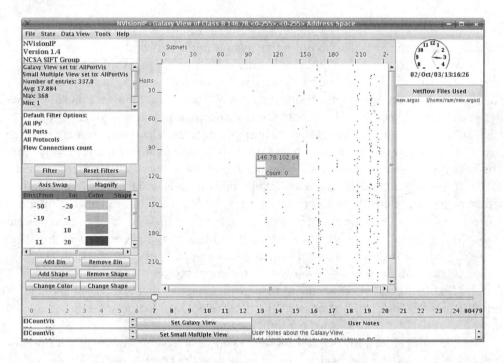

The National Center for Advanced Secure Systems built a Java-based visualization tool to analyze network traffic. The installation on my OS X was simple. The installer did all the right things. On my Ubuntu system, I had a bit more trouble. Starting the installer was not successful. After a failed attempt, I had to change into the /tmp/install.dir.*xxxx*/InstallerData (where *xxxx* represents a number) directory and run the installer manually with the following command:

```
java -classpath ./installer.zip com/zerog/ia/installer/Main
```

This did the trick, and the installer worked. I faced my second challenge when I tried to import some data. The supported input is textual Argus data (see www.qosient.com/argus). It took me a fair amount of time to actually figure out that I had to post-process my Argus file. The tool would not accept any input line that was not exactly 143 characters long. What I had to do was first generate an output file in Argus by running the following:

```
ra -A -c -G -n -t -r <file.argus> -
```

I then had to this output pipe into a series of commands to cut the length exactly to 143 characters:

```
sed -e 's/\r(\n)?/\n/' | awk '{ print substr($0, 1, 143) }' > out.argus
```

After I processed the data with this command, I was able to load it into NVisionIP.

The main screen of the tool contains a big area where a Class B network can be visualized. When loading your data, you need to specify the Class B that you own or the one that encloses your subnets. Activity of individual machines is then displayed as dots in the grid. You cannot change the color, zoom in on the data, hover over the data to display little sparklines, and so on. Looking at some data, I pretty quickly ran out of memory; even after instructing the virtual machine to use half a gig of RAM, I still ran out of memory. The tool has a few interesting and useful aspects. Chief among those is the fact that you can look at machine-centric views or analyze a smaller dataset fairly easily.

Rumint

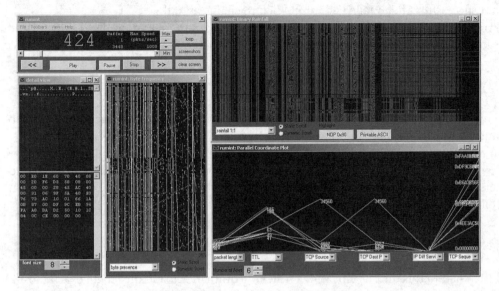

A visualization tool that is very focused on one application is rumint. The tool takes PCAP input (or captures traffic live from the network interface) to visualize it in various, fairly unconventional ways. From visualizing the packet captures showing the distribution of ASCII characters to parallel coordinate graphs of the most important packet header fields, rumint can display them all simultaneously. I find the parallel coordinate plots useful when analyzing network traffic. It shows at one glance how multiple packet fields are related. In addition, rumint displays the behavior over time, which is a new concept that greatly enhances the parallel coordinate view. The fact that rumint enables very simple interaction with the data through VCR-like controls makes it especially easy to analyze trends over time and see how network traffic develops.

Unfortunately, the amount of traffic that can be loaded into rumint is limited. It would be useful to allow arbitrary data files to be loaded, especially because packet captures tend to grow large very quickly.

Multi Router Traffic Grapher and Round Robin Database

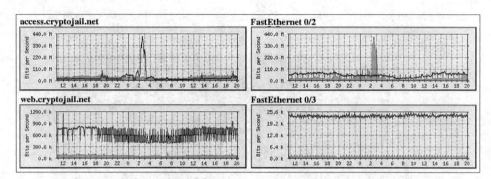

A tool commonly used in the networking world is the Multi Router Traffic Grapher (MRTG). MRTG is a tool to monitor the traffic load on network links. It generates HTML pages and provides a near real-time visual representation of this traffic. MRTG can be used not only to monitor traffic but any type of data that is made available via SNMP, such as host performance metrics or system logins.

MRTG uses a time-series[8] data store that is efficient at storing data in a compact way without expanding over time. It is not necessary to keep all the base data around for only graphing trends. Old data is unnecessary as long as aggregated information is kept around. For scenarios where data is not necessarily available via SNMP, and MRTG can therefore not be used. RRD, the Round Robin Database, is a tool implementing the concept of a time-series data store, too. It can be used via simple shell scripts or as a Perl module. These tools prove handy in scenarios where time-series data needs to be stored and quickly visualized.

---

[8]   A time-series is a sequence of data points representing measurements at specific time instances.

EtherApe

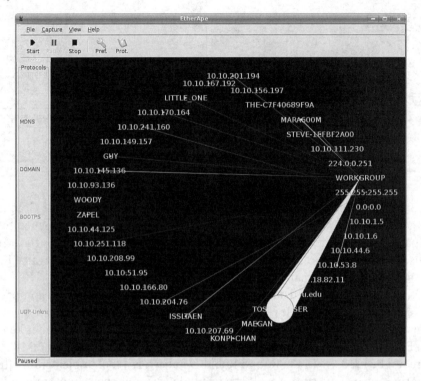

A simple visualization tool is EtherApe. It visualizes either traffic captured on the network interface or optionally reads PCAP files. EtherApe arranges all the communicating hosts in a single circle and highlights network communication by connecting the corresponding machines. Different colors are used to encode the different protocols. This helps you quickly learn the role of systems by looking at the differently colored lines connecting them. The width of the lines encodes the amount of traffic.

Alongside the graphical representation of communicating parties, you can also show statistics of used ports. These statistics can prove useful in identifying fluctuations in the type of network traffic observed.

OPEN SOURCE VISUALIZATION LIBRARIES

In some cases, you will find that existing tools do not meet your visualization needs. Either there is no tool that can deal with your exact use-cases or you might have to include a visualization capability into your own tools. One of the primary decision points for choosing a visualization library is the programming language it supports. This short look at visualization libraries considers both Java and non-Java libraries.

JAVA LIBRARIES

If you need to generate graphs out of a Java program, you can do so by using one of the many available libraries. There are commercial libraries, too, but the open source community provides several powerful libraries. The following is not a comprehensive list at all. These are libraries I came across during my visualization research. Likely, there are even better ones out there. At least this should be a starting point for your own research on existing libraries. You can find a good list of Java libraries at http://networkviz. sourceforge.net/ and at www.manageability.org/blog/stuff/open-source-graph-network-visualization-in-java/view. Many visualization libraries that you will find on the Internet are academic in nature. Often, they are not driven by a true community of open source developers that maintain and improve the code, but rather a research team that works on the libraries for a period of time. This can be the reason why documentation (and sometimes the quality of the code) is not very good. It would be an interesting project to have a look at a set of libraries or even open source tools and combine some of their functionalities.

In general, you will find that there are charting libraries and then there are data visualization libraries. I want to separate them because charting is not really that interesting. You can use Excel and Visual Basic if you want to chart something. Data visualization is much more interesting; this covers interactive link graphs, treemaps, zoomable parallel coordinates, and linked charts to support dynamic queries. When referring to visualization libraries, I am not including things such as Java 3D into the discussion. Although you could consider them visualization libraries, these types of libraries are meant to render graphs, not to visualize data and information.

Probably the best known Java graphing library that is being used for generating link graphs is JGraph. It provides all kinds of interaction capabilities, from zooming to drag and drop. JGraphT is based on the JGraph library. It provides mathematical graph-theory objects and algorithms on top of JGraph. Probably the biggest improvement over JGraph is the listeners to track modification events. The graph layouts are rendered by using JGraph.

A library that is in the same realm is OpenJGraph. Don't bother looking at it too closely; it has not gotten an update for more than 5 years. A library that is still in development is JUNG. By default, the library can load GML files. The library supports all kinds of algorithms, such as clustering or spanning-tree computation. The library makes an impression of being very mature and comes with a lot of code examples to get you started.

The Graph INterface librarY, or GINY for short, is yet another project concerned with visualizing link graphs. Its claim is that JGraph's APIs are much too complicated, and that's where GINY enters the stage. I have not used GINY and cannot comment on that claim.

A toolkit that I have been working with is the InfoVis Toolkit. When I looked at the library about a year ago, the capabilities and graph outputs seemed to match exactly what I was looking for. Unfortunately, along the path of implementing my data inputs and output capabilities around the toolkit, I ran into more and more limitations and issues that I think were bugs. The communications with the author never resulted in a bug fix or an update to the library. There have been no updates since the end of 2005.

If you are a real fan of GraphViz, you might want to consider the Grappa library. This is a Java wrapper for visualizing link graphs in GraphViz. It provides all kinds of features to visualize DOT files.

Another visualization library that seems very mature and easy to use is Prefuse. It was developed at U.C. Berkeley. Although the package has been developed for a long time, it is still in beta. Prefuse ships with a lot of example code that shows how to use the library to generate not just link graphs but also treemaps. Some of the features of Prefuse are the interactivity, the capability of animating the output, supporting dynamic queries, and an integrated search capability. Out of the box, the library provides an adapter for GML files. Yet another bonus point is Prefuse Flare, which is a visualization and animation tool for ActionScript and Adobe Flash. In the age of Web 2.0, this is a great step in the right direction.

NON-JAVA LIBRARIES

In the preceding section, I discussed some Java-based visualization libraries. If you are not familiar with Java or you need to use other programming languages, many visualization libraries are available. Again, I do not cover the entire field of visualization libraries. Consider this a starting point for your own journey.

Most people who need to generate visual output from within C++ have probably looked at the Boost Graph Library (BGL). As part of the Boost effort, BGL provides some standard interfaces and implementations for graph visualization. It provides the data structures necessary to efficiently store the graph data, algorithms to parse and operate on the graphs, and interfaces to plot the data, for example, by generating DOT output files.

Piccolo is a graphics library providing an abstraction on top of lower-level graphics APIs for Windows .NET and Java, and there is also a version for mobile devices. The availability of a mobile version makes this library fairly unique. Using the Piccolo library, you do not have to worry about the low-level details of these APIs. Piccolo handles boundary checking, event handling, graph interaction, animation, and so forth. Piccolo advertises a special zoomable user interface, which they call ZUI. The interface greatly improves interaction with graphs.

A project that goes in a completely different direction from all the other ones is Processing. It is a language for programming images. It does not just let users define and render graphs but also offers methods to support interaction and animation. The basic programming language follows a Java syntax, which makes it easy for people who already know Java to pick up the language. I played around with Processing and pretty quickly built a tool that plots 3D coordinates, which are stored in a file, onto the screen. It's fully animated and interactive. The 3D object rotates in space, and you can use the mouse to interact with it. What I found very slick as well is that the tool will generate a JAR with the entire code, executable on Linux, Windows, OS X, or it can even be used as an applet. This way you can prototype your graphs in the development environment that Processing offers and, once done, you can publish it as a full-blown executable. Many people have also contributed plugins to Processing, things such as a MySQL plugin for example. These plugins can significantly improve the productivity when using the Processing environment. This is definitely worth a closer look. You will be surprised how little code you need to write to generate an interactive graph.

CHARTING LIBRARIES

For completeness, I want to mention some of the charting libraries that I came across while working on this book. In the commercial space, you will find a lot of these libraries. Why would you want a commercial library? The benefit is that you get professional support and some guarantee that there will be bug fixes and new features in new releases of the software. With open source libraries, you generally don't have this security.

While searching for charting libraries, the one that came up most in the realm of Java is JFreeChart. It offers the capability to render a wide variety of charts. Unfortunately, there is no interactivity that comes out of the box. I am sure one could implement this on top of the library, but it is probably not too easy. If you need to publish your graphs via the Web, Cewolf is a JSP-based chart implementation that uses JFreeChart as the rendering engine.

The one charting tool that I have been using the most is Chart Director.[9] The library provides a nice set of charts that you can choose from. As with all libraries, you have to write some code to map your data to the data types and formats the charting library

---

[9] www.advsofteng.com

expects. I am a big fan of CSV files and of making things simple for the user. Therefore, I wrote a few Perl scripts that take mostly categorical data as input and maps them to various types of charts, starting with bar charts, extending to line graphs with trend lines and box plots. These scripts are merely wrappers around the Chart Director libraries, but they simplified my life enormously while generating a lot of the graphs in this book. You can find the scripts in the AfterGlow tarballs.[10] Chart Director has implementations for many programming languages, ranging from Java to Python to Perl and so on.

There are many more charting libraries out there, and I have not spent a lot of time evaluating different ones. If you are looking in the commercial space (especially), I am sure you will find a library that satisfies all your needs.

LIBRARIES SUMMARY

I have discussed a fair amount of open source visualization libraries in this section. To give you a reference, Table 9-3 summarizes all the libraries again and lists some of the properties that should help you make a decision when having to choose a library for your own needs.

Table 9-3   Open Source Visualization Libraries

Name	Language	URL	Input Data Type	Graph Output	Inter-activity	License	Ani-mation	Actively Devel-oped
OpenJGraph	Java	openjgraph. sourceforge.net	—	Link graphs	Yes	LGPL	No	No
JGraph	Java	www.jgraph. com	XML	Link graphs	Yes	LGPL	No	Yes
JGraphT	Java	http://jgrapht. sourceforge.net	XML	Link graphs	Yes	LGPL	No	Yes
JUNG	Java	http://jung. sourceforge.net	GML	Link graphs	Yes	BSD	Yes	Yes
GINY	Java	http://csbi. sourceforge.net	—	Link graphs	No	BSD	No	No

---

[10] http://sf.net/projects/afterglow

Name	Language	URL	Input Data Type	Graph Output	Inter-activity	License	Ani-mation	Actively Devel-oped
InfoVis Toolkit	Java	http://ivtk.sourceforge.net	TM3	scatter plots, time series, parallel coordinates, link graphs, treemaps	Yes	X11 software license	No	No
Grappa	Java	www.research.att.com/~john/Grappa	DOT	link graphs	Yes	CPL	No	No
Prefuse	Java	http://prefuse.org	SQL, GML	Link graphs	BSD	Yes	Yes	Yes
Processing	Scripted	http://processing.org	Various	various	Yes	LGPL	Yes	Yes
JFreeCharts	Java	www.jfree.org/jfreechart	Various	Charts	Yes	LGPL	No	Yes
Cewolf	Java/JSP	http://cewolf.sourceforge.net	Various	Charts	Yes	LGPL	No	Yes
Boost Graph Library	C++	www.boost.org/libs/graph	—	Link graphs	Yes	Boost software license	Yes	Yes
Piccolo	Java/C#	www.cs.umd.edu/hcil/piccolo/	—	—	Yes	BSD license	Yes	Reduced effort

ONLINE TOOLS

In the past year, a lot of applications have moved onto the Web. It is pretty amazing what services we have available via a browser interface today. The visualization world is no different. A few projects offer online visualization. These sites offer the capability to upload data to then visualize it. There are definitely issues associated with that model. Privacy comes to mind and protection of proprietary information. However, the possibilities that these services are opening up are quite amazing. The concept of people sharing data to visualize it and make it available for everyone else to see it is fairly crazy. Let's take a closer look at two of these services and one service from Google, which goes in a slightly different direction.

SWIVEL

If you navigate to www.swivel.com, you find yourself staring at a website that looks like a blog, with the possible exception of displaying a large number of charts. These are all examples where people uploaded some sort of data to then generate a chart. A user can **explore**, **share**, and **upload** data. Without even uploading any data, a user can browse the content that all the other Swivel users have uploaded and graphed. Interesting data and charts can be shared with other people via email or a comment can be added to existing charts. Finally, if a user wants to generate graphs of his own data, he can go ahead and upload it. The data format that Swivel accepts is CSV. Once data is uploaded, you can tag, describe, and annotate your data. You get a quick overview of the data you uploaded, and Swivel proposes some graphs that you can draw. You can then even compare other graphs with the one you just generated, whether from your own dataset or with data from other datasets. Very slick! The different chart types and capabilities are definitely limited, but Swivel nevertheless provides a quick and easy way to chart some of your data and share all of it with a broader community.

It is probably interesting to note that the main point of Swivel is not the visualization aspect, but the aspect of sharing data. A lot of interesting data is made available via this site. The price of oil over the past n months is available, for example. Comparing this data against your own might show some interesting trends. Where Swivel shines with regard to datasets, it loses in terms of visualization. The only available charts are bar charts, line charts, and scatter plots. Although this might be enough to compare simple data, for more complex analysis I would miss my treemaps and parallel coordinates. One fact that I didn't notice until I read some reviews of the site on the Web was that Swivel uses Ploticus (discussed previously in this chapter) to visualize their data. Another fairly interesting feature of Swivel is the Access API. You can automatically upload data through the API and have it graphed. They even offer a toolbar for Excel to automatically upload your data. So, although Swivel has its limitations, there are also some definitely very interesting developments.

Many Eyes

Another website that follows the concept of sharing data online and letting users visualize their data is Many Eyes (www.many-eyes.com). Many Eyes, as opposed to Swivel, is much more focused on the aspects of data visualization than it is on sharing data. The site offers an amazing number of graphs that you can choose from to visualize your data: zoomable geo maps, treemaps, line charts, bar charts, scatter plots, bubble graphs, all kinds of stacked charts, area graphs, word clouds, pie charts, and link graphs. I was pleasantly surprised to see that link graphs are supported. I uploaded some data, which turned out to be not as easy as in Swivel, and created a link graph. It worked like a charm. The site claims that tab-separated data is accepted for upload. I discovered that not to be true. I had to open up my CSV file in Excel to then copy and paste it into the online form. Not really what I prefer. I would rather point the tool to my CSV file (as in Swivel) to have it uploaded. Once the data is visualized, Many Eyes offers all kinds of interaction capabilities. Nodes can be moved around, data selected, and in the case of maps, you can even zoom in and out.

Many Eyes is not relying on a third-party visualization library to graph the data (as Swivel is). They implemented their own libraries, all based on Java. I hope that they will add some parallel coordinates at some point. That is really the only graph that I miss at this point. Another feature that would be interesting to have is the support for dynamic queries. Displaying multiple graphs at the same time and letting the user interact with them, while all the graphs simultaneously update, would be a nice additional feature.

Google Maps and Google Earth

Google Maps (maps.google.com) and (the later) Google Earth (earth.google.com) are two tools that changed how a lot of people use cartographic information. Google came up with a fast way to serve maps, with a simple, yet functional user interface and a rich scripting API. A search based on a variety of properties takes the user to any location in the world. Markers are used to indicate positions, and polygon lines can be added to show paths on a map. You have seen this all.

The API offered by Google Maps[11] enables you to embed maps in your own websites. By using JavaScript, you can define longitudes and latitudes that define locations on a map. With different calls, you can add markers and your own text bubbles as popups. You can find a great tutorial describing all the individual options at http://econym.googlepages.com/index.htm.

---

[11] http://code.google.com/apis/maps/

One way to load location information to mark up a map is via a simple text file that contains lines similar to this one:

```
41.82589|-72.10040|&lt; Text<br>And even more&gt;|MarkerName
```

This line contains the longitude and the latitude of a map location, along with a description for the location and a label for the marker. The description can be HTML and can, for example, contain images. The API then offers a special call to load this file from within your website. All of this can be found in part 9 of the aforementioned tutorial.

If an XML file is used rather than a text file to provide the data, you can display not only individual locations, but also polygon lines by using a markup similar to this:

```
<line colour="#008800" width="8" html="green line clicked">
   <point lat="43.9078" lng="-79.0264" />
   <point lat="44.1037" lng="-79.6294" />
   <point lat="43.5908" lng="-79.2567" />
   <point lat="44.2248" lng="-79.2567" />
</line>
```

The features so far can be used to map static content. By using AJAX, you can turn a map into a real-time monitor. You can find a complete tutorial on how to build a real-time website monitoring infrastructure at http://vega.rd.no/article/mapping-website-visitors-in-real-time.

Google Earth works similarly to Google Maps. To map locations to the map, Google Earth uses a special markup language called Keyhole Markup Language (KML). KML files can be loaded into Google Earth and contain markups for the locations of interest. A sample KML file extract looks like this:

```
<Placemark>
   <name>83.59.15.2,Madrid</name>
   <description>Attacked 03/20/08 12:13:22</description>
   <Style>
     <IconStyle><Icon>
       <href>root://icons/palette-3.png</href>
       <x>64</x><y>96</y><w>32</w><h>32</h>
     </Icon></IconStyle>
   </Style>
   <Point><coordinates>-3.6833,40.4,0</coordinates></Point>
</Placemark>
```

Similar to the format of the Google Maps input, you provide a name for a marker, a description, an icon style, and then the coordinates for where the marker should be drawn on the globe. Google Earth has a feature that you can enable to refresh the KML file on a periodic basis. That way you can point it to a file hosted on a Web server. By periodically updating the file on the Web server, Google Earth is showing you a near real-time view of your data.

GOOGLE CHART API

Google has introduced a completely different approach to Web-based visualization. The new chart API[12] enables users to generate charts for their websites without the need to install any graph libraries on the Web server. The user just uses an HTML image tag (IMG) to call Google's service. By passing URL parameters, the user can pass the data and graph properties that he wants to use for generating the chart. Here is a simple example:

```
http://chart.apis.google.com/chart?cht=p3&chd=s:hW&chs=250x100&chl=Hello|World
```

You would embed this in your website, inside an IMG tag. The parameters to the Google API tell it to render a 3D pie chart (cht=p3), use 33 and 21 as the data for the 2 sectors (chd=s:hW), make the chart 250 by 100 pixels (chs=250x100), and label the sectors Hello and World (chl=Hello|World) . The data encoding part looks somewhat confusing. How is h and W mapped to 33 and 21? Google uses a simple translation mechanism to easily translate letters into numbers. There are other encoding mechanisms to easily encode values in the URL used for the image. You can read more on the developer page.

The interesting aspect of Google's API is that via a simple URL, you can render charts. Currently, the API supports line charts, pie charts, bar charts, scatter plots, and Venn diagrams. Before using the API, you definitely should consider some issues. Privacy is one of them. Make sure you are not passing any information that could be sensitive in any way. Another point to consider is for how long Google is going to support this API. Relying on Google might impose too much risk for your use-case. In all, I am yet again surprised by Google and how they could take something that had already been done (we have had charting libraries for the longest time) and put a completely new spin on it. Interesting.

---

[12] http://code.google.com/apis/chart

COMMERCIAL VISUALIZATION TOOLS

You might ask yourself why you would even look into commercial solutions to visualize your data. There are enough open source tools that can be used. There are quite a few arguments for commercial software over open source. The biggest drawback of commercial systems is certainly licensing or purchasing costs. However, you do get something in return for that money (support, for example). Commercial solutions have a company behind them that continues development of the product. If you are lucky, you even get to voice your opinion and have an impact on their road map. With open source tools, you never know. The developers might decide to stop developing any day. In a lot of cases, you will also find that the commercial solutions have many more features and are just not as rough around the edges as open source solutions.

I want to give you a short overview of some of the commercial tools available, but in no way do I want to grade them or make a product recommendation. I do not have enough experience with a lot of the tools to even attempt to write a review. This section should give you an overview of some of the tools and inspire you to take a look at some of them. I start with a more detailed description of Advizor, which is the tool I have a lot of hands-on experience with. I then introduce a number of other commercial solutions.

ADVIZOR

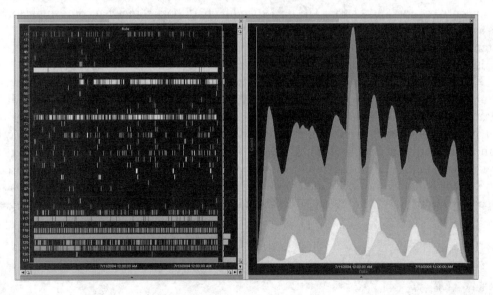

I learned about Advizor[13] at a customer site, where one of the security analysts was using it to visually analyze security data. I was fascinated by the capabilities of the tool and got in touch with the company to get my own copy. I ended up introducing Advizor to my company, and we decided to OEM the capability. This is why I was able to familiarize myself fairly well with the application.

Advizor comes in both a client and a server version. The server can be used to automatically update data and even serve the content via dynamic and interactive Web pages. The client can run independently of the server. If used with the server, it serves as a designer to define the data source and configure the graphs. The client can also be used as a stand-alone application. In that capacity, it enables the user to also browse the data after the displays have been built. The tool is highly interactive. All the graphical displays are linked. The displays update almost instantaneously, making dynamic queries a breeze. The amount of control over the individual graphs further helps you navigate the data. The set of supported charts is kept to the necessary ones that you would expect, as well as maps, treemaps, and parallel coordinates. The support for link graphs is complex, to say the least. You have to process your data specifically to get them working correctly. The same is true for maps.[14]

The data input is flexible. The best data source to use is a database where you store your data. To access the data, Advizor asks you to enter a query that is executed every time you load the data. This will then pull all the records from the database. You can also use CSV as a data source. My experiences with that were a bit disappointing. As soon as the loading process finds a bad data entry, for example, not enough columns, or a string where the column was defined to contain an integer, it aborts instead of discarding that record or offering a way to solve the problem. This can be frustrating if you deal with large datasets.

I have used Advizor a lot for interactive data analysis. It is truly easy to configure powerful, flexible displays that help to quickly discover anomalies and suspicious entries. In terms of analyzing computer security or networking data, there are a few shortcomings or limitations. One limitation that was quite annoying is that IP addresses were treated as strings, making it impossible to sort them correctly.[15]

Some of the newer capabilities are moving in the direction of decision support. Predictive analysis is one of the features. When you choose a field in the dataset, for example, this feature indicates which other data fields are determining the value of this field. In a set of Web access logs, it could, for example, determine whether the country

---

[13] http://advizorsolutions.com

[14] I submitted a feature request to make that easier.

[15] This is another thing that I submitted a feature request for.

that a connection originates in determines the websites accessed. It could turn out that connections from Asian countries always hit the English pages and not the translated ones, hinting at a possible problem with the site's setup. This can be used to analyze dependencies among the individual data fields and possibly to predict trends.

OTHER COMMERCIAL VISUALIZATION TOOLS

The features I outlined for Advizor are matched by pretty much all the other commercial visualization tools. There are slight differences, and some tools might be better at one or the other aspect. A general trend visible in almost all visualization tools is the movement toward more intelligence in the sense of data mining capabilities.

While looking around for commercial visualization solutions, I found a diverse set of them. It ranged from more consulting-driven approaches such as Oculus through some very research-centric systems such as StarLight, to huge corporations such as Tibco that sell visualization tools.

In the area of programming libraries for visualization, I came across Oculus (www.oculusinfo.com). The company offers libraries for both Java and .NET, as well as an add-on for Microsoft Excel. The main business seems to be consulting engagements where these development libraries are used to develop custom applications for customers. The main visual display design evolves around a 3D view in the center of the screen, surrounded by charts on each side. The charts emphasize some data dimension with 2D graphs. One aspect that scared me a little about the Java library was the fact that the current white paper references Java 1.1 and Netscape 4.0. I hope the library is not really that out of date.

A visualization tool that evolved out of a United States research lab is StarLight (http://starlight.pnl.gov). Initially, the tool was developed to analyze intelligence information, such as social ties to terrorist cells. The sophisticated and highly scalable architecture can be used to analyze huge amounts of data. At this point, this is probably the tool that scales the best. However, the tool is not generally available. Although it seems that StarLight can be purchased, it is still owned by the Pacific Northwest National Laboratory and not by a commercial concern (one reason it is still a bit rough around the edges). I hope that some company either picks this product up or a new company is formed around the technology.

Purple Insight (www.purpleinsight.com) is a company I came across about two years ago. The product provides an interesting set of data mining tools that are coupled with visualization. This approach is really promising. For example, the Column Importance feature enables you to rank columns based on their influence on the values of another column (i.e., data dimension). This can be a really interesting tool to quickly browse data and see which data dimensions are of importance. Evidence classifier and clustering are two more data mining applications that help you browse and understand the data. All of these steps are visually supported, providing the user with a visual understanding of the outcome. The drawback is that the tool tries to overutilize 3D displays. Some of the visualizations are really hard to read and suffer greatly from occlusion. Nevertheless, I think the data mining focus is incredibly useful.

Continuing the journey through visualization tools, we need to talk about Tableau (www.tableausoftware.com). The company definitely does justice to the visualization field. Their website is simple and provides the visitor with quick access to the most important information. Trying to get a feeling for the application is as easy as watching a few minutes of the online instruction videos. The definite strength of this product is its ease of use. You can tell that this product has been sold for a while and customers have been using it. The product interactions are nicely done. Drag and drop of data dimensions and interaction with the charts themselves make analysis really simple, whether you are looking for relationships in data dimensions or for trends and patterns. The easy-to-use interface updates immediately after you change the configuration. This makes the data exploration process really smooth.

SpotFire (http://spotfire.tibco.com), a product now owned by Tibco, is yet another highly interactive and easy-to-use visualization tool. In many ways, Tableau and SpotFire resemble each other. They both focus on easy interaction and simple, but expressive graphs. SpotFire makes it easy to share information between users. Export features built in to the user interface enable the user to export selections of the data into an external tool (Excel, for example).

Other tools that support visualization use-cases are mathematical and statistical packages, such as Mathematica (www.wolfram.com) and MatLab (www.mathworks.com). These tools are similar to the R package that I discussed a little earlier and are mainly used for statistical or mathematical visualizations. And, many more visualization applications are on the market. The list I presented here should give you a starting point and a feel for what you can expect in the commercial visualization market. Do your own research to find the tool that fits exactly your needs.

SUMMARY

In this last chapter of the book, I surveyed freely available visualization tools and libraries. These tools are mainly the ones that I have been using while writing this book to visualize my security data. The freely available tools come in all states of maturity. Some of them are in fairly experimental mode, whereas others are amazingly well polished. After introducing about 20 freely available tools, I switched to discussing open source visualization libraries that you can use in your own programs. Often, freely available tools do not provide the flexibility you need, and it is appropriate to write some custom code. If you plan to integrate some visualization capability into your own programs, you need to look at these libraries. One of the new developments is that of full-featured visualization services offered through the Internet. The projects I introduced are the leading ones at this time.

If you do not find the desired visualization capabilities in the freely available space, you can turn to commercial solutions. I discuss them only marginally here. It would be a project of its own to survey all the available commercial visualization tools. But with all this information, you should now be ready to go out and perform your own security visualization.

Index

Page numbers followed by *n* denote footnotes.

D

H

BOOKS ONLINE

ENABLED

THIS BOOK IS SAFARI ENABLED

INCLUDES FREE 45-DAY ACCESS TO THE ONLINE EDITION

The Safari® Enabled icon on the cover of your favorite technology book means the book is available through Safari Bookshelf. When you buy this book, you get free access to the online edition for 45 days.

Safari Bookshelf is an electronic reference library that lets you easily search thousands of technical books, find code samples, download chapters, and access technical information whenever and wherever you need it.

TO GAIN 45-DAY SAFARI ENABLED ACCESS TO THIS BOOK:

- Go to **informit.com/safarienabled**

- Complete the brief registration form

- Enter the coupon code found in the front of this book on the "Copyright" page

If you have difficulty registering on Safari Bookshelf or accessing the online edition, please e-mail customer-service@safaribooksonline.com.

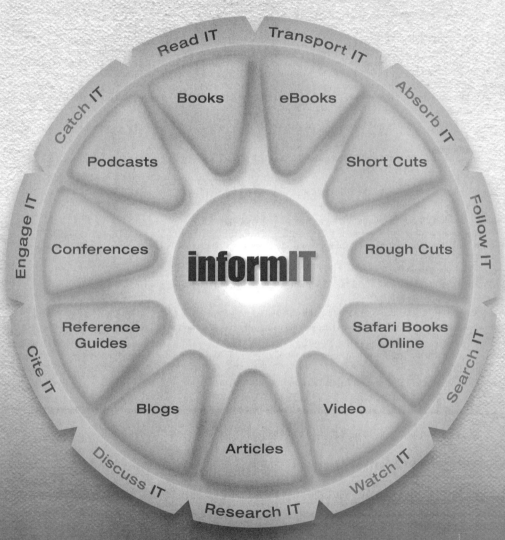

CD-ROM Warranty

The DAVIX Operating System is based on SLAX and is licensed under the GNU Public License V. 2. For more information, please see:

www.gnu.org/licenses/gpl.html

or

www.slax.org

The Davix Manual is licensed under the GNU FDL v. 1.2:

www.gnu.org/copyleft/fdl.html#SEC1

The visualization tools included on this CD are licensed and/or copyrighted as follows:

TimeSearcher 1 and TreeMap 4.1 are included with permission from the University of Maryland Human-Computer Interaction Lab. For information about documentation and licensing, please see:

www.cs.umd.edu/hcil/treemap
www.cs.umd.edu/hcil/timesearcher

ChartDirector is included courtesy of Advanced Software Engineering. For full information, please see:

www.advsofteng.com/index.html

KineticsKit: povexport is included courtesy of Markus Gritsch

The following tools are covered by their own license, which allow for redistribution in this package:

expat, libxcv, gd, Java3D, vpython, Numeric (Numpy)

Gnuplot is copyrighted but freely distributed (i.e., you don't have to pay for it).For more information, see:

www.gnuplot.info

Graphviz is licensed under the Common Public License Version 1.0, chapter 2a, 3:

www.graphviz.org/License.php

TNV is covered by the following licenses: MIT License Piccolo: BSD License, jpcap: MPL 1.1 hsqldb: HSQL License (BSD style license) mysql-j: GPLv2

The following tools are licensed under the following GNU Public Licenses:

GPL

Crypt::Rijndael, LGL, VRML, Free WRL, NVisionIP

GPL v.2

libtool, Tulip, Ggobi, rserv, Ploticus, EtherApe, dbus, dbus-glib, libbonobo, libbonoboui, gail, gcc, gnome-keyring, gnome-media, gnome-vfs, gconf, orbit2, libidmef, Afterglow, Parvis, Walrus, lesstif, GUESS, InetVis, Real Time 3D Graph Visualizer, Rumint, gltail, MRTG, R, gcc-gfortran, RMySQL, Imtest, multcomp, mvtnorm, rgl, tseries, zoo

GPL v.3

Mondrian, Rcmdr, RcmdrPlugin.FactoMine, RcmdrPlugin.HH, RcmdrPlugin.TeachingDemosRcmdrPlugin.epack, FactoMineR, HH, care, effects, leaps, relimp

The following tools are licensed under the LGPL v. 2.1:

Cytoscape, avahi, glib2, libgnome, libgnomeui, libgnomcanvas, libidl, FFTW, wine, DBI, abind

The following tools are licensed under the BSD License:

Shoki, pcre

The following tools are licensed under the Artistic License:

PyInline, TeachingDemos